Ireland and Germany:
Partners in European Recovery

Ireland's remarkable recovery is of crucial importance not only to the Irish people whose sacrifices made it possible but also to the people of Germany and Europe. In particular, Ireland and Germany's destinies have become highly related, to a point of strong mutual advantage: German and EU help for Ireland will return to benefit Germany and Europe, a fact already proven by how Ireland has used strong German assistance to stabilise its own economy, thereby helping to stabilise the Euro. By taking an early lead in fiscal consolidation and in reform of its financial regulatory environment and risk management systems, Ireland showed that a turnaround was possible. In this book, Ireland's contribution to the stabilisation of the Euro – of which the Irish Presidency in the first half of 2013 was a symbolic testament – is seen from the differing perspectives of those in both Germany and Ireland and from different fields of business, policy and politics. As well as a rich understanding of crisis and recovery, this mix of perspectives produces exciting ideas and messages for the common future that both countries will share beyond the crisis. The book underlines the importance of maintaining and deepening Ireland's competitive business model and of European support in the maintenance of key competitive advantages in overcoming the remaining challenges that still face Ireland's economy: the state of its banking system and the drive to restore full employment through innovation and internationalisation in its business sectors. Further, it shows how co-operation between the EU's largest and one of its smallest nations has helped carry Europe's economy through a severe crisis, enabling the European economy to survive a challenge that, divided, might well have destroyed it. Finally, this book reminds us that, despite its detractors and opponents, the European co-operation project has been, and very much still is, a success story.

Ralf Lissek, CEO of the German-Irish Chamber of Industry and Commerce presenting an early copy of *Ireland and Germany: Partners in European Recovery* to Jean-Claude Juncker.

Ireland and Germany: Partners in European Recovery

Edited by
Ralf Lissek and Marc Coleman

Published by
OAK TREE PRESS
19 Rutland Street, Cork, Ireland
www.oaktreepress.com / www.SuccessStore.com

© 2014 AHK Irland (Deutsch-Irische Industrie- und Handelskammer /
German-Irish Chamber of Industry and Commerce)

A catalogue record of this book is
available from the British Library.

ISBN 978 1 78119 141 5 (Hardback)
ISBN 978 1 78119 142 2 (Paperback)
ISBN 978 1 78119 143 9 (ePub)
ISBN 978 1 78119 144 6 (Kindle)

Cover images: Thinkstock.co.uk
Cover design by Kieran O'Connor Design.

Printed in Ireland by SPRINT-print Ltd

Contents

Exhibits

The Authors

Ralf Lissek (Editor / Author, **Chapter 1** and **Commentary / Chapter 7**), AHK Dublin (German-Irish Chamber of Industry and Commerce), Chief Executive Officer and initiator of this book.

John Corrigan (Author, **Commentary / Chapter 1**), National Treasury Management Agency, Chief Executive.

Dr. Jack Golden (Author, **Chapter 2**), CRH, Organisation Development Director.

Frank Mee (Author, **Commentary / Chapter 2**), Allianz Worldwide Care, Director of Finance and Information Technology.

Dr. Peter Breuer (Author, **Chapter 3**), IMF, Economist, Resident Representative to Ireland.

Marc Coleman (Editor / Author, **Chapter 4** and **Commentary / Chapter 7**), Economist, broadcaster, former ECB economist.

Brian Hayes (Author, **Commentary / Chapter 4**), Department of Public Expenditure and Reform, Minister of State.

Dr. Stefan Gerlach (Author, **Chapter 5**), Central Bank of Ireland, Deputy Governor.

Werner Schwanberg (Author, **Commentary / Chapter 5**), WGZ Bank Ireland, Managing Director.

Christoph Müller (Author, **Chapter 6**), Aer Lingus, Chief Executive Officer.

Dr. Eric Schweitzer (Author, **Chapter 7**), Deutsche Industrie- und Handelskammertag (DIHK), President.

Dr. Joachim Pfeiffer (Author, **Chapter 8**), CDU/CSU party, Spokesperson for the Committee for the Economy and Energy in the German Parliament.

Dr. Volker Treier (Author, **Chapter 9**), Deutsche Industrie- und Handelskammertag (DIHK), Deputy CEO.

Acknowledgements

We would like to thank everyone involved in the writing and production of *Ireland and Germany: Partners in European Recovery*, including Farid Assouad, Ralph Biedinger, Gabriel D'Arcy, Helen Dunne, Jean Fleming, Franziska Gross, Uli Hoppe, Victor Hrymak, Declan Kearney, Clare Lissek, Alan Manahan, Yvonne McCarthy, Brian Murphy, Ilja Notnagel, Johnny Pollock, Paul Sheehy, Sean Sheehy, Sandra Sheeran, Laurence Simms, Tony Spollen, Niamh Sweeney – and Brian O'Kane, the publisher, for his patience.

Ralf Lissek and Marc Coleman, Editors

Foreword

Ireland and Germany have long enjoyed excellent relations, politically, culturally and economically. Indeed, our relationship has never been better.

Over the last number of years, we have seen our relationship deepen and intensify as we worked together to move Europe forward, particularly during the Irish Presidency of the Council of the European Union last year. In fact, Irish Presidencies of the Council have often coincided with the most important developments for our countries and for Europe – for example, German reunification in 1990 and the accession of 10 new Member States in 2004. Our 2013 Presidency was no exception as, at a time of real challenge, we worked together to deliver stability, jobs and growth for Europe.

We in Ireland are determined to build on our achievements and to further enhance our ties in the period ahead. In doing this, we are building on solid ground and are already seeing signs of increased trade, employment and tourism.

Total trade between our two countries now amounts to more than €23bn. While total merchandise trade decreased in 2013, our food and beverages sector enjoyed an impressive increase in exports to Germany of 22 per cent. The beneficial nature to both sides of the trading relationship was reinforced by an increase in imports from Germany of 8 per cent.

The number of German tourists coming to Ireland increased with early indications for 2013 showing a record numbers of visitors here – almost half a million people. The positive outlook for 2014 is underpinned by increased air access between our two countries.

I commend the work of the German-Irish Chamber of Industry and Commerce in publishing this book. I know the Chamber supports the extensive business relations between Irish and German companies. Over 300 German companies employ an estimated 20,000 people in Ireland. However, trade and investment works positively both ways, with 58 Irish companies providing employment to 14,000 people in Germany and 480 Irish companies exporting high quality products and services to Germany.

The German economy continued to record growth in 2013 and is looking at strong growth in 2014 through increased trade and consumer spending. The Irish Embassy in Berlin, working closely with the State agencies, continues to work with our partners on the areas that are vital to our ongoing recovery. This has included supporting the work of the German Irish Chamber of Industry and Commerce, including last December when the Embassy hosted the German launch of the Chamber's publication, *German-Irish Business: The Story of Success.*

I think it is important to recall that – despite its challenges – the EU is a success story. Germany and Ireland together, and in their distinctive contributions, have played key roles in this success story. I am convinced that we will continue do so in future. There is much to do, but we know that our joint efforts to stabilise the economy and emerge from crisis will continue and will succeed. German-Irish relations will grow from strength to strength. I have nothing but optimism for our future joint endeavours.

Enda Kenny TD
An Taoiseach (Irish Prime Minister)
February 2014

Executive Summary

2008 to 2020: The Road to Recovery

Ireland's record in foreign direct investment and export led growth is the strongest in Europe, driven by a strategic role as a gateway to Europe for US companies. Ireland's recovery reflects this and puts Ireland in a very different place to other countries subject to the Troika. However, serious challenges remain in regard to debt, public spending and other necessary reforms.

Ireland's steady recovery – forecast to continue between now and 2020 – is built on a resilient population, a political commitment to reform, a vibrant business sector and Ireland's continued success as a world champion in foreign direct investment and as a leading gateway to Europe for multinational companies. Maintaining all these qualities in Ireland is vital to Europe's recovery and support from Ireland's partners is critical in this regard.

Commentary: Ireland's Recovery

When Ireland lost the confidence of investors and was obliged to request an EU/IMF Programme of Assistance in November 2010, the National Treasury Management Agency (NTMA) took the strategic decision to implement a programme of pro-active engagement with investors so as to work towards a successful return to the markets at the end of the programme. The continued outperformance by the Government of the fiscal targets set in the EU/IMF Programme, the transparent and credible exercise of re-capitalising and restructuring the Irish banks in 2011 and the restoration of competitiveness to the economy gradually regained the trust of investors.

The decision by US investors, mainly but not exclusively hedge funds, to enter the Irish Government bond market in mid-2011 when yields were at historically high levels eventually led to other more traditional "real money" investors re-entering the market and replacing the hedge funds as yields declined. Developments in Europe also helped Ireland's progress towards full market re-entry – especially Mr. Draghi's promise to do "whatever it takes", the IBRC promissory note arrangement and the term extensions on Ireland's EFSF and EFSM loans. Following Ireland's exit from the programme in December 2013 without a precautionary credit line, the NTMA was able to raise €3.75bn in the markets in early January 2014. Further issuance by way of regular scheduled auctions is planned as Ireland has normalised its presence in the markets.

Ireland's Business Model

Ireland has shown resilience and flexibility in adapting its economy and business model, not just in this crisis but also during four decades as a member of the European project. This explains its transition from a small agricultural economy, whose exports were dominated by Britain, into one of the world's most globalised and diverse economies.

Significant challenges remain to achieve the full potential of Ireland's dynamic economic model, such as overcoming the lack of credit to business, improving the ability of SMEs to export and retaining Ireland's competitive tax regime.

Commentary: A Case Study on Foreign Direct Investment into Ireland: Allianz Worldwide Care Limited

Many global international financial services companies are now located in Ireland due to a combination of success factors, of which Ireland's taxation regime is just one. Allianz Group, which employs 144,000 people and has 78 million customers, is a leading example.

A stable business environment, supportive government agencies and access to well-educated and entrepreneurial staff enabled the financial services sector to grow strongly and recover quickly after the crisis. Retaining Ireland's competitiveness in this area, however, will require action in relation to the still high costs imposed on the economy by its more sheltered sectors.

Crisis Response and Remaining Challenges

Although below initial forecasts, Ireland's growth rate has exceeded the Euro area average and indicators suggest a recovery may be emerging. Following a substantial rise in the fiscal deficit and a sharp increase in public debt during the crisis, phased consolidation has significantly improved the fiscal position while social cohesion was maintained. Banking reforms since the crisis have supported financial stability.

Continued determined policy implementation is needed on a range of fronts before Ireland can be judged to have fully recovered from the crisis. With the fiscal deficit still high and public debt very elevated, further consolidation is needed in the coming years to put debt firmly on a declining path and help to ensure Ireland's return to market financing is lasting. Intensified efforts are needed to ensure banks and mortgage borrowers in arrears conclude durable solutions so that a revival in lending can contribute to a sustained domestic demand recovery.

Spending and Reform: Renewing the Momentum

Ireland's fiscal adjustment has been impressive and orderly. The Government has tried to cushion weaker sections of the community, while improving efficiency in the public sector, and achieving reductions in public pay levels.

While Ireland's public sector has improved in terms of efficiency – more is now being done with fewer resources – Ireland's major challenge now is to judge the effectiveness of public spending. Also notwithstanding significant reductions, public pay in Ireland remains well above Eurozone levels and closer analysis of the reasons and justification for this is necessary.

A new Government Department of Public Expenditure and Reform has been created to drive greater efficiency and effectiveness. From improving the cost of delivering public services, the emphasis under new reform plans to be announced in 2014 will shift to improving the quality of public services.

Commentary: The Reform Dividend
The Irish public service faces an unprecedented challenge to deliver services faster, better and more cost-effectively than before. To this end, plans for reform have been published in two waves, the first in November 2011 and the second in January 2014.

While the first plan was necessitated by the need to reduce public sector spending in tandem with fiscal consolidation with an obvious focus on cost and efficiency, the second will broaden the scope of reform and improve public service delivery and effectiveness.

Banking and Finance: Back to Stability

The Irish banking system has emerged from the crisis restructured, significantly smaller and significantly better regulated than before. Under overarching European structures – such as the Single Supervisory Mechanism, which sees the ECB take responsibility for EU-wide financial supervision – Ireland's financial sector is now governed by improved Central Bank legislation, tighter capital requirements and improved risk management.

The challenges of mortgage arrears, continued reliance on short-term funding and other funding risks remain for the Irish banking sector. Restructuring work is ongoing and a particular focus will be needed on addressing the problem of weak credit flow to small and medium-sized business. The Government is committed to addressing this in its *Medium Term Economic Strategy*.

Commentary: The International Financial Services Centre during the Irish Banking Crisis: An IFSC Perspective
Despite having attracted a large variety of international financial organisations, the IFSC was not part of Ireland's financial crisis. IFSC companies in difficulty during the crisis were a rare exception and even then were not involved in Ireland's bailout programme.

This notwithstanding, as a result of the crisis the IFSC is now subject to an improved regime. The upgrade of Ireland's investment rating shows that, amongst other things, financial regulation in Ireland has restored confidence in Ireland's financial sector and, at the same time, has taken a proportionate risk-based approach to determining supervisory needs.

The Dynamics of Ireland's Labour Market

During the crisis Ireland has remained an excellent location for business. By restoring lost competitiveness and implementing structural reforms, the Government aims to make Ireland in this decade the best small country in the world in which to do business.

Investment in training and skills development will be critical to achieving this. While this investment should focus on the future needs of the labour market, action to initiate policy in this area is needed now.

Germany's "Mittelstand": The Seven Pillars of Success

The success of the German economy in the last few years is in large part due to the hard work of the country's business enterprises. Internal restructuring, coupled with increased international orientation and investment in research and development, has laid the foundations. The process also has been fostered by the Government through reforms to the labour market and the corporate tax regime.

Germany is a strong location with an unusual mix of enterprises. It is home to successful, large, publicly-quoted companies, countless highly-committed small businesses – and a broad *Mittelstand*. These companies, in many cases family-owned, are not always in the limelight; they are, however, highly innovative and – as hidden champions – successful on the world markets.

Commentary: Is an Irish "Mittelstand" Possible?

Ireland's small size has been an obstacle to date to achieving size and scale in its small and medium-sized enterprise sector. This, in turn, has affected the sector's capacity to export. Despite this, a thriving SME sector has survived the crisis and retains many of the characteristics of Germany's "Mittelstand", with a strong export performance among some subsectors.

Dynamic Government policy is assisting the sector, but serious challenges remain. These include gaining access to financing and achieving the scale needed to export. Under the right conditions, Irish firms could, over time, replicate for the traded services sector the success that Germany's Mittelstand has achieved in manufacturing. In its *Medium Term Economic Strategy* the Government is looking to other countries, particularly Germany, for inspiration on improving conditions for SMEs and there are many positive opportunities for both countries to exchange good policy and practice. In particular, Germany's long-term orientation and the related access to support of strong banking and education systems could be instrumental in achieving the full potential of Ireland's SME sector.

Ireland and Germany: Partners in European Recovery

The European sovereign debt crisis may be a critical turning point in Europe's history. If Europeans learn from their mistakes, the European integration process and the formation of a more stable union can be accelerated. Only as a union can Europe make its voice heard in international affairs.

As is evident in light of Ireland's successful adjustment process, reform efforts are yielding results and overall European recovery is on track. Given the substantial remaining challenges, it is nonetheless critical to maintain the reform momentum. The ongoing consolidation of public finances and the implementation of structural reforms are necessary to increase competitiveness and ensure sustained growth in the Eurozone.

What Did Countries in Europe Do to Get Back to Stability?

The economic crisis reflects not just systemic problems with the global and European economies, but mistakes in each Member State. A mix of European-wide action and national reforms is gradually overcoming the crisis. An increasingly stable Euro, improving government financial balances and rising exports are signs that the situation in Europe is better than it looks.

A comparison of Ireland's performance with other adjustment programmes shows how well Ireland has done, but also how many significant challenges remain at European and national level, challenges that in spite of its salutary performance, apply in some cases to Ireland as well.

CHAPTER 1

2008 to 2020: The Road to Recovery

Ralf Lissek

Key Messages

- Ireland's record in foreign direct investment and export-led growth is the strongest in Europe, driven by a strategic role as a gateway to Europe for US companies. Ireland's recovery reflects this and puts Ireland in a very different place to other countries subject to the Troika. However serious challenges remain in regard to debt, public spending and other necessary reforms.
- Ireland's steady recovery – forecast to continue between now and 2020 – is built on a resilient population, a political commitment to reform, a vibrant business sector and Ireland's continued success as a world champion in foreign direct investment and as a leading gateway to Europe for multinational companies. Maintaining all these qualities in Ireland is vital to Europe's recovery and support from Ireland's partners is critical in this regard.

Introduction

Ireland is a country with a remarkable history of recovery and renewal. With its recent economic crisis and turnaround, this is no less the case. But Ireland's strong efforts to overcome the current crisis have presented it with the serious challenges of high debts in both the public and private spheres of its economy. The first challenge is now the subject of a Government target to reduce public debt significantly by 2020. Before the latest crisis hit, Ireland had spent two decades achieving a transition from being one of Europe's poorest countries to one of its richest. The latter years of this transition resulted in an overheating that left Ireland badly exposed when the global crisis came in 2008.

Despite the crisis and the changes it brought about in the State's relative economic position, Ireland retains many of the gains and most of the advantages it enjoyed from joining the European Economic Community (now the European Union) on 1 January 1973. The extent of those gains – which to a significant degree are still intact – is impressive. From just over half of the EU average in 1997, Ireland's economic output *per capita* is now comparable to the Eurozone average, if we use GNP *per capita*, and one-fifth higher than the Eurozone average if we use GDP *per capita*.[1] More importantly, at the time of writing, the Irish economy is experiencing good growth rates and strong growth in employment, positive signs for the future.

Exhibit 1.1: Eurozone GDP *per capita* by Purchasing Power Parity*

	2012
Germany	115
Greece	72
Ireland	121
Portugal	68
Eurozone	**100**

Source: IMF *World Economic Outlook Database 2013*.
* Purchasing power parity adjusts for relative price levels in different countries.

This table reflects an average economic growth rate that, over the last four decades, even accounting for a recent deep recession, remains the highest in the EU. Between 1972 and 2012, GDP and GNP grew in real terms by 458 and 332 per cent, respectively.[2] This growth is loaded towards recent decades and was driven by a strong export performance that followed Ireland's commitment to Economic and Monetary Union in 1992. Between that year and 2012, export volumes have risen by 295 per cent.[3] Unfortunately the later years of the growth phase were not based on export growth but were achieved with an unsustainable accumulation of debt that has hampered Ireland's ability to grow. Nonetheless, signs are emerging that the economy's capacity to grow – if not at the rates seen during the boom – is returning.

Ireland's "Weltmeister" performance in foreign direct investment is one of the reasons. According to the US Bureau of Economic Analysis, US firms' investments in Ireland ($189bn) since 1990 have exceeded their investment in Germany and the combined US investment in the so-called BRIC countries of Brazil, Russia, India and China.[4] Turning this advantage into domestic growth and more employment faces an obstacle, namely the levels of public and private debt. On one hand, Ireland has

---

[1] Ireland's successful foreign direct investment policies mean that its Gross Domestic Product (which includes foreign-owned company activity) is approximately one-fifth higher than Gross National Product (which excludes foreign-owned company activity). GDP is a standard measure for international comparisons.

[2] 1972 data from Department of Finance, *Budget and Economic Statistics 2013*; Central Statistics Office.

[3] Department of Finance, *Budget and Economic Statistics 2013*; Central Statistics Office.

[4] Quinlan, Joseph (2012). *The Irish-US Economic Relationship*, American Chamber of Commerce in Ireland.

shown it can excel: Ireland's Industrial Development Agency – a world leader in attracting foreign direct investment – has pioneered Ireland's crucial role as a gateway to Europe for multinational firms, particularly from the US. Indigenously-owned exporters also have performed well, thanks to Enterprise Ireland, the State agency tasked with assisting indigenous firms. From a fall in exports in 2009, indigenous exports grew by 12 per cent in 2011 and by a further 6.3 per cent in 2012.[5]

But, on the other hand, this cannot flatter the serious impact of the global crisis on Ireland. Nor can it remove the need for Europe to support Ireland's recovery. The case for that support is not just strengthened by Ireland's recent adjustment efforts, but also by the excellent use it has made of its EU membership in the past. There are few more solid signs of how Ireland has used EU membership to transform itself than its population growth.

Exhibit 1.2: Ireland's Population Rose 54 per cent since EU Membership

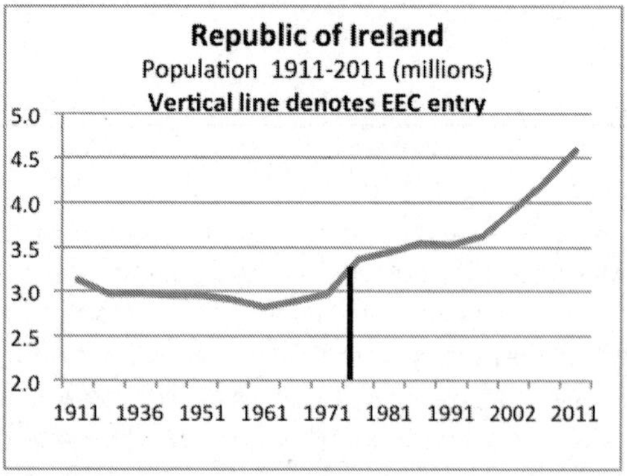

Republic of Ireland
Population 1911-2011 (millions)
Vertical line denotes EEC entry

Source: Central Statistics Office, Census data, 1911-2011.

When it voted to join the EEC in 1972, the population of the (Republic of) Ireland had been stable at approximately 3 million since a century before, the legacy of a famine that had stunted development for over a century. Between 1971 and 2011, Ireland's population – as measured by successive census returns – rose by a staggering 54 per cent. Through most of this time, Ireland's living standards increased. Emigration is acting to slow that growth rate, but there are other factors pulling in the opposite direction: Ireland has one of Europe's highest birth rates and is still experiencing strong inward migration. For these reasons, between 2006 and 2011 – a period that includes the three worst years of the crisis, during which living standards fell – Ireland's population rose by a further third of a million persons.

---

[5]   Enterprise Ireland, *Annual Reports 2011 and 2012*.

But what future awaits Ireland's growing young population? A land of full employment and prosperity or of unemployment and indebtedness?

The Irish people are renowned for their optimism and belief that the best will happen. It can happen. But policymakers and Ireland's partners in Europe will play a decisive role in determining whether it will.

Exhibit 1.3: Ireland's Unsustainable Boom

	2004	2005	2006	2007
Population (000s)	4,045	4,134	4,233	4,376
GDP growth (% change y-o-y)	4.2	6.1	5.5	5.0
GNP growth (% change y-o-y)	3.8	6.0	6.5	3.6
Unit Labour Costs (Index 2000=100)	95.8	100.0	103.5	108.7
Export growth (% change y-o-y)	7.6	4.4	5.0	8.4
Balance of Payments (Current Account) as % GDP	-0.7	-4.1	-4.1	-6.2
Private Sector Credit (€bn, end Dec)	91.0	115.4	134.1	148.6
of which mortgage finance (€bn, end Dec)	73.1	94.3	110.6	123.0
Employment (000s)	1,871.1	1,962.8	2,053.6	2,143.1
Unemployment % GDP	4.5	4.4	4.5	4.7
Personal Disposable Income (€m)	74,810	81,377	86,188	93,561
Per capita (€)	18,494	19,685	20,361	21,380
Gen. Gov't Balance as % GDP	1.4	1.6	2.9	0.2
Gen. Gov't Debt as % GDP	29.4	27.2	24.6	24.9
Total Gov't expenditure (€bn)	45.7	50.8	56.1	62.9
as % GNP	35.9	36.6	36.4	38.6

Source: Department of Finance, *Budget and Economic Statistics 2013*; CSO.
Note: Balance of Payments, General Government Balance and Debt figures are provided as a percentage of GDP, while Total Government Expenditure figures are provided as a percentage of GNP. This reflects standard reporting in *Budget and Economic Statistics*.

2004 – 2007: An Unsustainable Boom

Between 2004 and the end of 2007 Ireland embarked on an unsustainable expansion, departing from a sound business model of competitiveness-based growth. As Exhibit 1.3 above shows, growth was strong on the surface. Underneath that surface, however, were clear signs of a rapid deterioration in competitiveness as well as warnings of imminent financial trouble. In just four short years, unit labour costs rose by 13.5 per cent. From broad balance in 2004, the balance of payments on current account became a large deficit of 6.2 per cent of GDP by 2007. While employment rose by a quarter of a million persons in this period and personal disposable incomes also grew, a glance at the growth rate in private sector credit showed this to be unsustainable. By 2007 one in seven Irish workers and one in five male workers were employed in the construction industry. As can be seen from **Exhibit 1.4** below, average growth considerably outstripped inflation in several crucial sectors of the labour force, eroding a position of strong competitiveness in the late 1990s. The general price rise of 44.8 per cent between 1998 and 2008 was already high by European standards. In some sectors such as Computing, Research & Development, and Wholesale and Business Services, wage growth over the period was not far above inflation. In the public sector (excluding the health sector), wages rose by 70.9 per cent, well above inflation.

Exhibit 1.4: Wage Growth in Different Sectors of the Economy

Average weekly earnings €	1998	1999	2000	2001	2002	2003	2004	2005	2006	2007	2008	% change 98-08
Public Sector (exc. health)	555.1	578.3	611.5	671.8	704.3	734.9	797.1	844.2	882	922.5	948.9	**70.9**
Wholesale	471.2	489.6	527.2	558.0	583.7	598.8	626.4	665.5	703.3	711.7	737.7	**56.5**
Hotels & Restaurants	286.3	303.8	322	339.3	347.1	367.5	395.8	418.7	431.2	446.3	465.2	**62.5**
Computing, Research & Development	531.8	563.6	613.9	642.6	626.9	645.8	676.9	708.1	720.7	767.2	824.2	**55.0**
Business Services	456.9	480.6	513.5	551.5	561.4	585.5	619	642.9	679	705.3	723.6	**58.4**
Consumer Price Index (Dec 2001 =100)	87.2	88.7	93.6	98.2	102.7	106.3	108.6	111.3	115.7	121.3	126.3	**44.8**

Source: Central Statistics Office Statistical Databank.

In relation to the Computing, Research & Development sector, high wage growth is likely to reflect the success of a competitive and internationally traded sector. The Web Summit of October 2013 is a demonstration of how Ireland has excelled in foreign direct investment from multinationals (which, in the information technology area, are mainly focused on hardware) to vibrant software and social media industries. In the public sector, price rises reflect the impact of successive national wage agreements – partly reflecting legitimate claims to a share in the growth of the economy – and, in particular, the impact in 2002 of the public sector benchmarking awards. According to the data above, public pay was on average already relatively high compared to other sectors by 2001. Given the frequent description of Ireland's crisis as a "banking crisis", it is interesting to note a related issue to that of public sector pay. Compared to a €31bn liability in relation to the so-called Promissory Note[6] burden, analysis conducted in October 2013[7] suggests that the contingent liability to the State arising from public sector pensions is as high as €116bn, approximately three times the cost to the Irish taxpayer arising from the bailout of financial institutions.

2008-2011: Crisis

The fall in Ireland's economic position from 2008 was as rapid as the growth in the years immediately preceding the crisis. Precipitated by a global economic downturn, Ireland experienced one of the most sudden and rapid declines in modern economic history.

The most startling impact of the crisis was that Ireland went from a low level of public debt – a mere 24.9 per cent of GDP in 2007 – to a country where national debt significantly exceeded 100 per cent of GDP by 2011 (though debt is expected to have peaked in 2013). This sudden deterioration resulted from several factors. Amongst these, a series of injections into Ireland's banking system was the most obvious and commented upon. However, a continuation of high levels of public spending built up in the years preceding the banking crisis, and the sharp fall in property-related tax revenues on which the State had become too dependent, are as significant (if not more significant) in explaining this deterioration.

Troubled by excessive residential and commercial property lending, the banking system found itself increasingly dependent on Government support. This process culminated in the nationalisation of Anglo Irish Bank and the Irish Nationwide Building Society and the addition to the national debt of obligations relating to the promissory note worth €31bn.[8] This burden was later reduced by the wind-up of the Irish Bank Resolution Corporation.[9] However, other factors, such as a significantly high burden of public spending, were also evident. Between 2004 and 2007, public expenditure rose dramatically from €45.7bn to €62.9bn, equating to a 37 per cent increase.

---

[6]   See **Annex II: Glossary.**

[7]   Barnes, Sebastian & Smyth, Diarmaid (2013). *The Government's Balance Sheet After the Crisis: A Comprehensive Perspective,* IFAC.

[8]   Ireland's experience of bank recapitalisation and the recovery of its banking sector is discussed in **Chapter 5.**

[9]   The entity formed in 2011 from the merger of Anglo Irish Bank and the Irish Nationwide Building Society.

Exhibit 1.5: 2008 to 2011: Financial and Economic Crisis

	2008	2009	2010	2011
Population (000s)	4,485	4,533	4,555	4,575
GDP growth (% change y-o-y)	-2.2	-6.4	-1.1	2.2
GNP growth (% change y-o-y)	-1.8	-9.8	0.5	-1.6
Unit Labour Costs (Index 2005=100)	116.1	113.1	105.5	101.3
Export growth (% change y-o-y)	1.1	-3.8	6.4	5.4
Bal. of Payments (Current Account) as % GDP	-6.6	-2.8	1.4	1.5
Employment (000s)*	2,128	1,961	1,882	1,849
Unemployment (000s)	145	268	303	317
Unemployment % Labour force	6.4	12.0	13.8	14.6
Personal Disposable Income (€m)	101,515	95,260	88,700	87,428
Per capita	*22,634*	*21,015*	*19,473*	*19,110*
Gen. Gov't Balance as % GDP**	-7.4	-13.7*	-30.6*	-13.1*
"Underlying" Gen. Gov't Balance as % GDP	-7.4	-11.2	-10.6	-8.9
Gen. Gov't Debt as % GDP	44.2	64.4	91.2	104.1
Total Gov't expenditure (€bn)	68.7	75.9	69.0	76.5
as % GNP	44.4	56.7	52.3	58.5

Source: Department of Finance, *Budget and Economic Statistics 2013*; CSO.
* Rounded to nearest 1,000.
** Deficits from 2009 to 2011 reflect Eurostat requirements to include as Government spending funding for recapitalisation of some banks. "Underlying" General Government Balance figures in row below exclude impact on Government finances of bank support.

Between 2008 and 2011, the construction sector collapsed, contributing greatly to the loss of a total of 280,000 jobs in the economy. Personal disposable incomes declined in *per capita* terms by 12 per cent and the unemployment rate rose from 4.7 per cent to 14.6 per cent between 2007 and 2011. From budget balances that were in surplus or in balance before the crisis, Ireland's "underlying" deficit[10] rose to 11.2 per cent of GDP by 2009, although some progress was made in reducing this between 2010 and 2011.

While it would have been less severe without the banking crisis, it is clear that Ireland's economy and public finances both would have needed to correct themselves significantly even had such a crisis not occurred. Although stemming from a strongly competitive economy in its earlier years – export-driven growth linked to indigenous and foreign direct investment firms – Ireland's strong rates of growth became overly influenced by low interest rates, beginning in the late 1990s

---

[10] The budget deficit excluding the impact of bank recapitalisation costs.

until well into the middle of the following decade. The reliance of Government finances on revenues from unstable property-related taxation during this time disguised the long-term unsustainability of very strong rises in public expenditure that also occurred at that time. Particularly strong were rises in public pay and related pension obligations.

Public servants have since made a strong contribution to the recovery, agreeing to reductions in earnings such as the pensions levy applied in January 2009, pay cuts averaging 7.5 per cent implemented as part of Budget 2010 and a further cut in incomes as part of the Haddington Road Agreement. It also should be more widely accepted than it is that many in the public sector – particularly frontline staff – earn modest wages, especially when Ireland's cost of living is taken into account. However, as data from the second quarter of 2013, from the CSO's *Earnings and Labour Costs* release, shows, the average weekly earnings for the 377,300 staff working in the State sector was €928.76 as against €623.17 in the private sector. It has been argued that this differential – 49 per cent – reflects greater qualifications and skill levels in the public sector.

That being said, such positive differentials between average earnings in the public and private sector of this magnitude are hard to find in most other Eurozone countries. One study suggests in relation to Eurozone public pay differentials that *"notable differences"* exist between member states, with *"Greece, Ireland, Italy, Portugal and Spain exhibiting higher public sector premia than in other countries"*.[11] This study preceded the Haddington Road Agreement, but occurred after the pension levy and pay reductions of January and December 2009 respectively and it suggests that neither the differentials between public and private pay that exist in Ireland, nor the levels of earnings underpinning them, exist in Germany. This is despite a level of public service provision in Germany that few would say is worse than in Ireland.

2012-2016: The Road to Recovery

Although recovery began in earnest in 2012, efforts to turn the Irish economy around were already underway from soon after the crisis began. In October 2008, again in April 2009 and once again in December 2009, Ireland enacted three emergency budgets whose effect is clear from the fall in personal disposable income shown in **Exhibit 1.5** above. In addition, a new regime of risk-based financial regulation – more stringent than that later required by the EU – was quickly put in place, although it must be said that Ireland's rapid adjustment was not just in the fiscal area. By 2011, the deterioration in competitiveness of earlier years had been significantly reversed and an impressive rate of export growth restored. The factors at work here include the success of Enterprise Ireland in

---

[11] Guajardo, J., Leigh, D. & Pescatori, A. (2011). "The Public Sector Pay Gap in a Selection of Euro Area Countries", ECB *Working Paper 1406*, December.

encouraging indigenous industries to internationalise their business, the continuing success of the IDA in attracting foreign investment to Ireland, the flexibility and dynamism of Ireland's business community and, above all, the responsiveness and flexibility of the Irish workforce and population in responding to crisis.

Of course, adjustment in the Irish economy is not complete. As later chapters elaborate, having exited from the bailout, Ireland now faces a new challenge of securing and consolidating the progress of the last few years and then restoring economic normality and prosperity. To that end, the Government published a strategy document that identifies ambitious, but realistic targets for reducing debt and unemployment by 2020.[12] By adjusting to crisis more quickly and robustly than any other country in the Eurozone – one of the advantages of a smaller economy – Ireland has shown leadership to the rest of Europe. And it has provided grounds for confidence that, if the political will is there, Ireland can achieve some normalisation of its economy by the end of this decade.

Some Irish commentators suggest that Ireland's misfortune results solely from Eurozone interest rates being set at a level that suited low growth countries in central Europe, such as France and Germany, but not high growth countries on the periphery. While the European Central Bank's mandate is to set monetary policy for the entire Eurozone, and without any regard to preferences of one country over another, it is certain that the ECB's monetary policy had very different effects on Ireland compared to Germany.

Exhibit 1.6: 2012 to 2016: The Road to Recovery

	2012	2013e	2014f	2015f	2016f
Population (000s)	4,585	4,612	4,638	4,665	4,691
GDP growth (% change y-o-y)	0.2	0.2	2.0	2.3	2.8
GNP growth (% change y-o-y)	2.0	1.0	1.7	1.7	2.1
Unemployment % Labour Force	14.7	13.5	12.4	11.8	11.4
Gen. Gov't Balance as % GDP	-8.2	-7.3	-4.8	-2.9	-2.4
Primary Balance as % of GDP	-4.5	-2.7	0.0	2.0	2.6
Gen. Gov't Debt as % GDP	117.4	124.1	120	118.4	114.6
Total Gov't expenditure (€bn)	70.0	67.1	64.9	63.7	64.5

Source: For 2012, Department of Finance, Budget and Economic
Statistics 2013; CSO. For 2013 and beyond: Department of Finance,
Budget 2014 Economic and Fiscal Outlook.

To some extent, the provision of structural funds to help prepare Ireland's economy for entry into EMU, as anticipated in the Maastricht process, were an

---

[12] Department of Finance, *Medium Term Economic Strategy 2014-2020*, December 2013.

opportunity to prepare Ireland for the rigours of monetary union. In 1996, an extensive study was prepared by the ESRI on the likely impact of EMU on Ireland. So it seems that the opportunities to discuss, prepare and decide for this momentous event were available and in some cases taken up. To another extent, however, the widespread nature of the crisis in the Eurozone indicates that there was also a systemic problem in the Eurozone. The mismatch between a centralised monetary policy and a disjointed system of banking regulation is a clear example of this now being rectified in moves towards a banking union. Recognising this in hindsight is important. In accepting the principle that the European Stability Mechanism can be used to assist with bank recapitalisation and that this might be applied retrospectively, the European Council decision of June 2012 has left the door open to doing just that. The question is whether this opportunity will have the support of Member State governments.

The Eurozone crisis was certainly one contributed to by specific nationally-induced problems. But it was also a crisis with a common dimension. The breakdown in the *Stability Pact* a decade ago is a development in which the larger member states share some responsibility for the collapse in fiscal discipline across the Eurozone. All things considered, it is hard to escape the conclusion that resolving the European crisis should involve accepting the clear and impressive efforts of countries like Ireland to accept and correct their mistakes and matching this by an acceptance of some common degree of responsibility at EU level also.

A Normal Economy by 2020: A Realistic Goal

On the basis of reasonable and prudent forecasts – the Government's latest full set of economic forecasts have been validated as prudent by both the EU Commission and the Independent Fiscal Advisory Council[13] (IFAC) – not only is a clear and solid recovery in prospect for Ireland between now and 2016, but the return to a full employment economy in the coming decade is at least conceivable if the right policies are pursued. Indeed, since the aforementioned forecasts were published,[14] employment figures[15] suggest that growth in the number of jobs is accelerating, as is the rate of economic growth. With the right assistance, Ireland's return to a position of some normality seems possible by the end of this decade.

Measures in recent budgets[16] are encouraging business investment and job creation to the point where employment has risen by 58,000 in the 12 months to

---

[13]   IFAC was established in 2011 and given statutory status and authority under the *Fiscal Responsibility Act, 2013*. This Act gives statutory effect to Irish voters' approval a year before of the *Fiscal Compact Treaty* referendum. IFAC has the task of monitoring of Ireland's fiscal forecasts on an independent basis according to the terms of the *Fiscal Compact Treaty*.

[14]   October 2013.

[15]   December 2013.

[16]   Ireland's fiscal turnaround and budgetary policies are discussed in **Chapter 3**.

September 2013. From a peak of 14.7 per cent reached in 2012, unemployment at the time of writing had already fallen to 12.8 per cent and job creation shows every sign of gathering pace in the years ahead. There is also a welcome fall in the number of long-term unemployed. The Government's *Medium Term Economic Strategy* suggests that, under the right growth conditions – and if the future policy decisions are right – unemployment could fall to below 6 per cent by 2020. While Government spending has remained high, a reduction in spending, both in absolute size and as a share of the economy, is now being targeted for 2016. More importantly the Government's latest strategy sets out a benchmark for the resolution of public debt that sees it falling from a peak at 124 per cent in 2013 to 93 per cent in 2020, somewhat lower than envisaged in the latest forecasts tabulated above. Subject to a supportive climate for growth, this benchmark looks realistic.

Ireland's five-year adjustment is beginning to pay off, not just in terms of an improving future outlook, but also in terms of fiscal stability. From a peak of 11.5 per cent of GDP attained in 2009, the underlying fiscal deficit will fall to below 3 per cent by 2015. In terms of Ireland's "primary balance" – the balance of revenues over spending excluding spending on debt interest – Ireland will already run a balanced budget next year and significant surpluses in 2015 and 2016. This will contribute to the reduction in public debt envisaged in the Government's economic strategy.

However, the size of Ireland's national debt remains an obstacle to growth and continued decisive action will be needed to achieve the significant progress that is possible.

A third related concern is how Irish banks will fare, next year, against both ECB stress testing and market assessment now that Ireland has exited the bailout. The banks' ability to lend to the economy is a crucial prerequisite for growth. The Government's economic strategy has set out a series of objectives to improve the availability of credit to small and medium-sized businesses and it is in talks with the *KreditAnsalt für Wiederaufbau* (KfW).

The challenges posed by the size of government debt, personal debts and the banking sector are daunting. Nonetheless Ireland's people, business community and Government are a significant way on the journey to recovery. In that regard, it is important to stress that Ireland's crisis was not caused by its tax regime, but rather weak banking regulation and that Ireland was the first country to put in place corrective financial regulation in response to the crisis and also – as **Chapter 5** will elaborate – has gone further than required by the EU in this regard. Ireland is now a country of good financial governance and risk management.

Ireland's Turnaround and Competitive Business Model

At the height of Ireland's crisis, several high profile economists advised Ireland to leave the Euro and pursue a competitive devaluation. The Irish economy, they argued, might be incapable of adjusting its price level to remain competitive within the discipline of the Eurozone. However, mirroring the impressive extent of Ireland's fiscal turnaround is also the manner in which – with the aid of a flexible, dynamic business community, a low business tax regime, supportive Government policies and highly professional State agencies – Ireland's competitiveness also has improved within the context of Euro membership. As **Chapter 2** will highlight, that adjustment has been stronger than seen in other countries affected by the crisis.

Exhibit 1.7: Projected Economic and Export Growth, 2014 to 2016

Y-o-Y % change	2014	2015	2016
GDP	1.8	2.5	2.5
Exports	1.5	3.0	3.5

Source: IMF, *World Economic Outlook*, October 2013.

Some features of Ireland's competitiveness were relatively unaffected by the crisis, such as the strength of Ireland's indigenous exports and the continued success in the area of foreign direct investment. For example, Intel's decision to design its newest microchip in Ireland, announced in October 2013, is a sign that Ireland's past success in attracting foreign direct investment has stayed with it and is destined to be part of its future business model. That model must not be undermined at this crucial time.

Initially that model was based on a highly educated, low wage English-speaking workforce, but is now more sophisticated and developed, thanks to which Ireland remains, in spite of the impact of the crisis, one of the world's most competitive economies. While Ireland's ranking in the World Economic Forum Global Competitiveness league declined from 11th place in 2001 to 29th position by 2010 it remained in the top 30 during the crisis. Now stabilised at 28th (2013/2014 index), Ireland's overall index score contains even more impressive results for more specific indicators of competitiveness, such as for Technological Adaptation (13th in the world), Goods and Labour Market Flexibility (11th and 16th respectively) and Business Sophistication (20th). This demonstrates that the Irish business model has strengthened and diversified its attractions from the low cost model of the 1990s. And if its current low rankings for Macroeconomic Environment (134th) and financial markets (85th) – legacies of the crisis which have weighed Ireland's overall performance down – can be overcome by economic recovery (and the signs are that they can) then Ireland stands every chance of regaining its position amongst the world's 20 most competitive economies. The growing number of leading high technology clusters – in pharmaceutical, information technology and biomedical sectors to name a few – shows a deepening and widening of success in established high technology areas, while the highly successful Dublin Web Summit of October 2013 shows Ireland's capacity to leverage growth in new areas.

While it was never the sole driving force of Ireland's high tech success, and is now matched by many more advantages, Ireland's business tax environment still remains a vital *sine qua non* for the country's continued economic recovery and future success. Recently, as a result of speculation in Washington, and more recently in Brussels and Berlin, there has been a focus on Ireland's competitive Corporation Tax regime. However, in its latest review of the Irish economy,[17] the OECD described Ireland's Corporation Tax as a "central element in its foreign direct investment model" and went on to add that it was "the best way to remain attractive for foreign direct investment vital for economic growth". Ireland is collaborating with the OECD initiative on Base Erosion Profit Sharing (BEPS) and, as elaborated in **Chapter 2**, shows a continued and longstanding commitment to international tax co-operation.

Having experienced one of the world's most remarkable rebirths as a nation and people in the last century, Ireland's recovery from this deep crisis demonstrates that its resilience and success have been carried forward into a new century. By giving a leading example of fiscal consolidation in the Eurozone, Ireland has made a significant contribution to stabilising the Euro. By continuing and deepening the policies that have resulted in this turnaround – and exploring and implementing new policies – Ireland can build on a successful exit from the Troika to the goal of restoring a prosperous full employment economy by or close to the year 2020.

The enormous sacrifices of Ireland's people and the resolve of its Government were instrumental in achieving Ireland's fiscal turnaround. But a fiscal turnaround will not address Ireland's outstanding issues relating to debt. Nor can a fiscal turnaround alone secure the prosperity and return to full employment that Ireland deserves after five years of exertion.

Ireland is playing its part in fulfilling its obligations, not only to the Eurozone and EU, but also playing its part in international collaboration on matters of taxation. Although far from being the only factor in its success, Ireland's business tax regime remains crucial to deepening high technology activity, to attracting new investment and to stimulating the vital indigenous sector. That regime must not be blamed for a crisis with deep roots in global financial governance, as well as in domestic policy mistakes. Ireland has dealt with its domestic failures – failures of financial regulation and fiscal mismanagement – early on and thoroughly. It has also exited its adjustment programme, while several other Eurozone countries are still implementing their own.

Ireland has secured its own turnaround with European help. In doing so, it has helped secure Europe and the Euro's future – and, most important, helped itself.

---

[17]   OECD, *Economic Survey: Ireland*, September 2013.

COMMENTARY: CHAPTER 1

Ireland's Recovery

John Corrigan

Key Messages

- When Ireland lost the confidence of investors and was obliged to request an EU/IMF Programme of Assistance in November 2010, the National Treasury Management Agency (NTMA) took the strategic decision to implement a programme of pro-active engagement with investors so as to work towards a successful return to the markets at the end of the programme. The continued outperformance by the Government of the fiscal targets set in the EU/IMF Programme, the transparent and credible exercise of re-capitalising and restructuring the Irish banks in 2011 and the restoration of competitiveness to the economy gradually regained the trust of investors.

- The decision by US investors, mainly but not exclusively hedge funds, to enter the Irish Government bond market in mid-2011 when yields were at historically high levels eventually led to other more traditional "real money" investors re-entering the market and replacing the hedge funds as yields declined. Developments in Europe also helped Ireland's progress towards full market re-entry – especially Mr. Draghi's promise to do "whatever it takes", the IBRC promissory note arrangement and the term extensions on Ireland's EFSF and EFSM loans. Following Ireland's exit from the programme in December 2013 without a precautionary credit line, the NTMA was able to raise €3.75bn in the markets in early January 2014. Further issuance by way of regular scheduled auctions is planned as Ireland has normalised its presence in the markets.

When the Irish Government announced on 21 November 2010 that it had formally requested a programme of assistance from the EU/IMF the loss of confidence with investors was confirmed, although investor confidence had been sorely tested in the preceding months; Ireland's 10-year bond yield was 8.12 per cent at the time of the bailout, up from a figure of 4.67 per cent six months earlier. Conditions were to become even more testing, with 10-year yields in excess of 14 per cent in July 2011. The reaction of the rating agencies was swift – Moody's downgraded the Irish rating by a record five notches (from Aa2 to Baa1) on 17 December. That move had been preceded by less dramatic, but still punitive, moves on the part of the other rating agencies: Standard and Poor's had cut the rate by two notches (from AA- to A) on 23 November, while Fitch had imposed a three-notch downgrade (from A+ to BBB+) on 9 December.

In those circumstances the NTMA took the decision that it was necessary to engage with investors in a pro-active manner to lay the foundations for Ireland's eventual return to the markets at the end of the programme of assistance – a return which was still far distant and indeed doubted by many commentators who envisaged the necessity of either a second EU/IMF programme or sovereign debt restructuring. The NTMA's plan was to visit investors in the main financial centres in Europe, the US and Asia twice each year. The principal narrative at those meetings was that the Government was committed to delivering on all the commitments it had entered into with the Troika. In relation to the public finances, this involved a specific schedule for the phased reduction of the Government budget deficit to a level of less than 3 per cent of GDP over the period to 2015 and, perhaps more importantly, would entail the achievement of a primary budget surplus of sufficient size to stabilise and subsequently reduce the debt to GDP ratio. A credible assertion of a path towards debt sustainability was of key importance for investors. The NTMA's narrative with investors also included the measures taken to restore competitiveness in the economy – particularly the "internal devaluation" that was required in the absence of the traditional policy tool in such circumstances: currency devaluation. The resizing and restructuring of the banking sector also featured largely in the presentations and discussions – this was of key focus when the NTMA hit the road immediately after the €24bn round of bank recapitalisation in March 2011. Investors were interested also in assessing the risk that the various contingent liabilities overhanging the Government's balance sheet might be crystallised and become actual direct liabilities of the Government. The main contingent liabilities identified by investors related to the potential for further recapitalisation of the banks on top of the €64bn provided by the Government by the summer of 2011, the Government's guarantee of the €30bn in bonds issued by NAMA (as consideration for removing €74bn of land and development loans from the banks' balance sheets), the liabilities under the Eligible Liabilities Guarantee (ELG) scheme (the successor of the two-year blanket guarantee given to the banks by the Government in September 2008) and the Irish banks' drawing of Exceptional Liquidity Assistance (ELA) from the Central Bank of Ireland. Investors frequently expressed admiration for, and sought for a greater understanding of, the roots of the remarkable resilience and social cohesion of the Irish people in taking the painful steps required to deal with the crisis.

In the early investor meetings, the NTMA frequently faced hedge funds and the managers of the emerging markets, credit desks and high yield portfolios in the various investment houses, rather than, or sometimes in addition to, the "real money" investment managers, who because of their low risk appetite traditionally would invest mainly in bonds issued by developed country sovereigns. Investors in government guaranteed bonds issued by the Irish banks also featured largely in the investor meetings. In this initial period there were frequent, and sometimes vocal, complaints from the holders of subordinated debt issued by the Irish banks regarding the various liability management exercises that had seen some of those junior bonds forcibly repurchased at a steep discount. Typically the investors at that stage expressed concerns about the ability of the Irish Government to successfully navigate a way through the crisis without defaulting on its debt obligations. An even bigger concern for many investors was the risk of the break-up of the Euro.

The ability of the NTMA to point to the consistent outperformance by the Government in relation to the fiscal targets gradually won back the trust of investors. Especially important in this regard were the endorsements by the Troika in their quarterly reports of the steady progress Ireland was making and the fact that the targets were never relaxed.

An important turning point in Ireland's recovery came in March 2011 with the results of the stress tests on the Irish banks. The robustness and transparency of the exercise and the deep involvement of high calibre external institutions gave credibility to the exercise, which gradually convinced investors that on this occasion Ireland had truly come to terms with the scale of the recapitalisation and restructuring required for the Irish banks. However, the conversion of investors was not instant and the nadir for the Irish Government bond market was to come in July 2011 when Moody's downgraded the Irish credit rating to sub-investment (or "junk") status. The 10-year bond yield exceeded 14 per cent while the two-year yield reached a staggering 23 per cent.

The decision in July 2011 by a group of US/Canadian investors to invest €1.1bn to acquire a 34.9 per cent shareholding in Bank of Ireland represented a significant statement of confidence in Ireland by influential foreign investors. At about the same time in 2011 a number of hedge funds and traditional asset managers in the US began to purchase Irish government bonds. Some of these investors wished to take a contrarian view to a widely-held belief in sectors of the US investment community that the Euro would break up. They decided that the purchase of Irish Government bonds was the best way to reflect their investment view, given the prospect of significant capital gains should their view be vindicated (Irish Government bond prices ultimately doubled from the level pertaining in July 2011). This initiated a rally in Irish Government bonds, which led to the NTMA being able in January 2012 to execute its first capital market transaction since September 2010 – investors accepted an offer to switch €3.5bn of a bond due to mature in January 2014 into a new bond maturing in February 2015. Investors had regarded the redemption of the €11.8bn bond maturing in January 2014, immediately after the end of the EU/IMF programme, as a major obstacle to Ireland's successful return to the markets. The NTMA addressed the challenge posed by this "funding cliff" by means of this switch operation and a number of other transactions, including a subsequent switch and outright funding operation in July 2012.

The NTMA's process of re-engagement with the markets rapidly gathered pace over the course of 2012.

In May 2012 Ireland's voters approved the *EU Fiscal Treaty* by a 60 per cent to 40 per cent majority. The Euro area leaders issued a statement following their summit on 29 June about the imperative to break the vicious circle between banks and sovereigns and on 26 July ECB President Draghi issued his famous assurance that "the ECB is ready to do whatever it takes to preserve the Euro". Substance was given to this assurance with the announcement of the ECB's Outright Monetary Transactions (OMT) on 6 September 2012. Against this positive background the NTMA, on 5 July 2012, was able to hold its first Treasury Bill auction since September 2010. As a result of this auction, the trading desks in a large number of banks that wished to participate in the transaction applied to their risk committees to have lines reopened to enable them to take on exposure to Irish Government risk. In many cases these lines had been closed since the onset of the crisis. Subsequently, on 26 July 2012, the NTMA was able to issue bonds to raise €4.2bn in new money and switch a further €1bn from short-dated to longer-dated bonds. In August, the NTMA sold €1bn of long-dated amortising bonds to the local pensions industry.

With the continued rally in Irish Government bond yields during 2012, many of the hedge fund-type investors who had purchased when yields were at or close to their peak around mid-year 2011 sold their holdings so as to monetise their gains. At the same time, the traditional "real money" asset managers became more prominent in the market and took up the slack so that the market rally continued.

Exhibit 1.8: Irish Government 2-year and 10-year Bond Yields, 2000 to 2014

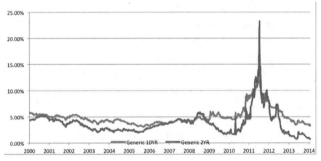

Entering the third and final year of the Troika programme in 2013, it was necessary for the NTMA to press on with the process of engaging with market participants so as to be able to fully fund the State without support from the end of 2013 onwards once the full amount of €67.5bn available under the EU/IMF programme had been drawn. The objective was to have enough cash on hand at end-2013 from long-term funding sources to cover the Exchequer's needs for 12 to 15 months ahead. In practice, this meant raising about €7bn to €8bn in the bond markets in 2013, in addition to the last monies to be drawn under the EU/IMF programme so as to have about €20bn cash at end year. The NTMA began its funding operation on 7 January 2013 with the syndicated issue by tap of €2.5bn of its existing five-year benchmark bond. Investors proved very receptive to the bond issue.

February 2013 saw a step-change improvement in the Government's funding requirements. IBRC was liquidated and the promissory notes (which the Government had issued to Anglo Irish Bank and Irish Nationwide Building Society prior to their being merged into Irish Bank Resolution Corporation on 1 July 2011) held by that institution and which required €3bn of borrowing by the NTMA each year were replaced with long-dated Government bonds. The net effect of this transaction was to reduce the NTMA's funding needs by about €2bn per year, or €20bn over the next decade. In addition, in a series of discussions among EU leaders in the early months of 2013, it was agreed to extend by seven years the maturities of Ireland's borrowings from the EFSF (€17.7bn) and EFSM (€22.5bn). Coincidentally, this had the effect of reducing the amount of debt to be refinanced in the markets by €20bn over the next 10 years. Thus the combined effect of this agreement and the replacement of the promissory notes was to reduce the NTMA's funding needs in the markets by €40bn over the next 10 years. Taking advantage of favourable market sentiment arising from these two boosts to Ireland's liquidity (by reducing refinancing risk) and solvency (the deals locked in lower interest cost for the long-term), the NTMA raised €5bn through the syndicated issue of a new 10-year benchmark bond on 13 March 2013 at a yield of 4.15 per cent. This deal attracted bids from over 400 good quality, and mainly "real money", investors based predominantly in mainland Europe, the UK and the US, but also including domestic investors who took up 18 per cent of the issue. This effectively secured all the funding the NTMA needed for the full year of 2013.

The transformation of the market from one driven early in the rally by "fast money" hedge fund-type investors with an high risk appetite to one dominated by the more traditional "real money" asset managers, insurance companies and pension funds which had commenced in 2012 continued. In particular, many real money investors in Europe came into the Irish market. These new investors were convinced that Ireland would be able to access the markets at yields compatible with debt sustainability. They also were assured by Mr. Draghi's commitment to do "whatever it takes" and were chasing a higher yield for some of their investments than could be had from investing in the AAA-rated bonds of core Eurozone countries. Irish yields were trading at a premium of well over two percentage points above the often sub-2 per cent yields in those countries.

The Irish Government's decision in November 2013 to exit the EU/IMF programme without requesting any type of precautionary credit line surprised many commentators but was taken in its stride by the bond market. The Government's decision proved to be well-founded and the NTMA was able to launch one of its most successful deals ever when it syndicated a new 10-year bond issue on 7 January 2014 at a yield of 3.54 per cent, 166 basis points over the 10-year German bond. The decision by Moody's on 17 January to restore Ireland's investment grade rating was seen generally as following the market but did open the prospect of new investors in Irish Government bonds whose mandates allow investments only where there is an investment grade rating from all the major credit rating agencies. It also qualified Ireland for some bond indices that it had been excluded from: this forces some investors to buy Irish bonds. This is particularly important for investors in Asia and the Middle East, but also for some European funds. Thus Ireland can be seen as having unequivocally regained full market access. The NTMA plans to validate that judgment by conducting a series of normal bond auctions over the course of 2014, just as the other smaller Eurozone countries will. It should be said that the continued ability to access the markets at sustainable rates is crucially dependent on the ability of the Government to follow a prudent fiscal policy for many years to come, where primary budget surpluses are sufficient to keep the debt burden, as exemplified by the debt to GDP ratio, on a downward trajectory.

CHAPTER 2

Ireland's Business Model

Dr Jack Golden

Key Messages

- Ireland has shown resilience and flexibility in adapting its economy and business model, not just in this crisis but also during four decades as a member of the European project. This explains its transition from a small agricultural economy, whose exports were dominated by Britain, into one of the world's most globalised and diverse economies.
- Significant challenges remain to achieve the full potential of Ireland's dynamic economic model: overcoming the lack of credit to business, improving the ability of SMEs to export and retaining Ireland's competitive tax regime.

Introduction

In 1972 Ireland was a small agricultural economy where two-thirds of exports were destined for its nearest neighbour. Living standards were below two-thirds of the European average. Forty years later, Ireland is now the third most open economy in the world.[18] Exports to its nearest neighbour, while vital, now account for one-fifth of its total exports. Despite four years of recession, living standards have remained at or above the EU average (Ireland's GDP *per capita* is 121 per cent of the EU average).[19] This compares with the situation before Ireland joined the European Economic Community (EEC) when living standards of the average Irish person lagged far behind that of the average German or French person. The transition is not a once-off. The success of Ireland's business model is that it has never stopped adapting to change.

---

[18] EY (Ernst & Young) Globalisation Index 2012.

[19] The gap between GDP and GNP (the former is around a fifth greater than the latter) means that GDP *per capita* overstates Ireland's living standards. However the use of GDP *per capita* may be justified for two reasons: First, GDP *per capita* is a standard international measure and, second, the continued success of foreign direct investment, which the higher GDP figure reflects, is a positive sign for the future of the economy (see **Chapter 4**).

In the 1970s and 1980s the Common Agricultural Policy was instrumental in raising incomes and economic activity in Ireland's less developed rural regions. In the 1980s decades of work by Ireland's Industrial Development Authority began to pay off. In 1985 Microsoft became the first leading global information technology firm to locate its international headquarters in Ireland. Another key turning point in Ireland's business model was the commitment of its voters in 1992 to Economic and Monetary Union (EMU). This marked the transition from targeting foreign direct investment on the basis of low labour costs, competitive business taxation and a highly educated workforce, to a new phase of stressing Ireland as a bridge to the world's largest single market.

High value added and export-driven clusters in information technology, medicare, biotechnology, pharmaceuticals and other industries now are a key feature of Ireland's economy. The arrival in more recent years of global social media giants Facebook and Twitter shows this process is both continuous and constantly renewing itself.

From purely export-driven growth seen in the 1980s and early 1990s, the commitment to EMU saw the beginning of a more domestically-driven economic model. By 2000, Ireland had attained full employment and was one of the fastest-growing economies in the developed world. But in that year it was still one of the world's most competitive economies, ranked 4th in a leading global indicator.[20] The balance between export growth and domestic growth still was reasonably healthy.

Soon after, however, this balance was disturbed as increasingly dominant domestic growth became over-reliant on high levels of public spending and bank lending. Growth in construction activity – initially benign and a necessary response to a rapidly-growing population – began to spin out of control. At one point close to one in five male workers was working in the sector.

By 2007, the Irish business model looked healthy on the surface. But high levels of debt and State spending were to leave Ireland badly exposed to the global crisis to come. But even as crisis struck, changes were occurring in this model that are now helping Ireland recover: until the 1990s Ireland's business model was based on an industrial policy that used capital grants to attract high technology manufacturing-related foreign investment. From 1994 the EU began restricting the size of capital grants to industry. Ahead of the game, Ireland had started to shift policy and the *Lisbon Agenda* of 2000 – to create the world's most "dynamic and competitive knowledge based economy" – gave further impetus to this change.

Ireland evolved from having an industrial strategy to developing a broader "Enterprise Policy", which included encouraging indigenous industries in high growth areas, especially in traded services, an area of huge potential growth for Ireland's small and open island economy

As alluded to in the previous chapter, and shown more clearly below, this transition was helped by a significant improvement in cost-competitiveness

---

[20] World Economic Forum Global Competitiveness rankings 2000/2001.

between 2008 and 2012. A number of focused policies, such as the *Action Plan for Jobs* and various budgetary initiatives that have assisted business start-up, innovation and job creation in the economy, also have contributed to the success of Ireland's business model.

But challenges remain. Some – despite improving competitiveness, Ireland remains a relatively high cost country in which to do business – are the result of past economic policy mistakes. Others – Irish small and medium-sized enterprises, unlike their German counterparts, lack access to a domestic market of sufficient size and scale to develop export capacity easily – are more structural. And some challenges are more related to the recent crisis, particularly the challenge of gaining access to credit. At the time of writing, Ireland's banking system was still normalising. The ECB's stress testing of Ireland's banks expected in 2014 will be a decisive threshold in this regard. Another new challenge is that, with manufacturing now accounting for a smaller share of employment and the economy than in the 1990s, multinational manufacturing companies' high productivity will be therefore less able to drive economic growth rates of the kind seen in the 1990s and early 2000s. Other sectors must make a greater contribution if Ireland's growth is to reach the levels needed to restore prosperity.

Fortunately, the latest overhaul of Ireland's business model has seen the Government implement innovative policies that go a considerable way towards to addressing these challenges. These are elaborated below. But first it is worth looking at the values that underpin Ireland's business model and its ability to adapt to change.

Values Underpinning Ireland's Business Model

The perception that Ireland's business model is solely dependent on its taxation policy is completely false. A number of core values serve to underpin a comprehensive set of enterprise policies aimed at supporting and continuously developing the manufacturing and service sectors of the economy.

Investment in attracting foreign companies to establish in Ireland and in developing indigenous industry has been fundamental to Ireland's success. This has been reinforced by a focus on **innovation** and the increasing degree of **interdependence** established between indigenous and multinational enterprises. The creation of industry **clusters** also has been a key feature that is increasingly visible, as has the impact of **culture** and a keen focus on **competitiveness**.

Investment: Foreign Direct Investment

After decades of anaemic growth following independence, the new Irish State quickly grasped the importance to Ireland's development of trade investment from abroad. Close geographical location made Britain the most important trading partner, while close historic ties made the US a logical target for investment. The US quickly became a dominant force in foreign direct investment. But that investment is now more diversified, both geographically and across sectors. Increasingly, internationally traded services are showing a capacity to complement the role played up to now by high technology manufacturing companies. Foreign direct investment is now also a "two-way street", with Irish companies investing significantly abroad out of all proportion to Ireland's small size as a nation.

Founded in 1949, the Industrial Development Authority (IDA) pioneered foreign investment in the Irish economy. It was an essential factor in the country's transformation and Ireland's "Weltmeister" status in this field is one many other small nations have sought to emulate.

According to data from the US Bureau of Economic Analysis,[21] US investment in Ireland rose in 2011 by 20 per cent to $188.3bn. This means that Ireland receives more US multinational investment than Brazil, Russia, India and China combined.

According to the *IBM 2012 Global Location Trends Report* Ireland ranks first in the world for the quality and value of inward investment, first in Europe for jobs created in Research & Development and second in Europe and fourth in the world for the number of investment jobs per head of population.

Investment: Indigenous Industry

As well as promoting foreign direct investment, the Irish Government since the recession has been vigilant in promoting investment in indigenous small and medium-sized enterprises. Through a successful State agency, Enterprise Ireland, and through a range of Government policies (discussed below), indigenous industry has begun to recover impressively from the recession.

Further initiatives are strengthening that trend. Although the 2014 budget adjusted Ireland's fiscal position by less than requested by the Troika,[22] and whilst this attracted some adverse comment, the gap between the adjustment requested by the Troika and the adjustment that transpired (some €500m) was directed entirely at a package of incentives aimed at stimulating SMEs.

Initiatives to assist trade finance, tax exemptions for new entrepreneurs and a series of enhancements to tax incentives aimed at stimulating the reinvestment of capital gains and further investment in Research & Development were all features of this budget.

Tourism is the oldest and best-known source of foreign service income. The Government's 2014 budget reduced the Air Travel Departure Tax and maintained a reduced rate of VAT for the tourist industry with a view to boosting visitor numbers. This follows the "Gathering" initiative in 2013, aimed at encouraging significant numbers from the global Irish diaspora to return to the country for a

---

[21] Cited in Quinlan, Joseph (2012). *The Irish-US Economic Relationship*, American Chamber of Commerce Ireland.

[22] The Troika had requested a combined adjustment – incorporating tax increases and spending reductions – of €3.1bn, which compares to an adjustment of €2.6bn made on Budget Day.

range of family and community events. Measures designed to reinvigorate another established sector – one badly affected by the downturn – and steer it away from speculative activities of the kind that contributed to that crisis were also in evidence with initiatives such as the Home Renovation scheme, which aims to stimulate demand for small construction firm activity.

Interdependence

Ireland's success in attracting foreign direct investment might be seen as a case of over-dependence on foreign investors. It is anything but. Ireland's position is not one of dependence but of interdependence. Research by the American Chamber of Commerce in Ireland shows how Irish companies in the US directly employ more workers than subsidiaries of US companies do in Ireland.

Likewise, just as German companies are an important provider of jobs in Ireland, Irish companies such as CRH, Glen Dimplex and Kingspan provide thousands of jobs across Germany.

The interdependence of multinational companies based in Ireland and indigenous business is apparent at many levels, including customer-supplier arrangements, the exchange of talent within the country and internationally as well as the development of Irish multinationals that have expanded overseas in the last 40 years.

By 2012, internationally traded goods and services in the Irish economy were worth approximately €313bn – or one third of a trillion euro – equating to almost double Ireland's GDP. This is by far the highest level of any EU Member State and makes Ireland the most globalised Western economy and the third most open economy in the world after Hong Kong and Singapore.

More impressive still is how, as recession still held the domestic economy in its grip, Ireland's record on exports and foreign direct investment actually improved significantly: in 2010 export growth, for both multinational and indigenous firms, exceeded the rate of decline in the preceding year.

So whether one examines the World Economic Forum's Global Competitiveness Index, the EY Globalisation Index or the *IBM Global Location Trends* report, it is clear that Ireland is emerging from this crisis with its status as a leader in the globalised economy intact.

Innovation

Since its entry to the EEC as an agricultural country, Ireland's economy has grown strongly, due to the country's impressive capacity to constantly innovate. From the wave of high technology manufacturing firms that came to Ireland in the 1980s and early 1990s to the emergence of a strong domestic economy and consumer culture in the late 1990s and early 2000s, Ireland's business model is now going through perhaps its most interesting phase of innovation.

The emergence of new clusters in areas such as nanotechnology, health informatics, high technology, food and the internationalisation of construction expertise, to name a few, are not only as a result of the work of the IDA, but have been encouraged by various policy initiatives in the fields of research and development, innovation and incentivising investment.

In October 2007, the Smart Economy Framework, introduced under the National Reform Programme, prioritised innovation-driven enterprises and high quality employment. This built on the *Strategy for Science, Technology and Innovation* (2006-2013), which aimed to transform Ireland into a knowledge economy through increased research and development funding.

Launched in 2012, the *Action Plan for Jobs* aims to replace jobs lost during the crisis with more sustainable employment based on innovation, enterprise and exports. Under broad strategic objectives such as building competitive advantage, assisting indigenous industry to grow, helping company start-ups and deepening the impact of foreign direct investment, the plan contains hundreds of initiatives and so-called "disruptive reforms" that are identified as having the potential for job creation. As many as 12,000 jobs were created in the private sector during 2012 when the plan was introduced. Over 58,000 jobs were created in the 12 months to the third quarter of 2013[23] and a reinforcement of this positive trend is anticipated for the coming years.

The innovativeness of the Irish economy is reflected also in the success at catching a new wave of traded services growth. A strong opportunity, driven by demographic trends (such as the growth of the world's "middle income" population) as well as economic factors, this source of economic growth is less dependent on the global economic cycle and offers a small versatile economy like Ireland the chance to grow faster in the future. Between 2003 and 2012 inclusive, and in spite of recession affecting other parts of the economy, services exports from Ireland almost trebled, from €35.3bn to €90.3bn.[24] Unlike manufacturing exports, where the strong influence of the US has been evident to date, exports of traded services are more diversified across the globe.

Competitiveness

The striking feature of the competitiveness of the Irish business model is one it shares with German cars: its ability to turn sharply and at speed!

Relying on the speed and resilience of tens of thousands of small and medium-sized enterprises, that "roadholding" ability comes from a combination of factors more microeconomic than macroeconomic in nature. Between the onset of crisis in 2008 and 2012 Ireland achieved an astounding improvement in competitiveness of 40 per cent (shown in **Exhibit 2.1** below) as measured by the ECB's Harmonised Index of Competitiveness. While this was following a period in which

---

[23] Central Statistics Office, *Quarterly National Household Survey, Q3 2013*.

[24] Newman, Carol (2012). "Manufacturing and Internationally Traded Services", in O'Hagan, John & Newman, Carol, *The Economy of Ireland*, Gill & Macmillan; Central Statistics Office, *International Trade in Services Release 2012*, 30 September 2013.

competitiveness deteriorated, it demonstrates Ireland's resilience and its ability to adapt quickly to new circumstances (a fall in the line indicates a fall in relative costs and consequently a rise in competitiveness); Ireland's improvement in competitiveness exceeded the EU average and that of Germany and was considerably ahead of other bailout countries.

Exhibit 2.1: Ireland's Competitiveness Gain: A Dramatic Improvement since 2008

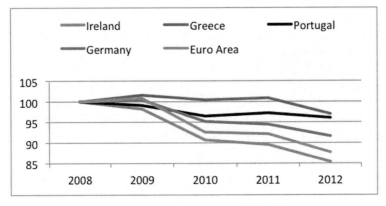

Source: ECB (index rebased so 2008 = 100).

Behind this improvement was the fact that price and wage levels fell relative to the rest of the Eurozone. Some economists had argued for Ireland to leave the Euro in order to be able to devalue its currency. But Ireland's experience to date shows that a real devaluation – an adjustment in business costs relative to its peers – has been achieved without sacrificing Euro membership. What is more this adaptability of Ireland's business model has reaped rewards in a strong rebound in exports after a year, 2009, in which many Eurozone countries, including Germany, experienced sharp export falls.

Exhibit 2.2: Ireland's Export Growth Percentage, 2008 to 2012

Country	Average	2008	2009	2010	2011	2012
Ireland	+1.7	-1.1	-3.8	6.4	5.4	1.6
Greece	-2.6	1.7	-19.4	5.2	0.3	-0.9
Portugal	-0.5	2.3	-11.9	0.8	8.1	2.0
Germany	+3.2	2.8	-13.0	15.2	8.0	3.2
Euro Area	+1.6	0.6	-12.7	11.6	6.3	2.3

Source: IMF, *World Economic Outlook*, October 2013.

Exhibit 2.2 demonstrates not only how Ireland's exports recovered strongly in 2010 but how they have risen to new levels and, while they are not as strong over the period as Germany's, they have been less volatile and have outperformed peer Troika countries.

Although exports slowed in 2012, due to international factors, export growth will be a crucial engine of recovery. The pick-up in growth from 2014 onwards, expected by the IMF in its latest *World Economic Outlook* forecasts, clearly relies on continued export growth.

Ireland's World Economic Forum Global Competitiveness ranking of 28th, according to the 2013/2014 Index, places it still in the top 30 most competitive economies in the world. As mentioned in **Chapter 1**, this overall performance is negatively impacted by low rankings for Macroeconomic Environment (134th) and Financial Markets (85th), a legacy of the crisis. As a result, Ireland's ranking understates the vigour and renewability of the country's business model. This vigour and renewability is shown by Ireland's rankings in other categories such as Technological Adaptation (13th), Goods Market Flexibility (11th), Labour Market Flexibility (16th) and Business Sophistication (20th), to name a few. Clearly Ireland can re-enter the list of top 20 most competitive economies in the world, and perhaps even the top 10. The fact that Intel has decided to design its newest microchip in Ireland, announced in October 2013, is an encouraging sign that it will.

Clusters

Some decades after the concept was first pioneered in Denmark, Ireland has achieved success in developing clusters of industries that have a potential to sink deeper roots into Ireland's economy.

The information technology cluster, comprising globally-recognised brand names such as Microsoft, Dell, Hewlett-Packard and Intel, is the first and best-known of these. Even before the recession, some traditional activity in this cluster moved from Ireland as business costs rose and more cost-competitive manufacturing centres emerged in the East. But as this happened new second and third generation clusters have come into being in response to both Government policies and the vigilance of the IDA. Among the second wave might be included pharmaceutical, medicare and biotechnology companies and Dublin's International Financial Services Centre (IFSC).

As in any dynamic economy, change is constant. But as some industries undergo adverse developments – activity in the pharmaceutical sector is being affected by the "patent cliff" – others experience growth. The announcement in 2013 of Deutsche Bank's intention to create 700 jobs in the IFSC is an example of such growth.

A third generation of clusters has emerged in recent years in areas such as software development, social media, green technology and cloud computing. A key measure in the 2013 *Action Plan for Jobs* is to make Ireland the leading country in Europe for "Big Data" (data generated and collected by companies and governments). This is a typical example of a market that is projected to grow rapidly and where Ireland can harness new economic vigour by strategically positioning itself to play up its advantages (pre-existing clusters, as well as the skill sets and supply chains for such industries, are already present in Ireland, if not yet in sufficient quantities) and play down its disadvantages (data analytics do not require location in areas of large population concentration so Ireland's peripheral location is not an obstacle to high growth in this sector).

By targeting these high value added and rapidly-growing sectors Ireland can offset the impact both of its relatively high cost base and the strong Euro.

A key challenge remains the matching of educational sector output to meet the demands of new sectors. From the high quality but generalist educational skills sought after during previous waves of development, demand for skills is becoming more specific. Among the strategic objectives identified in the 2013 *Action Plan for Jobs*, for instance, was to provide an additional 2,000 Information Communication Technology graduate level professionals. The challenge of keeping Ireland's educational system up to date in this regard is addressed in **Chapter 6**.

Culture
One of the key factors that has enabled Ireland's business model to adapt rapidly to changes in the global environment has been attributed to a culture in Ireland of flexibility and pragmatism as well as a highly-developed capacity to network in an organic and dynamic manner. Deficiencies in the regulatory system exposed by the financial crisis have been addressed and the quality of physical infrastructure is now comparable to other developed Western economies. While a competitive Corporation Tax regime is clearly an incentive for business, the cultural advantages of openness, flexibility and a unique capacity for networking have been pivotal in exploiting opportunities to provide a bridge between international, particularly American businesses and the European single market.

Ireland is a small country where family life and community are important values, reinforced by a strong tradition of intense verbal communication. These characteristics and the fact that Ireland is the only English-speaking country in the Eurozone have been successfully exploited in business-to-business communication for many years. Networking and communication skills are becoming even more important for the development of many emerging and high growth sectors like social media and cloud computing. The success of the Global Web Summit held in Dublin in 2013 is a clear indication that Ireland's business culture is well-suited to support the continued development of these sectors.

Further evidence of the dynamic nature and flexibility of the Irish business culture is demonstrated by the way the IDA has influenced government policy to ensure it has been continually adapted to the needs of multinational investors, making it a world leader in this field.

Challenges for Ireland's Business Model

Credit

Despite significant injections of taxpayers' money into Ireland's banks and capital adequacy ratios that remain good by international comparison – and in spite of signs of economic recovery – the rate of lending growth to business remains negative. The Government has taken several initiatives to boost credit availability to small business. The establishment of a Credit Review Office enables small business owners to appeal declines for loans from specified banks. A Credit Guarantee Scheme has been established to guarantee €450m in additional bank lending to viable micro, small and medium enterprises. In addition, a Microfinance Fund has been created for firms with no more than 10 employees, with loans of up to €25,000 available for commercially viable proposals that do not meet conventional risk criteria applied by commercial banks.

The constraints, however, are not restricted to the supply side and there is evidence that companies are adapting a more cautious approach to borrowing. Many businesses have been through painful re-structuring processes since 2008 and are reluctant to put pressure on their balance sheets until they become convinced that the economic growth seen recently is sustainable. According to Central Bank data,[25] credit to non-financial corporations was falling by 4.5 per cent as of September 2013. For credit between one and five years – a crucial category for small to medium-sized enterprises – the rate of decline was 15 per cent. Given the constraints faced by the Government and caution being applied by banks in relation to the outcome of stress testing by the European Central Bank, shortage of credit and an unwillingness on the part of small and medium-sized enterprises to take risks may well act as constraints to short-term economic growth.

Internationalisation

The small size of Ireland's domestic market and Ireland's position as an island all combine to create significant obstacles for small and medium-sized Irish enterprises to internationalise their business.

For many, trading with mainland Britain is an obvious first step to exporting. However, for smaller firms, acquiring the necessary skills, distribution channels and credit lines – not to mention developing or accessing suitable logistical capacity – to make this first transition can be daunting.

Again Government is helping: Enterprise Ireland's Potential Exporters Division has been established to provide potential exporters with practical advice, information and market intelligence along with some training and development and funding assistance. While EU restrictions prevent aggressive forms of export assistance, new strategies should be explored with a view to transforming more

---

[25] Central Bank of Ireland, *Credit, Money and Banking Statistics*, November 2013.

Irish SMEs into successful export companies capable of exploiting huge opportunities for them in the global economy.

An opportunity exists for the development of specialist 'export acceleration' services in the private sector to help SMEs establish bases in foreign markets for products and services. The growth of non-traditional services that can be delivered to customers online has enormous potential but competition in this sector is extremely intense.

Taxation

Ireland's business model has been built by combining a number of core elements and is therefore not over-reliant on any single factor. At the same time, Ireland's competitive tax regime is fundamental to the success of that model and has been key to attracting foreign direct investment. The OECD[26] has rightly described it as a "central element in its foreign direct investment model" and as "the best way to remain attractive for foreign direct investment vital for economic growth". What needs to be stressed also is the extent to which Ireland has been a consistent collaborator with relevant international bodies in terms of maintaining a business model that is consistent with best international practice.

Recent criticism of the Irish taxation system emanating from countries competing for tax revenue from multinational companies has been largely based on inaccurate information. In 1956, Ireland introduced a zero rate of taxation on income from export sales in a bid to stimulate a stagnant economy but, on joining what was then known as the European Economic Community, Ireland agreed to phase out this zero rate. By 1980, Ireland's Corporation Tax rate on manufacturing had been increased to 10 per cent. In 1987, that rate was extended to the emerging international financial services sector. In a phased process negotiated with its European partners, Ireland harmonised the rate of Corporation Tax to 12.5 per cent – the currently applicable rate – by 2003.

Ireland's co-operation with other partners is also strong. Ireland has full exchange of tax information with its peers through a system of 69 double taxation agreements. In 2010 Ireland introduced mandatory disclosure rules to obtain early information about certain tax schemes and who has availed of them and to close down any schemes viewed as aggressive. In 2012, Ireland was one of the first countries to sign the *Foreign Account Tax Compliance Act* (FATCA) with the US.[27] FATCA is now recognised as the emerging global standard for automatic exchange of tax information.

International tax co-operation was also a key feature of Ireland's successful 2013 Presidency of the EU. Ireland's Presidency focused on tackling tax fraud and tax evasion. Following a meeting in Dublin of Economic and Finance Ministers in April 2013, Irish Finance Minister Michael Noonan and EU Commissioner for

---

[26]   OECD, *Economic Survey: Ireland*, September 2013.

[27]   September 2012.

Taxation, Algirdas Šemeta, identified a list of actions to strengthen and deepen collaboration against tax evasion and tax fraud at European level. The European Council conclusions on tax signed on 22 May 2013 – and adopted under an Irish Presidency of the EU – called for automatic exchange of information to be extended to an international level. To that end, Ireland is taking an active part in the OECD's Base Erosion Profit Shifting project. Lastly, a symbolic point might be noted: the 2013 G8 summit which led to the Lough Erne declaration – which assists public reporting by international companies on tax and profits – was signed on the island of Ireland.

The maintenance of a transparent, internationally-compliant and competitive Corporation Tax regime has been a fundamental element of successive Governments' policies and maintenance of the 12.5 per cent Corporation Tax rate remains a firm commitment of both Government and opposition political parties.

Conclusions

Like few other EU member states, Ireland has shown adaptability and resilience in updating and renewing its business model. From a small agricultural economy whose exports were dominated by its nearest neighbour, it is now one of the world's most open, most flexible, most high technology and diverse economies. Government policies – and the flexibility of Ireland's people and businesses – in adapting to change and challenge have been indispensable in this process.

Ireland's business model is one driven by strong values:

- Innovation in both business practice and government policy.
- Interdependence between Ireland and its trading and political partners.
- A dedication to investment in new and emerging technologies and sectors.
- Constant attention to maintaining and restoring the competitiveness of its economy, tax model and business sectors.
- The promotion of clusters of industry in both manufacturing and services that leverage Ireland's unique advantages and create opportunities for growth.
- A culture of business that stresses flexibility, adaptability and pragmatism.

Key challenges that face Ireland's business model now include improving access to credit and overcoming barriers to exporting – particularly for small and medium-sized enterprises – and ensuring that small, medium and larger firms continue to avail of Ireland's transparent and competitive tax regime.

COMMENTARY: CHAPTER 2

A Case Study on Foreign Direct Investment into Ireland: Allianz Worldwide Care Limited

Frank Mee

Key Messages

- Many global international financial services companies are now located in Ireland due to a combination of success factors, of which Ireland's taxation regime is just one. Allianz Group, which employs 144,000 people and has 78 million customers, is a leading example.
- A stable business environment, supportive government agencies and access to well-educated and entrepreneurial staff enabled the financial services sector to grow strongly and recover quickly after the crisis. Retaining Ireland's competitiveness in this area, however, will require action in relation to the still high costs imposed on the economy by its more sheltered sectors.

Introduction

While Ireland's Corporation Tax policy gets all the headlines as a key reason for the country's attractiveness for foreign direct investment (FDI), it is in reality just one of the reasons for Ireland's success in this area and in many cases is a subsidiary reason. Other factors like Ireland's pro-business environment, lack of bureaucracy, good labour pool and favourable labour laws are also key factors. Ireland has enjoyed unprecedented success in attracting FDI, even when some of the advantages were mitigated during the economic collapse in the 2008 to 2012 period. While it is still an attractive location, there is a need for a Government focus in certain areas, such as costs, personal tax and maintenance of the 12.5 per cent Corporation Tax rate, in order to maintain that advantage.

Jack Golden, in **Chapter 2, Ireland's Business Model**, sets out the strategy of successive Irish Governments in creating a business model designed to create a pro-business environment aimed at attracting FDI in key sectors. One of these sectors was international financial services. The International Financial Services Centre initiative from 1987 had the effect of creating a cluster of businesses in Dublin owned by most of the key global financial institutions in the banking, insurance and fund management arenas. Currently, there are over 500 such international financial services businesses in Ireland, mostly in Dublin, employing over 30,000 skilled employees.

This Commentary looks at a real-life example of a foreign direct investment into Ireland in international financial services. Allianz Group, which is headquartered in Munich, is one of the world's largest financial institutions with 144,000 employees insuring 78 million customers in more than 70 countries. Its asset management division has more than €1.4 trillion assets under management. In mid-1999, Allianz Group decided to locate its new international health business in Ireland. This case study looks at the background to that decision and how the business has developed in Ireland in the past 15 years.

Allianz and Ireland

In the late 1990s, the German health insurance subsidiary of Allianz Group had identified that many German companies had significant numbers of senior staff based overseas. These expatriate staff could not be covered by a German domestic health insurance policy. Allianz set up a working group to determine whether it would be viable to set up a new health insurance company to service such business. This was at the time that the EU insurance market had just been liberalised, allowing insurers authorised (licenced) in one EU State to sell insurance products into all other EU States using the freedom of services provisions of the *Treaty of Rome*. The working group concluded that there were not enough expatriate staff employed by German companies to warrant a new company servicing the German market only but there would be sufficient such business taking into account the whole EU market. The working group recommended that a new health insurance company be established by Allianz to service the expatriate staff of EU multinationals using freedom of services as allowed under the EU *Insurance Directives*. Their preliminary recommendation was that the business be located in The Netherlands. Following an intervention by Allianz Ireland management, the working group considered Ireland as a potential location. This resulted in a proposal being made to the Allianz Board of Management to establish the new business in Ireland, which was ratified by the Allianz Board in mid-1999.

There were a number of factors behind the decision to locate in Ireland back in 1999:

- A perception of Ireland being a good location for FDI, with a good business model.
- Significantly less bureaucracy in establishing a business in Ireland.
- More business-friendly corporate and regulatory environment.
- English-speaking country (English being the business language of most multinationals).
- Labour laws evenly balanced between workers' rights and employers' rights.
- Lower cost location.

- A substantial pool of foreign language skills.
- Existing Allianz Group operation to provide set-up support.
- Lower tax environment (a then Corporation Tax rate of 10 per cent).

The lower tax rate was not a major factor in the decision; it was more the "icing on the cake".

The new company, which was named Allianz Worldwide Care Limited, spent six months establishing itself and opened for business in Park West Business Campus on the outskirts of Dublin in April 2000.

So how has it worked out for Allianz? Currently, Allianz Worldwide Care has a premium income of circa €500m and makes in excess of €30m in annual profits. It has 825 employees, of which 650 are based in Ireland. The company also has significant overseas operations in Dubai, Belgium, China, Libya and Qatar. Approximately 42 per cent of the staff are Irish nationals; two-thirds of them are female, while the average age is 31. The staff come from 58 different countries, covering 27 different languages, making it the most diverse company in Allianz Group by some distance. In every year since 2003, it has beaten its premium income and profit targets, always by a wide margin. The company writes business in most countries throughout the world, with 60 per cent of its business being written outside the EU. Ninety per cent of its business is with multinationals and major organisations (a significant portion of which are *Fortune 500* companies) and 10 per cent is with individual expatriates. It insures over 350,000 expatriates and the company paid claims in almost 200 countries in 2013. While the initial target market was EU multinationals, the company quickly found new markets. Businesses headquartered outside the EU was an obvious first move and then the company moved into new niche markets such as inter-governmental organisations (IGOs), diplomatic services, international schools and shipping businesses. By any standards, this is a real success story.

The fact that the company is part of the Allianz Group and incorporates Allianz in its name was a significant factor in its success. The Allianz name opens all doors and gives potential clients a sense of solidity and financial strength. Furthermore, in the initial stages, Allianz helped its new Irish subsidiary through knowledge transfer and introductions to major corporate customers. Allianz's timing in setting up this new company designed to provide health insurance worldwide turned out to be inspired – it coincided with the confluence of a number of key factors:

- The rapid expansion of globalisation in the 2000s resulting in tens of thousands of high net worth expatriates being transferred annually from their mother countries to foreign subsidiaries / acquisitions. This continued apace during the recessionary 2008 – 2013 period in Western economies as multinationals poured resources into the developing and emerging economies which still had high single-digit and, in some cases, double-digit GDP growth rates.

- The development of the Internet on a global scale, which facilitated easy communication with an insured population scattered all over the world.
- The *Single Licence EU Insurance Directive* liberalised insurance laws in the EU, thus allowing insurers to sell into other EU markets on a freedom of services basis using their home country licence.

It is also fair to say that its Irish base has been a big factor in Allianz Worldwide Care's success. What were these success factors? In my view, they were:

- Ireland proved to be a significantly less bureaucratic country to establish a business than the European norm. The operations were set up quickly without fuss. In recent years, the company has had to establish smaller operations in other countries, all of which have proved to be significantly more complicated than the Irish experience. The Allianz Worldwide Care experience in Ireland bears out Ireland's very high position in the World Economic Forum's Competitiveness Index, the Ernst & Young Globalisation Index and the IBM Global Location Trends report.
- Allianz found an excellent labour pool in Ireland – both highly-educated Irish nationals with good insurance and business expertise and many young foreign nationals who had moved to Ireland and who provided the necessary foreign language skills to deal with medical providers worldwide and with insured members in their native languages. The required languages could be found in Ireland, even during the economic difficulties in the 2008 to 2013 period. It is fair to say that, like all English-speaking nations, Irish people do not have linguistic skills in the same league as Continental Europeans and it will always be necessary for multinationals established in Ireland to hire some non-nationals in order to get the right foreign language mix.
- For the first four years of the company's operations, Ireland still had a cost advantage over competing European nations. This disappeared during the boom times in the mid-2000s and, in some areas such as infrastructure and utilities, costs rose above the EU average. The economic collapse has brought back a sense of reality and most, but not all, costs have fallen again to a level that makes Ireland an attractive location. This is particularly so for new or growing companies that can hire from the large labour pool at relatively low salaries. Even during the boom times of the mid-2000s, Allianz Worldwide Care was able to get staff at salary rates lower than in competing economies. Allianz would now perceive overall Irish costs to be a neutral factor.
- Ireland has maintained its balanced labour laws, which gives the company the confidence to grow its business in Ireland. While predominantly Irish-based, the company now has employees in many countries and has found Irish labour laws significantly easier to deal with compared with its other locations.

- Irish people are good at doing business and relate well with key overseas executives. The company's staff in general are young, well-educated (almost all staff have a degree and many have post-graduate or professional qualifications) and very entrepreneurial. This entrepreneurial spirit – where nothing is impossible – has been one of the key reasons for the company's exponential growth. For example, we have found ways to enter difficult but potentially profitable markets such as Libya, Algeria, Mozambique, Angola and, last but not least, China.

- Despite the recent economic difficulties, Irish Governments have maintained a stable business environment, nowhere more so than in taxation policy where it has maintained its low tax policy. The 10 per cent tax rate applicable to international financial services companies was phased out at the end of 2002 and was replaced by a 12.5 per cent Corporation Tax rate applicable to all Irish companies, both those trading in the domestic market and those trading internationally. Despite significant pressure from certain countries, the 12.5 per cent Corporation Tax rate is treated as a red line by all Irish Governments, given its importance in attracting FDI into Ireland. While the low tax rate was not a deciding factor for Allianz in establishing its international health insurance company in Ireland, it is nonetheless a valuable benefit. Due to the company's exponential growth, it required significant additional regulatory capital. The bulk of the additional regulatory capital in the 2004 to 2013 period was in the form of retained profits rather than capital injections. The low tax rate allowed the company to accumulate the capital needed to fund its growth.

- The company has found Irish Government departments and organisations to be very helpful and anxious to help the company overcome any difficulties it faced over the years in establishing and growing its business. The Industrial Development Authority, Department of Finance, Department of Health and Department of Jobs, Enterprise & Innovation proved to be particularly helpful and senior executives were always available. Furthermore, Ireland has excellent telecommunications, as well as a stable of excellent business, legal and financial advisors that can deal with any legal, regulatory, actuarial or accounting issue and who are well-versed and experienced in dealing with multinational companies.

- International insurance companies look for fair, predictable and proportionate regulation in deciding on a location to establish a new business. In the period from initial licencing to 2008, the company had an excellent experience with Irish regulation. The regulator was very helpful in establishing the required freedom of services permissions and provided a very stable regulatory base. The collapse of many Irish banks in the 2008-2009 period resulted in a substantial and understandable toughening of financial regulation in Ireland and this tougher regulation applied to all financial institutions, including insurance companies. Like all other financial institutions, Allianz Worldwide Care experienced this tough regulation, which was an inevitable reaction as a brand new regulatory regime got to grips with the world (and Irish) financial crisis. For a period, Irish regulation was arguably tougher than almost anywhere but, in the past two years, has matured and, while still strong, would be regarded again by international insurers as fair, proportionate and predictable.

So in summary, while there were a few speed-bumps along the way, the Allianz Worldwide Care foreign direct investment experience in Ireland has been highly positive and this played a significant part in the successful establishment and development of the company's business.

Looking to the Future

As regards the future for new FDI projects in Ireland, there are lots of positives, but not everything is rosy in the garden. It is safe to assume that the Government will maintain its pro-business environment and laws. The maintenance of a low Corporation Tax rate is vital and all political parties treat this as a red line issue. However, arguably, the Government has to address the perceived aggressive use of the Irish tax code by some multinationals, such as the "Double Irish Dutch Sandwich" arrangement. If this goes unchecked, it may be very hard to maintain the 12.5 per cent Corporation Tax rate in face of pressure from other Western countries and the OECD. Another area for Government attention is the cost base. The boom-time cost levels that turned Ireland from a low-cost jurisdiction to a well-above-average cost jurisdiction have now been materially addressed. While wage level and private sector costs have reduced to attractive levels, this has not been the case with Government sector costs, such as the sheltered utility sector. More work needs to be done here. Finally, the requirement for the Government to bring the budget deficit back to within 3 per cent of GDP has required significant expenditure cutbacks and tax increases. Due to interest groups and to public sector union pressure, the Government has found it politically easier to raise personal taxes rather than to cut expenditure, with the result that personal taxes are now at a level where any further increase will impact negatively on foreign direct investment. The Irish Government and IDA Ireland are well aware that Ireland does not have a divine right to FDI and that multinationals will go where it best suits them. Given the track record of IDA Ireland and successive Irish Governments, and the relative importance of FDI to the Irish economy, I have no doubt but that the necessary focus and actions will be forthcoming. It is one thing that we are very good at!

CHAPTER 3

Crisis Response and Remaining Challenges[28]

Dr. Peter Breuer

Key Messages

- Although below initial forecasts, Ireland's growth rate has exceeded the Euro area average and indicators suggest a recovery may be emerging. Following a substantial rise in the fiscal deficit and a sharp increase in public debt during the crisis, phased consolidation has significantly improved the fiscal position while social cohesion was maintained. Banking reforms since the crisis have supported financial stability.
- Continued determined policy implementation is needed on a range of fronts before Ireland can be judged to have fully recovered from the crisis. With the fiscal deficit still high and public debt very elevated, further consolidation is needed in the coming years to put debt firmly on a declining path and help to ensure Ireland's return to market financing is lasting. Intensified efforts are needed to ensure banks and mortgage borrowers in arrears conclude durable solutions so that a revival in lending can contribute to a sustained domestic demand recovery.

Introduction

Ireland has achieved a tremendous amount in the three years since the EU/IMF-supported programme began in December 2010. Ireland's three-year programme supported by the EU and the IMF followed an exceptionally deep banking crisis and property boom-bust cycle. The Irish authorities have maintained steadfast implementation of programme policies through the final quarterly review of the programme and signs of nascent recovery are emerging. Yet, even as Ireland has pulled back from a deep banking crisis, it still faces a number of challenges as is common at the end of a programme supported by the Fund.

This chapter discusses the response by the authorities to the crisis, especially during their EU/IMF-supported programme, and outlines the remaining challenges

---

[28]   The author is very much indebted to the IMF's Ireland team for the analysis underlying this chapter.

that need to be tackled. In particular, it discusses (i) performance of the economy and macro-financial prospects and risks; (ii) the fiscal response to the emergence of large deficits and the continued need to put high public debt firmly on a downward path; (iii) the efforts to stabilise the financial sector and the need to improve asset quality and profitability prospects; and (iv) selected structural reforms.

Macroeconomy

Growth and Competitiveness

Economic growth during the EU/IMF-supported programme has been slower than projected, although exceeding the Euro area average (see **Exhibit 3.1**). After an export-led expansion of 2.2 per cent in 2011, growth slowed to 0.2 per cent in 2012 and turned negative in the first half of 2013 as exports were hit, partly reflecting the expiry of pharmaceutical patents, but also slow trading partner recovery. Expected cumulative growth in 2011-2013 of about 2.75 per cent falls short of the 5.25 per cent originally projected. However, expected Euro area growth of 0.5 per cent in 2011-2013 falls short of the October 2010 projections of 5.2 per cent to a greater extent. Ireland's cumulative growth in 2011-2013 is expected to match that of the UK.

Exhibit 3.1: Real GDP Growth

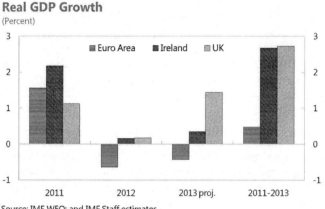

Source: IMF WEO; and IMF Staff estimates.

Competitiveness is improving, even as structural reform progress has been slower than hoped. During the boom until 2007-2008, Ireland's competitiveness deteriorated significantly but subsequent declines in unit labour costs and price level convergence with the Euro area have left Ireland with only a moderate degree of real effective exchange rate overvaluation, in the range of 5 to 10 per cent (see the IMF's *Article IV Staff Report on Ireland* from 2012). Flat nominal wages and low inflation suggest improvements in competitiveness can continue in coming years. Structural reforms have aimed to improve competition within the legal and medical services sectors, strengthen competition enforcement including by increasing resources, enhancing activation and training of the unemployed, and facilitating labour market adjustment in sectors hit hard by the crisis, although the implementation of some reforms is still being completed.

Private Debt Burdens

Heavy private sector debts weigh on the level of domestic demand. By boosting savings, households have reduced their nominal debts by 16 per cent in the past four and a half years, but debt burdens remain high at 198.3 per cent of disposable income in mid-2013 with savings likely to remain above normal levels for some time. SMEs face financing constraints on investment and job creation, often reflecting debt incurred for past property investments.

Among the highly-indebted households some are running arrears on their mortgage, currently some 6 per cent of households. Sustainable loan restructures will entail downward adjustments in consumption in some cases, while providing relief in others. But these direct near-term effects on consumption are likely to be outweighed by the broader medium-term benefit of improving banks' asset quality, thereby enabling banks to attract cheaper funding and facilitating a revival of mortgage lending. Resolving nonperforming mortgages also will ease fears around the "shadow housing inventory" from "underwater" mortgages, enhancing housing market turnover and reducing household uncertainty about wealth, altogether supporting domestic demand recovery. These benefits could be reversed, however, if widespread redefaults were to occur or debt service discipline were to weaken further.

Recovery Prospects and Risks

Higher trading partner growth is a key driver of Ireland's gradual recovery, with the IMF projecting 1.7 per cent year-on-year growth in 2014. The latest *World Economic Outlook* projections show Ireland's trading partner growth picking up from 0.4 per cent year-on-year in 2013 to 1.6 per cent in 2014, which is expected to allow net exports to boost Irish growth by just over 1 percentage point. Recent employment growth, of 3.2 per cent year-on-year in Q3 2013, appears to be continuing and is expected to support household incomes and confidence. Public consumption will continue to fall in coming years in line with the policy of public service numbers reductions and other expenditure consolidation.

Ireland's growth is projected to firm to about 2.5 per cent from 2015, even as heavy private sector debt burdens imply a protracted domestic demand recovery. Improvements in the external economic environment, less drag from fiscal consolidation, and a gradual revival of lending are key drivers. This growth rate is sustainable into the medium term as demographic trends support growth in the working age population of around 1 per cent over the next 10 years, declines in unemployment allow a period of employment growth in the order of 1.5 per cent without igniting wage pressures, and as Ireland's productivity rises about 1 per cent annually including as a result of continuing FDI inflows.

A number of uncertainties surround these recovery prospects, with near-term risks significant yet broadly balanced, though risks tilt to the downside in the medium term:

- **External environment:** Ireland's high degree of openness (exports account for around 110 per cent of GDP) makes it vulnerable to trading partner growth fluctuations. Weak external recovery could spill over also to domestic demand through consumer and business confidence. Nonetheless, recent indicators in some of Ireland's main trading partners are relatively positive, especially the UK, providing scope for upside risk.
- **Domestic demand:** Consumption prospects hinge importantly on a continuation of recent employment gains, supporting incomes and reducing uncertainties. The ongoing house price recovery is yet to be tested by the depressive effects of a potential rise in disposals of repossessed properties, though houses with primary dwelling mortgages in arrears account for only 6 per cent of all houses. Investment recovery is a potential upside risk given its low base (around 11 per cent of GDP).
- **Financial conditions:** The revival in credit growth and investment needed to sustain recovery over the medium term would be hindered if current efforts to resolve nonperforming loans and improve bank profitability were to fall short. If a later US Federal Reserve tapering were to impact the Euro area periphery more strongly, there could be adverse impacts on banks' access to and costs of market funding and thus to credit availability.

Fiscal Policy

Although Ireland had a balanced budget going into the crisis, booming revenues masked a significant weakening in the underlying fiscal position. After a period of rapid export-led growth in the 1990s where spending and tax revenues declined to low levels relative to GDP, public finances at the turn of the millennium were redirected toward improving social outcomes and expanding public services. Nominal primary spending rose 140 per cent over 2000-2008 (11 percentage points of GDP in structural terms), with welfare rates doubled (tripled in the case of the universal child benefit), the number of public servants enlarged by 35 per cent, and public wages raised 60 per cent. In comparison, *per capita* GDP growth was 45 per cent over 2000-2008 and 24 per cent over 2000-2011. The spending surge was accompanied by structural tax cuts: the already high entry point to Income Tax (25 per cent of *per capita* GDP in 2000) was doubled by 2009, while statutory Income Tax rates were lowered by five percentage points. With the benefit of hindsight, IMF staff estimates the structural primary deficit had widened to over 10 per cent of GDP in 2008, but this was hidden by a flood of property-related revenues during the boom years of 2003-2007.

Policy Response to Crisis

The crisis prompted a sharp course correction, with substantial consolidation implemented in recent years, significantly improving the fiscal position. Even before the start of the EU/IMF-supported programme, Ireland undertook substantial fiscal consolidation, reducing the structural primary deficit by 5.25 per cent of GDP in 2009-2010. Steady fiscal consolidation has been a hallmark of the programme and key to restoring Ireland's policy credibility, with every fiscal target met during the programme. As a result, Ireland is expected to reduce its structural primary deficit to 0.5 per cent of GDP in 2013, a cumulative decline of around 4.5 percentage points since 2010 and of 10 percentage points since the onset of the crisis. Fiscal measures implemented during the programme total over €13bn or 8 per cent of GDP, two-thirds of them on the expenditure side.

The fiscal framework also has been strengthened. A general Government budget balance rule and a general Government debt rule were adopted as part of the *Fiscal Responsibility Act, 2012* (FRA), consistent with the *Stability and Growth Pact*. Budget 2012 introduced three-year aggregate and ministerial-level expenditure ceilings, which have been put on a statutory basis. The FRA also provided for the independence and adequate funding of the Irish Fiscal Advisory Council, which is responsible for providing an *ex ante* endorsement of the macroeconomic forecasts underpinning the budget and for assessing the soundness of the government's budgetary projections and fiscal stance. Measures to enhance transparency include the authorities' action plan on fiscal reporting, forecasting and risk analysis and the launch of a quarterly *Government Finance Statistics* publication.

Remaining Challenges

Public debt is expected to reach 124 per cent of GDP in 2013, although this partly reflects high cash buffers. Netting out financial assets from public debt, about half of the increase since 2008 is accounted for by bank support amounting to 40 per cent of GDP. Under the IMF staff's baseline scenario, the public debt-to-GDP ratio declines to 112 per cent of GDP by 2018 as the economic recovery gains traction. However, public debt sustainability remains fragile as these projected declines in public debt are subject to risk from lower growth, contingent liabilities, or a combination of both.

Budget execution has once more been solid in 2013, including the smooth introduction of the Local Property Tax and the social cohesion demonstrated by reaching the Haddington Road Agreement on public sector pay and pensions. The deficit for 2013 is expected at about 7 per cent of GDP, well within the 7.5 per cent of GDP ceiling under the Excessive Deficit Procedure (EDP). Nonetheless, the fiscal deficit remains high, as a rising interest bill stemming from high debt offsets part of the major primary adjustment under the programme.

Putting public debt firmly on a downward path therefore requires sizeable further fiscal consolidation, while allowing room for economic recovery. Budget 2014 targets the primary balance and the Irish authorities are firmly committed to reaching a fiscal deficit below 3 per cent of GDP by 2015. This path incorporates a balanced pace of adjustment in coming years and is expected to put public debt on a declining trajectory, though subject to risks from growth prospects and contingent liabilities. Continued sound implementation of fiscal consolidation will be especially critical after the completion of the programme to help ensure Ireland's return to market financing is lasting.

Financial Sector Policy

The integration of the Irish financial system into the broader Euro area financial landscape, together with the apparently strong fiscal position of the sovereign, gave Irish banks the unfettered access to wholesale funding during the boom years that enabled their turbocharged asset expansion. In the five years to mid-2008, the net foreign liabilities of the Irish banking system jumped from about 20 per cent to about 70 per cent of GDP, and wholesale funding rose to 55 per cent of assets.

The Crisis and Policy Response Before the Programme

Ireland's property price downturn began in 2007. After facing heavy losses on property-related assets in the spring of 2008, the post-Lehman global financial turmoil tipped the vulnerable Irish banking system into a deep crisis. The banks suffered a run on wholesale funding in the fall of 2008 – prompting massive recourse to Eurosystem liquidity support. Government actions included a far-reaching guarantee from September 2008; the transfer of large distressed property development and commercial real estate loans from banks to the National Asset Management Agency (NAMA) from April 2009; large scale capital support for two failed banks (Anglo Irish Bank and Irish Nationwide Building Society); and major equity injections in other banks. For a time these actions maintained stability, yet the scale of capital support, and uncertainties about further support requirements, contributed to the Government losing market access and an escalation of pressures on banks' funding in 2010.

Policy Response during the Programme

The financial sector was stabilised by determined efforts to recapitalise and restructure the system, supported by the EU/IMF programme. The 2011 Prudential Capital Assessment Review (PCAR) stress-tested AIB, Bank of Ireland, and PermanentTSB (together the PCAR banks). Their capital was topped up by €24bn (15 per cent of GDP) based on the results of the exercise, coupled with a significant restructuring of the system. The PCAR banks reported an aggregate core tier 1 risk-based capital ratio of 14.1 per cent as of mid-2013 and provisions doubled between end-2010 and June 2013. However, bank support involved a heavy burden on the public sector, with gross costs of €64.1bn (40 per cent of GDP). Recovery of these costs is at an early stage, making progress with the disposal of Irish Life and the preference shares and contingent capital notes in Bank of Ireland.

Domestic deposits have stabilised since mid-2011, even as deposit rates have declined. Aided by substantial deleveraging of non-core assets, the loan-to-deposit ratio has come down from 190 per cent at end-2010 to 117 per cent in June 2013 and PCAR bank reliance on Eurosystem support is down from a peak of over €90bn to about €31bn.

The recent Balance Sheet Assessment (BSA) analysed the sufficiency of risk buffers in the three PCAR banks. It focused on the adequacy of provisions on an incurred loss basis and the appropriateness of internally-generated Basel risk weights, which fed into a point-in-time assessment of capital as of June 2013. As envisaged, the Central Bank of Ireland-led exercise engaged private sector contractors in project execution and a consulting firm for oversight and independent validation. This analysis found a further increase in provisions appropriate, taking into account *Impairment Provisioning and Disclosure Guidelines* updated by the Central Bank of Ireland (CBI) in May 2013, but did not find an immediate need for additional capital. Banks need to use the BSA results to guide a reallocation of their risk buffers from capital to provisions, which also will encourage more timely loan resolution. The BSA will inform the CBI's continuing supervisory dialogue with the banks on the adequate level of provisioning at year end.

Financial regulation and supervision were radically changed and improvements continue. In October 2011 a special resolution regime for banks and credit unions was enacted and in July 2013 the supervisory powers of the Central Bank were strengthened. The CBI has been strengthening banking supervision by increasing resources and operationalising its new risk-based supervisory approach.

Remaining Challenges: Non-performing Loans and Profitability
Banks' progress in resolving high nonperforming loans (NPLs) has been very slow and weak profitability also hinders a revival of lending. NPLs stand at 26.5 per cent of PCAR bank loans, led by commercial real estate loans (41 per cent), Irish residential mortgages (34 per cent) and business and SME loans (19 per cent). This high share of NPLs raises the cost of market funding and drains management resources that could be used for new lending. However, banks' progress in resolving NPLs has been very slow, prompting the CBI to establish targets for the resolution of residential mortgages and SME loans.

Focusing on mortgages, high unemployment and other shocks have led to arrears over 90 days on 17.4 per cent of the total value of mortgages outstanding for principal dwellings, and on 29.3 per cent of buy-to-let mortgages. The rise in mortgage arrears appears to be slowing recently, as banks' improved collection efforts appear to be containing early arrears cases and the stabilisation of house prices and decline in unemployment likely contributed as well, but a substantial stock of mortgages need to be resolved.

Banks are reporting progress in line with the CBI's Mortgage Arrears Resolution Targets (MART) framework, with the CBI announcing that banks reported they had met the end-September 2013 target for proposing solutions to 30 per cent of mortgages with arrears over 90 days. Banks' improving loan workout efforts are reflected in a lower share of short-term forbearance in mortgage restructurings. Banks now face targets to conclude solutions for 15 per cent of mortgages in arrears by end-2013, rising to 35 per cent of mortgage arrears cases by end-June 2014. Supporting this process, reforms of the *Personal Insolvency Act* established three new essentially non-judicial procedures for debt resolution and shortened the period of bankruptcy.

Overcoming insufficient engagement between banks and borrowers is critical to make this move from proposals for arrears solutions to conclusions in a timely manner. On the bank side, incentives to offer durable restructurings should be reinforced by introducing rules-based policies on the accounting for provisions, charge-offs, and interest accrual for unrestructured loans with prolonged arrears at end-2014. Where a bank falls materially behind targets, more directive supervisory guidance on resolution or outsourcing of workouts may be needed. Measures to strengthen borrowers' engagement toward sustainable solutions are needed. For cases where a loss of ownership is unavoidable, enhanced support for mortgage-to-rent solutions would help contain social costs.

In the case of small and medium-sized enterprises (SMEs), the resolution of distressed loans is proceeding, with both banks that dominate SME lending meeting their workout targets set by CBI in recent quarters. The number of loan restructures substantially exceeds cases of legal enforcement. To permit small businesses to apply for examinership – restructuring rather than liquidation – in Circuit Courts, where legal fees are generally lower, the authorities are fast-tracking recently published amendments to the *Companies Bill*. This is a welcome step forward, yet additional gains could be realised by further streamlining the role of Courts in examinership, drawing on experience with the Insolvency Service for households.

Even after significant profitability improvements in the first half of 2013 – reflecting the removal of the Eligible Liabilities Guarantee (ELG) scheme, reductions in staffing and branch numbers made in 2012, and declines in deposit rates – bank profitability remains weak, limiting banks' capacity to generate the capital needed to sustain lending. Profitability is particularly sensitive to prospects for new business volume, repricing of loans, and funding costs – each of which will depend on the macroeconomic environment and progress in balance sheet repair.

A key challenge remains the funding at an appropriately low rate of low-yielding mortgages that track the central bank policy rates. In aggregate the PCAR banks hold €48bn in tracker mortgages in Ireland with a low average margin over the policy rates of the ECB. Declines in these policy rates had outpaced reductions in bank funding costs, resulting in a significant cost of carry for tracker mortgages, although the profitability drag has eased somewhat with recent declines in deposit and market funding rates. Attracting funding from private counterparties at sufficiently low rates will be challenging.

Structural Reforms and Unemployment

Unemployment has eased from 15.1 per cent in early 2012 to a still high 12.5 per cent by late 2013, owing to a combination of job creation and emigration. However, the long-term jobless constitute some 58.4 per cent of all jobseekers, eroding labour force participation and work skills. Such high long-term unemployment, if unaddressed, could depress growth for years, requiring a combination of structural reforms and steps to support job creation.

Strong engagement with the long-term unemployed is important to ensure they actively seek work and acquire the skills needed to compete successfully for jobs when job growth picks up further. The continued roll-out of Intreo offices, providing a streamlined single point of contact for jobseekers, and the intended doubling of frontline case officers will be helpful in this regard, as will be outcome-based payments to private sector employment service providers. The recent review of further education and training highlights the need to better align training with the needs of the economy, and timely initiatives to achieve the strategic priorities set out in the review are critical, especially to ensure the long-term unemployed gain skills enabling them to return to work.

Initiatives to promote credit to SMEs, with the support of European partners such as the EIB and KfW, are positive for investment and job creation. In anticipation of the establishment of the Ireland Strategic Investment Fund, the National Pension Reserve Fund has committed, in partnership with private sector players, up to €950m in investments dedicated to providing equity financing and new lending to SMEs. A large number of potential transactions are at various stages of underwriting. Preparations for the disposal of up to €3bn in State assets are proceeding, with recent announcements regarding Bord Gáis Energy. These proceeds can help fund job-creating projects, including public-private partnerships.

Conclusions

Ireland has pulled back from an exceptionally deep banking crisis, significantly improved its fiscal position and regained its access to the international financial markets. Though below initial projections, economic growth has exceeded the Euro area average and indicators suggest a recovery may be emerging. Banking reforms have supported financial stability. Although the crisis and bank support led to a substantial rise in the fiscal deficit and a sharp increase in public debt, phased consolidation – initiated prior to the Fund arrangement but subsequently maintained – has significantly improved the fiscal position while social cohesion was maintained. Market access has been regained, also benefitting from EFSF/EFSM maturity extensions, the promissory notes transaction, and the broader easing in Euro area market tensions.

The Irish authorities recognise that continued sound policies are needed to support Ireland's growth and recently released a *Medium Term Economic Strategy* to cover the period from 2014 to 2020. The determination to articulate and implement such a strategy is most encouraging. Continued determined policy implementation is needed nonetheless on a range of fronts before Ireland can be judged to have fully recovered from the crisis. With the fiscal deficit still high and public debt very elevated, sizable further consolidation is needed in coming years to put debt firmly on a declining path and to help ensure Ireland's return to market financing is lasting. Slow progress in addressing mortgage arrears hinders a revival over time in lending that is needed for domestic demand recovery to become sustained, so intensified efforts are needed to ensure banks and mortgage borrowers in arrears conclude durable solutions. Banks also need to rebuild their profitability, although, in the context of low ECB policy rates, they face challenges from the structure of their assets. Efforts to improve employment services and further education and training should continue apace, especially to ensure the long-term unemployed remain in the workforce and acquire marketable skills.

CHAPTER 4

Spending and Reform:
Renewing the Momentum

Marc Coleman

Key Messages

- Ireland's fiscal adjustment has been impressive and orderly. The Government has tried to cushion weaker sections of the community, while improving efficiency in the public sector and achieving reductions in public pay levels.
- While Ireland's public sector has improved in terms of efficiency – more is now being done with fewer resources – Ireland's major challenge is to now judge the effectiveness of public spending. Also notwithstanding significant reductions, public pay in Ireland remains well above Eurozone levels and closer analysis of the reasons and justification for this is necessary.
- A new Government Department of Public Expenditure and Reform has been created to drive greater efficiency and effectiveness. From improving the cost of delivering public services, the emphasis under new reform plans to be announced in 2014 will shift to improving the quality of public services.

Introduction

With an emphasis on Ireland's spending levels and reform programme, this chapter examines Ireland's progress towards fiscal consolidation and does so in two respects: first in terms of its success in progressing towards adherence to the terms of the *Fiscal Compact Treaty* and, second, in terms of how the design of this consolidation (both the overall balance between spending consolidation and tax increases, as well as the particular design of spending reforms and tax increases) has affected Ireland's economic recovery. Looking to the longer term, the chapter looks for operational fiscal policy guidance at norms of spending and taxation as established in more fiscally stable Eurozone countries such as Germany in order to ask whether Ireland could emulate those norms. This discussion benefits from the recent publication by Government of a *Medium Term Economic Strategy*, which contains helpful benchmarks for the future.

The success of the Government in achieving its fiscal consolidation targets under the Troika programme is not only undoubted, but also impressive. According to Government forecasts – forecasts that are based on modest assumptions and vindicated by an independent body,[29] by 2015 Ireland's budget deficit will fall below 3 per cent of GDP, its primary balance will be in surplus and its debt to GDP ratio will be on a downward trajectory.

But the achievement of fiscal consolidation is one thing. Fiscal policies consistent with maximising growth are quite another. A crucial issue in any fiscal consolidation is whether it is achieved by reducing expenditure and cost-cutting reforms or by increases in taxation or by a mixture of both strategies. Ireland's burden of taxation was, contrary to some suggestions, never low. On the contrary, for a young neutral country with relatively low age-related spending pressures compared to Germany and relatively few military commitments, Ireland should be able to achieve similar levels of social provision and services as are available in Germany for lower cost. As shown in one study, when structural and demographic factors are adjusted for, the share of taxation in Ireland's economy in 2006, just two years before the crisis, was already above the EU average.[30] Therefore while some broadening of the tax base – in terms of shifting away from an overreliance on unstable property-related taxes – was warranted, there was no case for increasing the size of the overall tax burden. As is clear from any rational analysis, Ireland's fiscal sustainability crisis is caused by the combination of two factors on the spending side: first the impact of once-off but substantial bank recapitalisation obligations between 2009 and 2011 and, second, a staggering rise by €25bn in the annual level of total public spending between the years 2003 and 2008. The second development took place before the banking crisis impacted on public finances and, unlike that impact, is an annual rather than a once-off increase.

Irish Public Spending, 1997-2008

Like few other countries in Europe, and like few other times in European history, Ireland witnessed a staggering rise in public expenditure during its ill-fated boom. Initially justified to meet the needs of a growing population, public spending was to grow out of control in a manner that would badly expose Ireland when crisis struck in 2008. Until that year the damage done to Ireland's fiscal position was disguised by overreliance on property taxation (Stamp Duty) and other taxes related to property market activity (Capital Gains Tax and Capital Acquisitions Tax). On the back of strong credit growth (see **Chapter 1**), Stamp Duty, Capital Gains Tax and Capital Acquisitions Tax grew in 2005 by 30 per cent, 29 per cent and 31 per cent

---

[29] Irish Fiscal Advisory Council. See IFAC, *Fiscal Assessment Report* (26 November 2013).

[30] De Butleir, Donal & Thornhill, Don (2008). "The Agenda for Tax Reform: Playing To and Developing Our Strengths", *Dublin Economic Workshop*.

respectively and by 38 per cent, 54 per cent and 37 per cent respectively in 2006.[31] In 2007 rates of growth were modestly positive or negative, with strong declines from 2008 to 2011 inclusive.

In tandem, spending grew strongly also. The clear difference was that, while tax revenues would rapidly collapse during the crisis period of 2008 to 2011, spending reductions were politically less easy to achieve. Hence the clear emphasis on taxation increases during the early years of fiscal consolidation discussed below. **Exhibit 4.1** shows the dramatic extent of spending increases in the five years up to the crisis of 2008. From €43bn in 2003 to €68bn in 2008, spending rose by a staggering 58 per cent.

Exhibit 4.1: Spending Growth in Ireland, 2003 to 2012

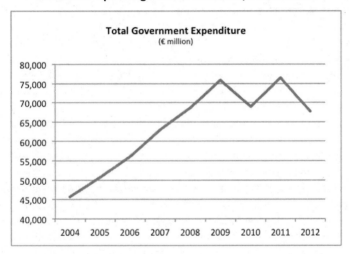

Source: Department of Finance.

It should be borne in mind that this came after a 10-year period in which the Irish economy may be seen to have been driven largely by healthy export-driven growth and which saw public spending more than double from €18bn in 1993 to €43bn in 2003. At 36 per cent of GNP and 31 per cent of GDP (see the note at the end of this chapter concerning the relevance of these two different measures), public expenditure was at a level consistent with the provision of good social protection and public services. As discussed above, and when adjusted for Ireland's relatively favourable current demographic situation compared to Germany, France and Italy (where age-related spending pressures are much greater), Ireland's tax burden during the period was above the EU average and therefore adequate to fund public services and provision according to the European social market model.

---

[31] Department of Finance, *Exchequer Returns.*

According to independent estimates, the optimal size of the State in terms of maximising social provision and growth potential is between 30 and 35 per cent of output.[32] And while a bigger role for Government may be valid and consistent with high growth and productivity, this is always, as is the case in some Nordic countries, a situation that has been developed patiently and where prolonged growth in indigenous productivity preceded spending growth by at least a decade. In Sweden, for instance, the ratio of public expenditure to GDP rose from 31 per cent in 1960 to 60.1 per cent over a two-decade period[33] and with a prior emphasis on first achieving the indigenous growth in high productivity industries that then formed a solid basis for greater taxes and spending. By contrast in Ireland public spending rose from 35.9 per cent of GNP in 2004 to 51 per cent in 2012, over a period of just eight years. During the first few years of this period productivity deteriorated substantially.

The pattern of spending shown in **Exhibit 4.2** shows clearly how, unlike the planned increase in Nordic countries, public spending in Ireland was rapidly implemented in the run up to an election year in 2007.

Despite reaching a level of spending adequate from the point of view of proper provision of social services, and despite having doubled in the preceding 10 years, some spending increases from 2003 nonetheless would have been justified in the ensuing years. But what is also clear from **Exhibit 4.2** is that the rate of spending rise was in well in excess of what might have been justified by any objective criteria. In 2004, a (modest) inflation rate of 2.1 per cent and population growth rate of 1.6 per cent, together, would have justified a rate of spending growth in the region of 4 per cent in order to preserve the capacity of the State to deliver services to a rising population in the context of a rising price level. In that year, spending growth was close to that benchmark. Population remained close to its 2 per cent average over the 2004 to 2007 period but inflation rose inexorably due to the loss of competitiveness discussed in earlier chapters. This, plus the onset of a general election in 2007, drove up spending growth to an annual rate of 12 per cent in 2007, the year before the crisis struck. It is also noteworthy that Germany breached the *Stability Pact* in 2002, a year in which it held Federal elections.

---

[32] See Tanzi (2000). *The Role of the State and the Quality of the Public Sector*, IMF Working Paper WP/00/36; also Tanzi and Schuknecht (1996). *The Growth of Government and the Reform of the State in Industrial Countries,* IMF Working Paper WP/95/130 and Tanzi (2004). *A Lower Tax Future? The Economic Role of the State in the 21st Century*, Politeia, Policy Series No.44.

[33] Tanzi and Schuknecht (2000). *The Role of the State and the Quality of the Public Sector*, IMF Working Paper WP/00/36.

Exhibit 4.2: Rates of Increase in Total Government Expenditure

% Annual change	2004	2005	2006	2007
Total Government Expenditure	5.1	11.1	10.6	12.1
Inflation	2.1	2.5	3.9	4.9
Population growth	1.6	2.2	2.4	3.4

Source: Department of Finance.

Since 2008 public spending appears to have been stabilised but not reduced. However, in a country whose population has risen by almost one-third of a million (8 per cent) since the onset of crisis and where unemployment has risen dramatically, this stabilisation remains a considerable achievement and understates the significant effort made in containing not only the effects of irresponsible policies before 2008 but also in containing demographic pressures that are unique in Europe and which, had they not been contained, could have driven spending further upwards. These are discussed further below. First, however, the nature of Ireland's fiscal correction should be examined.

Fiscal Consolidation So Far, 2008-2013

The Balance of Spending Reduction and Tax Increases

The *National Recovery Plan 2011-2014*[34] had committed Government to achieving two-thirds of the overall budgetary adjustment through expenditure savings and one-third through revenue raising measures. But as shown in **Exhibit 4.3**,[35] the total summation of expenditure reductions and attempted increases in taxation[36] increases were broadly balanced over the seven budgets of the correction period. The final column of **Exhibit 4.3** gives the ratio of spending reductions to tax increases. The even balance between spending reductions and tax increases may reflect the fact that, in practice, tax increases have proven to arouse less vocal political opposition, given that taxpayers are less organised in defending their interests.

---

[34] The *National Recovery Plan 2011-2014*, page 9.

[35] Note the figures presented are approximations but give a fair overall indication of the balance between expenditure reductions and tax increases as intended by successive governments during the crisis.

[36] Unlike spending reductions, whose efficacy is dependent and at the discretion of government implementation, the efficacy of attempts to increase taxation is subject to economic and behavioural reactions largely outside the control of government.

Exhibit 4.3: Balance of Spending Reduction and Tax Increases, 2008 to 2013

Budget	Spending Cuts (€bn)	Tax Increases (€bn)	Ratio SC/TI
October 2008	0.30	2.30	3/23
April 2009	1.20	2.70	4/9
December 2009	3.10	0.10	31/1
December 2010	2.20	2.40	11/12
December 2011	1.60	1.60	1/1
December 2012	1.85	1.65	37/33
October 2013	1.60	0.90	16/9
Total	**11.85**	**11.65**	**1/1**

Source: Calculated from Department of Finance Budget data.

The different experience with individual budgets suggests, however, that despite the stronger political opposition to them, the weight of evidence in favour of expenditure-based rather than tax-based adjustment is strengthened. The October 2008 budget cut €3 for every €23 targeted in additional taxes. The subsequent supplementary 2009 budget increased the share of spending reductions but remained strongly biased towards tax increases. Growth during 2009 was sharply lower than in any other year of the crisis. This outcome was undoubtedly affected by the global intensity of the crisis and any inferences as regards the effects of the first two crisis budgets on the economy are clouded in uncertainty. That being said, a contrast between the two subsequent budgets is interesting.

The first of these, the December 2009 budget, cut €31 for every €1 targeted in additional tax. This decisive shift towards avoidance of tax increases and towards radical spending reductions was followed by a brief recovery in the economy. Not only was the overall public pay level cut on average by 7.5 per cent in that budget; the previous January a pension levy[37] was imposed upon public servants. Further reductions to higher level pay were to follow.

After declining by 9.8 per cent in 2009 GNP grew by 0.5 per cent in 2010 and while GDP declined in that year by 1.1 per cent the performance of GDP in 2010 was a significant improvement on 2009 when it had declined by 6.4 per cent. Months after this budget consumer confidence began increasing and, after falling by a quarter of a million between September 2008 and March 2010, employment stabilised at 1.89 million for a six-month period. Compared with a 19 per cent fall in 2009, tax revenues fell by a much more modest 4 per cent and ended the year over €0.5bn ahead of Government forecasts.[38]

---

[37]   The Public Service Pension Reduction.

[38]   Department of Finance, Exchequer returns data for 2009, 2010 and 2011.

In March 2010, the Government committed to protecting levels of public pay and pensions that were amongst the highest in Europe and which according to independent evidence were – adjusting for various factors – some 12.5 per cent higher than private sector averages.[39] That evidence followed the aforementioned pension levy but preceded pay cuts implemented in December 2009. However another paper published subsequently[40] found that, with the exception of Portugal, Italy and Greece, the differential of average public sector pay compared to private sector pay in Ireland was significantly higher than in other Eurozone countries.

In May 2013, the Government agreed the *Public Service Stability Agreement 2013-2016*, implementing yet further reductions in public sector pay for those earning salaries of €65,000 or more.

As a result of these and other spending measures, the October 2013 budget, while not as favourable to expenditure reduction as the December 2009 budget, has achieved the most favourable balance in this regard of any other budget since the crisis began. The evidence is that this is assisting Ireland's economic recovery and jobs growth.

Ireland's Previous History of Consolidation

Theorists differ as regards whether spending reductions or tax increases constitute the best means of fiscal consolidation but on balance, evidence favours the former approach. While the recent paper *Expansionary Austerity: New International Evidence*[41] has been interpreted as warning against the effects of excessively rapid correction, its verdict on the impact of spending-based *versus* tax-based corrections on growth points clearly[42] towards spending-based consolidation as the least damaging approach. As far as practical evidence goes, the evidence for Ireland, both historical and more recent, clearly vindicates this view.

Between 1982 and 1986 inclusive the Government of the day responded to a fiscal crisis by increasing Total Government Expenditure from €10bn to over €13bn, a rise of almost one-third. As a share of GDP and GNP respectively, the size of Total Government Expenditure fell slightly but this was largely due to the impact of high inflation on the size of nominal output. In an attempt to finance this, marginal income tax rates were raised to as high as 65 per cent. The result was that, at a time when Europe and the US were recovering from the recession of the early

---

[39]   Barrett, A., Kearney, I. & Goggin, J. (2009). *Quarterly Economic Commentary, Autumn,* ESRI.

[40]   Giordani *et al.* (2001). *The Public Sector Pay Gap in a Selection of Euro Area Countries,* ECB Working Paper 1406.

[41]   Guajardo, J., Leigh, D. & Pescatori, A. (2011). *Expansionary Austerity: New International Evidence,* IMF Working Paper WP/11/158.

[42]   Figure 9, page 25 of Guajardo, J., Leigh, D. & Pescatori, A. (2011). *Expansionary Austerity: New International Evidence,* IMF Working Paper WP/11/158.

1980s, Ireland was paralysed by weak growth in the domestic economy. Despite some export-driven growth – annual GDP growth during the period averaged 1.3 per cent – GNP growth averaged a mere 0.4 per cent. The fiscal balance[43] remained substantially high at the end of this period at 11.4 per cent due to lower growth in the economy.

The contrast with the ensuing five year period 1987 to 1991 is instructive. It should be noted that Ireland devalued its currency in 1986 giving a short-term boost to exports. What is more remarkable, however, is the stark difference in approach to fiscal consolidation and, in particular, the difference attained in GNP growth (see the note below on differences between GDP and GNP for Ireland) between the two periods.

Between 1987 and 1991, Total Government Expenditure also rose from €13.1bn to €15.4bn; however, compared to the rise in the previous period – of approximately one-third – this rise of approximately 18 per cent was more modest and reflected tighter control of both current and capital spending. As a share of GNP, Total Government Expenditure fell from 54.7 per cent at the end of 1986 to 46 per cent, reflecting much stronger growth acceleration. From an average annual rate of 1.3 per cent in the 1982 to 1986 period, GDP growth accelerated to an average annual rate of 4.3 per cent in the 1987 to 1991 period. In earlier years this was due partly to the currency devaluation. However, the strong acceleration in the average annual rate of GNP growth, from just 0.4 per cent between 1982 and 1986 to 3.7 per cent in the ensuring period reflected a virtuous circle of spending control, falling debt and taxes and rising growth and employment, assisted initially to some degree by devaluation.

Why Has Current Spending Not Decreased?

Given the above evidence – and given the steep rise in public expenditure between 2003 and 2008 – one might ask why public expenditure has not been cut by more. **Exhibits 4.4** and **4.5** (see note at end of chapter about GNP and GDP) show that gross current expenditure has not decreased significantly as a share either of GNP or GDP since the onset of the crisis. What it does not show, however, are the significant upward pressures that – had they not been contained by action and reform – would have driven public spending up significantly.

---

[43] The standard measure for measuring the fiscal balance at the time was the Exchequer Balance.

Exhibit 4.4: Total Government Expenditure as a Share of GNP (%)[44]

	2004	2005	2006	2007	2008	2009	2010	2011	2012
Total Government Expenditure	35.9	36.6	36.4	38.6	44.4	56.7	52.3	58.5	51.0
of which Current	30.8	31.1	30.8	32.2	37.0	45.3	46.0	46.0	45.4
of which Capital	5.2	5.5	5.6	6.4	7.4	11.3	6.3	12.6	5.6

Source: Department of Finance.

Exhibit 4.5: Total Government Expenditure as a Share of GDP (%)

	2004	2005	2006	2007	2008	2009	2010	2011	2012
Total Government Expenditure	30.5	31.2	31.6	33.2	38.1	46.8	43.6	47.0	41.3
of which Current	26.1	26.5	26.8	27.7	31.8	37.4	38.4	36.9	36.8
of which Capital	4.4	4.7	4.9	5.5	6.3	9.3*	5.3*	10.1*	4.5

Source: Department of Finance.
* Affected by State investments in the financial and property sector.

It needs repeating that, since Ireland's crisis began, its population has risen by nearly one-third of a million persons. In a variety of ways this has increased public spending pressures in the areas of health, education and capital expenditure.

Aside from this population growth, changes in the composition of the age profile of the population are creating significant upward pressure on education spending. This would be the case regardless of the state of the economy. Since 2007, the number of primary and secondary students will have increased by 75,000 to a projected 889,300 in 2014. In other words one-fifth of Ireland's population is of school-going age. In addition and over this period the number of full-time third level students increased by 17,000 to 165,000. Given that one-quarter of Ireland's young and growing population is in the education system and incurring costs on the Exchequer, and given that their numbers are rising significantly, it is a significant achievement that non-pay expenditure has been maintained, barely rising from €1.9bn in 2007 to a projected €2bn in 2014.

At the same time the numbers of persons claiming unemployment assistance rose by one-quarter of a million. As a necessity, therefore, expenditure in this area rose from €1.4bn in 2007 to a projected €3.3bn in 2014.[45] Demographic pressures

---

[44] Note that capital spending figures are affected by bank recapitalisation measures for the years 2009 to 2011 inclusive.

[45] Estimated at the time of writing according to the latest available (October 2013) budgetary projections.

have contributed also to a rise in other social welfare spending from €13.8bn in 2007 to a projected €16bn by 2014.

Efficiency Reforms

In Ireland efforts at reforms – achieving the same outputs with fewer resources – have been significant. What may remain a challenge is to consider shifting emphasis from "efficiency reforms" to "effectiveness reforms". Efficiency stresses achieving the same results and outputs for fewer resources. There is little doubt that this is happening.

From €17.5bn in 2009, the public service pay cost has fallen to €14.5bn in 2014, a reduction of 17.5 per cent. Further, the number of persons working in the public service – which is not high by German standards[46] – has fallen by 30,000 between 2007 and 2014, a fall of 9 per cent. Clearly these reductions – achieved against a headwind of rising pressure to deliver services to a growing population – are an indication of overall efficiency gains.

However, a strong criticism of this adjustment is that the focus on reducing numbers employed in the public service would have been unnecessary but for the maintenance of public pay at levels that, despite aforementioned pay reductions, remain generous by EU standards. Arguably reducing jobs in the economy when average public pay remains above private sector average levels is unjustified. In Germany trade unions have emphasised the need to protect jobs and adjust pay if necessary to ensure employment in the public sector is maximised. In Ireland a considerable number of public sector jobs were shed at a time when public pay levels were protected by the Croke Park Agreement. But the fact that Ireland's public sector share of overall employment remains modest by EU standards suggests more could have been done to save jobs.

Aside from public pay, consolidation effort has relied significantly on capital spending. Excluding the impact of bank recapitalisation measures, capital spending on infrastructure has fallen from €9bn in 2008 to €3.3bn in 2014.[47] This may be criticised as taking a relatively easy route to spending reductions in that capital spending is usually easier to cut but more productive for the economy in the long run. On the other hand Ireland since 1993 enjoyed a decade and a half of extensive and substantial National Development Plans in which the country's infrastructure was radically transformed. Nonetheless, with Ireland facing renewed competitiveness pressures – and having fallen back from 4th to 21st position in the EU in terms of government capital infrastructure – spending is now becoming more important and a renewed momentum may be justified in this area.

---

[46]   Approximately one-sixth of Ireland's workforce is employed in its public sector.

[47]   Headline capital spending during the interim was affected by Government intervention in the banking and property sectors.

The Croke Park and Haddington Road Agreements

The other dimension to reform has been the improvement in micro level efficiency in the public sector. In March 2010 and in return for a commitment not to reduce pay or pensions or impose layoffs, Ireland's trade union movement agreed to the *Public Service Agreement 2010-2014* (the "Croke Park agreement") under which it agreed to call no industrial action and to co-operate with reforms aimed at increasing efficiency. This includes the redeployment of public servants, more flexible work practices and additional hours for primary, secondary and third level teachers.

In July 2013, this agreement was replaced by the *Public Service Stability Agreement 2013-2016* (the "Haddington Road agreement") under which further pay reductions of between 5.5 per cent and 10 per cent – depending on salary – were implemented for public servants earning €65,000 or more a year. In addition the Public Service Pension Reduction rates – levies on public pensions introduced in 2009 – were increased. Standard working hours were also increased, overtime rates were reduced and pay increments were suspended for a three year period.

Nonetheless, public pay and pensions remain, on average, considerably more generous than in either the private sector or in comparable EU countries. Recent earnings data[48] shows that average public service weekly earnings remain nearly one and a half times the level of private average earnings. While not directly comparable, this comparison does tend to re-enforce the message that the issues identified in aforementioned studies are still relevant. Earnings in the public sector also are rising faster than private sector levels.

Effectiveness Issues

Performing the same task with fewer resources than before is certainly an achievement in efficiency. It is not, however, necessarily an achievement in effectiveness. Effectiveness demands a more fundamental question: not whether we are doing the same thing more efficiently but, rather, whether we should be performing the same task at all.

Over the span of Ireland's history, Ireland's public service has served it well and in many areas Ireland's public servants are among the finest in Europe. However, the rapid rises in public pay and pensions between 2003 and 2008 have created public concern in relation to the fairness of the size of public expenditure and the burden created, particularly on those in more vulnerable forms of employment.

In some cases, this concern has led to rancour and division. A constructive approach to this issue may be to explore cross-country comparisons in public sector pay, adjusting for relative performance and cost of living. Instead of a divisive debate, a constructive comparison of international public service pay and

---

[48]   Central Statistics Office, *Earnings and Labour Costs Quarterly*, Q3 2013.

performance may help to resolve the issues above and ensure that public pay is fairly calibrated and associated with transparent and acceptable benchmarks.

As well as helping to judge future pay policy, such a comparison of public service effectiveness and productivity would be of assistance also in judging overall fiscal policy.

For instance it is often argued – most strongly by public employee representatives – that Ireland should emulate high Scandinavian levels of public expenditure and taxation on the basis that these countries also have high productivity and living standards. However, it does not follow that high public spending and tax levels automatically produce high productivity and living standards. Indeed the strongest increases in public spending in Ireland occurred at a time when productivity was declining sharply. In fact, research by the Institute of Public Administration[49] points to an interesting contrast between Ireland and Scandinavia. In Scandinavia's public administration, the gap between top and bottom pay levels is a ratio of 3.8; in Ireland, that ratio is 7.7. This indicates that there is considerably more inequality in the distribution of pay in Ireland's public sector. Research should be undertaken to establish whether these greater differentials are justified by higher productivity and performance at the top of Ireland's public service. This, in turn, may shed light on whether indeed there is a case for emulating Scandinavian economies by raising levels of State intervention in the economy or whether such an initiative would merely lead to higher costs without any improvement in economic performance.

Given evidence cited in this chapter, particularly by the authors Vitor Tanzi and Ludger Schuknecht (in relation to the optimal size of government) and Don Thornhill and Donal De Butleir (in relation to a properly adjusted and accurate measure of the size of Ireland's tax burden as a share of the economy), two very different possible conclusions also need to be considered: first that at 53.5 per cent of GNP, the size of Irish public spending is possibly well above a level that is required either for sustaining adequate public services and social provision optimal or in terms of optimising growth; and second that at nearly two-fifths of economic output – and more than this when adjusted for structural and demographic factors – the share of Ireland's economic output taken by tax revenue is already sufficient to fund adequate public services and social provision. In that eventuality, the case for Ireland to focus strongly, if not solely, on spending consolidation rather than tax reduction would be supported.

A Technical Note about GDP and GNP

Ireland's success in attracting foreign direct investment[50] has a statistical side effect that must be borne in mind when using either GDP or GNP as denominators for

---

[49]   Boyle, Richard (2011). *Public Sector Trends*, IPA.

[50]   See **Chapters 1** and **2**.

fiscal indicators. Gross Domestic Product (GDP) includes the output of all economic agents resident but not necessarily domiciled in Ireland. By contrast, Gross National Product includes the output of all economic agents domiciled but not necessarily resident in Ireland. The large presence of multinational firms means GDP is persistently larger than GNP by around one-fifth. The portion of Ireland's economic output that is attributable to GDP but not GNP is highly important to the economy, supporting many jobs and supply linkages. Compared to the output attributable to GNP, however, Ireland's competitive tax regime means that it is less accurate as an indicator of the economy's potential to generate tax revenues to support expenditure. Hence this chapter provides key fiscal measures both as a share of GDP (which is consistent with international practice) and GNP (which is a necessary "cross-check" given the nature of the Irish economy). GNP is also a better measure of the health of the domestic economy in that Ireland on occasions has experienced periods of healthy export-driven GDP growth whilst GNP growth remained weak. While the level of GNP will always be lower than GDP for Ireland (at least in the foreseeable future), a healthy recovery is characterised by strong real growth in both variables.

Exhibit 4.6: GDP and GNP for Ireland, 2004 to 2012

€m	2004	2005	2006	2007	2008	2009	2010	2011	2012	Average
GDP	150,024	162,897	177,573	189,655	180,249	162,284	158,097	162,600	163,938	
GNP	127,146	138,636	154,309	163,134	154,933	133,919	131,812	130,662	132,649	
Ratio	1.18	1.17	1.15	1.16	1.16	1.21	1.20	1.24	1.24	**1.19**

Source: Central Statistics Office.

COMMENTARY: CHAPTER 4
The Reform Dividend

Brian Hayes

Key Messages

- The Irish public service faces an unprecedented challenge to deliver services faster, better and more cost-effectively than before. To this end, plans for reform have been published in two waves, the first in November 2011 and the second in January 2014.
- While the first plan was necessitated by the need to reduce public sector spending in tandem with fiscal consolidation with an obvious focus on cost and efficiency, the second will broaden the scope of reform and improve public service delivery and effectiveness.

Introduction

Since taking office in 2011, far-reaching public service reform has been an essential part of the Government's strategy to meet the challenges we have faced in recent years. It was clear that the public service had to radically change what it does and how it does it.

The public service we create and provide to our citizens sharply defines the image we as a country project both at home and abroad. Never before has there been a greater need to deliver public services more effectively and more efficiently than now. We have had to reduce spending at a time when demand for services is greater than ever, given the confluence of a weak economy with a strong demography. Only through sustained radical reform can we continue to provide services, to protect the vulnerable members of our society, to drive job creation and to rebuild our economy.

A Vision for Public Service Reform

The public service is facing an unprecedented challenge to deliver services faster, better and more cost-effectively. All elements of the public service must work together to deliver value for money and quality public services. Our commitment to reform must be built on the core values of integrity, fairness, accountability and openness.

We must build a public service that has the flexibility, capacity and capability to respond to current and future challenges in an ever-changing global and local economic and business environment. Our vision is a public service that provides real value-for-money for the taxpayer by maximising efficiency and eliminating waste, and one that is innovative in providing citizen-centred services.

The Building Blocks for Reform

The success of this Government's public service reform programme is dependent on a robust focus on delivery and empowering public servants to deliver authentic reform locally. Established in 2011, the Department of Public Expenditure and Reform provided both the platform and opportunity to drive the many elements of the reform programme by integrating our approaches to reform and expenditure. In this context the Department's role is to facilitate, support and drive reform. While central administration empowers and supports each sector to deliver the necessary change, the Department of Public Expenditure and Reform leads on key cross-cutting initiatives and support.

The Government's commitment to public service reform was made clear by the decision to establish a dedicated Cabinet Minister to drive the reform agenda. This places reform at the centre of Government and cements the relationship between the reform and expenditure functions of Government.

A dedicated Reform and Delivery Office has been established to co-ordinate the various reform initiatives across the public service and to ensure a strategic and concerted implementation programme. This office is led by a Programme Director experienced in implementing major change and restructuring in the private sector. In addition, each Department and major Office has Change Delivery Teams to manage and drive the reform process in their organisations and sectors, as well as within the various bodies and agencies under their aegis.

The key driver in the reform process is the Cabinet Committee on Public Service Reform, which provides political direction and accountability for reform. The Cabinet Committee, which I attend, is chaired by the Taoiseach (Irish Prime Minister). It meets regularly to consider priority issues and ensure that overall progress is being achieved. In addition, an Advisory Group at Secretary General level provides support and advice on strategic issues to the Cabinet Committee.

A Reform Delivery Board, comprising Assistant Secretaries responsible for leading reform in each Government Department and major Office, meets regularly to oversee and monitor the delivery of public service reform at organisational and sectoral level, and provides assurance to the Reform and Delivery Office, and to the Cabinet Committee, that public service reform is being successfully delivered.

Laying the Foundation – the Public Service Reform Plan

In November 2011, the Irish Government launched a comprehensive *Public Service Reform Plan*, which outlined key commitments and actions for change across the public service. The Reform Plan set out five central themes for reform. These were:

- Placing customer service at the core of everything we do.
- Maximising new and innovative service delivery channels.
- Radically reducing our costs to drive better value for money.
- Leading, organising and working in new ways.
- A strong focus on implementation and delivery.

The Reform Plan contained some 70 recommendations and more than 200 actions, grouped under 14 main headings, as follows: Implementation; eGovernment, ICT, Information Sharing and Customer Service; Shared Services; Business Process Improvement; Procurement Reform; Property Asset Management; External Service Delivery; Rationalisation and Re-organisation; Public Expenditure Reform; Government Level Performance Management; Organisational Performance; Leadership and Individual Performance; Public Service Numbers, Workforce Planning and Redeployment; and Legislative and Political Reform.

Co-ordinated Action

Underpinning this integrated approach was the creation of high-level Integrated Reform Delivery Plans by each Department and major Office. This enables a clear understanding of the priority reform initiatives underway across the public service at both a cross-cutting and organisational level. These Departmental plans are aligned with the central *Public Service Reform Plan* and also capture the reforms for the associated sector where applicable.

Advancing on Several Fronts

It is clear that Ireland has a Government committed to reform. As a result of the economic and fiscal crises, a wide range of measures designed to save almost €30bn have been implemented. Over two-thirds of these adjustments have been on the expenditure side. Gross voted spending has been reduced from its peak of €63.1bn in 2009 to €54.6bn in 2013. This represents a reduction of approximately 13.5 per cent.

Public service numbers have now reduced by over 30,000 from a peak of 320,000 in 2008 to fewer than 290,000 currently. Achieving this target will require a further contribution from many but I am convinced there is a willingness to push forward in this regard.

Public servants already have had two pay reductions, totalling an average of 14 per cent. In addition, those earning over €65,000 have seen a further reduction since July 2013. From its peak of €17.5bn in 2009, the public service pay bill was reduced to €14.1bn this year, including the pension-related deduction. This is a reduction of almost 17.7 per cent. In addition, the numbers employed in the public service have fallen by almost 10 per cent.

The Reform Plan has changed how people are managed through the introduction of greater workforce flexibility and new working arrangements, as well as strengthening senior management and leadership capacity.

Redeployment arrangements are protecting frontline services as staff numbers fall by enabling staff to be moved to those areas of greatest need. We are implementing a framework for all sectors that seeks to put in place strategic workforce planning to ensure we have the right people in the right places at the right time. The *Public Service Stability Agreement 2013-2016*, known as the "Haddington Road Agreement", sets out the basis for the contribution of €1bn by the public service pay and pensions bill to our fiscal recovery, through a series of equitable and sustainable measures, which will allow for the creation of a more streamlined and unified public service.

In addition, new working arrangements have been introduced, including longer working hours, new rosters, standardised arrangements for annual leave and an improved performance management framework. A new single pension scheme, which commenced on 1 January 2013, will deliver significant long-term savings in public service pension costs. These are just some examples of how we are reforming the way our public service is managed.

Significant progress has been made on shared services. For example, PeoplePoint, the Civil Service HR and Pensions Shared Service Centre, is now operational. Once fully operational, the savings are estimated at €12.5m annually. The Government also approved the establishment of a single Civil Service Payroll Shared Service Centre. It is estimated that this initiative will achieve savings of €5.6m *per annum* when fully operational.

We also have approved the establishment of a National Shared Services Office to lead Civil Service shared services across the civil and public service and to provide direction for a whole-of-Government approach.

Opportunities for new ways of delivering services are being explored, with a view to reducing costs, increasing efficiency and allowing for greater focus of resources on core value-added activities. A programme of skills development has been put in place by the Reform and Delivery Office to improve the capacity and capability of public service managers in this area.

The Government's *eGovernment Strategy 2012-2015* ensures a strong focus on the citizen and better and more innovative use of technology to improve the citizen's experience of interacting with the public service. Over 400 public services are available from our central portal – www.gov.ie – with more to be added over time in line with the eGovernment strategy.

The management of public expenditure is being reformed through the introduction of Performance Budgeting, Medium-Term Expenditure Frameworks and a new *Public Spending Code*. Performance budgeting has resulted in a radical reformatting of estimates documentation so as to include performance information, together with the resources that are being provided. Moreover, all Government Departments and Offices are now publishing all purchase orders over €20,000 on a quarterly basis. The publication of balance sheets has also commenced.

2013 saw a major transformational change in the public procurement of goods and services – accounting for approximately €9bn of spending by the State. A National Procurement Office, led by a Chief Procurement Officer for the Public Service, has been established. This new office integrates procurement policy, strategy and operations. It will strengthen spend analytics and data management and, having much greater aggregation of purchasing across public bodies, achieve better value for money. A target of €500m in savings over three years has been identified.

Making Industrial Peace Benefit All

In considering how far we have come in reform of the public service, we must acknowledge the role of the *Public Service Stability Agreement 2013-2016* and the related pay reduction measures provided for under the *Financial Emergency Measures in the Public Interest Act, 2013*.

Achieving the general government deficit target of below 3 per cent of GDP by 2015 remains a challenging cornerstone of our economic policy. With pay and pensions accounting for 36 per cent of voted current expenditure, it is clear that a proportionate contribution of €1bn in savings is needed from the public service pay and pension bill by 2015.

Of this €1 billion in savings, the pay reduction to higher earners – those earning over €65,000 – will deliver approximately €210m, with other central measures, including pension reductions, delivering some €130m.

In addition to the obvious cost benefits, the Agreement provides us with the scope to progress the next phase of the Government's ambitious reform agenda and to deliver unprecedented increases in productivity across the public service. For example, the Agreement has provided for almost 15 million additional working hours in the public service, which will deliver significant efficiency savings.

In addition to these core changes, there have been numerous specific measures agreed at the sectoral level. These measures will help to deliver the greatest return for each sector both in terms of cost savings and efficiency gains.

Maintaining Momentum

In the two years since the Government's *Public Service Reform Plan* was published, a new phase of reform has been developed, building on the progress made on implementing the first Reform Plan and setting out an ambitious new phase in the reform programme.

This new plan, published in January 2014, outlines the key cross-cutting and sectoral reform initiatives that will be implemented over the next three years. It also looks further forward to address the ambition for reform towards 2020.

Better Delivery

The previous phase of reform had a necessarily strong focus on reducing the cost of delivering public services. This next phase of reform will continue that work but with a strengthened focus on the delivery of improved outcomes for service users. This will be centred on using alternative models of service delivery, including commissioning for specific outcomes; more online delivery of services; and a series of service delivery improvements at organisational level.

Securing the Reform Dividend

There have been major efficiency and productivity gains in the public service in recent years and we will build on these and deliver more. Under the new Reform Plan, the reform agenda will be about protecting and improving public services, and so over the period of this Plan, there will be an emphasis on 'Saving to Invest'. The State intends to free up resources by making existing processes more cost-effective and efficient and using the savings to invest in new or improved services.

More and More Open Data

Technology is shrinking the world and increasing people's expectations. A new Government *ICT Strategy* will be published early in 2014 that will address the use of new and emerging technologies, ensuring that eGovernment is designed around real needs and taking steps to improve take-up of Digital Government.

Openness Equals Accountability

Citizens must be able to clearly see that the public service is working fairly in its decision-making, in implementing policy and in delivering public services. The Government's political reform programme will focus on delivering greater openness, transparency and accountability to strengthen trust in government and public services and strengthen public governance.

The new *Public Service Reform Plan* also addresses a wide range of other issues. These include, for example, the implementation of shared services models; the evaluation of new business models for the delivery of non-core services; the reform of public procurement; property rationalisation; strengthening leadership; and human resource management reforms.

Conclusions

Ireland's reform programme has been dynamic and responsive. It must continue to be so. Ireland's difficulties in recent years have been reported on and viewed globally. I believe we have been radical in our solutions. The world has seen the benefits a reforming Government can bring.

We have emerged from a dire economic and fiscal situation and are determined to put the conditions for sustainable growth in place. To do so, Ireland must be adaptable to meet the new challenges and new opportunities that lie ahead. On this point I defer to Lewis Carroll's masterpiece, and the Queen's comments to Alice: *"... it takes all the running you can do, to keep in the same place. If you want to get somewhere else, you must run at least twice as fast as that!"*.

CHAPTER 5

Banking and Finance: Back to Stability[51]

Dr. Stefan Gerlach

Key Messages

- The Irish banking sector today looks very different from the pre-crisis. After registering extraordinary losses during the crisis, the sector has been recapitalised, downsized, experienced significant consolidation, and, in several cases, nationalisation.
- The difficulties encountered by the Irish banking sector during the financial crisis revealed a need for reform and improvement in a number of areas of financial sector operations and oversight. Both international and domestic policy have been important in shaping these changes, foremost of which has been the EU/IMF programme of support, which required a large number of structural, fiscal and financial reforms to be enacted.
- While much progress has been made, there are still several challenges ahead in restoring the State-supported banks to full viability and private ownership.

Introduction

Six years on from the onset of the global financial crisis, the Irish banking sector looks very different from its pre-crisis years. During the boom, the sector was characterised by rapid growth, high profit levels, negligible loan impairments and increasing levels of competition. After extraordinary losses during the crisis, the sector has been recapitalised, downsized, experienced significant consolidation, and, in several cases, nationalised. The sector still suffers from high levels of arrears and non-performing loans. Meanwhile the regulatory landscape also has changed dramatically, with supervisory and regulatory developments at both domestic and European levels having profound effects on the environment in which banks operate.

---

[51] I am very much indebted to Lars Frisell and, in particular, Yvonne McCarthy for their work on this chapter.

The Irish banking sector comprises three main groups – Irish-owned retail banks, non-Irish owned retail banks and banks in the International Financial Services Centre (IFSC). While the retail banks largely provide financial services to households and businesses at home, IFSC institutions mainly conduct their business with counterparties outside Ireland.[52]

This chapter explores some of the key changes that have taken place in the Irish banking sector since the financial crisis began and provides an assessment of the current outlook for the sector. In discussing specific banking sector developments, the focus is largely on Irish-owned retail banks, which have been most affected by the crisis. The remainder of this chapter is structured as follows: the next section provides a brief summary of the background to the banking crisis and the initial policy response; the following section details key changes in the banking supervision and regulation landscape since the onset of the crisis; and the final section concludes with an assessment of the banking sector in Ireland and an outline of the key challenges likely to face the sector in coming years.

Background To The Crisis

The years prior to the crisis witnessed several unsustainable trends in the Irish retail banking sector that made it particularly vulnerable when the financial crisis and the economic downturn came.[53] Against a backdrop of emerging imbalances in the domestic economy, the sector experienced dramatic balance sheet growth, driven primarily by property lending. Between 2000 and 2008, private sector credit grew by over 400 per cent, with property-related loans (commercial and retail) constituting 80 per cent of this growth.[54] To some extent this was driven by volume growth, which in turn was driven by very significant growth in the population. Simultaneously, however, property prices also grew at very significant rates; new house prices, for example, increased by 88 per cent between 2000 and 2007, when house prices peaked. **Exhibit 5.1** shows the sectoral composition of bank lending over the period 2002 to 2008.

To fund the growth in their balance sheets, banks became increasingly reliant on wholesale market funding, largely in the form of foreign borrowing by the banks. **Exhibit 5.2** shows the increasing funding gap – the difference between domestic lending and retail corporate deposits – that emerged over the period in the Irish financial system. The banks' demand for non-deposit funding grew at a particularly high rate over the period 2004 to 2007. This increase in non-deposit

---

[52] See Box 1 in the Central Bank's *Quarterly Bulletin, Q3 2013*, for a detailed account of developments in these three groups over the period 2003 to 2012.

[53] For a full exploration of these issues, see Chapter 2 of the *Report of the Commission of Investigation into the Banking Sector in Ireland* (2011).

[54] These figures are based on an internal Central Bank dataset that adjusts the series to reflect non-credit related transactions such as revaluations, securitisations and transfers to NAMA.

funding left banks highly exposed to fluctuations in international interest rates and to changes in market sentiment.

Exhibit 5.1: Sectoral Composition of Bank Lending (excluding financial intermediation)

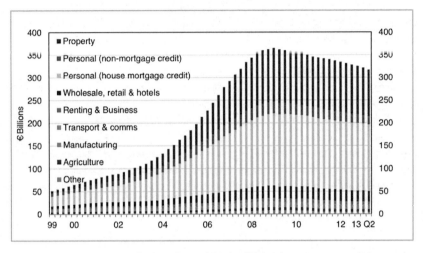

Source: Central Bank of Ireland.
Note: Series are adjusted to reflect non-credit related transactions such as revaluations, securitisations and transfers to NAMA.

Exhibit 5.2: Private Sector Credit and Deposit Levels in the Irish Financial System

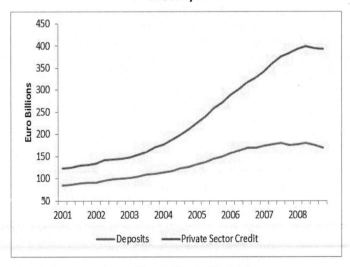

Source: Central Bank of Ireland.

In the years leading up to the crisis, a number of foreign banks entered the Irish banking sector.[55] This increased competition lead to a relaxation of underwriting standards and new mortgage products such as interest-only loans, equity releases and tracker rate mortgages. The first two products brought loan-to-value ratios as high as 100 per cent or more. This left borrowers and banks exposed to a downturn in the housing market, while tracker rate mortgages were based on the assumption that sufficient funding would continue to be available at near-ECB rates. The rate of acquisition of higher risk investment or buy-to-let properties by retail customers also rose over the period, while foreign competition also increased in the commercial property lending sector.

Against this background, when the financial and economic climate started to weaken in mid-2007, rents and property values in Ireland declined rapidly. This led to an increase in loan-to-value ratios and an erosion of the equity cushion on property loans. Coupled with the significant exposure to property-related borrowing and the potential for loan losses in a depressed economic environment, investor sentiment towards banks in the Irish market deteriorated significantly. In 2007, the cost of funding for Irish banks increased to well above the ECB rate. After the Lehman Brothers bankruptcy in September 2008, access to wholesale funding quickly drained for Irish banks.

Policy Response

Honohan *et al.* (2010)[56] and Honohan (2012)[57] provide a detailed overview of the early response of Irish policymakers to the financial crisis. Responding to the pressures in the banking sector, the Irish Government introduced a blanket guarantee scheme covering all Irish bank debt liabilities in September 2008. The overarching approach of the Irish Government since the guarantee involved cleansing the banks' balance sheets of bad assets and recapitalising the banks to sufficient levels. Specifically, efforts to stabilise the banking sector included several rounds of recapitalisations of the main Irish banks beginning in late-2008, the nationalisation of Anglo Irish Bank in January 2009, the issuance of promissory notes to bolster the capital position of Anglo Irish Bank from early 2010, the introduction of Exceptional Liquidity Assistance (ELA) in 2009 and the setting up of an asset management company (NAMA) in late-2009 to manage property-related loans.[58]

---

[55]   Bank of Scotland entered the Irish market in 1999 and Ulster Bank acquired First Active in 2004, giving it a substantial share of the residential mortgage market.

[56]   Honohan, P., Donovan, D., Gorecki, P. & Mottiar, R. (2010). *The Irish Banking Crisis: Regulatory and Financial Stability Policy*, Central Bank of Ireland.

[57]   Honohan, P. (2012). "Recapitalisation of Failed Banks – Some Lessons from the Irish Experience", address at the *44th Annual Money, Macro and Finance Conference*, Trinity College, Dublin, 7 September.

[58]   The initial capitalisation plan was announced in December 2008 when €2bn was to be

NAMA was set up to purchase the large property loans of the Irish banks at a "long-term economic value" so that expected losses in relation to these loans would be immediately crystallised by the banks. Furthermore, the Central Bank undertook an assessment of the future capital requirements of Irish banks (known as Prudential Capital Assessment Review (PCAR)), the details of which were published in March 2010.[59] The outcome was a requirement for a further €11bn of new capital for Allied Irish Bank (AIB), Bank of Ireland (BOI) and Educational Building Society (EBS) and approximately €20bn for Anglo Irish Bank and Irish Nationwide Building Society (INBS). By end-August 2010, it became clear that previously estimated losses on NAMA-related transfers would be higher than anticipated. Further capital injections were required and the decision was made to wind down Anglo Irish Bank.[60]

In November 2010, a programme of support from the EU/IMF was announced for Ireland, totalling €85bn (including a contribution of €17.5bn from Ireland's own resources). The primary objective of the programme was to rebuild international confidence in the Irish economy and the banking system. This programme provided a strong foundation for a reformed and restructured banking sector. It involved a number of financial sector reform commitments that would be key to shaping the Irish banking sector.[61] These commitments were primarily aimed at downsizing and re-organising the Irish banking system to a sustainable structure. For example, the programme required the running down of non-core assets for Irish banks, an increase in resources for banking supervision, reform of the personal insolvency regime, measures to deal with mortgage arrears as well as ensuring a sufficient supply of credit to viable businesses.

Reform – How Things Changed

The difficulties encountered by the Irish banking sector during the financial crisis revealed a need for reform and improvement in a number of areas of financial sector operations and oversight. Both international and domestic policy have been

---

injected into each of AIB and BOI (plus a commitment to underwrite a further €1bn each in new equity to be issued), and €1.5bn was to be injected into Anglo Irish Bank. As time progressed, events overtook this announcement and Anglo Irish Bank was nationalised in January 2009; and the initial injections into AIB and BOI were increased to €3.5bn each.

[59] Further details are available at http://www.centralbank.ie.

[60] The new capital requirements were announced on 30 September 2010. AIB was deemed to require a further €3bn in new capital, Anglo Irish Bank a further €12bn and INBS was to require almost €3bn in additional capital.

[61] Full details of these financial sector commitments are available in the *Memorandum of Economic and Financial Policies* (http://www.finance.gov.ie/documents/ publications/ reports/2010/EUIMFmemo.pdf), while details of the progress on such are available in IMF country reports and reviews of the extended arrangement. The latest review is accessible at http://www.imf.org/external/pubs/cat/longres.aspx?sk=40978.0.

important in shaping these changes, foremost of which has been the EU/IMF programme of support, which required a large number of structural, fiscal and financial reforms to be enacted. An overview of the most important changes shaping the current structure of banking and finance in Ireland is provided in this section.

European Level

To address weaknesses and heterogeneity in the assessment of financial sector risks in Europe, as revealed by the crisis, the European Union developed a new financial supervision framework for Europe.[62] This framework came into force on 16 December 2010. Central to this framework was the establishment of the European Systemic Risk Board (ESRB). This body was tasked with contributing *"to the prevention or mitigation of systemic risks to financial stability in the EU that arise from developments within the financial system and taking into account macro-economic developments, so as to avoid widespread financial distress".*[63] To this aim, the ESRB would issue warnings and recommendations that were subject to a "comply or explain" mechanism. The board also has consultative powers in a number of areas. However, at inception the ESRB had no legal power to enforce recommendations; that responsibility remained with national authorities.

The most significant development at European level, which will have a sizeable impact on the Irish banking environment over the short- to medium-term, is the establishment of the Single Supervisory Mechanism (SSM). In 2014, the ECB will take over prudential supervisory responsibility for all credit institutions in the Euro area, with a decentralised approach for the less significant ones, and potential opt-in from other non-Euro area Member States.

Finally, a new regulatory framework for banks is introduced with the *Capital Requirements Regulation* and *Directive* in January 2014, which transposes the so-called Basel III requirements.[64] Most importantly, the framework will phase in significantly stricter capital and liquidity requirements. The *Directive* also covers issues in relation to governance and remuneration practices. While the new requirements will contribute to more stable banking systems in the future, it also

---

[62] In November 2008, a High Level Group, chaired by Mr Jacques De Larosière was mandated by the EU Commission to propose recommendations on how to strengthen European supervisory arrangements. The report of the group, commonly referred to as the *De Larosière Report*, was published in February 2009.

[63] ESRB (2013). *The Consequences of the Single Supervisory Mechanism for Europe's Macro-prudential Policy Framework*, Reports of the Advisory Scientific Committee, September.

[64] Bank for International Settlements, *Basel III: A Global Regulatory Framework for More Resilient Banks and Banking Systems* (original version: Dec 2010, Revised version: June 2011) and *Basel III: International Framework for Liquidity Risk Management, Standards and Monitoring* (original version: Dec 2010, revised version: Jan 2013).

pose challenges for Irish banks in the short-term as they are still largely dependent on short-term funding and have yet to return to profitability.[65]

National Level

Following the *Central Bank Reform Act, 2010,* the Central Bank of Ireland is now responsible for both central banking and financial regulation.[66] Further enhancements of the supervisory and enforcement powers of the Central Bank were made with the passing of the *Central Bank (Supervision and Enforcement) Act, 2013*. This Act ensures that many of the provisions of the Central Bank (for example, direction-making powers) are harmonised across all regulated financial service providers rather than being applicable to one industry sector alone. This can be contrasted with the situation prior to the Act in which the legislative powers available to the Central Bank to perform its functions in a particular industry sector was typically governed by the sector-specific legislation involved.

Regulatory policy and objectives have been refocused within this new unitary organisation, both relating to oversight at an individual institution level (micro-prudential) and at a system-wide financial stability level (macro-prudential). The Central Bank also has targeted improved standards of governance and fitness and probity in financial institutions in Ireland. Clear requirements for the directors and boards of banks and other financial entities have been set out in the Central Bank's *Corporate Governance for Credit Institutions and Insurance Undertakings*, while the statutory *Fitness and Probity Standards* strengthen the Central Bank's role in relation to senior appointments in regulated financial entities.

Regarding supervision, it has been identified that the supervisory culture in Ireland and other countries was too deferential towards the banking industry in the period preceding the crisis. Honohan *et al.* (2010)[67] provide an overview of the flaws in the supervision of financial institutions in Ireland preceding the crisis: too few resources were dedicated to the task of supervision; supervisory practice was too focused on verifying the governance and risk management models of financial institutions rather than attempting an independent assessment of risk; and there was also a degree of complacency about the likely-performance of seemingly well-governed banks that proved unwarranted.

---

[65] As for several other European banks, the issue of deferred tax assets (DTA) is of particular interest. After several years of incurring significant losses, Irish banks now have sizeable contingent tax claims on the State, against which they may offset future corporate tax. Under the new requirements DTA no longer count as regulatory capital.

[66] The new structure replaced the previous related entities, the Central Bank and the Financial Services Authority of Ireland and the Financial Regulator. The Act became effective on 1 October 2010.

[67] Honohan, P., Donovan, D., Gorecki, P. & Mottiar, R. (2010). *The Irish Banking Crisis: Regulatory and Financial Stability Policy*, Central Bank of Ireland.

The crisis brought recognition that significant change was needed. In response, the Central Bank reshaped its approach to banking supervision, expanding its resources and increasing its focus on quantitative and financial analysis, setting up a new risk panel comprising external risk advisors and introducing a dedicated enforcement team.[68] Central to these changes was an underlying change in the supervisory culture; the Central Bank's focus is now on delivering an assertive, risk-based and challenging approach to banking supervision underpinned by a credible enforcement deterrent.

To aid its altered approach to supervision, the Central Bank developed a new risk assessment framework: the Prudential Risk and Impact System (PRISM). The framework was introduced in 2011 and was designed to provide a structured framework for institution supervision and to enhance the Central Bank's ability to deliver judgement-based, outcome-focused regulation. The system requires supervisors to form judgements about the risks each institution presents and then to develop appropriate risk mitigation programmes to reduce unacceptable risks to an acceptable level.

PRISM involves the segmentation of regulated institutions into different impact categories, where these categories are assigned on the basis of quantitative data. There are four impact categories reflecting an institution's relative importance based on *inter alia* size, turnover and client base and there are four engagement models to match these impact categories. The highest impact institutions receive the highest level of engagement, with dedicated supervision teams following a pro-active programme of supervision. The forward-looking assessment of risks, the provisions and capital set aside to cover them, and the review of liquidity and funding are at the centre of the Central Bank supervisory process. This is complemented by assessment of fitness and probity, governance, business model and profitability analyses.

In the autumn of 2013, the Central Bank conducted a comprehensive Balance Sheet Assessment and Asset Quality Review of the three main domestic retail banks (AIB, BOI and PTSB) to review loan classifications, provisions, and regulatory risk weights.

Further non-statutory guidelines have been issued by the Central Bank to deal with the crisis in the banking sector. For example, the Central Bank's *Consumer Protection Code* sets out conduct of business requirements applicable to a wide range of financial services provided in Ireland. In the spring of 2013, the Bank launched quantitative targets for mortgage arrears resolution.

---

[68]   Central Bank of Ireland, *Banking Supervision: Our New Approach* (June 2010); Central Bank of Ireland, *Banking Supervision: Our Approach 2011 Update* (June 2011).

Current Assessment and Key Challenges

The Irish banking sector today looks very different after the crisis. In line with requirements under the EU/IMF programme of support, there has been a significant reduction in the size of the sector and a considerable restructuring of operations to focus on core domestic activities. In 2008, the total assets of the Irish banking sector (retail and IFSC banks) amounted to over €1,400bn (equivalent to 789 per cent of GDP). Irish-owned retail banks accounted for about 44 per cent of this. By 2012, total assets of the resident banking system had declined to €859bn (525 per cent of GDP), of which 51 per cent was accounted for by Irish-owned retail banks.

Considerable restructuring has taken place in the retail banking sector that serves the domestic economy. Three of the major banks in the Irish-owned retail sector are no longer in existence (Anglo Irish Bank, INBS and EBS). Remaining significant domestic institutions include AIB and BOI. Following significant recapitalisations and the transfer of impaired property loans to NAMA, these banks are now in a much stronger position than when the crisis hit.

Recent months have seen considerable improvement in international investor sentiment towards Irish banks, and domestic banks have issued some secured debt and reduced their reliance on central bank funding. Bank balance sheet deleveraging has also continued and capital ratios are currently well in excess of regulatory requirements. However, while much progress has been made, there are still several challenges ahead in restoring the State-supported banks to full viability and private ownership. These include:

- **Profitability:** Bank profitability has been adversely affected by a number of factors including loan impairments, weakness in both the domestic and European economy, a low level of new lending, a high proportion of low-yielding "tracker" mortgages, and relatively high funding costs. While improvements have been made, the future earnings capacity of domestic banks remains challenging; banks are planning for further cost reductions which should bolster margins. However, certain aspects are outside their control. For example, the cost of future debt issuance is dependent upon positive investor sentiment. Furthermore, the upcoming Balance Sheet Assessment and the 2014 stress tests bring uncertainty about future loan provisions.

- **Loan arrears and credit risk:** Continued growth in non-performing loans remains a challenge for Ireland's banks. The stock of impaired loans reached €57bn, or 27 per cent of the value of outstanding loans, in the second quarter of 2013. While the pace of deterioration has slowed from recent quarters, efforts to deal with distressed loans so far have proved inadequate. In the case of mortgages, for example, banks have tended to favour temporary forbearance measures. However, a new target-based framework to deal with mortgage arrears, known as the Mortgage

Arrears Resolution Targets (MART), was introduced in March 2013, following a set of measures to facilitate arrears resolution.[69] Early indications on progress under the MART, albeit on unaudited data, are positive.[70]

- **Funding risks:** Domestic banks have made a lot of progress in dealing with funding challenges since the crisis involving a reduction in official sector support, recent debt issuance, and reductions in deposit rates. However, funding conditions remain vulnerable to swings in market sentiment and banks are still predominantly reliant on short-term funding.

Against this backdrop, the Irish authorities continue to work on restructuring and strengthening the Irish banking sector. The main aim of these efforts is to get the domestic banks to a position where they can support the economic recovery in Ireland by providing the necessary credit to consumers and businesses. In this regard, a strong focus remains on lending to small and medium-sized enterprises, a key sector for job creation.[71]

---

[69] For example, the *Code of Conduct on Mortgage Arrears* has been revised, new personal insolvency legislation has been enacted, the Insolvency Service of Ireland has been established and previous legal obstacles to the instigation of repossession proceedings have been removed.

[70] On introduction, the MART required banks to propose viable solutions for 50 per cent of mortgage holders who were in more than 90 days arrears, by the end of 2013. Further targets, requiring mortgage lenders to reach sustainable conclusions with at least 15 per cent of borrowers more than 90 days in arrears before the end of the year and 25 per cent by March 2014 were announced in September 2013.

[71] For example, an independent Credit Review Office was established in April 2010 to assist SMEs that were refused credit by the pillar banks. The Irish government also has introduced a Credit Guarantee Scheme and Micro-finance Scheme to boost the availability of credit to viable businesses.

COMMENTARY: CHAPTER 5

The International Financial Services Centre During the Irish Bank Crisis: An IFSC Perspective[72]

Werner Schwanberg

Key Messages

- Despite having attracted a large variety of international financial organisations, the IFSC was not part of Ireland's financial crisis. IFSC companies in difficulty during the crisis were a rare exception and even then were not involved in Ireland's bailout programme.
- This notwithstanding, as a result of the crisis the IFSC is now subject to an improved regime. The upgrade of Ireland's investment rating shows that, amongst other things, financial regulation in Ireland has restored confidence in Ireland's financial sector and, at the same time, has taken a proportionate risk-based approach to determining supervisory needs.

Introduction

In his chapter **Banking and Finance: Back to Stability** above, Dr. Stefan Gerlach, Deputy Governor of the Central Bank of Ireland, refers to the three main groups of the Irish banking sector: namely Irish-owned retail banks, non-Irish owned retail banks and banks in the International Financial Services Centre (IFSC). Given my background, I will concentrate on the last: IFSC banks and, in particular, German-owned IFSC banks.

I joined Dresdner Bank in Ireland in 1991 as a client relations manager of their Asset Management subsidiary, the first German-owned financial institution to be established under the IFSC regime. Dresdner's presence in Dublin subsequently developed into a total of three companies, one of which was a fully licensed bank. I headed this bank until 2003 when, following internal restructuring, the group reduced its global international presence and also withdrew from Ireland. In 2006, I was appointed CEO of WGZ Bank Ireland plc, another German-owned bank in Dublin, a position I have held since then. Beside these executive roles, I have joined boards of other Irish financial services companies as a non-executive director.

---

[72] The author thanks John Wright and Christine Pisch for their valuable assistance in writing this Commentary.

The History of the IFSC

To understand the motivation for establishing an international financial services centre, one has to look at the problems of the Irish economy during the mid-1980s. Fuelled by over-spending, over-borrowing and an overvalued currency tied to the Exchange Rate Mechanism (ERM), the country struggled with a weak economy, high interest rates, high unemployment, mass emigration and labour market unrest leading to intensive industrial strike actions. In 1986 the Irish currency, the Punt, was devalued.

Successive Governments tried to tackle the multitude of challenges and improvements were achieved by economic and welfare reforms, tax cuts, etc. In search for further economic stimulus, politicians engaged in a dialogue with Irish business leaders. In one instance this led to the idea of establishing an international financial services centre that would attract foreign investment, create jobs and lead to infrastructural enhancement in neglected parts of Dublin.

The idea of the IFSC was born. The basic concept was relatively simple and showed similarities with previous projects – for example, the Shannon Free Zone, which was established in 1959. This had brought a number of multinationals from various industries to Ireland. The IFSC targeted solely financial services companies, which were willing to actively trade in Dublin, would commit to employ a minimum number of staff in line with accepted business plans and lastly would agree to move their offices into the Dublin Docklands, which were to be developed accordingly. In return, successful applicants were given a special Corporation Tax rate of 10 per cent (the general Corporation Tax rate in Ireland at the time was 40 per cent), and some rent allowances. All conditions were laid down in a so-called "tax certificate", which was issued by the Department of Finance. Fears of the domestic financial sector were eliminated by imposing a ban on business with Irish counterparties. A ban also was imposed on business with private clients.

The key sponsors of the scheme were the prominent Irish businessman, Dermot Desmond, who is said to have created the concept, and the then Taoiseach (Prime Minister), Charles Haughey, who saw its potential, took it on board and defended it against scepticism and opposition from parts of the civil service and the Irish domestic banks, which feared overwhelming competition from abroad. At EU level, the measures did not raise any objections on the basis that the tax concessions were time-restricted to 2000, which was later extended under certain circumstances to 2005.

Beside the fiscal advantages, Ireland also could offer a well-educated work force, some of whom had already gathered international experience mainly in the US and the UK and were eager to return home and secure employment in areas that would use their expertise gained abroad.

The IFSC Today

Successive Irish Governments have supported the IFSC since its inception, irrespective of their political allegiance. Twenty-seven years on, it has proven to be a major success and a boost to the Irish economy. Over 500 firms have been established, covering banking, insurance, funds and asset management, leasing, securitisation, payments and money transmission and corporate treasury. They provide direct employment to 33,000 people, plus 6,000 employed by indigenous firms, and operate in 20 different counties throughout Ireland. The IFSC companies contribute 7.4 per cent of Irish GDP.[73] Long gone is the ring-fenced Corporation Tax of 10 per cent, which was replaced by a general Corporation Tax for trading income of 12.5 per cent. Also, the conditions connected to a tax certificate, or, indeed, the tax certificate itself, were no longer necessary.

The Impact of Recent Financial Crises on IFSC Banks

Global Events

Like everyone else, from 2007 banks in the IFSC or their parent companies were affected in different ways and to a varying degree by the challenges emanating from such events as the US subprime crisis, the collapse of Icelandic banks, the Lehman Brothers demise and, in more recent times, the Eurozone financial crisis.

The impact on the IFSC banks often depended on the situation of the parent groups. For instance, if the parent bank received capital assistance from the State in which it was domiciled, then it often faced pressure to consolidate its affairs, shed non-core business and streamline the group structure. There were also technical factors at play, such as losses carried forward at group level that sometimes diminished the enthusiasm for operations in locations like Ireland. As a result, a number of European banks reviewed their position and, in some cases, started to wind up their companies in Ireland. This was very much a European issue and did not affect the US banks to the same extent.

The bottom line was that:

- IFSC banks in severe financial difficulties due to the financial crisis were a rare exception. Where problems occurred, the parent companies bailed them out.
- No IFSC bank cost the Irish taxpayer a single Euro.

The Irish banking crisis

The problems resulting from the property boom in Ireland and the failing of the domestic banks had no direct impact on the international financial services community in the IFSC. However, it was soon to feel some indirect side-effects radiating from the crisis.

---

[73] http://www.ifscireland.ie/facts-figures.

First, Ireland's international reputation suffered severely from the financial difficulties it was experiencing and from the necessity to enter into a bailout programme with the EU/IMF to the tune of €67 billion.[74] The reputational damage was exacerbated by sometimes misleading or exaggerated media reports, both at home and abroad. These were particularly troubling during 2009 and 2010 and most certainly had an influence on decision-makers at global financial institutions when it came to considering Dublin for capital investment. The Irish responded by co-operating fully with the international lenders and the terms of the bailout programme and by implementing a vast array of measures to reduce public expenditure and enhance revenue. This was, and is, a difficult and painful process that put significant burdens on the general public. In addition, the Government and diplomatic representatives, together with organisations such as the IDA and the German-Irish Chamber of Commerce, launched an extensive information campaign inside and outside of Ireland to explain what efforts were being made by the country to overcome the crisis and why the fundamentals of its economy were in much better shape than those of other economies in trouble.

The results are well-known. Ireland successfully returned to the capital markets, is fully funded into 2015 and exited the bailout programme in December 2013. In 2014, the State issued a benchmark 10-year 3.4 per cent bond, raising €3.75bn out of a €8bn target for the year (the corresponding rate in 2011 peaked at 15 per cent). Also, in early 2014, the rating agency Moody's upgraded Ireland's rating to investment grade levels with a positive outlook. While there are undoubtedly remaining challenges, not least the legacy burdens of the bank and property crisis, the country's reputation has been restored after this remarkable comeback and that is reflected in current media reports and comments from its European partners.

A second side-effect for IFSC firms that resulted from the Irish banking crisis was the country's approach to financial regulation. The failing Irish banks triggered severe criticism of the Irish regulator, the Central Bank of Ireland (CBI), resulting in calls for tougher regulation. This required a substantial increase in resources and staff numbers. In addition, expertise was brought in from other jurisdictions. Principles-based regulation was replaced by rules-based regulation. A mandatory corporate governance code[75] was introduced for banks and insurance undertakings, together with a number of other measures. While this was an understandable and necessary reaction to the domestic banking crisis, it posed an irritant for the international financial services industry in the IFSC. The regulator's approach initially showed little proportionality and an IFSC wholesale bank with 20 staff suddenly faced similar regulatory challenges as the domestic banks. The dilemma for international banks and insurance operations was that, on the one

---

[74]   The total programme of €85bn included €17bn cash and pension reserves.
[75]   Central Bank of Ireland, *Corporate Governance Code for Credit Institutions and Insurance Undertakings 2010*.

hand, they wanted sophisticated regulation but, on the other hand, they also wanted appropriate proportionality applied. Again, global financial institutions had concerns about what they perceived to be undue regulatory burdens on their Irish subsidiaries and, in some cases, this would have found its way into their strategic planning. However, since then the CBI has adopted a risk-based approach by classifying institutions in risk categories that determine the intensity of supervisory engagement. This, in my opinion, has brought the necessary level of proportionality to Irish bank supervision.

Conclusion

The financial crisis, both globally generated and home-made, has rocked the "IFSC boat" slightly but it did not cause any major damage as experienced in other parts of the market. Ireland still offers the same advantages to international financial services investors as before:

- A significant financial services centre with major international players present.
- A stable political environment.
- A transparent and attractive Corporate Tax regime.
- A pool of well-educated professionals.
- Regulation to EU standards
- An economic link between the US and the EU as the only English-speaking country in the Eurozone.

In my view, Ireland and the IFSC continue to have a lot to offer to any internationally-positioned financial services group with sound business plan, a solid risk strategy and a focus on profitability.

CHAPTER 6

The Dynamics of Ireland's Labour Market

Christoph Müller[76]

Key Messages

- After four years in the country, I can say that I find Ireland a great place to do business. Taoiseach Enda Kenny and the Irish Government plan to take this a step further, to make Ireland the best small country in the world in which to do business.
- In order to achieve this objective, we need to invest in training and skills development. While this investment should focus on the future needs of the labour market, action is needed now.

Introduction

The Irish economy has been through a period of absolute and unprecedented devastation in recent years. Most of the European economies have suffered during the economic crisis, but the small and open nature of the Irish economy has meant that the effects here have been far more pronounced than at the core of Europe. The waves grew in size as they moved out from the core and Ireland, as a small open economy on the periphery, has borne the brunt.

Whereas certain countries in mainland Europe bounced back as early as 2010, some of them even facing into a second crisis, Ireland has not yet moved on from this monumental set-back to its economic output.

This is not to say that Ireland did not have its own particular economic dynamics that caused, and perhaps amplified, the economic meltdown. The failure of government, the general body politic, economic policymakers, regulators, financial institutions, large sectors of the economy and countless vested interest groups have all been well debated and documented over the course of this crisis. It is not my intention to go over that well-worn ground but rather to look specifically at what I see as the most significant result of economic collapse and the greatest challenge facing our economy: the jobs crisis.

---

[76] The author would like to acknowledge the assistance of EY, Goodbody and Davy with this chapter.

The Current Situation

Before going into the specifics of the current situation, it is important to recognise some important underlying facts:

- The growth rate of the Irish population is the highest amongst the European membership states and at the current rate of job creation the gap between supply and demand will grow.
- This growing gap means that any solution to tackling overall unemployment will have to focus firmly on tackling youth unemployment.
- It is not sufficient to compare the current situation with the pre-crisis so-called Celtic Tiger years but, in particular, the period of the 1990s needs special attention as a blueprint for the way forward. Those early years of the Celtic Tiger period created an entrepreneurial foundation of growing economic prosperity and competitiveness in Ireland. Most of the factors that led to this prosperity are still available to us today.

The consensus view of the Irish labour market currently is that it has stabilised. While there has been an increase in total employment of 33,800 in the year to Q2 2013, unemployment has remained extremely high with 300,700 people unemployed, representing an unemployment rate of 13.9 per cent in the year to Q2.[77] At the time of writing, it appears that Q3 may see the statistics improve somewhat but full employment is still a very long way away.

The modest growth in employment is underpinned by moderate economic growth, which although low is higher than the majority of EU countries.

Exhibit 6.1: GDP, GNP and Unemployment in Ireland, 2003 to 2012

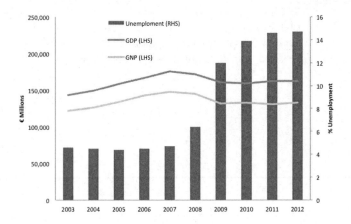

Source: Central Statistics Office.

---

[77]   Central Statistics Office, *Quarterly Household Survey, Q2 2013*.

The overall balance of employment, however, is composed of many, sometimes contradictory, trends. **Exhibit 6.2** illustrates the magnitude of the different movements.

Exhibit 6.2: Irish Employment Growth, 2005 to 2013

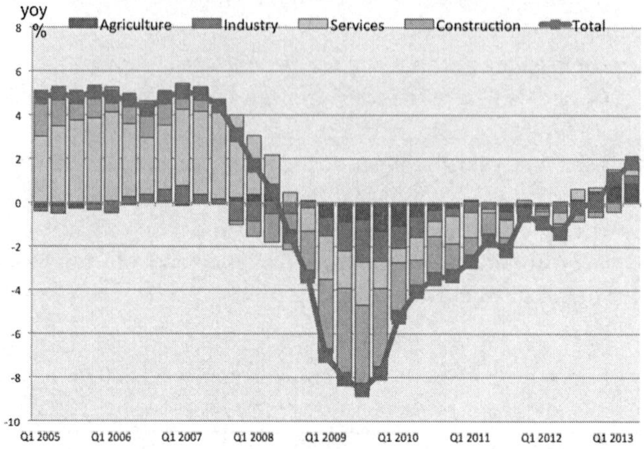

Source: Central Statistics Office.

The strongest contraction has been suffered in the construction area. Not only has this resulted in the largest increase in unemployment but it also has reversed the inflow of migrant construction workers into the Irish labour market.

The services sector is showing signs of growth again and, in particular, the growth of the hotel, restaurant and retail sectors suggest that the domestic economy and labour market are stabilising. **Exhibit 6.3** illustrates the projected job gains and losses in Ireland from 2012 and projected into 2014.

Exhibit 6.3: Job Gains and Losses in Ireland, 2012 to 2014

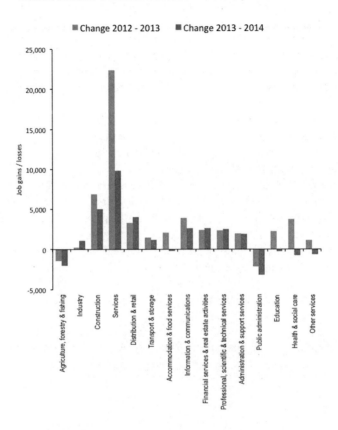

Source: Central Statistics Office.

It appears that, for the first year since the crisis hit in 2008, employment will actually expand in 2013.

Increased Flexibility

Also on the positive side, the Irish labour market seems to have gained flexibility.

In 2012, there were over 250,000 transitions in the labour market, with 130,000 people transitioning from unemployment to employment and a further 120,000 moving in the opposite direction. A further quarter of a million people changed occupation, employer or both during this period. While this flexibility is welcomed, it appears to be happening at the lower skilled end of the market, which calls into question the ability of individuals to find sustainable employment and the systems in place to match the supply and demand for skills in the market place.

A further positive to be observed is a fall in the rate of long-term unemployment, which decreased from 9.2 per cent to 8.1 per cent over the year to Q2 2013.[78]

While unemployment is falling, the highest rates of unemployment continue to be observed amongst the under-25s, those who were previously employed in construction, and those with the lowest levels of educational qualifications.

The fact that unemployment is highest in the construction sector is unlikely to surprise anyone, given the disproportionate amount of activity in this area up until 2007. Neither is it surprising to hear that unemployment is lowest in the services sector and particularly in the Information Technology, Scientific and Technical sectors. What is surprising, however, is that our labour market continues to be characterised by significant skills shortages.

According to the *National Skills Bulletin 2013*, we have a shortage of labour in the Information & Communications Technology Sector, Science, Engineering, Financial, Healthcare, Customer Service (foreign language-related) and Specialist Sales occupations.

This shortage is causing a new wave of extremely highly qualified immigration into Ireland with some noticeable economic side-effects. Immigration is naturally highest into urban areas but particularly into the greater Dublin area, where demand for housing is putting upward pressure on prices with a strong effect on the cost of living.

Exhibit 6.4: Unemployment in Ireland by Age Group, 1998 to 2013

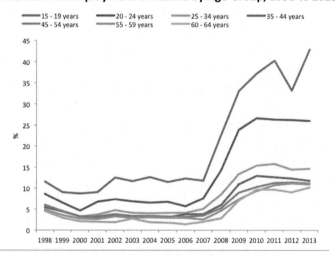

Source: Central Statistics Office.

---

[78] Central Statistics Office, *Quarterly Household Survey, Q2 2013*.

Exhibit 6.5: Unemployment and Educational Attainment in Ireland, 2013

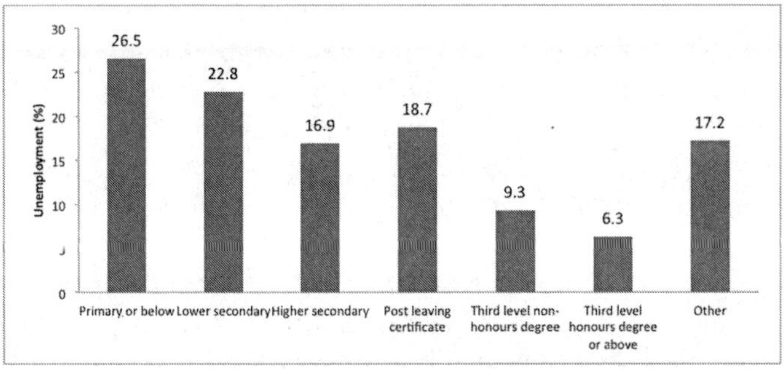

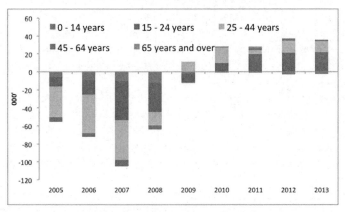

Source: Ernst & Young.

Whereas downward pressure on nominal wages needs to continue for increased export attractiveness, this new 'white collar' migration causes upward pressure on nominal wages in the service sector in urban areas.

Exhibit 6.6: Net Migration in Ireland by Age Group

Source: Central Statistics Office.

Even though the comparison might not be entirely fair, it is worth recognising that the large scale migration from East to West Germany in the last 20 years could not be stopped or at best slowed by government intervention and artificial job creation. Real sustainable jobs were created on the basis of available skills. Neither domestic nor foreign investment can afford to have many years of lead time without any income stream until the necessary skill base has been built.

Ireland and Germany: The Same Problem at a Different Time – Is the Solution the Same?

During the economic boom period up until 2008, the Irish Government's employment policy seemed to focus on driving high levels of economic activity, which would support jobs growth. The Irish economy doubled in size over the course of the 1990s and unemployment dropped from a high of 17 per cent in the late 1980s to a level of only 4.7 per cent in 2007. The period of the 1990s is often referred to as "the real half" of the Celtic Tiger as productivity was growing, entrepreneurship was on the rise, Irish international competitiveness was growing and the period was generally characterised by increases in production and domestic investment rather than the increases in consumption that characterised the period from 2000 to 2007.

Ireland was able to attract significant foreign investment, which to some degree was stimulated by corporate tax incentives but was mainly the result of a very attractive wage differential between Ireland and continental European countries. For example, labour-intensive aircraft maintenance and call centres created many jobs, not strictly confined to Dublin but also in other areas of the country.

During the same period uncompetitively high unit labour costs caused record unemployment levels in Germany, resulting in Germany becoming the proverbial "sick man of Europe". Germany had lost its competitiveness and youth and long-term unemployment were at record levels as a result. The gap between East and West Germany opened further and the economy continued on two different velocities.

Since the German situation was not dissimilar to the current Irish profile, we should question whether Ireland can use the same medicine to recover.

Without any doubt the German wage austerity of almost 10 years, coupled with low levels of inflation, boosted German competitiveness. A sharp increase in productivity at constant nominal wages over a 15-year period brought unit labour costs to very low levels.

In retrospect, the task of returning Germany's competitiveness within 10 years of the re-unification was quite a herculean one. It was only possible by maintaining almost constant consumer prices and increased competition in domestic retail and telecommunications price reductions, which caused the price of the consumer basket to fall relative to most other European countries.

In Ireland, recent wage austerity measures have brought about a reduction in nominal wages but the overall cost of living (CPI) has not supported wage austerity, as the real cost of living has continued to increase. The private sector-related part of the cost of living basket indeed has fallen but the State-controlled part has increased, resulting in less disposable income. Public charges such as the TV licence, waste charges, increased road taxes and property taxes have increased to high levels and discretionary spending has been curbed, particularly amongst those with lower incomes. Overall the cost of living in Ireland is higher than in Germany and is very close to the Nordic countries with their expensive welfare systems.

Exhibit 6.7: Price Level Index for Household Final Consumption Expenditure, 2011 (EU27=100)

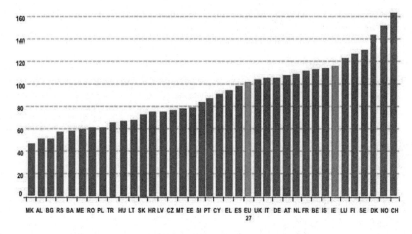

Source: Eurostat (European Commission).

Exhibit 6.8: Price Developments in Ireland – Public Sector *versus* Private Sector

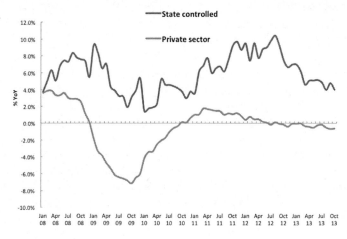

Source: Central Statistics Office.

This rising cost of living threatens the competitiveness of the Irish export sector and our ability to attract foreign investment as well as reducing our ability to create economic stimulus through increasing private consumption. The problem has been recognised and consumer-related charges are now also falling in certain areas. The suspension of the Air Travel Departure Tax and a reduction in the level of Value Added Tax for hotels and restaurants are good examples of stimulus measures increasing consumer spending.

During the boom period, the Irish Exchequer enjoyed sizeable surpluses and Government policy decisions led to high increases in welfare benefits. Social welfare benefit levels increased to levels comparable with the Nordic countries but, as was observed in a report by the Organisation for Economic Co-operation and Development (OECD) in 2009, the Nordic countries had much higher levels of investment in activation measures to reduce unemployment – that is, they focused more resources on returning the unemployed to the workforce than in the Irish system.

The current public debate about a reduction in absolute payments and also a reduction in beneficiaries and the increasing cost of living in urban areas is timely.

The Unemployment Trap

When assessing this phenomenon, it is important to look at the two potential problems and solutions.

A private household opting for social welfare because it is higher than what it would receive from paid employment is perfectly rational economic behaviour. On the one hand, one could take the view that welfare payments are at too high a level. This is the conclusion the Government appears to have reached, evidenced by its recent reduction in welfare benefits for the under-25 age group. Some economists identify this as the cause of a recent decrease in youth unemployment.

On the other hand, it can be argued that wage levels for unskilled work are too low, which makes entry to the labour market unattractive. Those who make this case relate high youth unemployment to low levels of market demand; and as such they argue that reducing welfare rates for the youth will not encourage them into jobs as the jobs simply do not exist. It will simply increase hardship for our youth.

There is no doubt that the relatively high welfare levels in Ireland create some level of moral hazard. We hear anecdotally of those who do not want to work as they are better off on welfare. Further anecdotal stories abound of those availing of the generous benefit system whilst residing outside the State, and of those working in cash employment and simultaneously drawing benefits.

Undoubtedly these examples exist but it is near impossible to identify to what extent. The solution to the unemployment trap most likely lies in creating attractive paths out of unemployment. Where direct jobs are not available, activation measures are needed from State agencies to get people into skills training that is aligned to areas of genuine and increasing demand in the economy. Activation measures also are needed to keep people close to the employment market. When individuals become long-term unemployed, the prospect of returning to employment becomes more remote and many research studies exist that show that young people who experience unemployment suffer a so-called "wage scarring" for the rest of their lives. This has significant knock-on effects for society and the economy.

As noted earlier, one of the aspects of the Irish welfare system that stands out is the peculiar combination of high social welfare levels and low activation measures. This is most likely the greatest contributor to the unemployment trap and needs to be addressed.

Youth Unemployment has Trebled

Youth unemployment is now the major focus in Ireland. As many as 30 per cent of our youth are unemployed – that is 65,000 young people without work, which is an unsustainable situation.

Exhibit 6.9: Youth Unemployment Rate and Ratio in Ireland, 2004 to 2013

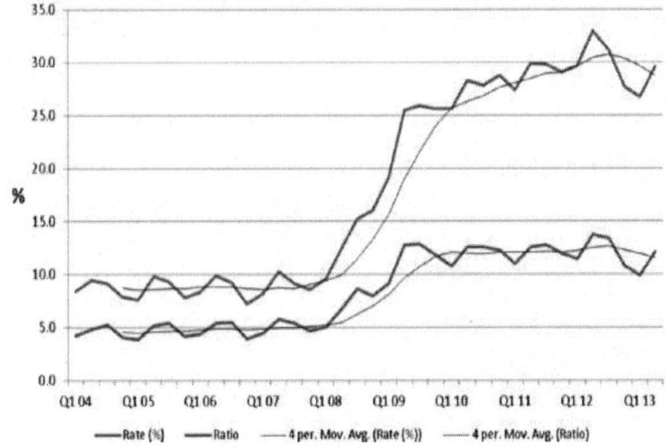

Source: Central Statistics Office.

The sharp rise in youth unemployment in the recession mirrored the fall in the number of young people with jobs. The situation is improving, though. Central Statistics Office data from Q2 2013 shows a drop in the number of young people unemployed to 64,700, which is a drop of nearly 12,000 *versus* the same point in 2012. This is encouraging but much more needs to be done, since we have demographical evidence that the job market will continue to remain under pressure from young people entering their professional life.

The high rate of youth unemployment is of course primarily a result of the economic crisis and the resulting fall in levels of overall demand; but is also, in my view, the result of a mismatch between supply and demand for specific skills.

An observation that I have made since I have come to Ireland is that anything other than a university education is now perceived as inferior. That is quite unique in the world and has not always been the case in Ireland.

I note that this was also recently observed by the international vocational education awarding body, City and Guilds. The organisation surveyed the attitudes of more than 500 young people in Ireland towards vocational training and found that: *"There is an apparent lack of awareness of what vocational education really means and the opportunities that can be offered. A major shift in attitude is required to give vocational education the status it deserves as a worthy career path for young people"*.

The report also found that: *"Young people typically saw vocational education as less challenging and less prestigious than academic education; 32 per cent saw it as a route for the less able, and 26 per cent saw vocational education as a low status option"*.

It is my firmly-held view that we cannot run an economy entirely based on university graduates primarily provided for the Dublin-based financial and IT services industries. Rather, we need a healthier pyramid of skills and qualifications, not only embracing what is often referred to as "blue collar" but also crafts and more practical skills, including practical and recognised qualifications across a range of all economic activities.

There are a number of tasks that must be undertaken to achieve this:

- To rebalance supply and demand in the labour market, we need to educate families, schoolteachers and the entire society that non-academic education should be promoted as something that is at least equal to academic education. A mismatch exists at all levels in the Irish labour market. Maths, ICT, and science-based qualifications are in undersupply whereas fully qualified accountants and lawyers are leaving the country to find jobs in the UK, Canada and Australia.

- We need an overhaul of our dual-education system. Non-academic skills attainment needs to be re-branded. Its brand is currently flawed as it is wrongly perceived as only being appropriate for those who "didn't make it to university". In Germany over 60 per cent of high school graduates participate in the system each year. That means that, for school-leavers completing the equivalent of the Leaving Certificate, the automatic path is not into a university or other third level institute, it is into vocational training. The job opportunities after the successful completion of an apprenticeship and later as a "Meister" are regarded as equal or even superior. In fact, most SMEs in Germany are founded by graduates of the dual educational system.

- We need to focus on young people gaining more practical skills training. Those coming out of university often lack the practical experience that can get them the first foothold in the jobs market. University students are not required to accomplish on-the-job training. In most EU countries this has become an almost mandatory part of the curriculum, not by law but by convention. When employers are sourcing graduates, they are looking for future employees who are well-trained in a company, in addition to their academic skills.

- We have to increase the scope of non-academic qualifications available to our workforce. If we use the German dual education system as an example, the 350 different apprenticeships and traineeships available *via* the German Chambers of Commerce outnumber what is available here in Ireland by four to one. This is similar in other European countries with a similar history of manufacturing to Germany's.

- The organisation and administration of the practical and vocational education cannot be entirely left to the State. It is fundamentally important that the business community and business organisations are fully involved in the co-ordination of the demand and supply of workforce skills. Membership organisations such as Chambers of Commerce are best positioned to step into this gap as they are directly connected to their members and are acutely aware of the labour force challenges facing them.

- We need to encourage and incentivise employers to offer traineeships, apprenticeships and internships; this cannot wait any longer. While not all employers are in a position to offer apprenticeships, partnerships could be considered as an alternative. At Aer Lingus, we are currently working on a pilot project to supply trained mechanics not only for our own business but also for small and medium-sized companies that are too small to train their own resources. In our most recent round of recruitment for 20 apprenticeships in aviation mechanics and avionics, we received more than 2,000 applications – 100 applicants for every open position!

- The qualification obtained in practical or vocational traineeships needs to become a form of internationally accepted certificate in order to have currency in the international job market. The Irish diaspora around the world are an impressive testament not only that Irish skills are highly in demand globally but also that the Irish work ethic and the ability of Irish workers to integrate quickly in foreign environments could make "Trained in Ireland" a successful brand.

- Proper vocational training not only supplies the immediate labour market but it also drives entrepreneurship. During my work and travel around the globe, I have always been impressed with how many German former apprentices ended up as entrepreneurs based on an internationally accepted job qualification. Not only the proverbial German brewer, baker and carpenter but also mechanics and laboratory technicians. This is similar for hotel specialists from Switzerland, water engineers from the Netherlands and chefs from France. In our industry, the aviation sector, qualifications are often based on international safety and certification standards and the prevailing language is English and so it is not surprising that airlines, aircraft maintenance companies and aviation leasing companies all around the world are peppered with managers and owners who learned their trade in Ireland. This could be the case for many other sectors of the economy.

Current Government Policy

Government policy is adapting to the crisis. While it focuses on driving a return to economic growth, increased competitiveness and improved productivity as a way of creating jobs, it also realises that systems need to be put in place to keep the unemployed close to the labour market. This includes new programmes of job-search assistance, sanctions for those who do not engage with the services offered and for those who cannot return to the workforce quickly, and provision of education and training.

Training and Education: Matching Supply and Demand

There are a number of Irish Government programmes aimed at providing access to training and education for young unemployed persons:

- The Youthreach programme provides 6,000 integrated education and training places for early school-leavers between the ages of 15 and 20 years of age who have no qualifications or vocational training. Almost all participants are under the age of 25; approximately two-thirds are aged 18 and under.
- The Vocational Training Opportunities Scheme provides 5,000 places on a range of courses to meet the education and training needs of long-term unemployed people over 21 years of age. It is particularly aimed at unemployed people who are early school-leavers. Approximately one-fifth of participants are under 25 years of age.
- The Back to Education Allowance allows unemployed people to return to full-time education in approved courses while continuing to receive income support.
- Out of approximately 27,000 people who participated in a FÁS training course in 2012 (excluding apprenticeships, evening courses, and Youthreach), almost 10,000 were aged under 25.
- The MOMENTUM scheme managed by FÁS offers 6,500 places to long-term jobseekers on training courses providing skills that are in demand in sectors where there are job opportunities. The training includes on-the

job training and the development of workplace skills. Over 1,250 of these
places are assigned to those under the age of 25.

These programmes are led by Government agencies and are aimed at providing
skills to address unemployment but need to be better connected to the current
and future requirements of employers in the marketplace.

Additionally, employers need to take a more active role in providing skills and
qualifications for the workforce than is currently the case. Apprenticeships in the
Irish system seemed focused on "trades" rather than providing recognised
qualifications for a broader range of employment activities in the business services
sector of the economy.

Businesses must identify their future labour needs and then partner with
Government agencies in the actual provision of the skills required to meet those
needs. In Germany, the content of the occupational training is determined by the
employer. Furthermore the entry qualification and criteria of the candidates, the
qualification of the trainer and, of course, the content and minimum qualification
standards for the interim and final examination and the issuing of the certificate
are set by the employers. State intervention exists at a minimal level in order to
ensure that short-term needs of employers do not impede the broader educational
and economic goals.

Two-speed Economies: The Challenge of Job Creation in Rural Areas

Both Ireland and Germany are facing specific problems with the geographical
distribution of work. The following heat maps of both economies illustrate in an
impressive way the slow reaction of national labour markets to changed demand.

Germany has not resolved the structural challenge of the job market after
reunification. The picture illustrates that the more rural areas in East Germany
suffer significantly higher unemployment; a picture very similar to Ireland. In the
former Eastern States of Germany, where unemployment is highest, the job
creation in urban areas is significantly higher than in rural areas.

However in the South of Germany, the exact opposite is the case. Bavaria and
Baden Wuertemberg have full employment mainly in rural areas. When I recently
travelled through the countryside in the South I got accustomed to a very similar
picture for hundreds of kilometres: a typical "Mittelstand" SME in a small town
with large billboards advertising qualified jobs in all disciplines and on all levels,
from engineers to mechanics, from physicians to PAs.

**Exhibit 6.10: Registered Percentage Unemployment Rates in
Germany by District, October 2013**

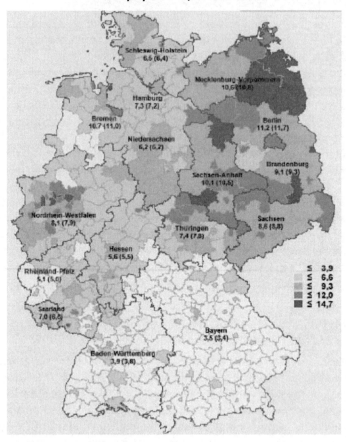

Source: German Federal Agency for Statistics.

Ireland's two speeds are very distinct between Dublin/Cork and the rest of the
country. As I explained earlier, a boom in the Dublin area always has the imminent
risk of overheating. The main question remains how to create a sufficient amount
of jobs in the rest of the country.

Exhibit 6.11: Regional Unemployment Rates in Ireland, 2013

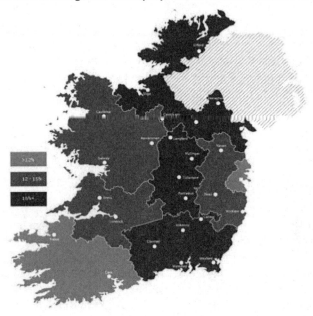

Source: Ernst & Young.

Exhibit 6.12: Regional Unemployment in Ireland, 2007 to 2013

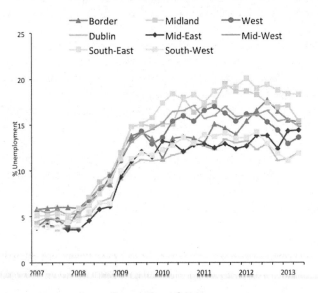

Source: Ernst & Young.

Important inroads have been made in promoting Ireland as an inbound tourism destination, but with two main impediments to the overall good news:

- Service jobs in the lower income bracket are mainly occupied by non-Irish citizens. This is an anomaly that does not exist in Northern Ireland.
- The strong seasonality does not provide full time employment on an annualised basis. A similar problem in Switzerland some decades ago resulted in the emergence of a hotel school business using the off-season for training and education.

The establishment of a more "Mittelstand"-type economy requires a long-term perspective with a sequential set of actions.

Entrepreneurship

In the last couple of years, the vast majority of white collar jobs were created by large corporate multinational companies – foreign investment. Nearly 1,000 multinational corporations (MNCs) have chosen Ireland as their European base. These corporations like the "can do" business culture in Ireland and are not only attracted by the Corporation Tax rate, as is often the external perception, but also see the successes of previous foreign direct investors and the skills of our workforce as major attractions.

The majority of these MNC investors are from the United States. A fact that is often missed in this relationship is that the investment flows both ways. Recent research by the American Chamber of Commerce shows that the employment balance favours the US rather than Ireland – that is, Irish firms directly employ 136,100 US workers in America, while US firms employ 115,000 Irish workers in Ireland.

The creation of new businesses in Ireland is, however, below the European average. One might speculate what the true reason for this is – risk adversity, lack of aspiration etc. but an observation is shared: top talent from universities is almost entirely absorbed by the large corporates in Ireland.

But the classic approach to company foundation is mostly founded in non-academic curriculums. A young person, having completed a traineeship in Information Technology after secondary school, will be in a job at approximately the age of 21. Not only will they be able to deliver an appreciated service but also they will have the proven credentials and reputation to ask for credit, and to employ and train their own people.

The most important driver in my opinion is the self-confidence of a young person to be able to produce, offer and sell something entirely made by him or herself in the early years of their career.

The scope for MBA graduates and lawyers to found their own companies is, in today's consolidated world, rather limited, as opposed to newer occupations like agricultural service specialists, audiovisual media technicians, biological laboratory technicians and so forth. One of my own classmates trained as a watchmaker and jeweller after school and had his own company with 10 employees at the age of 25.

In Ireland, too often the State is in demand to regulate the labour market. But in this particular field it obviously needs a catalyst to overcome the "chicken and egg" situation. It is too late to train the entrepreneurs of today but we have to start to train the entrepreneurs of tomorrow. And we must start as early as possible during their school education. Not only is this needed to create the appetite to explore new careers in a new economy but also to foster summer internships in companies, small or large, in services, crafts or industrial manufacturing – perhaps even in another country.

We do not have enough SMEs in new occupations to train the critical mass of graduates from our own resources. This is where our pilot project will try to explore ways to provide the basis of a "train the trainer" concept.

Languages

The importance of languages in education and training has become a modern feature of the global economy. Whereas certain small countries in Europe like The Netherlands, Belgium and Luxembourg are famous for their advanced language skills, from early childhood, neither Ireland nor Germany has traditionally excelled in this area.

Emigration in Ireland therefore was focused on the English-speaking world, still today the main footprint of the Irish diaspora. More and more the focus of Ireland's export market is shifting into Europe and the BRIC countries and consequently the language skills should follow suit.

Germany and France have been traditionally focused on their own mother tongue but in recent years some important progress has been made.

Ireland and Germany are starting from similar points. More emphasis on foreign languages will foster both countries' abilities to exchange skilled people and more importantly to trade with each other.

In the Irish context, two short-term opportunities for the job market need to be mentioned.

There are significant employment opportunities in Ireland for jobseekers with a foreign language. One call centre near Dublin has over 1,000 employees but less than 10 have an Irish passport. These opportunities are entirely absorbed by foreign labour and foreign students looking for part-time employment. One can almost say that the ability to speak a language fluently, other than English, is a certain guarantee of employment in Ireland.

And there is a short-term opportunity abroad. The German job market currently has a strong demand for qualified labour and this will continue for the foreseeable future. The demographics for Germany and Ireland are complementary and the cultural fit is very strong. Young Irish people with the ability or the preparedness to speak or learn German have good employment possibilities in the German economy, either to "learn and return" or to stay and to further contribute to each other's understanding.

A significant number of young, German-speaking Spaniards are currently entering the German job market and are much welcomed by the local industry.

Conclusions

The Irish labour market is predominantly working on the problems at hand. Some progress has been made but the final structure towards which we are progressing is still somewhat unclear. A further emphasis on the service industry with financial services, IT and pharmaceuticals is projected.

But under risk management scrutiny, these job categories are under permanent pressure from lower cost countries. We have seen major shifts of the financial service industry around the globe as a consequence of minor changes in taxation or other incentives. To balance this exposure, the Irish economy has to rebuild a second backbone in manufacturing or truly skill-based specialities and also must encourage domestic investment.

Ernst & Young's *Economic Eye* forecasts the following job gains (and losses) in Ireland between now and 2020:

Exhibit 6.13: Job Gains and Losses in Ireland, 2013 to 2020

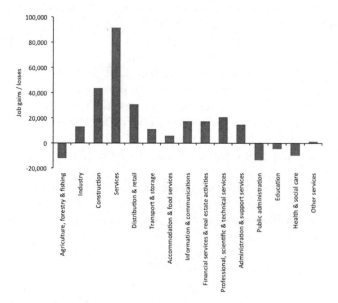

Source: Central Statistics Office.

The agricultural sector had deteriorated during the Celtic Tiger years to almost insignificance. A global surge in the trade of food and agricultural goods has propelled this segment of the economy to becoming one of the main engines of growth. This should serve as a good example of the structural changes required.

Out goes the romantic image of the Irish farmer posing with his sheep for a photo with the tourist and in with an entirely new high tech industry. Now PhDs in food processing, IT specialists for precision farming, robot engineering and manufacturing of milking robots, chemical engineers for hygiene control and many more qualifications in crafts like mechanics are required to defend Ireland's position in this rapidly growing industry.

Opportunities exist for Ireland to increase its levels of trade with its mainland European EU partners. Apart from the instant commercial effect, this would open the possibility to provide workplace qualifications that are recognised across Europe. This can either be the "Trained in Ireland" vision or the long-term investment in training abroad: "Learn and Return".

Migration in and out of a small open economy such as Ireland's is inevitable. If qualifications were more uniform across Europe, the ability to work overseas, gather work experience and return to Ireland would be enhanced.

It is vital for all parts of the Irish economy to provide jobs in all income brackets and in all levels of qualification. This requires a common understanding by all participants, families, company employees, trade unions and the Government to work together and pull in the same direction.

CHAPTER 7

Germany's "Mittelstand": The Seven Pillars of Success

Eric Schweitzer

Key Messages

- The success of the German economy in the last few years is in large part due to the hard work of the country's business enterprises. Internal restructuring, coupled with increased international orientation and investment in research and development, has laid the foundations. The process also has been fostered by the Government through reforms to the labour market and the corporate tax regime.
- Germany is a strong location with an unusual mix of enterprises. It is home to successful, large, publicly-quoted companies, countless highly-committed small businesses – and a broad *Mittelstand*. These companies, in many cases family-owned, are not always in the limelight; they are, however, highly innovative and – as hidden champions – successful on the world markets.

From the "Sick Man" of Europe to a Role Model for Others?

In May 2005, an *Economist* cover article was devoted to "The real sick man of Europe". The country it was referring to was Germany, where the picture it presented at the time was characterised by high levels of unemployment and low growth rates. So some of what Ireland and other European Union states with a sovereign debt crisis are currently going through are problems of a kind that Germany also had to deal with in the first half of the past decade.

Seven years later, the picture in Germany has changed markedly. The headline now reads: "Germany's economic model – what it offers to the world". Low unemployment, a strong industrial base and a broad SME sector – these are the things that people associate with the German economy at the present time.

To be sure, both pictures are an exaggeration. It is nevertheless true: Germany has gone through a time of tough changes, but these have definitely moved us forward. Firms have developed new markets, especially in Eastern Europe and many emerging countries throughout the world. They have undertaken radical restructuring measures in their business operations. They have spent on R&D, and succeeded in placing products as a result. The process placed heavy burdens on the employers and employees alike. The government also responded – for example, in 2003, when it launched the *Agenda 2010* to underpin its new course. As a result, the labour market was made more flexible, business taxes were cut, and since then, moderate wage settlements have strengthened the competitiveness of German firms on the world markets.

A Strong "Mittelstand"

One of the key roles in Germany's economy success story is played by the "Mittelstand", the small and medium-sized enterprise sector. The growth in employment between 2005 and 2010 – numbering no fewer than 1.8 million new jobs – was almost entirely due to the mid-market enterprises. The German term Mittelstand has come to be generally used in the Anglo-Saxon business press, where it no longer needs a translation. It has become a synonym for a successful economic model. As president of the DIHK, one question I am frequently asked by foreign delegations is: "What is the secret of the German Mittelstand?".

There is, in fact, no secret at all. After all, many countries have a small and medium-sized enterprise sector. But alongside the strong regional roots and the individualistic nature of many family entrepreneurs, the German Mittelstand is characterised by another aspect, and that is that many family enterprises have grown over several generations; indeed, they could now almost be described as "family-owned groups". At the same time, though, they have preserved their SME mindset, including the direct responsibility and commitment of the family.

Another factor for the success of the German SME sector is its international presence. On average, export-oriented Mittelstand businesses with annual sales of between €10m and €50m are active in 16 foreign markets. Even small firms with annual sales of less than €500,000 do business with six markets on average. This makes them resilient – a drop in business in one place can be made up for by success in another. While 98 per cent of the approximately 350,000 German exporters are SME enterprises, alongside European markets, they are increasingly turning their sights also on more distant, up-and-coming markets such as China, India or Indonesia.

And a further success factor: the German Mittelstand is a driver of innovation. As many as 30,000 German enterprises – a large proportion of them SMEs – have their own research departments.

In this way, thanks to bold ideas and persistence, many mid-market enterprises have captured market niches for themselves where, with their specialist products and services, they are able to garner success. And finally, to complete the picture, they offer tailor-made after-sales service, including also on foreign markets. So despite not being of giant size, these companies are up among the leaders everywhere in the world. Indeed, some of them are operations with as few as 200,

100 or an even smaller number of employees. In Germany, they have come to be known as "Hidden Champions". Germany has around 1,300 enterprises that belong in this category – more than any other country in the world. The next biggest – but a long way behind – is the USA, with around 350.

But why is it that Germany has so many of these "Hidden Champions"? One explanation could be special structural factors: small and medium-sized enterprises tend to be bigger in Germany than elsewhere. On average, they employ seven people – twice as many as in France, Spain or Italy. The reason is that Germany has a strong industrial sector. And industrial firms tend to be bigger than, say, service or commercial firms. Almost a quarter of Germany's GDP is generated by the industrial Mittelstand. In Spain and the UK, the figure is around 16 per cent; in France only 13 per cent.

The Seven Pillars of Success

But far more important than numbers are the special sense of identity and the special culture of the German Mittelstand. The "Mittelstand business model" is built on seven pillars:

- **First: Ownership and management are in the same hands.** More than 90 per cent of all German enterprises are majority-owned and run by family members. Consequently, the principle of liability, which is so important for a market economy, applies fully and directly. The actors harvest the fruits of their decisions. But they also have to carry the can if something goes wrong.
- **Second: Long-termism.** A family enterprise would be ill-advised to base its decisions primarily on short-term key figures and quarterly accounts. Rather, one key consideration that is always present when business decisions are being taken is: what will its effects be for my children or my successor? This focus also can help SMEs to persist on a chosen course even when the returns are temporarily low. The long-view approach is also supported by the specifics of the German banking system, namely the three-pillar model of private-sector banks, publicly-owned *Sparkassen*, and the co-operatively-owned financial institutions. This model offers enterprises a large bandwidth for securing their long-term financing. The Mittelstand is therefore never far away from a financing partner that will also support sustainable business strategies. This model is complemented also by State-owned development banks: at federal level by the KfW banking group, and at the level of the *Länder*, the individual federal states, by state development banks and also by "guarantor banks" (*Bürgschaftsbanken*), which can step in to fill the gap when SMEs lack security for borrowing.
- **Third: Nearness to customers.** Many successful SME businesses owe their success to specialist products in market niches. This calls for the ability to

supply after-sales service. And to complete the picture, these firms offer flexibility and short decision-making channels. They also attach importance to having an international presence on the ground. DIHK surveys reveal that more and more firms are increasingly investing in regions far away from Germany.

- **Fourth: Close ties to the workforce.** "The firm must feel like a family," is a view expressed by the heads of many Mittelstand businesses. They set great store by their team of qualified, long-standing personnel. The low level of staff fluctuation fosters a strong team spirit, which in turn promotes productivity. This attitude is further reinforced by the increasing shortage of skilled personnel – caused by demographic developments – which are also making themselves felt in Germany. The strong sense of loyalty of, and towards, the workforce is further promoted by Germany's dual training system. Young people are integrated into an enterprise at an early stage and undergo training that is specifically geared to the needs of the company and the labour market. The success of this model is reflected not least in the relatively low level of youth unemployment in Germany.

- **Fifth: Close ties to the home region.** Involvement in the region beyond what is strictly required either for business considerations or by law helps to foster the image of the company in the local community. Mittelstand enterprises assume civic responsibility for their regions. The term "corporate social responsibility", which has now also been newly adopted in Germany, merely describes a reality that in fact has been lived here for decades. Firms support culture and education in the region, promote projects for disadvantaged young people, and have an involvement in playschools, schools and sports facilities, to name just a few.

- **Sixth: A broad-based Mittelstand policy, not a selective one.** Support and promotion for the Mittelstand in Germany is not aimed at the development of specific sectors or enterprises. A balanced sectoral structure makes the economy resilient in the face of crises. Despite all the causes for criticism that may exist in detail, there is a basic understanding in Germany that what the Mittelstand needs to be competitive is equality of opportunity – or at the very least, no one putting spokes in their wheels.

- **Seventh: Support on the ground and worldwide.** "Germany is often singled out as having the most effective and integrated business support infrastructure."[79] For example, the local "IHKs" – the chambers of industry and commerce – represent the interests of the SME sector towards the local political parties. Their umbrella organisation, the *Deutsche Industrie-*

[79] Lord Heseltine of Thenford, *No Stone Unturned in Pursuit of Growth*, transcript of oral evidence to the House of Commons Business, Innovation and Skills Committee, October 2012.

und Handelskammertag (DIHK), performs the same role in the political arena in Berlin and Brussels. The presence of the local IHK organisations on the ground makes it possible even for smaller SME owners to meet face-to-face with politicians on any topic. The IHKs also offer a range of services, such as support in connection with starting-up a business or advice on energy efficiency and financing. They perform tasks on behalf of the State, such as issuing certificates of origin for exporters, but with a minimum of red tape. But first and foremost, they play a leading role in the context of the dual training system. Through the network of German chambers of commerce abroad – the "AHKs" – in more than 120 locations in 85 countries, the IHK organisation also provides bridges to international markets. For initial soundings of the market environment in Asia, for example, a Mittelstand business has no need to travel there itself. Instead, it can call on a local AHK to provide support. In this way, the AHKs save the SME sector transaction costs on a very significant scale and are therefore an important pillar in Germany's export success.

However, I do not want to forget that the success of the German Mittelstand also owes something to sheer good fortune. Germany lies right at the heart of Europe. Every market in the EU can be reached from here in 48 hours by rail, in 24 hours by road and in three hours by air.

What Can Be Learned from This?

Can the German Mittelstand be copied? I fear the answer is "No!". The German Mittelstand culture is also partly the product of German history. For a long period in the area that forms Germany today, there were hundreds of small and even mini-states, each with narrowly-defined local markets. These small economic areas were late in being given a broader framework – first in the form of a nation state, and later in the shape of Europe. For centuries, German enterprises and their predecessors have learned to specialise and engage in cross-border trading activities, but at the same time to stay in close touch with their home region. The regional aspect was, and still is, a factor of very substantial importance in Germany, including also in business.

At the same time, though, there are other factors that could just as easily be put in place elsewhere. Many countries are interested in the dual training system – not least in view of the high levels of youth unemployment in the wake of the Eurozone debt crisis. In this area, the IHKs and AHKs have a strong role to play with their own initiatives. Parts of the tried-and-tested support system offered by the State-owned KfW development bank, the development banks of the federal states, or the guarantor banks and *Mittelständische Beteiligungsgesellschaften* that provide seed or investment capital for SMEs could be of interest to other countries. As well as credit schemes, the system also includes support in the form of consultancy. One example of this are the KfW's "Round Tables" for firms in financial difficulties: with the IHK acting as moderator, the entrepreneur, banks and creditors sit down together to look for ways past the bottleneck. In the wake of a Round Table, nearly 70 per cent of businesses are back on a financially even keel, and also back on course for the market.

The biggest challenge I see facing the German Mittelstand in the coming years is the increasing shortage of skilled workers. The demographic development is hitting Germany hard. By the year 2025, the German labour market will be six million people short. Our dual vocational training system provides a good base, but will be insufficient by itself. We have to tap into every available potential. That includes further training and the employment of older people, greater compatibility between family and work, and a welcoming culture for skilled workers from other countries. After all, one thing is absolutely certain: without smart people, no business model can work, least of all the German Mittelstand business model.

COMMENTARY: CHAPTER 7

Is an Irish "Mittelstand" Possible?

Marc Coleman and Ralf Lissek

Key Messages

- Ireland's small size has been an obstacle to date to achieving size and scale in its small and medium-sized enterprise sector. This, in turn, has affected the sector's capacity to export. Despite this, a thriving SME sector has survived the crisis and retains many of the characteristics of Germany's "Mittelstand", with a strong export performance among some subsectors.
- Dynamic Government policy is assisting the sector, but serious challenges remain. These include gaining access to financing and achieving the scale needed to export. Under the right conditions, Irish firms could, over time, replicate for the traded services sector the success that Germany's Mittelstand has achieved in manufacturing. In its *Medium Term Economic Strategy* the Government is looking to other countries, particularly Germany, for inspiration on improving conditions for SMEs and there are many positive opportunities for both countries to exchange good policy and practice. In particular, Germany's long-term orientation and the

related access to support of strong banking and education systems could be instrumental in achieving the full potential of Ireland's SME sector.

Ireland and Germany: A "Seven Pillars" Comparison

Even if transposing Germany's Mittelstand directly onto Ireland's economy is not completely feasible, nonetheless a comparison of Ireland and Germany under the "Seven Pillars" in this chapter is illuminating.

These seven pillars are:

- Owner management.
- A long-term orientation.
- A close relationship with customers and ability to retain their custom by innovating to meet their needs.
- A strong bond between management and workers.
- Strong links to their local region.
- A broad consensus in Germany that the Mittelstand model should be protected and promoted.
- A strong network of worldwide support through the IHK.

Striking differences emerge, as do subtle similarities. Both point to the possibility of creating a business culture built uniquely on Irish values but drawing, where relevant, from established and transportable strengths of the German system: durability, long-term orientation and solid support from well-designed educational and credit systems. Likewise, the flexibility and adaptability of Ireland's business model with its blend of European and American elements, discussed in **Chapter 2**, can be an inspiration to German companies.

A comparison of the two should be preceded by a recognition of two obvious – and already alluded to – differences: Ireland's smaller size and its more peripheral location. Ireland's smaller size means that more modest thresholds of staff numbers and turnover should be used. Whereas, in Germany, firms with up to 500 employees may be considered part of the Mittelstand, it is more pragmatic to consider in regard to Ireland the standard applied by the EU Commission[80] in defining the concept of "Small and Medium-sized Enterprise" (SME), which closely correlates to the German concept of "Kleinere und Mittlere Unternehmungen" (KMU).

On the edge of Europe and as an island, Ireland's location greatly affects the ability of its SME sector to generate firms the size and scale of which are the norm in Germany. This consideration also explains the relative importance to Ireland of its tax regime as a compensating factor in overcoming strong locational advantages of countries like France, Germany, Belgium and The Netherlands.

---

[80] *Commission Recommendation 2003/361/EC* issued on 20 May 2003.

In relation to the first pillar, according to one study Ireland had as of 2012 around 242,000 "owner-manager" firms[81] (in its latest *Medium Term Economic Strategy 2014-2020* the Government puts the figure at 180,000). The remainder of this chapter analyses subset of the SME sector for which detailed data is available from both the Central Statistics Office's *Census of Industrial Production* and *Annual Services Inquiry*.

The second pillar concerns the long-term orientation of durability and perspective that characterises the German Mittelstand. Three observations may be made here. First, the rate of Irish owner-managers remains relatively high by OECD standards, despite four years of crisis. Therefore, there is in Ireland a potential to build and sustain an Irish-style "Mittelstand", provided other conditions permit. However, recently there is also evidence that a higher proportion of Irish entrepreneurs than is usual either in the OECD or EU turn to entrepreneurship out of necessity.[82] Particularly in sectors related to property, there has been a relatively high rate of attrition in Ireland's SME sector. Therefore, the German Mittelstand seems more stable than the Irish SME sector. However, this can be seen partly as a residue of the crisis with Ireland's SME sector hopefully now entering a more stable, long-term oriented phase. One challenge to be overcome in this respect is that the strength and solidity of Germany's financial system, which, as noted above, is a key support for the long-term orientation of its Mittelstand, is an advantage not yet replicated in Ireland. As discussed in **Chapter 2**, the Irish Government has already taken several steps to address the availability of credit to Irish firms. This is perhaps one area where Germany can be of assistance in pointing to German State-funded investment banks, such as the KfW Bankengruppe, as a possible inspiration for new sources of capital. The *Medium Term Economic Strategy* notes the difficulty of Irish SMEs in accessing long-term funding, given the changes in the financial regulatory regime. It also suggests increasing the use of more short-term equity financing, a tradition that is relatively weak in Europe compared to the US. According to its strategy, the Government aims to create an Irish Strategic Investment Fund – inspired by Germany's KfW – and to use funds from the National Pension Reserve Fund to improve access to capital for Irish SMEs. Careful consideration will be needed to align the types and maturity of funding to be made available with the Government's enterprise and sectoral strategies.

The third pillar of Germany's Mittelstand relates to the closeness to customers and ability to specialise. Here again, Ireland's relative small size plays a role in shaping the way its SME sector has evolved.

---

[81]   Table 1, page 29, Fitzsimons, Paula & O'Gorman, Colm (2013). *Entrepreneurship in Ireland* (Global Entrepreneurship Monitor).

[82]   Page 28, Fitzsimons, Paula & O'Gorman, Colm (2013). *Entrepreneurship in Ireland* (Global Entrepreneurship Monitor).

Exhibit 7.1 shows data from the Services sector. The plurality of firms (21.2 per cent) fall into the "Professional Scientific and Technical" category and, in reality, this captures a lot of small legal, accounting, tax advisory and medical professionals which, in turn, reflects the relatively smaller size of Irish towns and villages and the need to replicate such services to serve more rural parts of the economy. The next largest sector is the Retail sector accounting for 17.1 per cent, with accommodation (tourism) accounting for 12.4 per cent.

Exhibit 7.1: Services SMEs by Sector in Ireland[83]

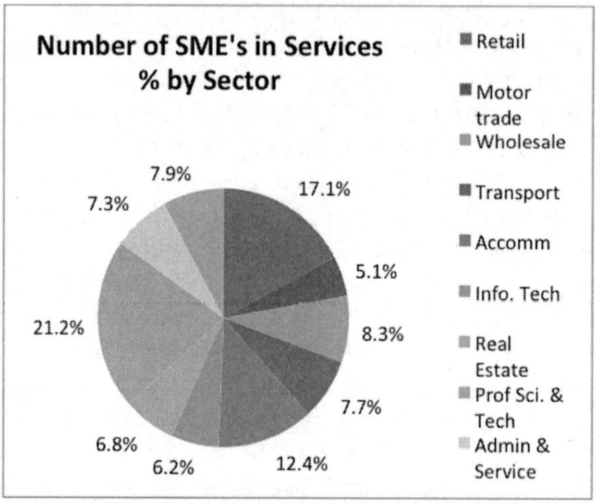

Source: Central Statistics Office, *2011 Annual Services Inquiry.*

Ireland's SME Sector: Overall Size and Manufacturing / Services Balance

Manufacturing[84] data available for 2011 is summarised in **Exhibit 7.2** below.[85] Here the SME sector accounted for approximately 94,000 jobs and €18.6bn in turnover.

Exhibit 7.2 shows a healthy propensity to export across manufacturing SMEs, with 27 per cent of very small businesses (thresholds of €200,000 or less) exporting and an overall average across all SMEs of 38 per cent. While not directly comparable with the statistic quoted for the share of Germany's exports accounted for by Mittelstand[86] firms, the share of Irish SMEs engaged in exporting is a healthy

---

[83] Latest data is for 2011 and is from Central Statistics Office, *Annual Services Inquiry.*

[84] Latest data is for 2011 and is from Central Statistics Office, *Census of Industrial Production.*

[85] Aggregating manufacturing and services data is difficult, due to differences in the manner in which the *Census of Industrial Production* and *Annual Services Inquiry* are conducted.

[86] That 98 per cent of all German exports are from Mittelstand companies.

sign. However, this relates to a manufacturing sector that is relatively small in comparison with the German one in terms of the share of employment and overall turnover accounted for.

What about the propensity of Ireland's services SMEs to export? According to recent survey evidence, the positive news is that a majority (66 per cent) of those starting a business in Ireland in 2012 expected to have at least some exports.[87]

Exhibit 7.2: Manufacturing SMEs in Ireland

		< €200k	€200k - €1m	€1m - €5m	€5m - €10m	€10m - €50m	Total
Number of Enterprises		584	2,097	1,432	337	450	**4,900**
Prop/Family engaged		658	1,611	656	79	99	**3,103**
Total engaged		1,742	11,793	22,964	13,557	41,910	**91,966**
Labour Costs	€m	32.2	316.6	721.3	485.8	1555.4	**3,111.3**
Turnover	€m	69.2	1,105.0	3,127.5	2,383.8	9,481.8	**16,167.3**
% Turnover Exported	%	27.2	23.4	24.9	34.4	44.8	**38**
Ind. Tax	€m	0.4 m	9.5 m	29.3 m	19.2 m	64.0 m	**122.4**
Average employed		*4.1*	*6.4*	*16.5*	*40.5*	*93.4*	***19.4***

Source: Central Statistics Office, *2011 Census of Industrial Production.*

Judging by a sectoral breakdown of the services sector, as provided above, it is unlikely that Ireland's service sector SMEs are yet dominated by exporting firms.

However, as detailed in **Exhibit 7.3** below, with 122,169 firms employing around 600,000 persons – of which almost one-third of a million are employed full-time, accounting for €111bn in turnover – the strategy discussed in **Chapter 2** of promoting the traded services sector could reap further large benefits to Ireland's economy. It is not impossible that Ireland could become – albeit on a smaller scale – to its traded services sector what Germany has become in terms of its manufacturing sector: a centre of global exporting excellence.

---

[87] Page 43, Fitzsimons, Paula & O'Gorman, Colm (2013). *Entrepreneurship in Ireland* (Global Entrepreneurship Monitor).

Exhibit 7.3: Services SMEs in Ireland

	Retail	Motor	Wholesale	Transport	Accom	Info. Tech	Real Estate	Prof Sci. & Tech	Admin & Service	Other	Total
Number of enterprises	20,942	6,205	10,111	9,366	15,184	7,533	8,290	25,907	8,971	9,660	**122,169**
Turnover (€m)	15,755	6,693	48,140	6,943	7,143	5,564	1,461	9,007	7,508	2,814	**111,032**
Persons	107,807	24,883	73,021	39,903	131,757	26,725	19,214	85,127	49,919	46,026	**604,382**
of which full time	49,158	16,548	55,887	25,130	57,519	17,185	5,088	47,180	30,803	21,215	**325,713**

Source: Central Statistics Office, *2011 Annual Services Inquiry.*

Exhibit 7.4: Summary Table

	Manufacturing	Services	Total
Turnover (€m)	16,167	111,032	127,199
Employment	95,069	604,382 (325,713 full-time)	699,451 (counting part-time)

Source: Central Statistics Office, *2011 Annual Services Inquiry* and *2011 Census of Industrial Production.*

The summary position of Ireland's SME sector as measured by official statistics – and according to the latest available data – is presented above in **Exhibit 7.4**. While not exactly comparable, the summary table gives a rough guide to the total level of employment (approximately 700,000) and turnover (approximately €120bn). Given the estimates contained in the Government's *Medium Term Economic Strategy*, these estimates may be a little on the high side.

Qualitative Issues

But how does this quantitative assessment of the size of Ireland's SME sector compare with other qualitative characteristics of the German Mittelstand?

The fourth characteristic of Germany's Mittelstand – strong links between management and workers – is one that mixes personal (the "family feeling") and policy (dual vocational training) aspects. Here, the relationship in Germany between management and workers is a special one. But it is by no means one that cannot be replicated outside Germany. And while Germany's system of dual vocational training is not directly replicable elsewhere, Ireland is undergoing an interesting discussion on the future of its third level education system. Ireland has an impressive record of producing third level graduates. The emergence from the crisis offers an opportunity to strengthen and deepen the links between industry and third level education, not only at the level of high technology research and development, but also in those sectors that are crucial to job creation, particularly in smaller towns and rural areas that, at present at least, are less likely to benefit from high technology employment.

The fifth characteristic of Germany's Mittelstand is harder to replicate in Ireland, given the country's small population and island location. For many German Mittelstand companies, the catchment population in their local region – before they even expand into the rest of Germany – already often exceeds the national domestic market accessible to an Irish company. Here, the internationalisation of Ireland's SME sector presents difficulties that are unenviable. However, what is enviable is the evidence cited above concerning the willingness of new Irish entrepreneurs to engage in exporting and also Ireland's proud status of being one of the most globalised economies in the world. Clearly, there is a challenge and an opportunity to ensure that Ireland's SME sector is as successful and representative of this characteristic of Ireland's economic position as its high technology sector. Here, the strong support of Enterprise Ireland in helping Irish firms is already impressive, although logistical issues and the goal of Irish SMEs in attaining economies of scale are remaining challenges.

In this respect, the sixth characteristic of Germany's Mittelstand may be helpful. Ireland already enjoys a strong political consensus in support of its competitive tax regime and this undoubtedly reflects the success of the IDA as a world leader in attracting foreign direct investment. Recent policy initiatives by Ireland – the *Action Plan for Jobs* and the 2014 budget, which introduced several incentives for small business – suggest Ireland is also working towards a consensus in favour of a strong successful enterprise policy. Such a policy will require many more initiatives and much patience to develop. In particular, whereas multinational corporations – a key (but far from the only) source of Ireland's exporting success to date – have the size and resources to source skilled workers and engage in research and development, Ireland's SME sector will require expertise and access to credit in order to do so. The success of Irish policy in promoting exports and jobs in its SME sector to date – despite significant challenges – indicates that efforts here can be richly rewarded. Given the success of both Enterprise Ireland in incubating indigenous SMEs and the IDA in attracting large MNCs, strengthening collaboration between the two and strengthening supply chain links between indigenous firms and MNCs deserves as much effort as possible.

In relation to the seventh pillar of Germany's Mittelstand – family-owned association support, the availability worldwide of support for German firms is guaranteed by the IHK and AHK network. In Ireland, Enterprise Ireland and Ireland's highly skilled diplomatic service performs excellent work on behalf of Irish firms around the world. The further development, integration and continued refocusing of this network according to new priorities and new opportunities can only work to Ireland's benefit.

Last but not least, it is worth pointing out some areas where Irish SMEs show some interesting characteristics, among them some surprising similarities with their German counterparts.

According to the Global Entrepreneurship Monitor report,[88] there is a tendency for Irish early stage entrepreneurs to be somewhat younger than their German counterparts. There is also a tendency for established enterprises to come from more "extractive" industries (table V, page 76) such as (farming, fishing) than is the case in Germany (3 per cent). This may be seen as a negative, but in fact it is not. In a world with hundreds of millions of consumers in the "middle class" category, Ireland's national brand as a source of excellence in food production gives it a huge advantage that many German firms would envy. This goes to the heart of the question of whether Ireland should develop a Mittelstand. The challenge is not to copy Germany, but to leverage those aspects of Germany's success to exploit Ireland's own unique advantages.

Further evidence from this source suggests that this is more than possible as the international orientation (table R, page 72) of Irish and German entrepreneurs are broadly similar. The higher percentage of German firms with no customers outside Germany (46 per cent compared to 34 per cent for Ireland) reflects the larger domestic market enjoyed by German SMEs. Government policy may help in overcoming Ireland's relative disadvantage here. Also Ireland's targeting of the traded service sector (discussed in **Chapter 2**) makes its small domestic market less relevant, given that barriers to exporting services, as distinct from goods, are generally either less onerous or, where they are onerous, at least less dependent on the challenge of achieving scale.

But perhaps the most hopeful sign of potential for Ireland's SME sector is that Irish and German entrepreneurs are quite similar in their attitude to innovation (table T, page 74). In fact, fewer (51 per cent) of Irish early stage entrepreneurs offer a product that is not new compared to German equivalents (60 per cent). Irish early entrepreneurs are also more likely (23 per cent) than German equivalents (15 per cent) to use new technology, although somewhat less likely (8 per cent *versus* 14 per cent) to use the very latest technology.

In conclusion, no economic model can be transposed directly from one country to another without regard to national conditions. This being said, some transferrable aspects of Germany's Mittelstand present huge opportunity. In particular, Germany's long-term orientation and the related access to support of strong banking and education systems could be instrumental in achieving the full potential of Ireland's SME sector. That sector faces logistical disadvantages that German firms – with their large regional and national markets and their easy accessibility across land borders to export markets – do not. However, Ireland is developing potential in the field of traded services. With continued support from

---

[88]   Table N, page 68 and Table O, page 69, Fitzsimons, Paula & O'Gorman, Colm (2013). *Entrepreneurship in Ireland* (Global Entrepreneurship Monitor).

State agencies and well-targeted policies, this offers potential for Ireland to develop its own brand of Mittelstand suited to its own unique advantages and national characteristics.

CHAPTER 8

Ireland and Germany:
Partners in European Recovery

Dr. Joachim Pfeiffer

Key Messages

- The European sovereign debt crisis may be a critical turning point in Europe's history. If Europeans learn from their mistakes, the European integration process and the formation of a more stable union can be accelerated. Only as a union can Europe make its voice heard in international affairs.

- As is evident in light of Ireland's successful adjustment process, reform efforts are yielding results and overall European recovery is on track. Given the substantial remaining challenges, it is nonetheless critical to maintain the reform momentum. The ongoing consolidation of public finances and the implementation of structural reforms are necessary to increase competitiveness and ensure sustained growth in the Eurozone.

A Critical Turning Point for Europe

In retrospect, the crisis Europe is currently experiencing may come to be viewed as the critical turning point in Europe's path toward the formation of a more stable union and deeper integration. Hopefully, these will be remembered as the times when Europe joined forces and gathered the strength to speak with one voice.

The European sovereign debt crisis has exposed gaps in our economic and currency union. The stability of the European Union and the single currency has been severely strained. However, it is incumbent on all Eurozone member states to preserve our union and to anticipate the challenges awaiting us in the future. The debt crisis may be our chance to increase the resilience of the single currency and to build a stronger union. Let us hope that dealing with the crisis helps us see our mistakes and learn from them. Given the severe problems in some Euro area countries unearthed by the crisis, decision-makers in politics, economics and finance are faced with the task to push for painful reforms and a continued consolidation process. This task also entails demonstrating in particular to the citizens of crisis-hit countries that the sacrifices and the patience shown throughout the necessary process of adjustment ultimately pay off. Meanwhile, each citizen has to contribute to the reform efforts and thereby help to create a more stable framework for Europe's future.

Evidence is mounting that Europe is on the right track, making a strong rebound from the severe crisis that struck some Eurozone member states. Ireland's impressive evolution from the first country to receive assistance from the European Financial Stability Facility to the first country strong enough to exit the bailout programme proves that the swift implementation of comprehensive reforms leads to recovery and subsequent financial independence. As an essential model of recovery and a source of leadership in Europe at key moments such as the recent EU Presidency, Ireland plays a decisive role in ensuring the union's stability. Moreover, Ireland's successful response to the crisis gives hope to those countries currently exposed to severe hardship as a result of fundamental structural problems. Adding to the overall positive outlook is Spain's announcement to follow in Ireland's footsteps and leave the bailout programme in 2014. Spain's and Ireland's unassisted programme exits prove that the Eurogroup's strategy is starting to deliver results.

Germany, on the other hand, finds itself in the position of a somewhat reluctant leader in European economic and financial affairs as its economy performed quite strongly throughout the crisis. With its growth-oriented employment policy boosting domestic consumption, high industrial competitiveness and its export strength, Germany has been able to mitigate the impact of the crisis on its national economy. At the same time, Germany has shown solidarity by offering extraordinary support to its European partners. In its effort to underpin the Euro, Germany has pushed for reforms in crisis-hit countries. This has caused some to criticise Germany and some to ask for more financial assistance. However, we have to remember not to overburden the German economy and thereby put the stability of the entire Euro area at risk. A stable German economy is closely tied to the stability of the European Union and *vice versa*. Moreover, despite the strong performance of the German economy, it is important to note that Germany already has gone through a process of painful reforms similar to those currently enacted in some Eurozone countries. Meanwhile, Germany, likewise, faces a number of tough challenges in the future, not least due to population ageing and its federalist system. In order to remain competitive, Germany, too, will be forced to undergo further structural reforms.

Challenges remain to be overcome in the entire Eurozone. In order to preserve Europe's strength, the adjustment process currently underway in several countries needs to be continued. Critical reforms need to be enacted, and the efforts at fiscal consolidation need to be carried on. To ensure we are on the right path we should take a step back and recap what has been achieved so far. This includes reassessing the causes of the sovereign debt crisis, re-evaluating the measures adopted to initiate the adjustment process, and identifying the remaining challenges. Given both Ireland and Germany have developed effective means to deal with the crisis, we can draw on their respective experience in our analysis. Ireland and Germany can share insights and thereby significantly contribute to the resolution of the sovereign debt crisis. Given the already high level of mutual dependence, the current challenges offer a number of opportunities for closer cooperation on future policy measures.

Several questions can guide us through the process of European recovery: What can we learn from the German and the Irish experience throughout the European debt crisis respectively? What contribution can Ireland and Germany make to European recovery? What remains to be done? Before we turn to the re-evaluation of German and Irish responses to the crisis, however, it is important to reassess the causes that led to the crisis and to review the actual role the Euro played in the crisis that has been named after it.

The Euro and the European Sovereign Debt Crisis

Europe's current crisis is commonly equated with a crisis of its currency. This is evident in the term "Euro crisis" commonly used to refer to it. This term, however, is misleading and creates a spurious relationship between the Euro and the unfolding crisis. The Euro is not at the root of the current crisis. Rather, the currency union worked as a magnifier that exposed existing structural problems in some Eurozone countries and reminded us that we had lived beyond our means.

In fact, for more than a decade, the Euro proved more stable, both internally and externally, than the Deutschmark ever was. Throughout the history of the Deutschmark from 1948 to 2001, prices on average increased at an annual rate of 2.6 per cent. During the first 10 years following the Euro's introduction, Euro area annual inflation was merely 1.6 per cent. Upon its introduction, the Euro brought a new dynamic to the single market, mainly by making it more efficient. Among other things, it increased price transparency, eliminated currency exchange costs, significantly lowered the barriers to international trade, and enhanced labour market mobility. For businesses, the Euro has significantly reduced uncertainty. Prior to the Euro's introduction, pan-European businesses had to hedge against currency fluctuations. In a currency union this has become unnecessary, saving the German economy alone €10bn each year. Currency devaluation has become impossible, plainly exposing structural differences among Eurozone countries. In addition to that, the Euro guarantees stable exchange rates with other currencies, such as the US dollar. As a result of its strong performance, the Euro has become the second most important reserve currency after the US dollar (**Exhibits 8.1** and **8.2**).

Exhibit 8.1: The Euro / Dollar Exchange Rate

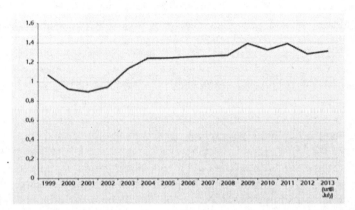

Source: German Federal Ministry of Finance, *Moving Towards a Stability Union*.

Exhibit 8.2: The Euro as a Global Reserve Currency

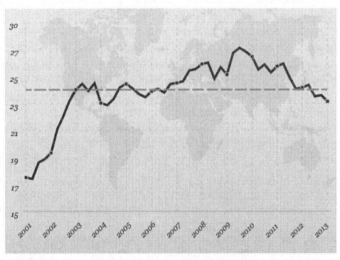

Source: German Federal Ministry of Finance, *Benefits of the Euro*.

Instead of stemming from the Euro itself, the European debt crisis has manifold causes. Primary among them were failures in economic and fiscal policy and an overall lack of fiscal policy co-ordination, which allowed Euro area Member States to live beyond their means. Recurring budget deficits, steadily rising public debt and high levels of public expenditure were the result of relatively lax oversight. These basic deficiencies were further aggravated by the global financial and economic downturn. Leading up to the European debt crisis, the global financial and economic crisis unfolded in four stages. First, the US real estate market's subprime crisis exposed the dangerous link between the real estate market and financial products. Mortgages on American homes had been packaged up with financial products and traded on a global scale. The loss of confidence in the international financial system that resulted from the Lehman Brothers bankruptcy characterised the second stage of the crisis. As this affected the real economy, it led to the third stage, the global economic crisis. The European sovereign debt crisis represents the fourth stage of the crisis. Though this debt crisis had been there before, it has been severely aggravated by the bursting of the property bubble and the financial crisis. Unless this cycle is broken, the sovereign debt crisis could turn into a new financial crisis and set off another vicious circle.

The high levels of Government debt accumulated by some Eurozone members cannot be attributed to the introduction of the common currency. Instead, high debt levels resulted from the setting of false priorities in national economic and financial policies. The introduction of the Euro in fact gave today's crisis-stricken countries some leeway. From 1995 onwards the mere announcement of the new currency led to a considerable reduction in the premium paid by southern countries – compared to Germany – on Government bonds. Greece, for instance, only spent 4.7 per cent of its gross domestic product (GDP) on interest payments in 2005, compared to more than 11 per cent in the mid-1990s. But instead of devising policies to increase their competitiveness, countries like Greece and Portugal significantly increased State spending, even before the most recent escalation of the crisis. Public sectors became bloated and social expenditures underwent a massive expansion – in Greece's case, from approximately 19 per cent of GDP in 1995 to more than 25 per cent in 2007. In Portugal the increase in the level of social expenditure was similarly dramatic. At the same time, these countries' economies suffered a loss of competitiveness. The result of this policy stance is a high level of Government debt and a lack of structural reform, due to which the competitiveness of the economy is severely weakened.

Realising that the Euro is not to blame for the European debt crisis is the first step to moving on and building a European stability union. As Europeans, we have to discover the enormous potential we have if we continue along the path of integration. Already now the Euro unites one of the biggest trading blocks in the world. However, to realise Europe's true economic potential, we have to overcome several flaws inherent in the build-up of our currency union and go through a process of structural and fiscal adjustments, including a significant reduction of high debt levels.

European Crisis Management

In a joint European effort to prevent the crisis from spreading and affecting the stability of the Eurozone and the single currency, several steps have been taken.

Various measures operating at the European and the national level have been implemented and form the main pillars of a sustainable economic and financial architecture for the Eurozone. Through this, we have paved the way for the Eurozone to enhance its competitiveness and increase economic growth rates.

The European Level

Decisive progress has been made in setting the European economic and currency union on a stronger institutional foundation. Since the *Maastricht Treaty* lacked an effective enforcement mechanism, it allowed Germany and France to violate the deficit criteria set out in the treaty and thereby contribute to the dilution of the treaty framework at a very early stage. In the year of the Euro cash changeover, this behaviour set the wrong standard early on in the history of Europe's single currency. In the wake of the crisis, Eurozone leaders have agreed on several instruments and measures designed to build a more stable, competitive and sustainable Eurozone. Among others, these comprise tighter EU budget surveillance by means of the European fiscal compact and a stronger *Stability and Growth Pact*, improved co-ordination in the economic policy realm, for instance through the *Euro Plus Pact* and the European Semester, and higher standards for the regulation of financial markets. Just recently, on 22 November 2013, the Eurogroup assessed the Commission's opinions on draft national budgets and the overall Eurozone fiscal outlook for the first time.

Helping to restore market confidence in the Euro, the banking union is of utmost importance among the remaining tasks. Through the establishment of a common European banking surveillance at the European Central Bank, more effective instruments to prevent national banking crises from impacting the real economy become available. With banks becoming increasingly Europeanised, supervisory structures need to follow suit and adjust to the changing environment. As the second pillar of the banking union, the Single Resolution Mechanism (SRM) with a Single Bank Resolution Fund (SRF) serves as a means to prevent further bank bailouts by taxpayers. The compromise reached by Euro finance ministers on 18 December 2013 will ensure that the costs of resolving banks will be imposed first on the bank's shareholders and creditors. Only if that is insufficient will the bank-paid SRF be used to cover additional costs. We need clear bail-in rules to clarify who is covering the costs of capital shortfalls possibly exposed by the 2014 stress test. In addition to that, the crisis resolution mechanism inherent in the European Stability Mechanism (ESM) is another characteristic of the Eurozone's enhanced institutional architecture.

Extensive financial assistance to the crisis-hit countries has been provided through the rescue funds. Moreover, the increase in the European Investment Bank's capital was a step in the right direction, fostering private investments and promoting the European growth agenda. In the battle against Europe's high youth unemployment – in October 2013, the Euro area youth unemployment rate was

24.4 per cent – several European and national initiatives have been launched because Europe cannot afford a "lost generation". At the youth unemployment summit in Paris in November, European leaders came together to devise strategies to provide security to young people across Europe. The financial instruments necessary to address this crucial problem will be available through the €6bn EU fund for young people from January 2014 on. Meanwhile, our focus must be on creating more flexibility and mobility on the labour market as offering Europe's younger generation a viable perspective is crucial to Europe's future.

In addition to the measures taken at the European level, each country had to devise its own strategy to deal with the crisis. Faced with severe domestic imbalances, Ireland adopted an ambitious adjustment programme. Looking at Ireland's experience helps us evaluate the effectiveness of the policies adopted so far.

Ireland's Swift and Comprehensive Return to the Markets – From Celtic Tiger to European Front Runner

Being the first country to enter the bailout programme of the EU and the IMF, Ireland has returned to the markets in December 2013. Ireland's example confirms that the combination of fiscal consolidation and the implementation of structural reforms ultimately pays off. After three quarters of negative economic growth rates, growth picked up again in September 2013. For 2014, GDP is forecast to grow by 2 per cent. The Irish Government's announcement that no follow-up programme will be required is further proof of Ireland's regained strength. Meeting all targets set by the adjustment programme, Ireland has turned into a role model for other crisis-hit countries over the last three years. Ireland's decision re-assures the markets and international lenders that the adoption of comprehensive austerity measures merits their confidence. Ireland is now in a position to make a sustainable return to the markets, needing no further loans to do so.

When analysing Ireland's economic performance, we have to consider the specific circumstances that led to the outbreak of the debt crisis in Ireland. In contrast to other countries, Ireland's crisis was fundamentally a banking crisis. Before Ireland was hit by the financial crisis in 2008, it had a solid budget and Government debt was low. Unlike Greece, in Ireland's case there was no public mismanagement to blame for the crisis. Instead, low interest rates and banking supervision, which in hindsight proved too lax, led to an unchecked expansion of bank loans. This spurred an increase in consumption and fed a growing property bubble, with the property market peaking in 2007-2008. The bursting of the bubble necessitated a write-down of home loans, which in turn caused the banking crisis. As a result, the Irish Government saw itself forced to guarantee the bank's liabilities and endow the banks with fresh capital. In order to relieve Ireland's severely strained budget, the EU/IMF bailout programme provided financial assistance in the amount of about €68bn.

What distinguishes Ireland from other countries affected by the crisis is the fact that its reaction to the crisis was both rapid and comprehensive. In return for the financial assistance, Ireland agreed to a downsizing and re-organising of its banking system, to the consolidation of its public finances, and it furthermore vowed to adopt the measures necessary to increase its growth potential. Through sustained efforts to cut spending and raise revenue, Ireland has made steady progress in continuously reducing its deficit. Since Ireland was hit by the financial crisis in 2008, spending cuts and tax rises have amounted to €28bn, which corresponds to 17 per cent of today's GDP. The latest measures include spending cuts of €2.5bn in the 2014 budget presented by Michael Noonan to the parliament in October. At 4.8 per cent of GDP, the budget deficit in 2014 is expected to be within the 5.1 per cent limit set by the Excessive Deficit Procedure (EDP) established under the *Stability and Growth Pact*. Furthermore, the Irish Government has expressed its commitment to reducing the deficit to less than 3 per cent in 2015. In light of the 2010 deficit peak at almost 31 per cent of GDP, these figures are remarkable.

Apart from the consolidation of public finances, Ireland has gone through structural reforms that allow economic growth to gain new momentum. Underpinning Ireland's rising competitiveness, unit labour costs have fallen considerably. More precisely, over the 2009-2013 period, nominal unit labour costs have declined by an estimated 10 per cent.

Combined with the downsizing and re-organising of its banking system, Ireland has made significant progress in its economic recovery and has met all targets set by the troika of international lenders. The overall positive outlook is evident in several encouraging indicators. Goods exports, retail trade and consumer confidence are all increasing. Given its growth is largely driven by external trade, Ireland has been running a current account surplus since 2010. The property market continues to recover. Moreover, honouring Ireland's determination and tough austerity measures, market confidence has improved and will continue to do so. Yields on 10-year Irish sovereign bonds have declined significantly from double-digit figures to below 4 per cent.

Germany – A Strong Partner Throughout the Crisis

Germany so far has quite successfully dealt with the crisis. The German economy has grown continuously at an estimated overall real growth rate of 8.5 per cent from 2009 to 2013. Several key components can be singled out in analysing why Germany has largely defied the debt crisis.

The consolidation of our public finances has enabled the German Government to present a structurally balanced budget for 2014. Since 2010, Germany has reduced its structural deficit from approximately €46bn to zero. New borrowing has been reduced to €6.4bn, thereby reaching its lowest level in 40 years. As set out in the *Stability and Growth Pact*, Euro area states are to reduce debt to below 60 per cent of their economic output. Germany's new grand coalition has agreed on reducing the debt ratio from 81 per cent at the end of 2012 to less than 60 per cent of GDP within 10 years. Until the end of 2017, we aim to reduce debt to below 70 per cent of GDP.

In addition to fiscal consolidation, both a strong industrial sector and the German Mittelstand constitute crucial backbones of our economy. Being highly flexible and offering a wide product portfolio, the German Mittelstand is exceptionally competitive. As other components of the Mittelstand's success have been thoroughly assessed in **Chapter 7**, I refrain from going into further detail on this topic.

The labour market reforms we enacted several years ago constitute another pillar of our relative strength today. Overall, these reforms increased labour market flexibility with the help of several basic instruments. First, low-wage employment was expanded, particularly by means of the so-called "minijob". In addition to bringing many people into work, this reduced incentives for illegal work. Furthermore, the *Agenda 2010* reforms also introduced new regulations that caused an expansion of temporary work. By giving companies more leeway in adapting to changes in demand, particularly the latter is an effective instrument to enable people to return to employment. Additionally, during the crisis, short-time work was introduced to prohibit unemployment. As a result of these reforms, the German labour market has proved exceptionally resilient throughout the crisis. Except for a slight increase during the 2008-2009 financial and economic downturn, unemployment has decreased significantly since 2005. Since then it has been nearly halved. In September 2013, Germany's unemployment rate was 5.2 per cent. This makes Germany the country with the second-lowest unemployment rate among the 28 EU member states after Austria (4.9 per cent). With more than 42 million people in employment, we have reached a historic high. Our labour market's strength becomes even more evident when seen in a larger context. Against the overall OECD trend, German unemployment has barely increased during the 2008-2009 recession and steadily decreased since 2009 (**Exhibit 8.3**). However, our economy has not always been that strong. A decade ago, still struggling with the cost of reunification, Germany was labelled the "sick man of Europe". Recovery did not come overnight and required Germany to follow a path of tough structural reforms.

Exhibit 8.3: Unemployment in Germany

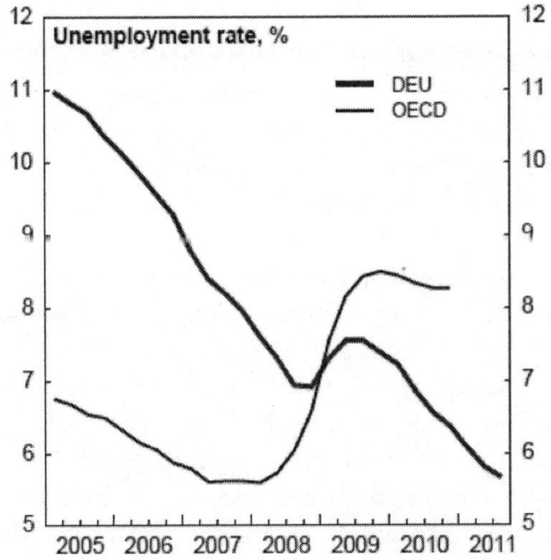

Source: OECD, Better Life, Economic Outlook and National Accounts databases.

Among the core themes identified by German economic policy are the fields of education as well as research, development and innovation as they build the foundation of long-term economic success and wealth in Germany. With additional investments of more than €13bn into education and research during the previous legislative period, we have provided a critical impulse that spurs future growth. As one of the main pillars of the German educational realm, the dual system of vocational training has helped us to have the lowest youth unemployment rate in Europe. Other countries like Austria, Denmark and Switzerland have strongly benefitted also from the system. Fostering the training of highly skilled workers is essential if we want to retain the overall strength of the German economy, particularly of the German industrial sector and the Mittelstand. It is therefore absolutely vital to realise that skilled labour is of equal necessity for our economy as academic education.

As the European Union's largest economy, Germany has helped initiate the comprehensive reform process currently underway in the Eurozone. Being able to do so because of a robust economy, Germany has demonstrated its solidarity to countries severely affected by the crisis. As a nation that has strongly benefited from the political and economic stability provided by the European Union, Germany recognises its large responsibility for the future of the union and the single currency. In short, Europe's unity is essential to Germany.

Adjustment processes similar to the one in Germany can be viewed in a number of Eurozone countries. While these processes continue to demand a high degree of endurance and commitment from many citizens in crisis-hit countries, it is critical to remember that the reforms need some time to kick in.

Structural Reforms and Consolidation Yielding Results

In line with the success achieved by Ireland, the adjustment process across Europe is beginning to yield results. The combination of institutional reforms at the European level and structural reforms, as well as the consolidation of public finances at the national level, has proved effective. Overall, we have seen that uncertainties which appeared in the context of the sovereign debt crisis have mostly been overcome. A significant reduction in the public budget deficits of Euro area countries has been achieved. At an average of 3.7 per cent of GDP in the second quarter of 2013, deficits have shrunk significantly compared with 6.4 per cent in 2009. The US budget deficit in 2013 by contrast amounts to 4.1 per cent of GDP, according to the Congressional Budget Office. With unit labour costs significantly declining in European crisis-hit countries, national economies have grown more competitive. Based on this, the level of exports is increasing. As a result, national current account balances in the Eurozone have levelled up. Countries severely affected by the crisis have achieved significant reductions in their current account deficits. Greece's deficit, for example, has dramatically declined from 18 per cent of GDP to an estimated 2.8 per cent in 2013 (**Exhibit 8.4**).

Exhibit 8.4: Current Account Balances

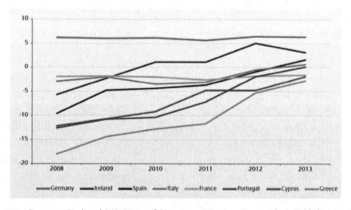

Source: German Federal Ministry of Finance, *Moving Towards a Stability Union.*

Corresponding to the overall positive trend, in the second quarter of 2013 the economy in the Eurozone grew at 0.3 per cent compared to the previous quarter. Gradually, growth is expected to become more domestic demand-driven and more robust in the course of 2014.

The Road Ahead

With regard to Ireland's future, Taoiseach Enda Kenny has stated correctly, that notwithstanding the enormous progress made so far, Ireland still faces "difficult economic decisions". Among the remaining challenges, unemployment and emigration are the most pressing issues. In September 2013, Ireland's unemployment rate was 13.6 per cent. Approximately 3,000 people still leave Ireland each month. In addition to that, Ireland's export-oriented economy generates a strong dependency on global economic growth, which means over the long-term domestic demand needs to be strengthened and the conditions for investment need to be further improved. This is a critical moment in Ireland's recovery and a critical moment in Europe's future. With the help of its European partners, Ireland has to continue the successful reform process. The Irish Government's announcement that it will publish a new *Medium Term Economic Strategy* to outline Ireland's return to prosperity, including a recommitment to reduce government borrowing, underlines the Government's determination to keep the reform momentum alive.

Though it has shown considerable resilience throughout the crisis, Germany faces major challenges in the coming years, too. Hence, it cannot afford to halt the reform efforts. Instead, we must develop an ambitious *Agenda 2030* to ensure our future competitiveness and sustainable growth rates. Germany, like all other Eurozone countries, needs to maintain the reform momentum by addressing several core issues. First, the constraints imposed by the existing system of German federalism have to be loosened; second, we have to foster a steady process of innovation, for instance through tax incentives in the field of research; third, we have to make substantial investments in infrastructure. Most importantly, Germany needs to anticipate rapid population ageing, which increasingly affects the labour market. In particular, we need to create effective instruments to tackle the skills shortage. To do so, among other things, the skilled labour campaign was launched to attract qualified professionals from abroad, the vocational training programme creates our future professionals, and we seek to make more effective use of our older employees' experience and potential. Furthermore, through an initiative for skilled labour, we seek to draw the attention of decision-makers in politics, economics and the unions to the importance of this issue and to encourage co-operation on it.

Against the background of the fundamental challenges Europe is faced with, we are in need of strong partnership towards consolidation and recovery. Both Ireland's good example – shown through sacrifice and rapid adjustment – and Germany's strength in underpinning the Euro are examples of this notion of European partnership. In fact, the resolution of the crisis offers new opportunities for higher levels of co-operation. In this spirit, Germany and Ireland have agreed on a joint initiative to improve the financing of the real economy and simplify the access to financial means for Ireland's SMEs. To this end, co-operation between the KfW and the Irish authorities is set to begin shortly.

With regard to the entire Eurozone, there are several core issues to be addressed. In many countries, high public and private debt levels persist. In light of an unemployment rate of 12.1 per cent in the Eurozone in October, more must be done to create higher labour market flexibility and mobility (**Exhibit 8.5**).

Exhibit 8.5: Unemployment Rates in EU (October 2013, seasonally adjusted)

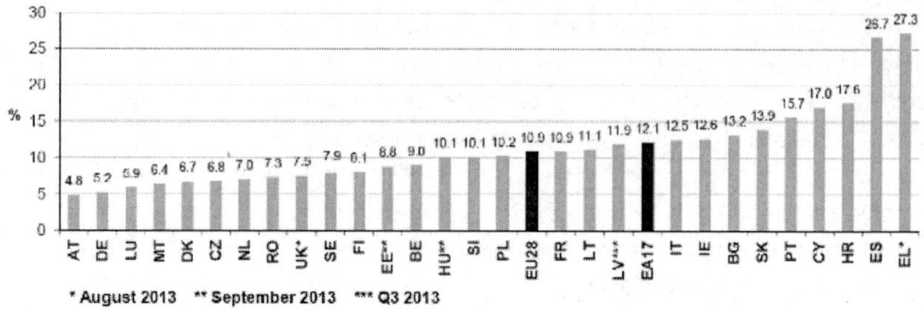

* August 2013   ** September 2013   *** Q3 2013

Source: Eurostat newsrelease *euroindicators*, November 2013.

To prevent future crises, banking regulation needs to be pushed as the current preferential regulatory treatment of sovereign exposures is insufficient and encourages financial institutions to invest in government bonds. This potentially dangerous sovereign-banking nexus needs to be dissolved. Banks should have to back their holdings of Government bonds with capital. Otherwise their solvency is directly threatened by a sovereign default, which could cause another financial crisis. At the same time, this creates false incentives as capital invested in Government bonds is not available for investments in small and medium-sized enterprises.

As expressed by the Eurogroup, crisis-hit countries need to maintain the reform momentum in order to overcome remaining challenges and to secure sustainable recoveries. Germany will support its partners throughout their continued reform efforts. Similar to the process both Germany and Ireland have gone through, it is essential that every single Eurozone member does its share by adopting the measures necessary to solve problems at the domestic level first. For the currency union to work, it is vital that everyone does their homework. The Irish experience, in particular, tells us that there is no alternative to the consolidation of public finances and structural reforms.

Conclusions

Despite all the predictions that it would fail, the Euro and Europe have survived and are consolidating and recovering. Now it is essential that the Eurozone moves on towards becoming a union of stability, with common values, credible rules and clear sanctions. We cannot afford to lose sight of necessary future consolidation. It is vital that we place our currency union on a solid fiscal footing and continue to steadily improve the institutional foundation of our economic and currency union. Meanwhile, we have to maintain the reform momentum and work hard to substantiate our claim on being a respected partner in the world economy. As the key to growth and employment, competitiveness is the crucial factor in ensuring Europe's future prosperity.

Europe's future will not be determined by the actions of single countries like Greece, Ireland or Germany. Rather it depends on what we are able to achieve as a union. It is about Europe as an economic power being in a steady process of co-operation and competition with other powers. If Europe is to play a significant role alongside major powers like the US and China, European countries have to join forces. The future European integration process should extend over a broad spectrum of policy areas, including the fields of foreign and security policy. Meanwhile, the crisis offers an opportunity for further labour market integration as it necessitates both greater flexibility and mobility. The sovereign debt crisis has not only exposed gaps in our monetary union, it has also accelerated the steps we take towards deeper integration. Like the single market, the Euro is a crucial instrument for as well as a commitment to European integration. Now it is incumbent on all of us to continue along the path towards the formation of a united Europe. In short, a stable single currency provides the foundation for a stronger Europe. Ensuring Europe's currency union will continue to require a number of brave political decisions in the future. Through partnership and commitment, Ireland and Germany can contribute to moving European integration to the next level.

Particularly in light of the considerable progress made by crisis-hit countries, most notably Ireland, it is essential that we begin to view the current crisis as a turning point leading to a sustainable European economic and fiscal policy. We have to become more conscious of our options and the immense value of Europe and our common currency. In the absence of the Euro, Europe's power to influence international politics and to push its interests would be dramatically reduced. The single currency fortifies Europe's growth potential and its overall economic power. The Euro is essentially a constant reminder of our need to work together and a harbinger of the future strength of a united Europe.

CHAPTER 9

What Did Countries in Europe Do to Get Back to Stability?

Volker Treier

Key Messages

- The economic crisis reflects not just systemic problems with the global and European economies, but mistakes in each Member State. A mix of European-wide action and national reforms is gradually overcoming crisis. An increasingly stable Euro, improving government financial balances and rising exports are signs that the situation in Europe is better than it looks.
- A comparison of Ireland's performance with other adjustment programmes shows how well Ireland has done, but also how many significant challenges remain at European and national level, challenges that in spite of its salutary performance apply in some cases to Ireland as well.

Introduction

The American writer Mark Twain once declared that "Wagner's music is better than it sounds". The same kind of sentiment could be accurately applied also to the current situation in Europe. If we view the fundamentals, Europe is already back in better shape than many people think.

Before looking at the progress that has been achieved, however, it is important to remind ourselves once more of the key causes of the crisis:

- **Cheap money:** Up to 2009 – and particularly in the USA – borrowing was available to everyone, whether with or without security. The borrowing was securitised, with European banks and investors buying large portions of it – but without first performing the necessary due diligence! It must be said, however, that not just house buyers in the USA but the property markets in Europe, too, benefited from the availability of easy money.
- **"Politics on tick":** The politicians gave promises, and the voters – and also businesses – demanded that they keep them. People got into the habit of expecting the State to give more in the way of benefits than was possible on the basis of the current revenue. Or to put it another way: the

politicians sold at a discount, and the people picked up the bargains. And it was not just in Euroland that this game was played; in Japan, the US and the UK, for example, the debt ratio also rose in some cases even much higher than in the Eurozone countries.

- **The culture of "turning a blind eye":** Anyone could have known how high the level of public borrowing in Greece really was. The volume of property lending by the Spanish banks was no state secret. And how poor the provision of training is for young people in many Member States is also well-known. But either people didn't want to know or didn't take the figures seriously. Today, no one can ignore the realities any more!

One birth defect of the currency union was unquestionably that the co-ordination of economic and financial policy within Europe was inadequate. And the fact that the stability and growth pact was watered down by France and Germany – the European heavyweights, of all countries – in 2005 did not help either.

Europe's standing has been damaged by the crisis. One way to rebuild confidence is to ensure that European policy is now geared uncompromisingly to encouraging growth and employment and safeguarding the soundness of government budgets and the financial markets. One thing that must not be allowed to happen – and indeed is not being allowed to happen – is that everyone should simply carry on as before.

Since the outbreak of the debt crisis, the EU and the Euro states have undertaken some important steps to instil more discipline into the Euro states and to create a more consistent monitoring system. A series of measures have been put in train. The following key reform steps stand out in particular:

- The *Fiscal Pact*, with an obligation on states to introduce national caps on borrowing.
- The European Stability Mechanism, with tough reform conditions for the recipients of payments under the mechanism.
- The co-ordination of economic policy with greater binding force at European level.

All these measures are aimed at putting a stop to "politics on tick" and "turning a blind eye". And it is right and proper that they are.

Another essential step is strengthening competitiveness. In this field, it goes without saying that the onus is primarily on the Member States themselves. It is right and proper that help is only available for self-help. Ultimately, effort is necessary in order to put the countries back on track, and so enable long-term growth. The goal must be to improve local working conditions for businesses in order to strengthen their ability to compete – even if it may now sound hackneyed to say so.

The results of the review of the reforms that we as the DIHK are conducting are impressive:

- Spain, for example, has put together a package of over 30 reforms – from the cap on borrowing to the facilitation of business start-ups.
- In Portugal, four public holidays have been abolished and privatisation has continued on an extensive scale.
- Ireland, too, has implemented a range of measures. Savings have been imposed in the field of public sector pay, and restrictions on competition in the field of legal services and pharmacies have been eliminated.

By any measure, the "withdrawal treatment" that Europe is currently undergoing is nothing short of remarkable. If applied to Germany, the savings made in the Greek budget in the last two years alone would be equivalent to almost €180bn! That would be tantamount to the cancellation of all administrative expenditure in Germany! That is an achievement that deserves enormous respect.

So it is worth taking a careful look. Far-reaching measures are being implemented at a tremendous pace. Europe is currently not taking the easy path; simply implementing new spending programmes with cheap money from the central banks is no solution. "Straw fires" are the very last thing Europe currently needs. They would be only a distraction and ultimately make it even more difficult to manage the crisis. It is essential to change structures.

There is no question that the reforms are painful – and that they take time. But they will pay off in the end. We in Germany know that from the *Agenda 2010*. Launched in 2003, it was not until 2006 that it became possible to start reaping any benefits. But this also makes it clear that the about-turn in the political course in the crisis countries comes very close to the limits of what the people there are willing to take. So it is all the more important for the reasons why the measures are necessary to be explained again and again. But it is equally important not to indulge in pessimism, but to look carefully at what has actually been achieved.

And some initial successes are visible: in the second quarter of 2013, the Eurozone managed to climb out of recession. The balance of payments and budget deficits of the crisis countries are slimming down, while exports are increasing. For 2014, the DIHK expects to see a return to growth both in the EU as a whole and the Eurozone, and in both cases bordering on 1 per cent. So things are moving in the right direction – even when one looks at the individual countries themselves.

Progress in Other Eurozone Countries

Portugal

In Portugal, the economy grew by no less than 1.1 per cent in the second quarter of 2013 compared to the previous quarter.[89] In terms of growth rates, therefore, Portugal is leading the whole of Europe. And more, the country is a model of good behaviour, with all the agreements negotiated with the Troika being met, despite

---

[89] *Eurostat*, October 2013.

setbacks. In 2014, the Government budget is even projected to achieve a primary surplus.

Growth in Portugal in 2014 will achieve an average positive rate of 0.8 per cent,[90] with growth accelerating to 1.5 per cent in 2015. In line with this improving growth trend, the budget deficit is projected to fall from 5.9 per cent of GDP in 2013 to 4 per cent in 2014 to 2.5 per cent in 2015, comfortably below the 3 per cent deficit. After several years of being in deficit, Portugal's current account balance also has turned positive, from a 1.9 per cent deficit in 2013 to a 0.9 per cent surplus estimated for 2013 and surpluses of 0.9 per cent and 1.0 per cent projected for 2014 and 2015 respectively.

The Economic Adjustment programme for Portugal was agreed in May 2011 following a request for assistance made in the previous month. It includes a joint financing package of €78bn covering the period until mid-2014, the burden of which is shared equally between the EU[91] and the Eurozone[92] and almost all of which has been disbursed at the time of writing.

As with Ireland, this aid package is conditional not just on strong fiscal consolidation but also on a package of structural reforms that aim to boost growth, create jobs and improve competitiveness and also on recapitalising and deleveraging the banking system. In contrast to Ireland at the time of writing, however, unemployment in Portugal showed little signs of falling and was projected to rise to 17.7 per cent in 2014 before falling very slightly in 2015.

In its latest quarterly review of the adjustment programme the EU Commission[93] has commented that "programme implementation is broadly on track" despite challenging circumstances. It also noted evidence of the recovery signalled in growth figures for the second quarter of 2013.

Portugal's exit from this adjustment programme is due in 2014. It remains to be seen whether, like Ireland, Portugal can exit without the requirement of an emergency credit facility, a facility that Irish authorities decided to do without. Finally as a share of GDP, Portugal's public debt burden in 2014, at 126.7 per cent, is projected to be close to that of Ireland.

Greece

In Greece, the growth outlook remains much more challenging than in Ireland, Portugal or Spain. As economic growth was either returning or as rates of economic decline were modest elsewhere, GDP in Greece continued to decline by significant, albeit moderating, rates until 2013 when, according to estimates at the

---

[90] EU Commission, *Autumn Forecasts*, October 2013.

[91] *Via* the European Financial Stability Mechanism (EFSM) (see **Annex II: Glossary**).

[92] *Via* the European Financial Stability Facility (EFSF) (see **Annex II: Glossary**).

[93] EU Commission, ECB, IMF, *The Economic Adjustment Programme for Portugal, Eighth and Ninth review*, November 2013.

time of writing,[94] GDP fell by 4 per cent. Growth, according to these estimates, was forecast to be a modest 0.6 per cent in 2014 but with significant acceleration, to 2.9 per cent, in 2015.

The budget deficit situation shows more signs of progress, however, with Greece's budgetary balance expected to meet the 3 per cent target by 2014 with a deficit of just 2 per cent of GDP. Greece is already running a "primary surplus".

Greece's better performance in regard to its budgetary balance most likely reflects the fact that it has little option but to outperform here: even compared to Ireland and Portugal – whose debt to GDP ratio both will exceed 120 per cent of GDP – Greece's public debt burden is significantly higher and is estimated to have peaked at 176.2 per cent in 2013, falling slightly to 175.9 per cent in 2014 and 170.9 per cent in 2015. Greece's balance on current account also remains negative, unlike that of Ireland, Portugal and Spain.

In contrast to Ireland, Greece's experience with financial adjustment has been more turbulent. Greece's Economic Adjustment programme dates from May 2010 and amounts to an overall package of €164.5bn until 2014, the largest amount of which is provided by the Eurozone.

In July 2011, a special "task force" for Greece was established, on the invitation of the Greek Government, both to co-ordinate technical assistance to Greece and to assist Greek authorities in defining the details of its legislative, regulatory and administrative aspects.

Unlike Ireland, Greece received a two-year extension in the length of its fiscal adjustment path in November of 2012. At the same time, a package of special measures – including a voluntary write-down some Government debt, interest rate reductions on bailout loans and an extension of loan maturities – aims to achieve a targeted reduction in Greece's debt to a more manageable 124 per cent by 2020.

Despite the turbulence of the preceding three years in relation to Greece, in July 2013 the Eurogroup noted with satisfaction that Greece's programme was broadly on track.[95] Progress on important structural reforms were noted, as was improving competitiveness in terms of labour costs. However, the number of issues facing Greece in the future is very significant on a number of fronts, including social cohesion, labour market reforms, improving the business environment and reforming Government revenue administration. Most challenging from an economic point of view is the unemployment rate in Greece, which at one-quarter of the labour force is far above that in Ireland or Portugal and is projected to remain so for some time.

---

[94]   EU Commission, *Autumn Forecasts*, October 2013.
[95]   EU Commission, ECB, IMF, *The Second Economic Adjustment Programme for Greece, Third Review*, July 2013.

Spain

In Spain, the rate of unemployment stopped rising in the third quarter of 2013. For the first time in two years, the economy once again recorded slight growth. And for 2014 and 2015, there are grounds for further optimism. From a negative average growth rate in 2013, GDP is projected to grow at the time of writing by 0.5 per cent and 1.7 per cent in 2014 and 2015 respectively.[96]

Spain requested assistance, predominantly in relation to stabilising its banking sector, in June 2012. This was later than Ireland, Greece or Portugal and in Spain's case adjustment is more focused on banking and shorter in duration from the Troika's point of view.

The budgetary balance appears to be making slower progress towards consolidation, with the EU Commission forecasting a 5.9 per cent deficit in 2014 and a 6.6 per cent deficit in 2015. Spain's debt is large but not quite as high in Ireland or Portugal (it is projected to reach 104.3 per cent in 2015). Like Portugal but later than Ireland, Spain has made the transition from a negative to a positive balance on its current account, indicating improved competitiveness.

In its review of Spain,[97] the EU Commission found that Spain's stabilisation and repair of its financial sector had "advanced further" and expressed confidence in the improved solvency position of Spain's banks. However, it noted that the budgetary situation remained "challenging". In contrast to Ireland, Portugal and Greece, issues relating to fiscal pressure from Spanish regions may be a factor in limiting the ability of central government to achieve fiscal consolidation with the same rapidity as is possible in smaller, more fiscally-centralised countries.

It should be said that while Spain is mentioned here, the ability to make comparison with Ireland is somewhat limited given the large difference in size between the Irish and Spanish economy. In one respect however, a contrast is noteworthy: like Greece, Spain has one of the EU's highest rate of unemployment, with one-quarter of the population out of work and a far higher proportion of young people out of work. The contrast with Ireland is all the more stark, given how Ireland has faced the pressures of a rising young population. In this respect both Greece and Spain, and to some extent Portugal, could justifiably look to Ireland and of course to Germany for inspiration in tackling the youth unemployment problem.

Latvia

For several reasons, Latvia is an interesting comparator country. First, it is the Eurozone's fastest growing economy on average – its GDP growth reached 5 per cent in 2012 and 4.2 per cent in 2013 and is projected to average 4 per cent in subsequent years. Second, as of 1 January 2014, Latvia is the Eurozone's newest

---

[96] EU Commission, *Autumn Forecasts*, October 2013.
[97] EU Commission, ECB, IMF, *Financial Assistance Programme for the Recapitalisation of Financial Institutions in Spain, Fourth Review*, November 2013.

Member State. Third, Latvia suffered a banking crisis not unlike Ireland's, with an excessively sized banking sector dependent on foreign credit. Fourth, like Ireland it is a small open economy with important economic relations with a large non-Eurozone neighbour (Russia). Fifth, although not a Eurozone member, Latvia's currency was pegged to the Euro and despite strong pressure to devalue its currency and abandon this peg, Latvia refused to do so, focusing instead on achieving a so-called "internal devaluation" of its currency whereby competitiveness was restored by reducing prices and wages in the domestic economy. This required great discipline on the part of the policy authorities. Last, where most other EU countries have spread fiscal consolidation over many years, Latvia concentrated its fiscal consolidation into a much shorter period, between 2008 and 2010.

The much more impressive growth rates for the Latvian economy suggest that, according to economic criteria, its adjustment process has been exemplary – the social consequences have not been uncontroversial however.

When global liquidity froze in September 2008, this led to the collapse of Latvia's second largest bank, Parex Bank. Confronted with the sizeable cost of recapitalising it, Latvia called in the IMF and EU Commission for assistance.[98] A package of €7.5bn was agreed as part of a co-ordinated international effort involving the EU and IMF.

In June 2009, the Latvian government, trade unions and employers agreed on deep public spending cuts, the size and extent of which are remarkable in that the budget deficit was reduced by 4 per cent of GDP in one single budget. In some cases administrative budgets to some arms of government were cut by up to 50 per cent. Public salaries were cut significantly and to an even greater extent than in Ireland and core welfare rates were cut more modestly.

As remarkable as the size of this adjustment is, equally is the fact that it took place during a month of European and local elections. A subsequent budget in December led to the departure from government of the largest coalition party[99] and yet in spite of this the IMF in July of that year completed its third review of the Latvian economy under the assistance programme and deemed Latvia's progress sufficient to approve a further disbursement to the country. In spite of the depth of cuts and extent of political change, elections held the following October led to the re-election of the incumbent Prime Minister.

As in Greece, austerity produced political reaction in Latvia. But unlike Greece and much closer to Ireland's experience, Latvian political debate centred not about whether, but rather about how, austerity should be implemented. Furthermore the need for fiscal discipline – and in particular the need to maintain currency

---

[98]   Åslund, Anders and Dombrovskis, Valdis (2011). *How Latvia Came through the Financial Crisis*, Washington DC: Institute of International Economics.

[99]   The People's Party.

discipline – was supported by a public consensus that was strong enough to survive changes in the political make-up of government.

While Latvia faces strong social pressures and issues arising from the crisis, its success in overcoming severe fiscal and exchange rate pressures to become not only one of Europe's best economic growth performers but also the newest member of the Eurozone is impressive. At a time when many predicted that countries like Ireland and Greece might have to leave the Euro and that this could precipitate the break-up of the currency, the reverse has happened: Ireland and Greece remain inside the Euro at the time of writing and two new Member States – Estonia and Latvia – have joined its ranks since the crisis began. The expansion of the Euro in spite of such trying conditions is testament to the underlying strength of the European project.

Ireland

Ireland's progress in relation to its adjustment programme is discussed extensively in **Chapter 1** but a brief summary is provided here. In 2008 – in the infancy of the crisis – Ireland had already taken initiatives to begin fiscal consolidation. By 2009, work was already underway in Ireland to overhaul financial regulation and to tackle structural reform and public spending challenges. By 2010, Ireland had already made significant progress on this front, in spite of the need that year to avail of assistance in the form of a bailout. Ireland also made significant and early improvements to its current account balance position much earlier than peer countries, reflecting a decisive improvement in competitiveness. While not as abrupt or sudden as Latvia's, Ireland's adjustment programme has been successful. It is notable that in spite of Ireland's adjustment, its population has continued to increase due to high rates of childbirth as well as the fact that although youth emigration is high it is counterbalanced by continued significant immigration.

As noted in **Chapter 2**, Ireland has a business model that combines an excellent environment for international business, a competitive tax regime and clusters of high technology industry. It also benefits from a quickly adaptable policy regime that is constantly renewing and refocusing Ireland's economy to new trends and opportunities in the global economy. It has now exited its bailout successfully and without recourse to any emergency credit facility. Ireland has made progress also on job creation, with a notable and sizeable reduction in unemployment during the early stages of recovery.

Thanks to the very liberal and open economy that was already in place in Ireland before the crisis, the country has succeeded in coming out of crisis very quickly. However, the burden of the bank rescue continues to weigh on the economy. As an export nation ourselves, we in Germany are aware that, given the difficult climate on the "home market of Europe", it is not easy to increase exports. Nevertheless, the economy is growing, industrial output is stable, and even unemployment has started to fall, albeit slowly. However, this does not mean that an end to the Government debt crisis and the uncertainties on the financial markets has finally been achieved. There is still a lot to do. And we also still have to keep a watchful eye on a number of risks taken on board by the Eurozone countries and the ECB in the interests of overcoming the crisis.

Conclusion

It would be wrong to give up now, with the job half-done. All the reforms that have been put in place would be worth only half as much if they were to be stopped now or even reversed. The initial successes that have already been achieved are grounds for encouragement. They should serve as an incentive to continue along the same path, especially as there is now a slowly strengthening tailwind to provide an additional boost from behind.

Conclusion

The contributions collected in this book increase our understanding of what Ireland and Germany faced in this crisis. Each of the authors has taken seriously the point that, to avoid a repetition of crisis, we must learn from our experience, and we must do so quickly.

The crisis was a not just "a challenge" for us. It was a cruel blow to the livelihoods of families in Ireland and across Europe. It was also a serious threat to the European project itself. Ireland, Germany and all of Europe faced profound international scepticism, and we must acknowledge that it was sometimes warranted.

The recovery that is underway in Ireland and our exit from the EU/IMF programme, on schedule and with no strings attached, is something that Europe's critics have had to recognise as a real and substantial sign of progress. It was an achievement made possible by the determination of our people, and by the support of Germany and our other partners in Europe.

Ireland's return to a sustainable economic path is not the kind of progress that could have been achieved through ambiguous promises or gimmicks. It required painstaking planning, cooperation and delivery. We had to implement a very difficult set of decisions and reforms, with real consequences for families struggling to balance their household budgets every month. We had to deliver an adjustment of taxation and spending that by next year will amount to 20 per cent of our GDP, while trying to support economic growth and reduce unemployment.

I am glad to say that this difficult reality was recognised by our partners in Europe and that there was flexibility in terms of renegotiating key terms of the programme and reducing the interest rate. We were able also to find a solution to the issue of the Anglo Irish Bank promissory note. These were important factors in Ireland's successful exit from the programme.

This book does not pretend that Ireland's exit from the programme is either the end of the story, or the most important way that our efforts in partnership should be judged. Rather, we will – and should – be judged on how we manage economic recovery in a way that is felt in those same household budgets across Europe – jobs, growth and confidence in the future.

This book examines a lot of the issues we will have to face as we continue to drive the recovery within Ireland and across Europe. There remain important questions for us, including how we deliver on the promise we made as European leaders to break the vicious circle between bank and sovereign debt. Ireland faced the consequences of this destructive dynamic earlier than most and before there were structures in place to protect European financial stability. The Irish people are still living with the heavy legacy of that period.

I want to thank the German-Irish Chamber of Commerce, under the leadership of Ralf Lissek, for bringing together these contributors to advance the debate, and for their ongoing work to strengthen further the relationship between our countries.

What these articles do collectively is bring out with great clarity one of the distinctive features of the European project – that it is a dynamic union of both small and large states. What unites us above all as Member States is not equivalent size, or similar economies, or identical interests. It is a deeper relationship of peoples, and a commitment to a better, safer, more stable and, at the same time, more vibrant Europe.

Ireland will continue to play its part in that project and in the immediate task of driving Europe's economic recovery and its deeper cohesion. We know that, in doing so, we will be working in a spirit of true friendship and mutual support with Germany, and our partners all over Europe.

Eamon Gilmore
Tánaiste (Deputy Prime Minister) and Minister for Foreign Affairs and Trade

ANNEX I
Chronology of Crisis & Recovery

2008

14/15 March	Bear Stearns goes bankrupt. George Bush addresses economic conference in New York on global economy.
15 September	Lehman Brothers goes bankrupt, beginning a global liquidity crisis in which the interbank lending market ceases to function: the result is a funding crisis for banks.
18 September	Irish Financial Services Regulatory Authority introduces a ban on short selling of financial stocks.
30 September	Dáil Éireann enacts legislation guaranteeing deposits, loans and bonds worth €440bn for six domestic financial institutions: Allied Irish Banks, Anglo Irish Bank, Bank of Ireland, Irish Life and Permanent, EBS and Irish Nationwide.
14 October	Normally held in December, Ireland's Government brings forward the annual budget by two months in order to address the ensuing crisis and implements tax increases and spending reductions. A series of peaceful demonstrations ensued.
21 December	Government announces intention to inject €5.5bn into three main lenders: Bank of Ireland, Allied Irish Banks and Anglo Irish Bank.

2009

15 January	The Irish Government nationalises Anglo Irish Bank to prevent its collapse.
January	In emergency legislation, the Government introduces a levy on public servants to fund their pension entitlements.
11 February	The Irish Government announces intention to inject €7bn into Bank of Ireland and Allied Irish Banks and receives a 25 per cent stake in both banks.

March	To facilitate lending to Anglo Irish Bank – whose collateral did not meet the standard for Eurosystem monetary operations – the Central Bank of Ireland agrees to provide "Exceptional Liquidity Assistance" (see **Annex II: Glossary**). These loans were underwritten by the Irish Government under the *Credit Institutions Financial Stability Act, 2009* and resulted in the State acquiring obligations.
7 April	In the second emergency budget in just six months, the Irish Government implements significant increases in taxation.
April	The Government announces the intention to establish the National Asset Management Agency (NAMA), a vehicle designed to manage property loans from five financial institutions covered by the bank guarantee scheme enacted in September 2009 (see **Annex II: Glossary**).
29 May	The Irish Government injects €4bn into Anglo Irish Bank following rising losses at the institution.
September	NAMA is established.
9 December	In its third emergency budget in just 14 months, the Irish Government implements cuts in public service pay and social welfare payments. The domestic economy in the following year shows a modest recovery in terms of Gross National Product (see **Chapter 4**), which rises by 0.5 per cent year on year.

2010

19 February	The Government takes its first direct stake in Bank of Ireland.
March	The Government concludes the so-called "Croke Park Agreement" with public sector unions. This commits the unions to reforms and a pay freeze in return for a commitment to no further reductions in pay or pensions.
30 March	NAMA buys its first batch of property loans from Irish banks at a discount of 47 per cent. This higher discount requires affected banks to raise more capital than previously thought necessary. The Central Bank requires lenders to hold a minimum of 8 per cent Tier 1 capital by the end of the year. The Government injects a further €8.3bn into Anglo Irish Bank and takes control of Irish Nationwide.
31 March	Anglo Irish Bank reports the biggest corporate loss in Irish history (€12.7bn).
13 May	The Government takes an 18 per cent stake in Allied Irish Banks.
9 June	The State injects a further €3bn into Bank of Ireland.

25 August	Standard and Poor's cuts Ireland's long-term bond rating to AA. This follows a cut in July by Moody's and is followed by further warnings of likely future downgrades.
30 September	The Central Bank of Ireland estimates that the final State injection into the banking system could be as high as €34.3bn, considerably higher than previous estimates.
October	The *Central Bank Reform Act, 2010* creates a new, reformed and fully integrated Central Bank of Ireland to oversee Ireland's financial and banking system. The Act also raises obligations on financial service providers to control lending and compliance and extends the powers of the Central Bank to police the banking system.
November	The Government agrees to an €85bn rescue package with the EU and IMF in return for a four-year programme of tax increases and spending cuts.
7 December	Reversing the policy of the previous year, the Irish Government implements a budget focusing on tax increases. The domestic economy, as measured by GNP, returns to negative growth in 2011 after a year of modest recovery

2011

February	A month after Dáil Éireann approves the Finance Bill enacting the previous December's budget, the Government collapses and an election is held in which the main opposition Fine Gael party falls just short of a majority and a Fine Gael-Labour coalition is formed.
1 July	The Irish Bank Resolution Corporation is formed following a court order. This formalises the State's take-over of Anglo Irish Bank and Irish Nationwide Building Society.
July	Moody's downgrades Ireland's debt rating. As part of a wider reform of public finances, the Government establishes the Irish Fiscal Advisory Council (IFAC) to monitor government fiscal policy.
December	The Irish Government introduces a budget balancing tax increases and spending cuts.

2012

June	Irish voters approve by a substantial majority to enshrine the *Treaty on Stability, Co-ordination and Governance in the Economic and Monetary Union* into the Irish *Constitution*.

December	The Irish Government's budget pursues a policy of mixing tax increases with spending reductions. The Government implements the *Fiscal Responsibility Act, 2012* to give statutory effect to the approval of the *Treaty on Stability, Co-ordination and Governance in the Economic and Monetary Union*.

2013

February	With ECB approval, the Irish Bank Resolution Corporation (see above) is liquidated. Its debts are assumed by the Irish Exchequer but on more favourable terms: the interest rate on debt is reduced and repayment of the principal of the debt is deferred from 2023 until 2053. This move results in significant savings to the Irish Exchequer.
July	IFAC (see above) is put on a financially independent footing to enhance its freedom and independence in commenting on budgetary policy.
19 September	Official economic statistics confirm the return of GDP to growth in the second quarter of 2012.
15 October	In the first budget implemented under the terms of the *Fiscal Responsibility Act, 2012*, the Irish Government's forecasts are approved by IFAC. The balance in this budget shifts more clearly in the direction of reducing expenditure.
26 November	Official employment figures confirm a rise of 3.8 per cent in the numbers of full-time employed in the economy. The figures also confirm that the rate of employment growth is increasing.
18 December	The Irish Government publishes *A Strategy for Growth*, which aims to attain full employment and reduce public debt by one quarter between 2014 and 2020.

ANNEX II
Glossary

Croke Park Agreement: An agreement between the Irish Government and Ireland's public service unions covering the civil service and State agency sector between 2010 and 2014 and agreed in March 2010. Following cuts in public service pay and pensions implemented during 2009, the agreement – so called because it was concluded after trade union meetings in Croke Park – set out an action plan for public service reform and a reduction in public service numbers in return for a ban on any further cuts in public service pay or pension rates. The agreement was widely criticised for preserving rates of public sector pay that, in some areas, are seen to be too high. In 2014, the Croke Park Agreement was replaced by the so-called "Haddington Road Agreement" (see below).

Eligible Liabilities Guarantee: The Credit Institutions (Eligible Liabilities Guarantee) Scheme came into effect on December 2009 and provides for unconditional and irrevocable State guarantees for specified bank liabilities (including deposits) up to five years in maturity by participating institutions joining the scheme. The scheme is operated by the National Treasury Management Agency (NTMA) (see below). The inclusion in the scheme of senior unsecured bonds and notes was a matter of public controversy and resulted in obligations of some €35bn to bondholders in Anglo Irish Bank and other institutions. These obligations were subsumed into the Irish Bank Resolution Corporation and in 2013 became part of Ireland's national debt under a deal to restructure Ireland's bank related so-called "promissory note" debt.

European Financial Stability Facility (EFSF): The European Financial Stability Facility was created by the Euro area Member States on 9 May 2010 within the framework of the Ecofin Council. With a mandate is to safeguard financial stability in Europe by providing financial assistance to Euro area Member States within the framework of a macro-economic adjustment programmes, it can borrow up to €440bn and raises loans with the support of the Deutsche Finanz Agentur (German Finance Agency). Its first bonds were issued in January 2011 and over 2011 and 2012 it provided some €18bn in lending to Ireland. Since September 2012, the EFSM has been confined to handling money transfers and programme monitoring for Ireland, Portugal and Greece and its broader functions have been subsumed by the European Stability Mechanism (ESM) (see below)

European Financial Stability Mechanism (EFSM): In operation since May 2010, this fund was created as a response to the Euro crisis. Backed by the EU Commission, the fund is supported by EU Member States and can raise up to

€60bn. Under the "Troika programme", the EFSM provided loans of €22.4bn to Ireland between 2010 and 2013. Since September 2012, the EFSM has been confined to handling money transfers and programme monitoring for Ireland, Portugal and Greece and its broader functions have been subsumed by the European Stability Mechanism (ESM) (see below)

European Stability Mechanism (ESM): Established in September 2012, this aims to safeguard Eurozone Member States in difficulty by providing instant access to financial assistance. As a result of the *Fiscal Stability Treaty* (see below), the ESM was established replacing most of the functions of the European Financial Stability Mechanism (EFSM) and European Financial Stability Facility (EFSF) (see above). It receives paid-in capital from Eurozone countries of up to €700bn and can approve bailouts of up to €500bn (the remaining being retained as a capital reserve). Ireland's bailout accounted for €67.5bn.

European System of Central Banks (ESCB): The ESCB is the group of all central banks and includes the ECB and the central banks of all EU Member States (including those not in the Eurozone).

European Systemic Risk Board (ESRB): Established in December 2010, this board is tasked with macro-prudential oversight of the EU's financial system. The ESRB is hosted and supported by the European Central Bank (ECB).

Eurosystem: The Eurosystem is the monetary authority of the Eurozone and encompasses the European Central Banks (ECB) and the central banks of individual Eurozone Member States.

Exceptional Liquidity Assistance (ELA): This was a lending facility provided by Ireland's Central Bank to Anglo Irish Bank in 2009. From late 2008, financial markets had ceased lending to the institution and when its assets declined sharply in value it was not able to offer counterparty collateral for standard Eurosystem refinancing operations conducted by the European System of Central Banks (ESCB) (see above). Instead under a "Master Loan Repurchase Agreement" a series of loans were made from the Central Bank to Anglo Irish Bank. The total value of these loans reached €38.4bn by mid-2011. As direct funding of banks by the European System of Central Banks (ESCB) is prohibited[100] under legal statutes governing it, these loans required the Irish Government to assume ultimate responsibility for them. Thus they became the responsibility of Irish taxpayers in the form of a "promissory note" (see below)

---

[100] However Article 32.4 of the legal statue governing the Eurosystem states that "The Governing Coucil may decide that national central banks shall be indemnified against cost incurred in connection with the issue of banknotes or in exceptional circumstances for specific losses arising from monetary policy operations taken for the ESCB". This has been taken by some as a vague justification for the ESCB sharing Ireland's ELA loan losses (Whelan, Karl "ELA, Promissory Notes and All That: The Fiscal Costs of Anglo Irish Bank", UCD Working Paper Series WP12/06 February 2012).

issued by the Government as a form of collateral to banks availing of ELA loans from the Irish Central Bank.

Fiscal Stability Treaty / Fiscal Compact Treaty: See *Treaty on Stability, Co-ordination and Governance in the Economic and Monetary Union*.

Haddington Road Agreement: An agreement concluded between the Irish Government and Irish public service unions in May 2013, and taking effect from 1 July 2013, to achieve €1bn in reduced public pay costs by 2015. The agreement includes a commitment to reduce pay levels in excess of €65,000 a year, along with a commitment to greater flexibility in work practices and restructuring.

Irish Bank Resolution Corporation (IBRC): The IBRC arose from the merging in 2011 of Ireland's two most troubled banks, Anglo Irish Bank and Irish Nation wide Building Society. Under the *Credit Institutions Stabilisation Act, 2010*, the latter's assets and liabilities were transferred to Anglo Irish Bank and a new merged entity was created.

Irish Fiscal Advisory Council (IFAC): Established in 2011, IFAC is an independent body monitoring Ireland's adherence to EU budgetary and fiscal strictures. Following the ratification of the *Fiscal Stability Treaty* (see above), IFAC was put on a statutory footing in 2013 and approved Ireland's budget for the first time in October 2013.

Irish Strategic Investment Fund (ISIF): Expected to be created in 2014, the ISIF is an investment vehicle to channel €6.4bn worth of assets held by the National Pension Reserve Fund (NPRF) (see below) into areas of strategic importance to Ireland to support growth and job creation in the years ahead. Areas of importance include investment in infrastructure and lending to small and medium-sized enterprises.

National Asset Management Agency (NAMA): NAMA was established in December 2009 to take ownership of troubled property loans and underlying assets from Irish banks, thus assisting the repair of their balance sheets. Loans with a book value of €77bn – but an estimated 2009 market value of €47bn – were purchased from five troubled financial institutions for €54bn in exchange for bonds which were then used as collateral. The premium paid for the loans in excess of the 2009 market value reflected the confidence at the time that Ireland's recovery would ensure a return on this investment.

National Pension Reserve Fund (NPRF): The NPRF was established in 2001 to meet as much as possible of the cost of Ireland's social welfare and public service pensions from 2025 onwards. The NPRF is controlled and managed by the NTMA. In 2009, NPRF resources were used for the purposes of bank recapitalisation and in 2010 regular payments into the fund were suspended. In September 2011, the Government announced its intention to establish the Irish Strategic Investment Fund (ISIF) (see above) which will channel resources from the NPRF towards productive investment in the Irish economy.

National Treasury Management Agency (NTMA): This State body has a commercial remit to provide asset and liability management services to government. It has evolved from a single function agency – managing solely Ireland's national debt – to managing a more complex mix of public assets and liabilities including the National Pension Reserve Fund (NPRF) (see above), National Asset Management Agency (NAMA) and others.

Primary Budget Balance: This is a measure of the Government's fiscal balance, which excludes the impact of annual interest debt payments. It helps give a clearer picture of the State's ability to meet standard day-to-day public spending obligations from taxation.

Promissory Note: This is a legal instrument with which a borrower promises in writing to pay a sum of money to a payee. In order to enable Irish banks to avail of ELA financing, the Irish Government issued them with promissory notes that could be used as collateral with Ireland's Central Bank (See "Exceptional Liquidity Assistance" above). These notes were transferred to the Irish Bank Resolution Corporation (IBRC) (see above) and on February 6 2013 this bank was liquidated and the promissory note debt was transformed into Irish Government bonds.

Single Resolution Mechanism (SRM): Agreed in December 2013 (but at the time of writing not yet finalised), the proposed *Banking Recovery and Resolution Directive* will make losses for senior bondholders and large savers a permanent feature of the EU's response to banking crises. The objective is to end taxpayer funded bailouts of European banks. A key outstanding issue is whether – as suggested by the terms of an agreement at an EU summit in June 2012 – Ireland's bank bailout, which incurred significant taxpayer costs to bailing out bondholders (see ELA above), will be subject to retrospective inclusion in the terms of the SRM.

Single Supervisory Mechanism (SSM): This is a mechanism established under the SRM (see above) to monitor EU banks. The SSM will be hosted by the European Central Bank and will begin its first supervisory reports at the end of 2014.

Structurally Adjusted Budget Balance: This is a measure of a government's fiscal balance which corrects for the impact of the economic cycle to give a clearer measure of the governments underlying fiscal discipline.

***Treaty on Stability, Co-ordination and Governance in the Economic and Monetary Union*:** Referred to as the "Fiscal Stability Treaty", this is an intergovernmental treaty signed on March 2012 by all Member States of the EU except the Czech Republic and UK and which entered into force on 1 January 2013. It binds participating countries to introduce "implementation law" establishing targets, guidelines, monitoring procedures and disciplines according to the fiscal objectives laid out in the Treaty. Ireland is the only country to have ratified the Treaty in a public referendum in June 2012.

Irland und Deutschland:
Partner im Europäischen Aufschwung

Irland hat eine erstaunliche Erholung erlebt. Diese ist von großer Bedeutung nicht nur für die Iren, deren Opferbereitschaft diesen Aufschwung möglich gemacht hat, sondern auch für die Menschen in Deutschland und in Europa insgesamt. Die Schicksale von Irland und Deutschland stehen nun in enger Beziehung, was beiden Ländern große Vorteile bringt: Die deutsche und die EU-Hilfe für Irland werden sich für Deutschland und Europa bezahlt machen. Dies ist bereits durch die Art und Weise erwiesen, wie Irland die starke deutsche Unterstützung zur Stabilisierung seiner eigenen Volkswirtschaft genutzt und damit zur Stabilisierung des Euros beigetragen hat. Durch frühzeitige finanzielle Konsolidierung und energische Reformen bei der Finanzregulierung und beim Risikomanagement hat Irland gezeigt, dass ein Umschwung möglich ist. In diesem Buch wird Irlands Beitrag zur Stabilisierung des Euros aus verschiedenen deutschen wie auch irischen Blickwinkeln und aus der Perspektive unterschiedlicher Geschäftsfelder sowie der Politik beleuchtet. Neben einem tiefgehenden Verständnis der Krise und des Aufschwungs bietet diese Mischung verschiedener Betrachtungsweisen spannende Impulse und Botschaften für die gemeinsame Zukunft beider Länder. Das Buch hebt hervor, wie wichtig es ist, das wettbewerbsfähige irische Geschäftsmodell aufrechtzuerhalten und zu vertiefen. Die europäische Unterstützung ist für Irland unabdingbar. Das Land muss seine zentralen Wettbewerbsvorteile erhalten, um die verbleibenden Aufgaben für die irische Wirtschaft zu bewältigen. Das Bankensystem muss repariert werden, neuer Schwung ist nötig, um durch Innovation und Internationalisierung zur Vollbeschäftigung zurückzukehren. Darüber hinaus zeigt das Buch auf, wie die Zusammenarbeit zwischen der größten und einer der kleinsten EU-Nationen geholfen hat, Europas Wirtschaft durch eine schwere Krise zu führen und eine Herausforderung zu überstehen, die sie bei einer getrennten Herangehensweise durchaus hätte zerstören können. Und schließlich erinnert uns dieses Buch daran, dass das europäische Projekt – trotz seiner Kritiker und Gegner – stets eine Erfolgsgeschichte war und noch immer ist.

Ralf Lissek, Geschäftsführer der Deutsch-Irischen Industrie-und Handelskammer überreicht Jean-Claude Juncker eine der ersten Ausgaben von "Irland und Deutschland: Partner im Europäischen Aufschwung".

Irland und Deutschland: Partner im Europäischen Aufschwung

Ralf Lissek und Marc Coleman
Herausgeber

Herausgeber
OAK TREE PRESS
19 Rutland Street, Cork, Irland
www.oaktreepress.com / www.SuccessStore.com

Eine Titelaufnahme dieses Buchs liegt bei der British Library vor.

ISBN 978 1 78119 141 5 (gebundene Ausgabe)
ISBN 978 1 78119 142 2 (broschierte Ausgabe)
ISBN 978 1 78119 143 9 (ePub-Format)
ISBN 978 1 78119 144 6 (Kindle)

Umschlagfoto: Thinkstock.co.uk
Umschlagdesign von Kieran O'Connor Design.

Für die einzelnen Kapitel sind die jeweiligen Autoren verantwortlich. Die
darin vertretenen Meinungen werden von der Deutsch-Irischen
Handelskammer sowie vom Verlag nicht unbedingt geteilt. Weder die
AHK Irland noch der Verlag können für etwaige Fehler oder
Auslassungen in den Übersetzungen verantwortlich gemacht werden.

Inhaltsverzeichnis

Illustrationen

Die Autoren

Ralf Lissek (Herausgeber / Autor, **Kapitel 1** und **Kommentar / Kapitel 7**), AHK Dublin (Deutsch-Irische Industrie- und Handelskammer), Geschäftsführer und Initiator dieses Buches.

John Corrigan (Autor, **Kommentar / Kapitel 1**), National Treasury Management Agency, Hauptgeschäftsführer.

Dr. Jack Golden (Autor, **Kapitel 2**), CRH, Direktor Organisationsentwicklung.

Frank Mee (Autor, **Kommentar / Kapitel 2**), Allianz Worldwide Care, Direktor Finanzen und Informationstechnologie.

Dr. Peter Breuer (Autor, **Kapitel 3**), IWF, Wirtschaftswissenschaftler, Landeskoordinator für Irland.

Marc Coleman (Herausgeber / Autor, **Kapitel 4** und **Kommentar / Kapitel 7**), Wirtschaftswissenschaftler, Broadcaster, ehemaliger EZB-Ökonom.

Brian Hayes (Autor, **Kommentar / Kapitel 4**), Ministerium für öffentliche Ausgaben und Reform, Staatsminister.

Dr. Stefan Gerlach (Autor, **Kapitel 5**), Irische Zentralbank, Stellvertretender Präsident.

Werner Schwanberg (Autor, **Kommentar / Kapitel 5**), WGZ Bank Ireland, Geschäftsführer.

Christoph Müller (Autor, **Kapitel 6**), Aer Lingus, Vorstandsvorsitzender.

Dr. Eric Schweitzer (Autor, **Kapitel 7**), Deutsche Industrie- und Handelskammertag (DIHK), Präsident.

Dr. Joachim Pfeiffer (Autor, **Kapitel 8**), CDU/CSU, Sprecher der Arbeitsgruppe Wirtschaft und Energie im deutschen Bundestag.

Dr. Volker Treier (Autor, **Kapitel 9**), Deutsche Industrie- und Handelskammertag (DIHK), Stellvertretender Hauptgeschäftsführer.

Danksagung

Wir möchten uns bei allen bedanken, die beim Verfassen und bei der Erstellung von *Irland und Deutschland: Partner im Europäischen Aufschwung* mitgewirkt haben, einschließlich Farid Assouad, Ralph Biedinger, Gabriel D'Arcy, Helen Dunne, Jean Fleming, Franziska Gross, Uli Hoppe, Victor Hrymak, Declan Kearney, Clare Lissek, Alan Manahan, Yvonne McCarthy, Brian Murphy, Ilja Notnagel, Johnny Pollock, Paul Sheehy, Sean Sheehy, Sandra Sheeran, Laurence Simms, Tony Spollen, Niamh Sweeney – und Brian O'Kane, dem Publisher, für seine Geduld.

Ralf Lissek und Marc Coleman, Herausgeber

Vorwort

Irland und Deutschland haben schon seit Langem sehr gute Beziehungen, sowohl politisch, kulturell als auch wirtschaftlich. Unser Verhältnis ist in der Tat so gut wie nie zuvor.

Unser Verhältnis hat sich über die letzten Jahre vertieft und intensiviert. Wir haben gemeinsam daran gearbeitet, Europa voranzutreiben, insbesondere während der irischen Ratspräsidentschaft im letzten Jahr.

Die irischen Ratspräsidentschaften trafen oft mit den wichtigsten Entwicklungen für unsere Länder und für Europa zusammen – zum Beispiel der deutschen Wiedervereinigung 1990 und dem Beitritt von 10 neuen Mitgliedsstaaten im Jahr 2004. Unsere Ratspräsidentschaft 2013 war hier keine Ausnahme, da wir zu Zeiten ernster Herausforderungen gemeinsam daran gearbeitet haben, Stabilität, Arbeit und Wachstum für Europa zu schaffen.

Wir in Irland sind entschlossen, auf unseren Erfolgen aufzubauen und unsere Verbindungen auch in der Zukunft weiter zu stärken. Dabei bauen wir auf festem Grund und können bereits jetzt Anzeichen für vermehrten Handel, Beschäftigung und Tourismus erkennen.

Das gesamte Handelsvolumen zwischen unseren beiden Ländern beläuft sich zurzeit auf mehr als 23 Mrd. Euro. Wenn auch das Gesamtvolumen des Warenhandels im Jahr 2013 zurückgegangen ist, so hat doch unser Getränke- und Lebensmittelsektor eine beeindruckende Zunahme von Exporten nach Deutschland in Höhe von 22 Prozent erfahren. Wie günstig diese Handelsbeziehung für beide Seiten ist, demonstriert auch die Zunahme der Importe aus Deutschland um 8 Prozent.

Die Zahl der deutschen Touristen in Irland nahm zu; erste Zahlen für 2013 deuten auf einen Rekord von fast einer halben Million Besuchern hin. Bessere Flugverbindungen zwischen unseren beiden Ländern lassen auf positive Aussichten für 2014 hoffen.

Ich spreche der Deutsch-Irischen Industrie- und Handelskammer meine Anerkennung für die Veröffentlichung dieses Buches aus. Ich weiß, dass die Kammer die umfangreichen Geschäftsbeziehungen zwischen irischen und deutschen Unternehmen unterstützt. Mehr als 300 deutsche Unternehmen beschäftigen rund 20.000 Menschen in Irland. Handel und Investitionen funktionieren jedoch in beiden Richtungen, denn 58 irische Unternehmen bieten Beschäftigung für 14.000 Menschen in Deutschland, und 480 irische Unternehmen exportieren qualitativ hochwertige Produkte und Dienstleistungen nach Deutschland.

Die deutsche Wirtschaft hat auch 2013 weiterhin Wachstum verbuchen können und erwartet für 2014 weiteres starkes Wachstum durch erhöhtes Handelsaufkommen und gestiegene Konsumausgaben. Die irische Botschaft in Berlin, die eng mit den Regierungsbehorden kooperiert, arbeitet mit unseren Partnern an den Bereichen, die für unseren anhaltenden Aufschwung unverzichtbar sind. Dazu gehört die Unterstützung für die Arbeit der Deutsch-Irischen Industrie- und Handelskammer, zum Beispiel im letzten Dezember, als die Botschaft zur deutschen Präsentation der von der Kammer herausgegebenen Veröffentlichung „German-Irish Business: Eine Erfolgsgeschichte" eingeladen hatte.

Ich finde es wichtig, daran zu erinnern, dass die EU – trotz aller Herausforderungen – eine Erfolgsgeschichte ist. Deutschland und Irland haben sowohl gemeinsam als auch durch ihre ureigenen Beiträge Schlüsselfunktionen in dieser Erfolgsgeschichte übernommen. Ich bin überzeugt, dass wir das auch weiterhin tun werden. Es gibt noch viel zu tun, und wir wissen: Wenn wir unsere gemeinsamen Anstrengungen zur Stabilisierung der Wirtschaft aufrechterhalten, kommen wir gemeinsam erfolgreich aus der Krise. Die deutsch-irischen Beziehungen werden immer besser. Ich bin voller Zuversicht für unsere zukünftigen gemeinsamen Unterfangen.

Enda Kenny TD
An Taoiseach (irischer Premierminister)
Februar 2014

Zusammenfassung

2008 bis 2020: Der Weg zur Erholung

Irlands Bilanz an ausländischen Direktinvestitionen und exportgetragenem Wachstum ist die stärkste in ganz Europa, unterstützt von der Rolle als europäische Anlaufstelle für US-amerikanische Unternehmen. Irlands Erholung spiegelt dies wider. Sie versetzt das Land in eine ganz andere Lage im Vergleich zu den anderen Teilnehmern an EU/IWF-Hilfsprogrammen. Für Irland Es bleiben schwere Aufgaben im Hinblick auf Verschuldung, öffentliche Ausgaben und nötige Strukturreformen.

Irlands Aufschwung – dessen Fortsetzung bis 2020 prognostiziert wird – beruht auf mehreren Faktoren: seiner anpassungsfähigen Bevölkerung; dem politischen Bekenntnis zu Reformen; einer dynamischen Unternehmerschaft; und dem bereits erwähnten Erfolg beim Anwerben ausländischer Direktinvestitionen, der die Insel zum führenden europäischen Standort für multinationale Unternehmen gemacht hat. All diese Qualitäten in Irland zu erhalten, ist auch für die Erholung Europas unerlässlich. Die Iren sind dabei auf die Unterstützung ihrer EU-Partner angewiesen.

KOMMENTAR: Irlands Wiederaufschwung

Im November 2010 verlor Irland das Vertrauen der Anleger und musste um ein EU/IWF-Hilfsprogramm bitten. Damals entschloss sich die NTMA dazu, aktiv auf die Anleger zuzugehen. Damit sollten die Voraussetzungen für Irlands spätere Rückkehr auf die Märkte am Ende des Hilfsprogramms geschaffen werden. Mit der durchgängigen Übererfüllung der im EU/IWF-Programm festgelegten finanziellen Zielvorgaben durch die Regierung, der transparenten und glaubwürdigen Durchführung der Rekapitalisierung und Umstrukturierung der irischen Banken im Jahr 2011 und mit der Wiederherstellung der Wettbewerbsfähigkeit in der Wirtschaft wurde das Vertrauen der Anleger allmählich wiedergewonnen.

Mitte des Jahres 2011, als die Zinserträge historische Höchststände erreichten, entschieden sich US-Anleger – überwiegend, aber nicht ausschließlich Hedgefonds – zum Kauf irischer Staatsanleihen. Später kamen auch eher traditionelle „Real-Money"-Investoren in den Markt zurück. Sie ersetzten die Hedgefonds, als die Zinserträge fielen. Auch Entwicklungen in Europa unterstützten die Fortschritte Irlands: vor allem Mario Draghis Versprechen, „alles zu tun"; das Arrangement hinsichtlich der IBRC-Schuldverschreibungen; und die Laufzeitverlängerung für Irlands EFSF- und EFSM-Darlehen. Nach Irlands Ausstieg aus dem Programm ohne vorsorgliche Kreditlinie im Dezember 2013 konnte die NTMA Anfang Januar 2014

3,75 Mrd. Euro in den Märkten beschaffen. Seit Irland wieder normal am Marktgeschehen teilnimmt, sind weitere Emissionen in Form regelmäßiger Auktionen geplant.

Irlands Geschäftsmodell

Irland hat Belastbarkeit und Flexibilität bei der Anpassung seines Wirtschafts- und Geschäftsmodells bewiesen, nicht nur in dieser Krise, sondern auch über vier Jahrzehnte als Teil des Projektes Europa. Dies erklärt seinen Übergang von einer kleinen Agrarwirtschaft, deren Exporte von Großbritannien dominiert wurden, zu einer der weltweit am stärksten globalisierten und vielseitigsten Volkswirtschaften.

Es bleiben bedeutsame Herausforderungen, um das volle Potenzial des dynamischen Wirtschaftsmodells Irlands auszuschöpfen, wie zum Beispiel die Überwindung der mangelnden Kreditvergabe an Unternehmen und die Verbesserung der Exportfähigkeit von KMU bei gleichzeitiger Beibehaltung des günstigen irischen Steuersystems.

KOMMENTAR: Eine Fallstudie zu ausländischen Direktinvestitionen in Irland: Allianz Worldwide Care Limited

Viele weltweit agierende internationale Finanzdienstleister unterhalten heute Standorte in Irland aufgrund einer Kombination von Erfolgsfaktoren, von denen das irische Steuersystem nur einer ist. Die Allianz Gruppe, die 144.000 Mitarbeiter beschäftigt und 78 Mio Kunden hat, ist ein gutes Beispiel dafür.

Ein stabiles Geschäftsumfeld, unterstützende Regierungsbehörden und der Zugang zu gut ausgebildeten und unternehmerisch denkenden Mitarbeitern ermöglichten dem Finanzdienstleistungssektor ein starkes Wachstum und eine schnelle Erholung nach der Krise. Um Irlands Wettbewerbsfähigkeit aufrechtzuerhalten, müssen jedoch die nach wie vor hohen Kosten in Angriff genommen werden, die der Wirtschaft durch ihre geschützteren Sektoren auferlegt werden.

Reaktion auf die Krise und weitere bestehende Herausforderungen

Zwar liegt Irlands Wachstumsrate unterhalb der anfänglichen Prognosen, doch hat sie den Durchschnitt des Euroraums übertroffen. Es gibt Anzeichen für eine Erholung. Nach der deutlichen Erhöhung des Haushaltsdefizits und dem steilen Anstieg der Staatsverschuldung während der Krise hat eine schrittweise Konsolidierung die Finanzlage deutlich verbessert, ohne den Zusammenhalt der Gesellschaft zu gefährden. Reformen des Bankensektors nach der Krise haben zur finanziellen Stabilität beigetragen.

Eine weiterhin entschlossene Umsetzung politischer Entscheidungen an verschiedenen Fronten ist vonnöten, bevor die Einschätzung gestattet ist, Irland

habe sich vollständig von der Krise erholt. Haushaltsdefizit und Staatsverschuldung sind weiterhin hoch. In den nächsten Jahren ist eine weitere Konsolidierung notwendig. Die Schulden müssen kontinuierlich sinken, damit Irlands Rückkehr zur Marktfinanzierung von Dauer ist. Intensive Bemühungen müssen darauf abzielen, dass Banken und Hypothekenschuldner, die mit ihren Rückzahlungen im Rückstand sind, zu dauerhaften Lösungen kommen. Dann kann eine Neubelebung des Kreditgeschäfts zu einer nachhaltigen Erholung der Binnennachfrage beitragen.

Ausgaben und Reform: Neuer Schwung

Irlands finanzpolitische Anpassungen waren eindrucksvoll und systematisch. Die Regierung hat versucht, schwächere Teile der Gesellschaft abzusichern. Gleichzeitig hat sie die Effizienz des öffentlichen Sektors verbessert und Senkungen bei den Gehältern im öffentlichen Dienst erreicht.

Während die Effizienz des öffentlichen Sektors größer geworden ist – es wird nun mit weniger Ressourcen mehr getan –, besteht nun die größte Herausforderung für Irland darin, die Wirksamkeit öffentlicher Ausgaben zu beurteilen. Auch liegen die Gehälter im öffentlichen Dienst trotz erheblicher Kürzungen weiterhin deutlich über denen der Eurozone. Dafür ist eine eingehendere Analyse der Gründe und eine Rechtfertigung notwendig.

Das neue Ministerium für öffentliche Ausgaben und Reform (Department of Public Expenditure and Reform) wirkt auf größere Effizienz und Wirksamkeit hin. Neuen Reformplänen zufolge, die 2014 veröffentlicht werden sollen, wird sich der Schwerpunkt von der Senkung der Kosten für die Bereitstellung öffentlicher Dienste hin zur Verbesserung der Qualität der öffentlichen Dienste verlagern.

KOMMENTAR: Die Reformdividende

Der öffentliche Dienst in Irland steht vor der beispiellosen Herausforderung, Leistungen schneller, besser und kostengünstiger als bisher bereitzustellen. Zu diesem Zweck wurden Reformpläne in zwei Schritten veröffentlicht, der erste im November 2011 und der zweite im Januar 2014.

Der erste Plan war bedingt durch die Notwendigkeit, die öffentlichen Ausgaben zu reduzieren. Dabei lag der Schwerpunkt klar auf Kosten und Effizienz. Der zweite Plan wird den Umfang der Reformen ausweiten und die Leistung und Effektivität des öffentlichen Dienstes verbessern.

Banken und Finanzen: Zurück zur Stabilität

Das irische Bankensystem ist neu geordnet, deutlich kleiner und wesentlich besser reguliert aus der Krise gekommen.

Neben den übergreifenden europäischen Strukturen – wie zum Beispiel dem Einheitlichen Bankenaufsichtsmechanismus (SSM), der vorsieht, dass die EZB die Verantwortung für eine europaweite Finanzaufsicht übernimmt – hat es der irische

Bankensektor auch zuhause mit strengerer Regulierung zu tun. Dafür sorgen das neue Zentralbankgesetz, strengere Eigenkapitalanforderungen und ein verbessertes Risikomanagement.

Hypothekenzahlungsruckstande, fortdauernde Abhängigkeit von kurzfristigen Finanzierungen und andere Finanzierungsrisiken stellen den irischen Bankensektor vor anhaltende Herausforderungen. Eine Umstrukturierung ist im Gange. Dabei gilt dem Problem des schwachen Kreditflusses an kleine und mittlere Unternehmen besonderes Augenmerk. Die Regierung muss sich damit in ihrer mittelfristigen Wirtschaftsstrategie auseinandersetzen.

KOMMENTAR: Das International Financial Services Centre während der Bankenkrise: eine IFSC-Perspektive

Obwohl es eine Vielzahl unterschiedlicher internationaler Finanzorganisationen beherbergte, war das IFSC nicht Teil der irischen Finanzkrise. Nur wenige Firmen im IFSC gerieten durch die Krise in Schwierigkeiten, und auch diese nahmen keine Hilfe durch das Rettungsprogramm in Anspruch.

Dennoch unterliegt das IFSC infolge der Krise nun einer verbesserten Ordnung. Die finanzwirtschaftliche Regulierung hat das Vertrauen in den irischen Finanzsektor wiederhergestellt, die Ratingsagenturen haben das Land aufgewertet. Die neue Regulierung verfolgt einen verhältnismäßigen und risikobasierten Ansatz.

Die Dynamik des irischen Arbeitsmarktes

Auch während der Krise blieb Irland ein ausgezeichneter Standort für Unternehmen. Durch die Wiederherstellung der verlorenen Wettbewerbsfähigkeit und die Umsetzung von Strukturreformen zielt die Regierung darauf ab, Irland in dieser Dekade zum besten kleineren Land der Welt für Unternehmen zu machen.

Dafür sind Investitionen in die Ausbildung, insbesondere von Facharbeitern, ausschlaggebend. Sie sollten sich auf den zukünftigen Bedarf des Arbeitsmarktes konzentrieren. Die politischen Rahmenbedingungen müssen jetzt geschaffen werden.

Deutschlands Mittelstand: Die sieben Säulen des Erfolgs

Der Erfolg der deutschen Wirtschaft in den vergangenen Jahren ist zu einem großen Teil den großen Anstrengungen der Wirtschaftsunternehmen des Landes zu verdanken. Interne Umstrukturierungen, gekoppelt an eine zunehmende internationale Ausrichtung, sowie Investitionen in Forschung und Entwicklung bildeten den Grundstein hierfür. Der Prozess wurde seitens der Regierung durch Arbeitsmarktreformen und das Körperschaftssteuersystem unterstützt.

Deutschland ist ein starker Standort mit einer ungewöhnlichen Mischung an Unternehmen. Es ist die Heimat von erfolgreichen, großen, öffentlich notierten

Firmen, unzähligen hochengagierten kleinen Geschäften – und einem breiten Mittelstand. Diese Firmen, in vielen Fällen im Familienbesitz, stehen nicht immer im Rampenlicht. Sie sind dennoch hoch innovativ und – als „hidden Champions" – erfolgreich auf den Weltmärkten.

KOMMENTAR: Ist ein irischer Mittelstand möglich?
Die geringe Größe des Landes war bisher ein Hindernis, wenn es darum ging, kleine und mittlere Unternehmen in Irland zu einer kostengünstigen Größe zu führen. Dies beeinträchtigte wiederum die Exportkapazitäten dieses Sektors. Immerhin hat ein florierender KMU-Sektor die Krise überlebt. Er zeigt viele der für den deutschen Mittelstand typischen Eigenschaften. Dazu gehört in einigen Teilsektoren ein starker Außenhandel.

Der Sektor wird durch eine dynamische Regierungspolitik unterstützt, jedoch gibt es erhebliche Herausforderungen. Dazu gehören der Zugang zu Krediten sowie das Erreichen einer für den Export notwendigen Größe. Unter den richtigen Bedingungen könnten irische Unternehmen mit der Zeit für den Dienstleistungssektor den Erfolg nachbilden, den der deutsche Mittelstand im verarbeitenden Sektor erreicht hat. In ihrer mittelfristigen Wirtschaftsstrategie („Medium Term Economic Strategy") schaut die Regierung auf andere Länder, insbesondere auf Deutschland, und sucht nach Anregungen, wie sie KMU besser helfen kann. Dabei erschließen sich für beide Länder viele positive Möglichkeiten zum Austausch bewährter Konzepte und Verfahren. Insbesondere die deutsche Langfristorientierung und damit zusammenhängend die Unterstützung durch ein starkes Finanz- und Ausbildungssystem könnten dem irischen KMU-Sektor bei der Ausschöpfung seines Potenzials helfen.

Irland und Deutschland: Partner im Europäischen Aufschwung

Die europäische Schuldenkrise kann ein kritischer Wendepunkt in der Geschichte Europas sein. Wenn die Europäer aus ihren Fehlern lernen, können der Integrationsprozess und die Bildung einer stabileren Union beschleunigt werden. Nur als Verbund kann Europa seiner Stimme in internationalen Angelegenheiten Geltung verschaffen.

Wie Irlands erfolgreicher Anpassungsprozess anschaulich zeigt, zeitigen die Reformbemühungen Erfolge. Die europäische Erholung ist insgesamt auf dem richtigen Weg. Angesichts der beträchtlichen, noch verbleibenden Herausforderungen ist es wichtig, den Reformeifer aufrechtzuerhalten. Die fortdauernde Konsolidierung der öffentlichen Finanzen und die Umsetzung von Strukturreformen sind erforderlich, um die Wettbewerbsfähigkeit zu erhöhen und ein anhaltendes Wachstum in Europa zu gewährleisten.

Was haben europäische Staaten getan, um zur Stabilität zurückzukehren?

Die Wirtschaftskrise spiegelt nicht nur systemische Probleme der globalen und europäischen Volkswirtschaften wider, sondern auch Fehler in den einzelnen Mitgliedsstaaten. Eine Mischung aus europaweiter Aktion und nationalen Reformen überwindet die Krise schrittweise. Ein zunehmend stabiler Euro, sich bessernde Finanzsalden der Regierungen und steigende Exporte sind Zeichen dafür, dass die Lage in Europa besser ist, als sie scheint.

Ein Vergleich der irischen Leistung mit anderen Anpassungsprogrammen zeigt, dass Irland seine Sache gut gemacht hat. Viele große Herausforderungen bleiben auf europäischer und auf nationaler Ebene bestehen. Das gilt, trotz der bisherigen Erfolge, auch für Irland.

2008 bis 2020: Der Weg zur Erholung

Ralf Lissek

Hauptaussagen

- Irlands Bilanz an ausländischen Direktinvestitionen und exportgetragenem Wachstum ist die stärkste in ganz Europa. Hinzu kommt die Rolle als erste Anlaufstelle in Europa für US-amerikanische Unternehmen. Irlands Erholung spiegelt diese Vorteile wider und versetzt das Land in eine ganz andere Lage als andere Länder, die der Troika unterliegen. Schwere Herausforderungen im Hinblick auf Verschuldung, öffentliche Ausgaben und andere Reformen bleiben jedoch bestehen.
- Irlands stetige Erholung, die bis 2020 anhalten soll, beruht auf einer leistungsfähigen Bevölkerung, dem Reformwillen der Politik, einer dynamischen Unternehmerschaft und Irlands anhaltendem Erfolg als Ziel ausländischer Direktinvestitionen und als wichtiger europäischer Anlaufpunkt für multinationale Unternehmen. All diese Vorzüge Irlands zu erhalten, ist unerlässlich für die Erholung Europas. Die Unterstützung durch Irlands Partner ist hierbei von entscheidender Bedeutung.

Einleitung

Irlands Geschichte kennt viele bemerkenswerte Beispiele von wirtschaftlicher Erholung und Erneuerung. Für die jüngste Wirtschaftskrise und die Trendwende gilt dies nicht minder. Allerdings haben die Bemühungen, die derzeitige Krise zu überwinden, dem Land die schwere Bürde hoher Schulden in öffentlichen wie in Privathaushalten aufgehalst. Die Regierung hat sich zum Ziel gesetzt, die Staatsverschuldung bis 2020 deutlich zu verringern. Vor Ausbruch der jüngsten Krise hatte Irland zwei Jahrzehnte damit verbracht, sich von einem der ärmsten Länder Europas zu einem der reichsten zu wandeln. Die letzten Jahre dieses Wandels führten zu einer Überhitzung, durch die Irland stark exponiert war, als die Krise 2008 kam.

Trotz der Krise und der Veränderungen, die sie für die relative wirtschaftliche Position des Landes brachte, hat sich Irland viele der Errungenschaften und die meisten Vorteile erhalten, die ihm der Beitritt zur Europäischen Wirtschaftsgemeinschaft (heute die Europäische Union) am 1. Januar 1973

brachte. Das Ausmaß dieser Errungenschaften – die in einem erheblichen Maß bis in die Gegenwart wirksam sind – ist beeindruckend. Ausgehend von gerade etwas über der Hälfte des EU-Durchschnitts im Jahr 1997 ist Irlands Pro-Kopf-Wirtschaftsleistung heute vergleichbar mit dem Durchschnitt der Eurozone, wenn wir das BNE pro Kopf betrachten; sie liegt sogar um ein Fünftel höher als der Durchschnitt der Eurozone, wenn wir das BIP pro Kopf zugrunde legen.[1] Zudem zeigt die irische Wirtschaft gute Wachstumsraten und ein starkes Beschäftigungswachstum – positive Anzeichen für die Zukunft.

Illustration 1.1: BIP pro Kopf in der Eurozone nach Kaufkraftparität*

	2012
Deutschland	115
Griechenland	72
Irland	121
Portugal	68
Eurozone	**100**

Quelle: IWF, "World Economic Outlook Database 2013".
* Kaufkraftparität berücksichtigt das relative Preisniveau der jeweiligen Länder.

Diese Tabelle spiegelt eine durchschnittliche Wirtschaftswachstumsrate wider, die über die letzten vier Jahrzehnte selbst unter Berücksichtigung der jüngsten tiefen Rezession die höchste in der EU ist. Zwischen 1972 und 2012 sind BIP und BNE real um 458 beziehungsweise 332 Prozent gewachsen.[2] Dieses Wachstum war in den letzten beiden Jahrzehnten besonders stark und wurde von einer starken Exportleistung getragen, die auf Irlands Bekenntnis zur Wirtschafts- und Währungsunion im Jahr 1992 folgte. Zwischen jenem Jahr und 2012 stieg das Exportvolumen um 295 Prozent.[3] Leider basierten die späteren Jahre der Wachstumsphase nicht auf einem Exportwachstum, sondern wurden durch eine unverantwortliche Anhäufung von Schulden erreicht, die Irlands Wachstumsfähigkeit einschränkte. Nun aber mehren sich die Anzeichen, dass die Konjunktur wieder anspringt, wenn auch nicht im gleichen Tempo wie zu Boomzeiten.

Zu den Gründen gehört, dass Irland als Weltmeister beim Werben um ausländische Direktinvestitionen gilt. Laut dem US-amerikanischen Bureau of

---

[1] Irlands Erfolg beim Werben um ausländische Direktinvestitionen bedeutet, dass sein Bruttoinlandsprodukt (das Unternehmensaktivitäten in ausländischer Hand einschließt) etwa ein Fünftel höher ist als das Bruttonationaleinkommen (das Unternehmensaktivitäten in ausländischer Hand ausschließt). Das BIP ist ein Standardmesswert für internationale Vergleiche.

[2] Daten des Jahres 1972 des irischen Finanzministeriums (Department of Finance), *Budget and Economic Statistics 2013*; Zentrales Statistikamt (Central Statistics Office).

[3] Finanzministerium (Department of Finance), *Budget and Economic Statistics 2013*; Zentrales Statistikamt (Central Statistics Office).

Economic Analysis übertrafen die Investitionen amerikanischer Firmen in Irland (189 Mrd. US-Dollar) seit 1990 nicht nur ihre Investitionen in Deutschland; sie lagen auch höher als die gesamten amerikanischen Investitionen in den sogenannten BRIC-Ländern Brasilien, Russland, Indien und China.[4] Diesen Vorteil gilt es in Binnenwachstum und mehr Beschäftigung umzuwandeln. Dabei steht der hohe öffentliche und private Schuldenstand im Weg.

Einerseits hat Irland gezeigt, dass es Herausragendes leisten kann: Die Industrial Development Agency – weltweit führend in der Anwerbung ausländischer Direktinvestoren – hat den Weg bereitet für Irlands entscheidende Rolle als Tor nach Europa für multinationale Unternehmen, insbesondere aus den USA. Auch einheimische Exporteure haben sich dank der staatlichen Fachagentur Enterprise Ireland gut entwickelt. Nach einem Rückgang im Jahr 2009 sind die Exporte einheimischer Betriebe 2011 um 12 Prozent und 2012 um weitere 6,3 Prozent gestiegen.[5]

Andererseits kann dies nicht die ernsten Auswirkungen der globalen Krise auf Irland verdecken. Für seine Erholung bleibt Irland auf die Unterstützung Europas angewiesen. Dafür gibt es gute Argumente: Irland hat in der Krise hohe Flexibilität gezeigt und sich auch in früheren Jahren schon seine EU-Mitgliedschaft zu Nutze gemacht. Kaum ein Indikator ist dafür aussagefähiger als sein Bevölkerungswachstum.

Illustration 1.2: Irlands Bevölkerung wuchs seit der EU-Mitgliedschaft um 54 Prozent

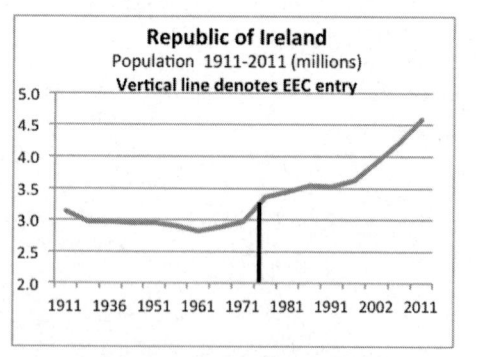

Republic of … = Republik Irland; Population… = Bevölkerung 1911-2011 (Mio);
Vertikal… = Senkrechte Linie markiert Beitritt zur EWG.
Quelle: Zentrales Statistikamt (Central Statistics Office),
„Volkszählungsdaten, 1911-2011".

---

[4] Quinlan, Joseph (2012). „The Irish-US Economic Relationship", Amerikanische Handelskammer Irland (American Chamber of Commerce Ireland).

[5] Enterprise Ireland, „Annual Reports 2011 and 2012".

Als die Bevölkerung (der Republik) Irland(s) 1972 für den Beitritt zur EWG stimmte, hatte sie seit einem Jahrhundert stabil bei etwa 3 Mio Menschen gelegen, eine Hinterlassenschaft der Hungersnot, die der wirtschaftlichen Entwicklung über ein Jahrhundert lang im Weg stand. Zwischen 1971 und 2011 wuchs Irlands Bevölkerung – gemessen anhand aufeinanderfolgender Volkszählungen – um atemberaubende 54 Prozent. Über den Großteil dieses Zeitraums stieg der Lebensstandard in Irland. Auswanderung bewirkt eine Verlangsamung dieser Wachstumsrate, doch gibt es andere Faktoren, die in die Gegenrichtung wirken: Irland hat eine der höchsten Geburtenraten Europas und verzeichnet nach wie vor starke Einwanderung. So wuchs Irlands Bevölkerung zwischen 2006 und 2011 um eine weitere Drittelmillion Menschen, also in dem Zeitraum, zu dem auch die drei schlimmsten Jahre der Krise mit stetig fallendem Lebensstandard gehören.

Welche Zukunft erwartet Irlands heranwachsende Jugend? Ein wohlhabendes Land mit Vollbeschäftigung oder anhaltende Arbeitslosigkeit und Verschuldung?

Die Iren sind bekannt für ihren Optimismus und ihr Vertrauen darauf, dass die Zukunft Gutes bringt. Das kann tatsächlich geschehen. Doch die politischen Entscheidungsträger und Irlands Partner in Europa werden entscheidend mitbestimmen, ob es auch wirklich eintritt.

Illustration 1.3: Irlands unhaltbarer Boom

	2004	2005	2006	2007
Bevölkerung (Tsd)	4.045	4.134	4.233	4.376
BIP-Wachstum (% Änderung z. Vorjahr)	4,2	6,1	5,5	5,0
BNE-Wachstum (% Änderung z. Vorjahr)	3,8	6,0	6,5	3,6
Lohnstückkosten (Index 2000=100)	95,8	100,0	103,5	108,7
Exportwachstum (% Änderung z. Vorjahr)	7,6	4,4	5,0	8,4
Zahlungsbilanz (Leistungsbilanz) als % BIP	-0,7	-4,1	-4,1	-6,2
Private Kredite (Mrd. Euro, Ende Dez.)	91,0	115,4	134,1	148,6
Davon über Hypothek finanziert (Mrd. Euro, Ende Dez.)	73,1	94,3	110,6	123,0
Beschäftigte (Tsd)	1.871,1	1.962,8	2.053,6	2.143,1
Arbeitslosigkeit %	4,5	4,4	4,5	4,7
Privates verfügbares Einkommen (Mio. Euro)	74.810	81.377	86.188	93.561
Pro Kopf (Euro)	18.494	19.685	20.361	21.380
Gesamtstaatl. Haushaltssaldo als % BIP	1,4	1,6	2,9	0,2
Gesamtstaatl. Verschuldung als % BIP	29,4	27,2	24,6	24,9
Staatl. Gesamtausgaben (Mrd. Euro)	45,7	50,8	56,1	62,9
als % BNE†	35,9	36,6	36,4	38,6

Quelle: Finanzministerium (Department of Finance), "Budget and Economic Statistics 2013"; Zentrales Statistikamt (Central Statistics Office).

Hinweis: Zahlungsbilanz, gesamtstaatlicher Haushaltssaldo und Verschuldung sind als Prozentsatz des BIP angegeben, während die staatlichen Gesamtausgaben als Prozentsatz des BNE angegeben sind. Dies entspricht der standardmäßigen Rechnungslegung in „Budget and Economic Statistics".

2004 – 2007: Unhaltbarer Boom

Zwischen 2004 und Ende 2007 ging Irland auf unverantwortlichen Expansionskurs und verabschiedete sich dabei vom soliden Geschäftsmodell eines auf Wettbewerbsfähigkeit basierenden Wachstums. Wie **Illustration 1.3** oben zeigt, war das Wachstum oberflächlich betrachtet stark. Doch unter dieser Oberfläche gab es klare Anzeichen einer rapiden Verschlechterung der Wettbewerbsfähigkeit sowie Warnzeichen für bevorstehende finanzielle Schwierigkeiten. In nur vier Jahren stiegen die Lohnstückkosten um 13,5 Prozent. Von einer ausgeglichenen Bilanz im Jahr 2004 rutschte die Handelsbilanz bis 2007 in ein erhebliches Defizit von 6,2 Prozent des BIP. Während die Beschäftigung in diesem Zeitraum um eine Viertelmillion Menschen anstieg und auch die privaten verfügbaren Einkommen zunahmen, verriet ein Blick auf die Wachstumsrate bei den privaten Krediten, dass

dies nicht durchzuhalten war. 2007 war eine von sieben irischen Arbeitskräften und sogar jeder fünfte männliche Arbeitnehmer in der Bauindustrie beschäftigt. Wie aus **Illustration 1.4** unten ersichtlich ist, überflügelte das durchschnittliche Wachstum die Inflation In mehreren entscheidenden Sektoren der Erwerbsbevölkerung erheblich, was die Position starker Wettbewerbsfähigkeit aus den späten 1990er Jahren aushöhlte. Der allgemeine Preisanstieg von 44,8 Prozent zwischen 1998 und 2008 war im europäischen Maßstab bereits hoch. In einigen Sektoren wie IT, Forschung und Entwicklung sowie Großhandel und Unternehmensdienstleistungen lag das Wachstum der Gehälter in diesem Zeitraum nicht weit über der Inflation. Im öffentlichen Sektor (ohne die Gesundheitsversorgung), stiegen die Löhne und Gehälter hingegen um 70,9 Prozent und damit deutlich über dem Inflationsniveau.

Illustration 1.4: Wachstum der Löhne und Gehälter in verschiedenen Wirtschaftsbereichen

Durchschnittl. wöchentl. Einkommen Euro	1998	1999	2000	2001	2002	2003	2004	2005	2006	2007	2008	% Änderung 98-08
Öffentl. Sektor (ohne Gesundheit)	555,1	578,3	611,5	671,8	704,3	734,9	797,1	844,2	882	922,5	948,9	**70,9**
Großhandel	471,2	489,6	527,2	558,0	583,7	598,8	626,4	665,5	703,3	711,7	737,7	**56,5**
Hotel & Gaststätten	286,3	303,8	322	339,3	347,1	367,5	395,8	418,7	431,2	446,3	465,2	**62,5**
IT, Forschung & Entwicklung	531,8	563,6	613,9	642,6	626,9	645,8	676,9	708,1	720,7	767,2	824,2	**55,0**
Unternehmens- dienstleistungen	456,9	480,6	513,5	551,5	561,4	585,5	619	642,9	679	705,3	723,6	**58,4**
Verbraucher- preisindex (Dez. 2001 =100)	87,2	88,7	93,6	98,2	102,7	106,3	108,6	111,3	115,7	121,3	126,3	**44,8**

Quelle: Zentrales Statistikamt (Central Statistics Office), „Statistikdatenbank".

In Sektoren wie IT, Forschung und Entwicklung spiegelt ein hohes Wachstum der Löhne und Gehälter mit hoher Wahrscheinlichkeit den Erfolg einer wettbewerbsfähigen und international leistungsstarken Branche wider. Das Web Summit im Oktober 2013 war ein anschauliches Beispiel dafür, wie hervorragend sich Irland um Direktinvestitionen multinationaler Unternehmen (die sich im IT-Bereich hauptsächlich auf Hardware konzentrieren) in die boomenden Software- und Social-Media-Branchen bemüht hat. Preisanstiege im öffentlichen Sektor waren Folge landesweiter Lohn- und Gehaltsabschlüsse, insbesondere nach dem Vergleichs mit dem privaten Sektor im Jahr 2002 (Benchmarking Awards). Teilweise

ging es dabei um legitime Ansprüche auf Teilhabe am Wirtschaftswachstum. Aber die o. a. Daten verdeutlichen auch, dass die öffentlichen Gehälter im Vergleich zu anderen Sektoren bereits 2001 im Durchschnitt relativ hoch lagen. Die Krise in Irland wird häufig als „Bankenkrise" beschrieben. Insofern ist ein Hinweis auf ein Problem, das mit der Bezahlung im öffentlichen Sektor zu tun hat, interessant. Die Verbindlichkeiten des Staates durch die Schuldverschreibungen (sogenannte ‚Promissory Notes"[6]) der Banken liegt bei 31 Mrd. Euro. Hingegen legt eine Analyse vom Oktober 2013[7] nahe: Durch die Pensionen des öffentlichen Sektors könnten sich letztlich Verbindlichkeiten von bis zu 116 Mrd. Euro ergeben, etwa dreimal so viel wie die Kosten des Rettungsprogramms für Finanzinstitute.

2008-2011: Krise

Der Niedergang der Wirtschaftslage in Irland ab 2008 geschah ebenso rapide wie das Wachstum in den Jahren unmittelbar vor der Krise. Ausgelöst durch einen weltweiten Abschwung erlebte Irland eine der plötzlichsten und schnellsten Talfahrten der modernen Wirtschaftsgeschichte.

Die schlimmste Auswirkung der Krise lag darin, dass Irland von einem Land mit niedriger öffentlicher Verschuldung – lediglich 24,9 Prozent des BIP im Jahr 2007 – bis 2011 zu einem Land wurde, in dem die Staatsverschuldung 100 Prozent des BIP deutlich überschritt. Immerhin soll 2013 der Schuldenhöchststand erreicht worden sein. Diese plötzliche Verschlechterung ist das Ergebnis mehrerer Faktoren. Besonders offenkundig und weithin diskutiert war dabei die Serie von Kapitalspritzen in Irlands Bankensystem. Doch gehören zu den Ursachen auch die öffentlichen Ausgaben auf dem in den Jahren vor der Bankenkrise aufgebauten, hohen Niveau sowie der immense Rückgang von Steuereinnahmen aus der Immobilienbranche, von denen der Staat zu abhängig geworden war. Diese Faktoren spielen eine wichtige, womöglich sogar wichtigere Rolle.

Durch übermäßige Kreditvergabe für Wohn- und gewerbliche Immobilien in Not geraten, gerieten die Banken zunehmend in Abhängigkeit von staatlicher Unterstützung. Dieser Prozess gipfelte in der Verstaatlichung der Anglo Irish Bank und der Irish Nationwide Building Society. Die Verpflichtungen aus den Schuldverschreibungen belasteten den Staatshaushalt mit neuen Schulden in Höhe von 31 Mrd. Euro.[8] Diese Belastung wurde später durch die Abwicklung der Irish Bank Resolution Corporation reduziert.[9] Doch waren auch andere Faktoren, wie eine sehr hohe Belastung durch öffentliche Ausgaben, offensichtlich. Zwischen

---

[6] Siehe **Anhang II: Glossar.**

[7] Barnes, Sebastian und Smyth, Diarmaid (2013). „The Government's Balance Sheet After the Crisis: A Comprehensive Perspective", IFAC.

[8] Irlands Erfahrungen mit der Rekapitalisierung der Banken und der Erholung seines Bankensektors sind in **Kapitel 5** erläutert.

[9] Das 2011 aus der Fusion der Anglo Irish Bank und der Irish Nationwide Building Society hervorgegangene Rechtsgebilde.

2004 und 2007 stiegen die öffentlichen Ausgaben drastisch von 45,7 Mrd. Euro auf 62,9 Mrd. Euro, was einem Anstieg von 37 Prozent entspricht.

Illustration 1.5: 2008 bis 2011: Finanz- und Wirtschaftskrise

	2008	2009	2010	2011
Bevölkerung (Tsd)	4.485	4.533	4.555	4.575
BIP-Wachstum (% Änderung z. Vorjahr)	-2,2	-6,4	-1,1	2,2
BNE-Wachstum (% Änderung z. Vorjahr)	-1,8	-9,8	0,5	-1,6
Lohnstückkosten (Index 2005=100)	116,1	113,1	105,5	101,3
Exportwachstum (% Änderung z. Vorjahr)	1,1	-3,8	6,4	5,4
Zahlungsbilanz (Leistungsbilanz) als % BIP	-6,6	-2,8	1,4	1,5
Beschäftigte (Tsd)	2.128	1.961	1.882	1.849
Arbeitslose (Tsd)	145	268	303	317
Arbeitslosigkeit % d. Erwerbsbevölkerung	6,4	12,0	13,8	14,6
Privates verfügbares Einkommen (Mio. Euro)	101.515	95.260	88.700	87.428
Pro Kopf	*22.634*	*21.015*	*19.473*	*19.110*
Gesamtstaatl. Haushaltssaldo als % BIP**	-7,4	-13,7*	-30,6*	-13,1*
„Eigentlicher" gesamtstaatl. Haushaltssaldo als % BIP	-7,4	-11,2	-10,6	-8,9
Gesamtstaatl. Verschuldung als % BIP	44,2	64,4	91,2	104,1
Staatl. Gesamtausgaben (Mrd. Euro)	68,7	75,9	69,0	76,5
als % BNE†	44,4	56,7	52,3	58,5

Quelle: Finanzministerium (Department of Finance), "Budget and Economic Statistics 2013"; Zentrales Statistikamt (Central Statistics Office).
* Auf Tausend gerundet.
** Defizite von 2009 bis 2011 spiegeln Eurostat-Vorgaben wider, wonach die Finanzierung der Rekapitalisierung einiger Banken als Staatsausgaben anzusetzen sind. Zahlen für den „eigentlichen" gesamtstaatl. Haushaltssaldo enthalten nicht die Auswirkungen der Bankenunterstützung auf die Staatsfinanzen.

Zwischen 2008 und 2011 brach der Bausektor zusammen und trug so einen großen Teil zum Verlust von insgesamt 280.000 Arbeitsplätzen in der Wirtschaft bei. Zwischen 2007 und 2011 sanken die privaten verfügbaren Einkommen pro Kopf um 12 Prozent, die Arbeitslosenquote stieg von 4,7 Prozent auf 14,6 Prozent. Von Haushaltssaldi, die vor der Krise im Plus oder ausgeglichen waren, stieg Irlands „eigentliches" Defizit[10] bis 2009 auf 11,2 Prozent des BIP, auch wenn zwischen 2010 und 2011 gewisse Fortschritte bei seiner Verringerung erzielt wurden.

---

[10]   Das Haushaltsdefizit ohne die Kosten der Bankenrekapitalisierung.

Zwar wäre die Situation ohne die Bankenkrise weniger ernst gewesen. Klar ist aber auch: Sowohl Irlands Wirtschaft als auch seine öffentlichen Finanzen bedurften selbst ohne eine solche Krise einer erheblichen Korrektur. In den frühen Boomjahren rührten Irlands hohe Wachstumsraten von einer stark wettbewerbsfähigen Wirtschaft her – es handelte sich um Export-orientiertes Wachstum, das sowohl einheimische Firmen wie auch ausländische Direktinvestoren generierten. Ab den späten 1990er Jahren bis weit in die Mitte des Folgejahrzehnts hinein beruhte das Wachstum zu sehr auf niedrigen Zinssätzen. Die Staatsfinanzen wurden zu abhängig von Steuer-Einnahmen aus dem stark zyklischen Immobiliensektor. Solange es diesem gutging, blieb verborgen, dass der sehr starke Anstieg bei den öffentlichen Ausgaben auf Dauer nicht haltbar war. Besonders hoch stiegen die Gehälter im öffentlichen Dienst und die damit einhergehenden Pensionsverpflichtungen.

Angestellte im öffentlichen Dienst haben seither einen großen Beitrag zur Sanierung geleistet und Einkommenseinbußen zugestimmt. Dazu gehören die im Januar 2009 eingeführte Pensionsabgabe, Gehaltskürzungen von durchschnittlich 7,5 Prozent im Rahmen des Haushalts 2010 sowie eine weitere Kürzung als Folge des „Haddington Road Agreement". Man sollte stärker als bisher anerkennen, dass viele Beschäftigte im öffentlichen Sektor – insbesondere die Angestellten im Kundenkontakt – bescheidene Gehälter beziehen, besonders wenn man die Lebenshaltungskosten in Irland berücksichtigt. Allerdings zeigen Daten aus dem zweiten Quartal 2013, veröffentlicht als „Earnings and Labour Costs" vom Zentralen Statistikamt (Central Statistics Office): Das durchschnittliche Wochengehalt für die 377.300 Staatsbediensteten liegt bei 928,76 Euro, im Privatsektor beträgt es 623,17 Euro. Zur Begründung dieses Unterschiedes von 49 Prozent werden höhere Qualifikationen und Kompetenzen im öffentlichen Sektor ins Feld geführt.

Gleichwohl sind Unterschiede von solcher Größenordnung zwischen den Durchschnittseinkommen im privaten und öffentlichen Sektor in anderen Ländern der Eurozone kaum zu finden. Eine entsprechende Studie weist darauf hin, dass in dieser Hinsicht zwischen den Mitgliedsstaaten *„spürbare Unterschiede"* bestehen, wobei *„Griechenland, Irland, Italien, Portugal und Spanien höhere Einkommen im öffentlichen Sektor haben als andere Länder"*.[11] Diese Studie bezog die Pensionsabgabe und die Gehaltskürzungen vom Januar bzw. Dezember 2009 in Irland bereits ein, konnte aber die Ergebnisse des Haddington Road Agreements nicht berücksichtigen. Aus dem Papier geht klar hervor: In Deutschland gibt es weder einen so erheblichen Unterschied zwischen öffentlichen und privatwirtschaftlichen Einkommen noch erreichen die ihnen zugrunde liegenden Gehälter ein ähnliches Niveau. Dabei dürfte kaum jemand behaupten, dass öffentliche Dienstleistungen in Deutschland schlechter seien als in Irland.

---

[11] Guajardo, J., Leigh, D. & Pescatori, A. (2001). "The Public Sector Pay Gap in a Selection of Euro Area Countries", EZB-Arbeitspapier 1406, Dezember.

2012-2016: Auf dem Weg zur Erholung

Eine echte Erholung ist erst seit 2012 spürbar. Bemühungen zur Gesundung der irischen Wirtschaft kamen aber bereits kurz nach Beginn der Krise in Gange. Im Oktober 2008, im April 2009 und noch einmal im Dezember 2009 verabschiedete das Parlament drei Nothaushalte, deren Auswirkung an dem in **Illustration 1.5** dargestellten Rückgang des verfügbaren Privateinkommens ablesbar ist. Außerdem wurde rasch ein neues System einer risikobasierten Finanzregulierung installiert – es fiel strenger aus als die später von der EU vorgegebenen Maßnahmen. Irlands Reformen beschränkten sich nicht auf den Finanzbereich. Bis 2011 war die Verschlechterung der Wettbewerbsfähigkeit aus früheren Jahren in erheblichem Maß rückgängig gemacht, die Exportwirtschaft erreichte wieder eindrucksvolle Wachstumsraten. Zu den hier wirksamen Faktoren gehört: der Erfolg von Enterprise Ireland bei der Ermunterung einheimischer Industrien zur Internationalisierung ihrer Geschäfte; der anhaltende Erfolg der IDA bei der Anwerbung ausländischer Investitionen nach Irland; die Flexibilität und Dynamik der irischen Unternehmerschaft; und nicht zuletzt die Anpassungsbereitschaft und Flexibilität der irischen Arbeitnehmer sowie der Bevölkerung insgesamt als Reaktion auf die Krise.

Natürlich ist die Anpassung der irischen Wirtschaft nicht abgeschlossen. Wie spätere Kapitel genauer ausführen werden, steht Irland nach seinem Ausstieg aus dem Rettungsprogramm nun vor einer neuen Herausforderung. Es muss die Fortschritte der vergangenen Jahre sichern und normalen Wohlstand wiederherstellen. Zu diesem Zweck veröffentlichte die Regierung ein Strategiedokument, das ehrgeizige, aber realistische Zielvorgaben für die Verringerung von Verschuldung und Arbeitslosigkeit bis 2020 benennt.[12] Indem es sich schneller und robuster an die Krise angepasst hat als jedes andere Land in der Eurozone – einer der Vorteile einer kleinen Volkswirtschaft –, hat Irland dem restlichen Europa Führungsstärke demonstriert. Den politischen Willen vorausgesetzt gibt es guten Grund zur Zuversicht, dass Irland bis zum Ende dieses Jahrzehnts eine gewisse Normalisierung seiner Wirtschaft erreichen kann.

Einige irische Kommentatoren sehen die Ursache für Irlands Unglück allein in der Eurozone: Die Niedrigzinsen der Europäischen Zentralbank EZB seien Ländern in Mitteleuropa mit geringem Wachstum, wie Frankreich und Deutschland, zugutegekommen, waren aber ungeeignet für Länder an der Peripherie mit hohem Wachstum. Aufgabe der EZB ist es eigentlich, die Geldpolitik für die gesamte Eurozone festzulegen, ohne Präferenz für ein Land gegenüber einem anderen. Dennoch steht fest, es steht jedoch außer Zweifel, dass die Entscheidungen der EZB sehr unterschiedliche Auswirkungen auf Irland im Vergleich zu Deutschland hatten.

---

[12]   Finanzministerium (Department of Finance), „Medium Term Economic Strategy 2014-2020", Dezember 2013.

Illustration 1.6: 2012 bis 2016: Der Weg zur Erholung

	2012	2013e	2014f	2015f	2016f
Bevölkerung (Tsd)	4.585	4.612	4.638	4.665	4.691
BIP-Wachstum (% Änderung z. Vorjahr)	0,2	0,2	2,0	2,3	2,8
BNE-Wachstum (% Änderung z. Vorjahr)	2,0	1,0	1,7	1,7	2,1
Arbeitslosigkeit % d. Erwerbsbevölkerung	14,7	13,5	12,4	11,8	11,4
Gesamtstaatl. Haushaltssaldo als % BIP*	-8,2	-7,3	-4,8	-2,9	-2,4
Primärsaldo als % des BIP	-4,5	-2,7	0,0	2,0	2,6
Gesamtstaatl. Verschuldung als % BIP	117,4	124,1	120	118,4	114,6
Staatl. Gesamtausgaben (Mrd. Euro)	70,0	67,1	64,9	63,7	64,5

Quelle: Für 2012: Finanzministerium (Department of Finance), "Budget and Economic Statistics 2013"; Zentrales Statistikamt (Central Statistics Office). Ab 2013: Finanzministerium (Department of Finance), „Budget 2014 Economic and Fiscal Outlook".

Wie im Maastricht-Vertrag vorgesehen standen Irland EU-Mittel aus den Strukturfonds zur Verfügung, um der Wirtschaft bei der Vorbereitung auf die Währungsunion zu helfen. 1996 erstellte das Wirtschaftsinstitut ESRI eine umfassende Studie zu den wahrscheinlichen Auswirkungen der EWU auf Irland. Es gab also einerseits Gelegenheiten zur Diskussion und zur entschlossenen Vorbereitung auf dieses einschneidende Ereignis; sie wurden auch in einigen Fällen genutzt. Zum anderen bestand jedoch in der Eurozone ein systemisches Problem, wie sich an der grossflächigen Verbreitung der Krise ablesen lässt. Die Diskrepanz zwischen einer zentralisierten Geldpolitik und einem fragmentierten System der Bankenregulierung ist dafür ein klares Beispiel. Dieses Problem wird nun durch die Schritte zur Bankenunion korrigiert. Dies im Nachhinein zu erkennen, ist wichtig. Der Europäische Rat hat im Juni 2012 den Grundsatz akzeptiert, dass der Europäische Stabilitätsmechanismus zur Unterstützung der Rekapitalisierung der Banken auch nachträglich angewandt werden kann. Allerdings bleibt die Frage bestehen, ob diese Möglichkeit die Unterstützung der Regierungen der Mitgliedsstaaten finden wird.

Zur Krise der Eurozone trugen sicherlich spezifische nationale Probleme bei. Doch war sie auch eine Krise mit einer gemeinschaftlichen Komponente. Durch die Aufweichung des Stabilitätspaktes vor einem Jahrzehnt haben die größeren Mitgliedsstaaten zum Verfall der Haushaltsdisziplin in der gesamten Eurozone beigetragen. Alles in allem kann man sich kaum der Schlussfolgerung entziehen: Zur Lösung der europäischen Krise gehören die Anerkennung der eindrucksvollen Bemühungen von Ländern wie Irland, ihre Fehler anzuerkennen und zu korrigieren, ebenso wie das Eingeständnis einer gemeinsamen Verantwortung auf EU-Ebene.

Rückkehr zur Normalität bis 2020: ein realistisches Ziel

Die neuesten Wirtschaftsprognosen der Regierung sind sowohl von der EU Kommission als auch vom irischen unabhängigen Finanzbeirat (Independent Fiscal Advisory Council, IFAC[13]) als solide bestätigt worden. Demzufolge darf Irland nicht nur eine deutliche und stabile Erholung zwischen jetzt und 2016 erwarten. Die Rückkehr zur Vollbeschäftigung im kommenden Jahrzehnt ist zumindest denkbar, falls die richtige Politik verfolgt wird. In der Tat legen seit der Veröffentlichung dieser Prognosen[14] die Beschäftigungszahlen[15] nahe, dass sich das Wachstum neuer Arbeitsplätze ebenso beschleunigt wie die Rate des Wirtschaftswachstums. Mit der richtigen Unterstützung erscheint Irlands Rückkehr zu einer gewissen Normalität bis zum Ende dieses Jahrzehnts möglich.

Maßnahmen in den jüngeren Haushalten[16] haben Unternehmensinvestitionen und die Schaffung von Arbeitsplätzen derart gefördert, dass die Beschäftigung in den 12 Monaten bis September 2013 um 58.000 gestiegen ist. Vom Höchststand von 14,7 Prozent im Jahr 2012 war die Arbeitslosigkeit zuletzt bereits auf 12,8 Prozent gefallen. Alles weist darauf hin, dass die Schaffung von Arbeitsplätzen in den kommenden Jahren an Tempo gewinnt. Auch gibt es einen willkommenen Rückgang der Zahl der Langzeitarbeitslosen. Die mittelfristige Wirtschaftsplanung der Regierung („Medium Term Economic Strategy") legt nahe, dass unter den richtigen Bedingungen – und wenn die zukünftigen politischen Entscheidungen die richtigen sind – die Arbeitslosigkeit bis 2020 auf unter 6 Prozent fallen könnte. Zwar sind die Staatsausgaben nach wie vor hoch, doch wird nun für 2016 eine Verringerung der Ausgaben, sowohl absolut als auch als Anteil an der Wirtschaft, angestrebt. Zudem legt die jüngste Strategie der Regierung einen Richtwert für den Abbau der Staatsverschuldung fest: Demnach soll sie nach dem Höchstwert von 124 Prozent im Jahr 2013 auf 93 Prozent im Jahr 2020 fallen und damit niedriger liegen als in früheren Prognosen vorgesehen. Unter der Voraussetzung, dass die Wirtschaft wächst, wirkt dieser Richtwert realistisch.

Irlands Anpassung über einen Zeitraum von fünf Jahren beginnt sich auszuzahlen. Sowohl die zukünftigen Prognosen wie auch die finanzielle Stabilität haben sich verbessert. Von einem Höchststand von 11,5 Prozent des BIP im Jahr 2009 wird das Haushaltsdefizit bis 2015 auf unter 3 Prozent fallen. Bezogen auf

---

[13] Der IFAC wurde 2011 eingerichtet und erhielt gemäß dem „Fiscal Responsibility Act, 2013" einen gesetzlich festgeschriebenen Status und gesetzlich festgeschriebene Befugnisse. Dieses Gesetz verleiht der ein Jahr zuvor von den irischen Wählern im Referendum erteilten Zustimmung zum Fiskalpakt Gesetzeswirkung. Der IFAC hat die Aufgabe, die Finanzprognosen für Irland unabhängig anhand der Bedingungen des Fiskalpaktes zu überwachen.

[14] Oktober 2013.

[15] Dezember 2013.

[16] Irlands finanzielle Trendwende und Haushaltspolitik werden in **Kapitel 3** erläutert.

sein „Primärsaldo" – der Saldo der Einnahmen und Ausgaben ohne Zahlungen für Schuldenzinsen – wird Irland bereits 2014 einen ausgeglichenen Haushalt aufweisen und kann 2015 und 2016 mit erheblichen Überschüssen rechnen. Dies wird zur Verringerung der Staatsverschuldung beitragen, wie sie in der Planung der der Regierung vorgesehen ist.

Die Höhe der irischen Staatsverschuldung bleibt jedoch weiterhin ein Wachstumshemmnis. Weitere entschlossene Maßnahmen werden notwendig sein, um durchaus mögliche bedeutende Fortschritte zu erzielen.

Die dritte, damit im Zusammenhang stehende Sorge ist die Frage, wie Irlands Banken 2014 abschneiden werden, und zwar sowohl im Stresstest der EZB wie auch in den Bewertungen durch die Märkte, nun, da Irland den Rettungsschirm verlassen hat. Die Fähigkeit der Banken, Kredite an die Wirtschaft auszureichen, ist eine entscheidende Voraussetzung für Wachstum. Die Wirtschaftsstrategie der Regierung hat eine Reihe von Zielvorgaben festgelegt, um kleinen und mittelständischen Unternehmen mehr Kredite zur Verfügung zu stellen. Dazu dienen auch Gespräche mit der Kreditanstalt für Wiederaufbau (KfW).

Die Staatsverschuldung, die Privatverschuldung und der Zustand des Bankensektors stellen beängstigende Herausforderungen dar. Aber die Menschen, die Unternehmerschaft und die Regierung Irlands haben bereits eine bedeutende Strecke auf dem Weg zur Erholung zurückgelegt. Man sollte betonen, dass Irlands Krise nicht von seinem Steuersystem verursacht wurde, sondern von einer recht schwachen Bankenregulierung. Zudem war Irland das erste Land, das als Reaktion auf die Krise eine bessere Finanzregulierung aufgebaut hat und – wie **Kapitel 5** näher beschrieben wird – in dieser Hinsicht auch weiter gegangen ist, als von der EU vorgegeben. Irland verfügt nun über gute Finanzaufsicht und gutes Risikomanagement.

Irlands Trendwende und wettbewerbsfähiges Geschäftsmodell

Auf der Höhe der Krise rieten mehrere bekannte Wirtschaftswissenschaftler dem Land, den Euro zu verlassen und die neue Währung erheblich abzuwerten. Die irische Wirtschaft, argumentierten sie, werde womöglich nicht in der Lage sein, ihr Preisniveau derart anzupassen, um in der Eurozone wettbewerbsfähig zu bleiben. Doch mit der finanziellen Trendwende Irlands geht auch neue Wettbewerbsfähigkeit innerhalb der Eurozone einher. Dazu hat die flexible, dynamische Unternehmerschaft ebenso beigetragen wie ein System niedriger Unternehmenssteuern, eine unterstützende Regierungspolitik und hochprofessionelle staatliche Agenturen. Wie **Kapitel 2** zeigen wird, geht diese Anpassung weiter als in allen anderen von der Krise betroffenen Ländern.

Illustration 1.7: Prognostiziertes Wirtschafts- und Exportwachstum, 2014 bis 2016

% Änderung zum Vorjahr	2014	2015	2016
BIP	1,8	2,5	2,5
Export	1,5	3,0	3,5

Quelle: IWF, "World Economic Outlook", Oktober 2013.

Einige Merkmale der irischen Wettbewerbsfähigkeit blieben von der Krise relativ verschont. Dazu gehören die Ausfuhren einheimischer Betriebe und der anhaltende Erfolg bei ausländischen Direktinvestoren. So gab Intel im Oktober 2013 bekannt, seinen neusten Mikrochip in Irland entwickeln zu wollen – ein Zeichen dafür, dass der frühere Erfolg bei der Anwerbung ausländischer Direktinvestitionen Irland treu geblieben ist und auch Teil seines zukünftigen Geschäftsmodells sein wird. Dieses Modell sollte zum jetzigen entscheidenden Zeitpunkt nicht gefährdet werden.

Zu Anfang beruhte dieses Modell vor allem auf einer hochgebildeten englischsprachigen Erwerbsbevölkerung mit geringem Einkommen. Mittlerweile ist es ausgeklügelter und weiter entwickelt, weshalb Irland trotz der Auswirkungen der Krise nach wie vor eine der weltweit wettbewerbsfähigsten Volkswirtschaften ist. Zwar fiel Irland in der Rangliste des Weltwirtschaftsforums zur Wettbewerbsfähigkeit vom 11. Platz im Jahr 2001 bis zum Jahr 2010 auf die 29. Position zurück. Auch während der Krise konnte es sich unter den Top 30 halten. Nunmehr auf Platz 28 (Index 2013/2014) stabilisiert, enthält Irlands Gesamtbewertung im Index noch eindrucksvollere Ergebnisse bei spezifischen Indikatoren: den 13. Platz für das „Technologische Anpassungsvermögen", die Flexibilität des Waren- und des Arbeitsmarktes (11. bzw. 16. Platz) sowie Ausdifferenziertheit des Wirtschaftslebens (20.). Das irische Geschäftsmodell hat also seine Anziehungskraft verstärkt und sich im Vergleich mit dem Niedrigkosten-Modell der 1990er Jahre differenziert. Die schwachen Platzierungen für das „Makroökonomische Umfeld" (134.) und die „Finanzmärkte" (85.) stellen Hinterlassenschaften der Krise dar, die schwer auf der Gesamtleistung Irlands lasten. Sobald diese durch den wirtschaftlichen Wiederaufschwung überwunden werden können (und die Zeichen sprechen dafür), hat Irland beste Chancen, seine Position unter den 20 wettbewerbsfähigsten Volkswirtschaften der Welt zurückzuerobern. Die wachsende Zahl führender Hochtechnologie-Cluster – beispielsweise in der Pharmazie, Informationstechnologie und Biomedizin – zeigt eine Vertiefung und Ausweitung des Erfolgs in etablierten Technologiebereichen. Der sehr erfolgreiche Web Summit im Oktober 2013 in Dublin verdeutlichte Irlands Fähigkeit, sich das Wachstum in neuen Bereichen zunutze zu machen.

Zwar war die Steuerpolitik nie die alleinige Triebkraft für Irlands High-Tech-Erfolg, zudem haben sich weitere Vorteile hinzugesellt. Doch bleiben niedrige

Unternehmenssteuern eine absolute Notwendigkeit für die weitere wirtschaftliche Erholung und den zukünftigen Erfolg des Landes. Vor kurzem stand aufgrund von Spekulationen in Washington, Brüssel und Berlin Irlands wettbewerbsfähiges System der Körperschaftssteuer im Fokus. Doch in ihrem jüngsten Bericht über die irische Wirtschaft[17] beschrieb die OECD Irlands Körperschaftssteuer als „zentrales Element seines Modells ausländischer Direktinvestitionen": Es sei „das beste Mittel, um für ausländische Direktinvestitionen, die entscheidend für das Wirtschaftswachstum sind, attraktiv zu bleiben". Irland arbeitet mit der OECD-Initiative gegen die Aushöhlung der steuerlichen Bemessungsgrundlage und Gewinnverlagerung („Base Erosion Profit Shifting") zusammen und kann, wie in **Kapitel 2** erläutert wird, auf anhaltendes und langjähriges Engagement in der internationalen Steuerzusammenarbeit verweisen.

Im vorigen Jahrhundert erlebte Irland eine bemerkenswerte Renaissance. Nun zeigt seine Erholung von der tiefen Krise, dass es seine Widerstandsfähigkeit und seinen Erfolg in das neue Jahrhundert mitgenommen hat. Als leuchtendes Beispiel für die finanzielle Konsolidierung in der Eurozone hat Irland einen bedeutsamen Beitrag zur Stabilisierung des Euro geleistet. Durch Fortsetzung und Vertiefung der Politik, die zu dieser Trendwende geführt hat kann Irland auf dem erfolgreichen Ausstieg aus dem Troika-Programm aufbauen und auf das Ziel einer florierenden Volkswirtschaft mit Vollbeschäftigung bis zum Jahr 2020 hinarbeiten.

Die enormen Opfer der Iren und die Entschlossenheit ihrer Regierung haben maßgeblich dazu beigetragen, die Trendwende für Irland herbeizuführen. Doch die grössere Ausgabendisziplin allein wird weder die noch ausstehenden Probleme Irlands bei der Staatsverschuldung lösen noch kann sie allein die Rückkehr zu Wohlstand und Vollbeschäftigung sichern, die Irland nach fünf Jahren der Kraftanstrengung verdient hat.

Irland erfüllt seine Verpflichtungen gegenüber der Eurozone und der EU und kooperiert auf globaler Ebene bei der Diskussion über Steuerfragen. Wenn es auch bei Weitem nicht den einzigen Erfolgsfaktor darstellt, so bleibt doch Irlands Unternehmensbesteuerung von ausschlaggebender Bedeutung für die Anwerbung neuer Investitionen, für weiteren Zuwachs bei der Hochtechnologie sowie für die Belebung der einheimischen Wirtschaft. Dieses Steuersystem darf nicht für eine Krise verantwortlich gemacht werden, die tief in der globalen Finanzordnung verwurzelt war und durch innenpolitische Fehlentscheidungen verstärkt wurde. Irland hat seine Fehler auf nationaler Ebene – das Scheitern der Finanzregulierung und fiskalische Misswirtschaft – frühzeitig und umfassend in Angriff genommen. Es hat darüber hinaus sein Anpassungsprogramm verlassen, während einige andere Länder der Eurozone ihre jeweiligen Programme noch immer umsetzen.

Irland hat seine Trendwende mit europäischer Hilfe erreicht. Es hat dazu beigetragen, Europa und die Zukunft des Euros zu sichern. Aber vor allem hat es sich selbst geholfen.

---

[17] OECD, „Economic Survey: Ireland", September 2013.

Kommentar: KAPITEL 1
Irlands Wiederaufschwung

John Corrigan

Hauptaussagen

- Als Irland das Vertrauen der Anleger verlor und im November 2010 um ein EU/IWF-Hilfsprogramm bitten musste, entwickelte die NTMA ein Programm, aktiv auf potenzielle Investoren zuzugehen. Ziel: die erfolgreiche Rückkehr in die Märkte am Ende des Programms. Mit der durchgängigen Übererfüllung der im EU/IWF-Programm festgelegten finanziellen Zielvorgaben durch die Regierung, der transparenten und glaubwürdigen Durchführung der Rekapitalisierung und Umstrukturierung der irischen Banken im Jahr 2011 und mit der Wiederherstellung der Wettbewerbsfähigkeit in der Wirtschaft wurde das Vertrauen der Anleger allmählich wiedergewonnen.

- Mitte des Jahres 2011, als die Zinserträge historische Höchststände erreichten, entschieden sich US-Anleger – überwiegend, aber nicht ausschließlich Hedgefonds – zum Kauf irischer Staatsanleihen. Dies bewegte andere, eher traditionelle „Real-Money"-Investoren zur Rückkehr in den Markt. Sie ersetzten die Hedgefonds, als die Zinserträge fielen. Auch Entwicklungen in Europa unterstützten Irland, darunter Draghis Versprechen, „alles zu tun", das Arrangement hinsichtlich der IBRC-Schuldverschreibungen und die Laufzeitverlängerung für Irlands EFSF- und EFSM-Darlehen. Nach Irlands Ausstieg aus dem Programm ohne vorsorgliche Kreditlinie im Dezember 2013 konnte die NTMA Anfang Januar 2014 3,75 Mrd. Euro im Markt beschaffen. Weitere Emissionen in Form regelmäßiger Auktionen sind vorgesehen, da Irland seine Präsenz auf dem Markt normalisiert hat.

Am 21. November 2010 gab die irische Regierung bekannt, dass sie offiziell um ein Hilfsprogramm im Rahmen des EU/IWF-Programms gebeten hatte. Damit wurde der Vertrauensverlust der Anleger bestätigt, deren Zuversicht bereits in den Monaten zuvor auf eine harte Probe gestellt worden war. Die Rendite für die 10-jährige irische Staatsanleihe war von 4,67 Prozent sechs Monate zuvor auf 8,12 Prozent zum Zeitpunkt dieser Rettungsaktion emporgeschnellt. Die Bedingungen sollten noch schwieriger werden: Im Juli 2011 notierten 10-jährige Anleihen bei über 14 Prozent. Die Reaktion der Ratingagenturen folgte auf dem Fuß. Standard & Poor's setzte am 23. November die Bewertung um zwei Stufen herab (von AA- auf

A), während Fitch am 9. Dezember eine Herabstufung um drei Stufen vornahm (von A+ auf BBB+). Am 17. Dezember stufte Moody's Irland um rekordverdächtige fünf Stufen herab (von Aa2 auf Baa1).

In dieser Lage fasste die NTMA den Entschluss, aktiv auf die Anleger zuzugehen. Damit sollten die Voraussetzungen für Irlands spätere Rückkehr auf die Märkte am Ende des Hilfsprogramms geschaffen werden. Diese Rückkehr lag in weiter Ferne, ja, sie wurde von vielen Kommentatoren angezweifelt, die entweder ein zweites EU/IWF-Hilfsprogramm oder eine Umstrukturierung der Staatsschulden vorhersagten. Die NTMA besuchte zweimal jährlich Investoren in den Hauptfinanzzentren in Europa, den USA und Asien. Der Grundtenor bei diesen Treffen lautete: Die Regierung will alle ihre Verpflichtungen gegenüber der Troika erfüllen. In Bezug auf die öffentlichen Finanzen beinhaltete dies einen genauen Zeitplan für die stufenweise Verringerung des Haushaltsdefizits auf weniger als 3 Prozent des BIP bis 2015. Hinzu kam, was vielleicht noch wichtiger war, das Erreichen eines primären Haushaltsüberschusses von ausreichender Größe, um das Verhältnis der Verschuldung zum BIP zu stabilisieren und dann zu reduzieren. Die glaubwürdige Darstellung eines Weges hin zur Schuldennachhaltigkeit war von ausschlaggebender Bedeutung für die Anleger.

Die Darlegungen der NTMA gegenüber den Investoren beinhalteten auch die Maßnahmen, die ergriffen wurden, um die Wettbewerbsfähigkeit in der Wirtschaft wiederherzustellen. Zur Sprache kam insbesondere die „innere Abwertung", die mangels des traditionellen politischen Mittels in solchen Umständen, sprich der Abwertung der Währung, erforderlich war. Die Schrumpfung und Umstrukturierung des Bankensektors spielte in den Präsentationen und Diskussionen ebenfalls eine große Rolle – ganz besonders im März 2011, als sich die NTMA unmittelbar nach der 24 Mrd. Euro teuren Bankenrekapitalisierungsrunde auf den Weg machte.

Die Anleger waren auch an einer Einschätzung des Risikos interessiert, dass sich die verschiedenen Eventualverbindlichkeiten, die die Bilanz der Regierung überschatteten, verdichten und zu tatsächlichen Verbindlichkeiten der Regierung werden könnten. Die wichtigsten angesprochenen Eventualverbindlichkeiten betrafen vier Szenarien: die Möglichkeit einer weiteren Rekapitalisierung der Banken zusätzlich zu den 64 Mrd. Euro, die von der Regierung bis zum Sommer 2011 bereitgestellt waren; die Regierungsgarantie für die von NAMA ausgegebenen Schuldverschreibungen im Wert von 30 Mrd. Euro (als Gegenleistung für die Übernahme von 74 Mrd. Euro an Land- und Erschließungsdarlehen aus den Bilanzen der Banken); die Verbindlichkeiten aus dem Programm „Eligible Liabilities Guarantee (ELG)", dem Nachfolger der zweijährigen pauschalen Bürgschaft der Regierung für die Banken vom September 2008; sowie die Inanspruchnahme von „Exceptional Liquidity Assistance (ELA)" von der irisches Zentralbank (Central Bank of Ireland) durch irische Banken. Die Anleger äußerten häufig Bewunderung für die bemerkenswerte Widerstandsfähigkeit und den sozialen Zusammenhalt der Iren trotz der schmerzhaften Maßnahmen, die zur

Bewältigung der Krise erforderlich waren. Sie versuchten, diese Eigenschaften besser zu verstehen.

In den ersten Investorengesprächen sah sich die NTMA seltener den „Real-Money"-Investmentmanagern gegenuber, die wegen ihrer geringen Risikofreude traditionell hauptsächlich in Anleihen von Industriestaaten investieren. Gesprächspartner waren häufig Hedgefonds und Manager von Zukunftsmärkten, Kreditabteilungen und ertragsstarken Portfolios in den verschiedenen Investmenthäusern. Auch Anleger in irischen Bankanleihen mit Staatsgarantie waren stark vertreten. In dieser Anfangsphase gab es regelmässig lautstarke Beschwerden der Inhaber nachrangiger Schuldverschreibungen der irischen Banken. Sie beklagten sich darüber, dass manche dieser nachrangigen Anleihen (junior bonds) mit einem starken Abschlag zwangsweise zurückgekauft wurden. Typischerweise äußerten die Anleger in dieser Phase Zweifel an der Fähigkeit der irischen Regierung, ihre Schuldenverpflichtungen pünktlich zu erfüllen. Eine noch größere Sorge vieler Investoren war die Gefahr des Auseinanderbrechens des Euro.

Dass die NTMA durchgängig darauf verweisen konnte, die Regierung habe ihre finanzielle Zielvorgabe übererfüllt, brachte allmählich das Vertrauen der Investoren zurück. Besonders wichtig waren die Quartalsberichte der Troika, in denen die beständigen Fortschritte Irlands bestätigt wurden. Zudem wurden die Zielvorgaben nie gelockert.

Ein wichtiger Wendepunkt in der Erholung Irlands kam im März 2011 mit den Ergebnissen des Stresstests der irischen Banken. Die Robustheit und Transparenz des Verfahrens und die intensive Einbeziehung hochkarätiger externer Institutionen verliehen dieser Übung Glaubwürdigkeit. Die Anleger kamen allmählich zu der Überzeugung, dass Irland dieses Mal wirklich die Rekapitalisierung und Umstrukturierung der irischen Banken in der geforderten Größenordnung bewältigt hatte. Die Umstimmung der Investoren erfolgte jedoch nicht augenblicklich und die Talsohle für den Markt für irische Staatsanleihen sollte im Juli 2011 erreicht werden, als Moody's die Kreditwürdigkeit Irlands auf Sub-Investment-Grade (also Ramschniveau) herabstufte. Die Rendite für die 10-jährigen Anleihen stieg auf über 14 Prozent, während die Rendite für 2-jährige Anleihen atemberaubende 23 Prozent erreichte.

Ebenfalls im Juli 2011 entschied sich eine Gruppe von US-amerikanischen und kanadischen Investoren, 1,1 Mrd. Euro in die Übernahme eines Anteils von 34,9 Prozent an der Bank of Ireland zu investieren. Dies stellte einen bedeutsamen Vertrauensbeweis einflussreicher ausländischer Investoren in Irland dar. Etwa zur gleichen Zeit begannen einige Hedgefonds und traditionelle Anlagemanager in den USA, irische Staatsanleihen zu kaufen. Einige dieser Investoren wollten ihren gegenteiligen Standpunkt zu dem in Teilen der US-amerikanischen Investment-Community weit verbreiteten Glauben verdeutlichen, der Euro werde auseinanderbrechen. Sie entschieden, dass der Kauf irischer Staatsanleihen der beste Weg sei, um ihren Investment-Standpunkt darzulegen – schliesslich konnten sie beträchtliche Kapitalerträge erwarten, falls sich ihre Ansicht als richtig erweisen

sollte (tatsächlich verdoppelte sich schließlich der Preis für irische Staatsanleihen gegenüber dem Preis vom Juli 2011).

Dies leitete eine Markterholung bei den irischen Staatsanleihen ein. Im Januar 2012 konnte die NTMA ihre erste Transaktion am Kapitalmarkt seit September 2010 durchführen – die Investoren nahmen das Angebot an, eine Anleihe über 3,5 Mrd. Euro, die im Januar 2014 fällig werden sollte, in eine neue Anleihe umzuwandeln, die im Februar 2015 fällig wird. Viele Anleger hatten die Auszahlung der Anleihe über 11,8 Mrd. Euro mit Fälligkeit im Januar 2014, unmittelbar nach dem Ende des EU/IWF-Programms, als Haupthürde für die erfolgreiche Rückkehr Irlands auf die Märkte betrachtet. Die NTMA meisterte die Herausforderung dieser „Finanzierungsklippe" mit Hilfe dieser Umwandlung und einer Anzahl weiterer Transaktionen, darunter einer nachfolgenden Umwandlung und einer Direktfinanzierung im Juli 2012.

Der von der NTMA vorangetriebene Prozess des Wiedereintritts in die Märkte nahm im Verlauf des Jahres 2012 rasch Fahrt auf.

Im Mai 2012 stimmten die irischen Wähler dem EU-Fiskalpakt mit einer Mehrheit von 60 Prozent zu 40 Prozent zu. Die Staats- und Regierungschefs des Euro-Währungsgebiets verabschiedeten nach ihrem Gipfel am 29. Juni eine Erklärung zur dringenden Notwendigkeit, den Teufelskreis zwischen Banken und Staatsanleihen zu durchbrechen. Am 26. Juli gab der Präsident der EZB, Mario Draghi, seine berühmte Zusicherung, dass „die EZB bereit [sei], alles zu tun, um den Euro zu retten". Dieser Zusicherung wurde durch die Bekanntgabe der „Outright Monetary Transactions (OMT)" der EZB am 6. September 2012 Substanz verliehen. Vor diesem positiven Hintergrund konnte die NTMA am 5. Juli 2012 ihre erste Auktion für neue Schatzwechsel seit September 2010 abhalten. Die Händler einer großen Anzahl von Banken wollten daran teilhaben. Sie wandten sich an ihre Risikoausschüsse, um Kreditlinien wieder öffnen zu lassen, die seit Ausbruch der Krise eingefroren waren. Am 26. Juli 2012 konnte die NTMA deshalb Anleihen zur Beschaffung von 4,2 Mrd. Euro an neuem Geld ausgeben und eine weitere Milliarde Euro von kurzfristigen in längerfristige Anleihen umwandeln. Im August verkaufte die NTMA langfristige, abschreibbare Anleihen im Wert von 1 Milliarde an die lokalen Pensionsversicherungen.

Die Renditen irischer Staatsanleihen erholten sich im Verlauf des Jahres 2012 kontinuierlich. Viele der Hedgefonds-Investoren, die etwa Mitte 2011 gekauft hatten, als die Renditen ihren Höchststand erreicht hatten, verkauften ihre Bestände, um ihre Gewinne zu Geld zu machen. Gleichzeitig traten die traditionellen „Real-Money"-Anlagemanager stärker in den Vordergrund und füllten die entstandene Lücke, so dass sich die Markterholung fortsetzte.

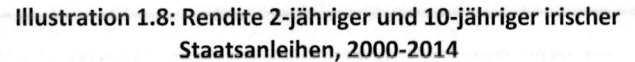

Illustration 1.8: Rendite 2-jähriger und 10-jähriger irischer Staatsanleihen, 2000-2014

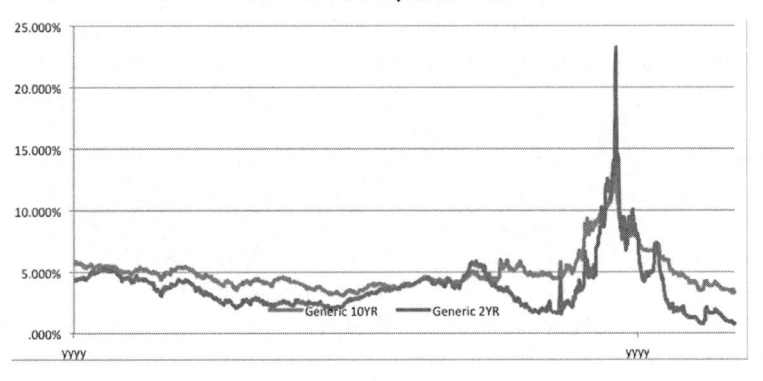

Generic ...YR = generisch ... Jahre

Im dritten und letzten Jahr des Troika-Programms 2013 musste die NTMA den Dialog mit Marktteilnehmern weiter vorantreiben. Von Ende 2013 an, wenn der gesamte im EU/IWF-Programm verfügbare Betrag von 67,5 Mrd. Euro aufgebraucht sein würde, musste sich der Staat ja ohne Hilfe finanzieren. Deshalb sollte Ende 2013 genug Geld aus langfristigen Finanzierungsquellen zur Verfügung stehen, um den Bedarf der Staatskasse für 12 bis 15 Monate abzudecken. In der Praxis bedeutete dies, 2013 zusätzlich zu den letzten Geldern aus dem EU/IWF-Programm etwa 7-8 Mrd. Euro auf den Anleihemärkten zu beschaffen, um am Ende des Jahres über etwa 20 Mrd. Euro an Barmitteln zu verfügen. Die NTMA begann diesen Finanzierungsprozess am 7. Januar 2013 mit der syndizierten Daueremission von 2,5 Mrd. Euro ihrer existierenden 5-jährigen Benchmark-Anleihe. Die Investoren zeigten sich gegenüber der Anleiheemission sehr aufgeschlossen.

Im Februar 2013 trat eine sprunghafte Verbesserung ein. Die IBRC wurde liquidiert. Sie war Inhaberin jener Schuldverschreibungen, welche die Regierung an die Anglo Irish Bank und die Irish Nationwide Building Society ausgegeben hatte, bevor diese am 1. Juli 2011 zur Irish Bank Resolution Corporation fusioniert wurden. Diese Papiere machten jedes Jahr eine Geldaufnahme durch die NTMA in Höhe von 3 Mrd. Euro erforderlich. Sie wurden nun durch langfristige Staatsanleihen ersetzt. Der Nettoeffekt dieser Transaktion lag in einer Verringerung des Finanzierungsbedarfs um etwa 2 Mrd. Euro pro Jahr oder 20 Mrd. Euro über das kommende Jahrzehnt. Außerdem vereinbarten die EU-Regierungschefs in den ersten Monaten des Jahres 2013, die Fälligkeitsfristen der von Irland aufgenommenen Kredite aus dem EFSF (17,7 Mrd. Euro) und dem EFSM (22,5 Mrd. Euro) um sieben Jahre zu verlängern. Dadurch wurde die Höhe der in den Märkten zu refinanzierenden Schulden über die nächsten zehn Jahre um weitere 20 Mrd. Euro reduziert. Der kombinierte Effekt dieser Vereinbarung sowie der

Umwandlung der Schuldverschreibungen ergab also eine Verringerung des Finanzierungsbedarfs der NTMA um 40 Mrd. Euro über die nächsten zehn Jahre.

Durch die gleichzeitig erhöhte Liquidität (durch Verringerung des Refinanzierungsrisikos) und bessere Solvenz Irlands (die Geschäftsabschlüsse sicherten langfristig niedrigere Zinskosten) war die Stimmung am Markt überaus günstig. Dies nutzte die NTMA und beschaffte am 13. März 2013 5 Mrd. Euro durch die syndizierte Emission einer neuen 10-jährigen Benchmark-Anleihe mit einer Rendite von 4,15 Prozent. Angebote kamen von über 400 guten, hauptsächlich „Real-Money"-Investoren vom europäischen Kontinent, Großbritannien und in den USA. Ausserdem erwarben einheimische Investoren 18 Prozent der Emission. Allein diese Transaktion sicherte praktisch die gesamte Finanzierung für das ganze Jahr 2013.

Im Lauf des Jahres setzte sich die 2012 begonnene Umwandlung von einem Markt, der zu Beginn der Erholung von „Fast-Money"-Hedgefonds-Investoren mit hoher Risikobereitschaft getragen wurde, zu einem Markt fort, in dem die traditionelleren „Real-Money"-Anlagemanager, Versicherungsgesellschaften und Pensionsfonds dominierten. Insbesondere Real-Money-Investoren aus Europa kamen auf den irischen Markt. Diese neuen Investoren waren überzeugt, dass Irland Marktzugang erhalten würde zu Renditen, die mit Schuldennachhaltigkeit vereinbar sin,. Außerdem hatte sie Draghis Zusicherung beruhigt, „alles zu tun". Sie waren auf der Suche nach Renditen, die mehr einbrachten als eine Investition in als AAA eingestufte Anleihen von Kernländern der Eurozone. Die irischen Renditen wurden mit deutlich mehr als 2 Prozentpunkten Aufgeld über den in diesen Ländern oftmals unter 2 Prozent liegenden Renditen gehandelt.

Dass die irische Regierung im November 2013 das EU/IWF-Programm ohne vorsorgliche Kreditlinie verließ, überraschte viele Kommentatoren, wurde vom Anleihenmarkt aber gelassen zur Kenntnis genommen. Die Entscheidung der Regierung hat sich als korrekt erwiesen. Die NTMA konnte eines ihrer erfolgreichsten Geschäfte überhaupt abschließen, als sie am 7. Januar 2014 eine neue Anleiheemission mit einer Laufzeit von 10 Jahren mit einer Rendite von 3,54 Prozent syndizierte, 166 Basispunkte über der deutschen Anleihe mit 10 Jahren Laufzeit. Die Entscheidung von Moody's am 17. Januar, Irlands Investment-Grade-Rating wiederherzustellen, wurde allgemein als Anpassung an den Markt gesehen. Sie eröffnete die Aussicht auf neue Investoren in irische Staatsanleihen, deren Mandate Investitionen nur dann gestatten, wenn ein Investment-Grade-Rating von allen großen Kredit-Ratingagenturen vorliegt. Außerdem wurde Irland von einigen Anleihe-Indizes wieder aufgenommen, was zur Folge hatte, dass einige Investoren zum Kauf irischer Anleihen gezwungen waren. Dies ist besonders wichtig für Anleger in Asien und im Nahen Osten, aber auch für einige europäische Fonds.

Irland hat ganz eindeutig wieder vollen Marktzugang erlangt. Die NTMA will diese Bewertung durch eine Reihe von normalen Anleiheauktionen während des Jahres 2014 bestätigen, genau wie die anderen kleineren Länder der Eurozone. Gewiss hängt die dauerhafte Fähigkeit zum Zugriff auf die Märkte zu nachhaltigen

Zinssätzen entscheidend von der Fähigkeit der Regierung ab, auf viele Jahre hinaus eine umsichtige Finanzpolitik zu betreiben. Primäre Haushaltsüberschüsse sollten ausreichen, um die Schuldenlast, festgemacht am Verhältnis von Verschuldung zum BIP, nach und nach abzubauen.

KAPITEL 2
Irlands Geschäftsmodell

Dr. Jack Golden

Hauptaussagen

- Irland hat Belastbarkeit und Flexibilität bei der Anpassung seines Wirtschafts- und Geschäftsmodells bewiesen, nicht nur in dieser Krise, sondern auch über vier Jahrzehnte als Teil des Projektes Europa. Dies erklärt seinen Übergang von einer kleinen Agrarwirtschaft, deren Exporte von Großbritannien dominiert wurden, zu einer der weltweit am stärksten globalisierten und vielseitigsten Volkswirtschaften.

- Es bleiben bedeutsame Herausforderungen, um das volle Potenzial des dynamischen Wirtschaftsmodells Irlands auszuschöpfen: Überwindung der mangelnden Kreditvergabe an Unternehmen, Verbesserung der Exportfähigkeit von KMU bei gleichzeitiger Beibehaltung des günstigen irischen Steuersystems.

Einleitung

1972 war Irland eine kleine Agrarwirtschaft, bei der zwei Drittel der Exporte für den unmittelbaren Nachbarn bestimmt waren. Der Lebensstandard lag unterhalb von zwei Dritteln des europäischen Durchschnitts. Vierzig Jahre später ist Irland die drittoffenste Volkswirtschaft der Welt.[18] Die Exporte an seinen unmittelbaren Nachbarn bleiben weiterhin sehr wichtig, machen nun jedoch ein Fünftel der Exporte insgesamt aus. Trotz vier Jahren Rezession ist der Lebensstandard auf Höhe des EU-Durchschnitts oder darüber geblieben (Irlands BIP pro Kopf beträgt 121 Prozent des EU-Durchschnitts).[19] Dies lässt sich mit der Situation vergleichen, bevor Irland der Europäischen Wirtschaftsgemeinschaft (EWG) beitrat. Damals lag der Lebensstandard des Durchschnitts-Iren weit hinter dem deutschen oder

---

[18] EY (Ernst & Young) Globalisierungsindex 2012.

[19] Der Abstand zwischen BIP und BNE (Ersteres ist etwa ein Fünftel größer als Letzteres) bedeutet, dass das BIP pro Kopf den Lebensstandard Irlands zu hoch angibt. Der Rückgriff auf das BIP pro Kopf ist jedoch aus zwei Gründen berechtigt: erstens ist das BIP pro Kopf ein internationaler Standardmaßstab und zweitens ist der anhaltende Erfolg ausländischer Direktinvestitionen, den das höhere BIP widerspiegelt, ein positives Zeichen für die Zukunft der Wirtschaft (siehe **Kapitel 4**).

französischen zurück. Die Veränderung ist keine Eintagsfliege. Der Erfolg des irischen Geschäftsmodells liegt darin, dass es nie aufgehört hat, sich Veränderungen anzupassen.

In den 1970er und 1980er Jahren war die Gemeinsame Agrarpolitik maßgeblich daran beteiligt, die Einkommen und Wirtschaftsaktivitäten in Irlands weniger entwickelten ländlichen Regionen zu steigern. In den 1980ern begann sich die jahrzehntelange Arbeit der irischen Behörde für industrielle Entwicklung, der Industrial Development Authority (IDA), auszuzahlen. 1985 wurde Microsoft das erste weltweit agierende, führende Unternehmen der Informationstechnologie, das sein internationales Hauptquartier in Irland aufschlug. Ein weiterer entscheidender Wendepunkt im irischen Geschäftsmodell war 1992 das Bekenntnis der irischen Wähler zur Wirtschafts- und Währungsunion (EWU). Dies markierte den Übergang von dem Ziel, ausländische Direktinvestitionen auf der Grundlage niedriger Arbeitskosten, günstiger Unternehmensbesteuerung und gut ausgebildeter Arbeitskräfte anzulocken, zu einer neuen Phase, in der Irland als Brücke zum größten Binnenmarkt der Welt hervorgehoben wurde.

Exportorientierte Cluster mit hohem Mehrwert in der Informationstechnologie, der Gesundheitsversorgung, der Biotechnik, der Pharmazeutik und anderen Branchen sind nun ein Hauptmerkmal der irischen Wirtschaft. Die Ankunft der globalen Social-Media-Giganten Facebook und Twitter in den letzten Jahren zeigt, dass dieser Prozess kontinuierlich ist und sich ständig selbst erneuert.

Ausgehend vom rein exportgetriebenen Wachstum der 1980er und frühen 1990er Jahre brachte das Bekenntnis zur EWU den Beginn eines stärker inländisch orientierten Geschäftsmodells. Bis 2000 hatte Irland Vollbeschäftigung erreicht und war eine der am schnellsten wachsenden Volkswirtschaften unter den Industrienationen. Gleichzeitig war es in jenem Jahr mit Rang 4 in einem führenden weltweiten Indikator[20] immer noch eine der wettbewerbsfähigsten Volkswirtschaften der Welt. Die Balance zwischen Exportwachstum und Binnenwachstum war immer noch einigermaßen gegeben.

Doch bald wurde diese Balance gestört, als sich ein zunehmend dominantes Binnenwachstum zu sehr auf hohe öffentliche Ausgaben und Bankenkredite zu stützen begann. Das Wachstum der Bauaktivitäten – anfangs als notwendige Reaktion auf eine schnell wachsende Bevölkerung noch positiv – geriet bald außer Kontrolle. Plötzlich war fast jeder fünfte männliche Arbeitnehmer in diesem Sektor beschäftigt.

Bis 2007 sah das irische Geschäftsmodell an der Oberfläche gesund aus. Doch sollten ein hoher Schuldenstand und hohe Staatsausgaben für die enorme Gefährdung Irlands in der herannahenden globalen Krise sorgen. Immerhin: Selbst als die Krise ausbrach, veränderte sich dieses Modell auf eine Weise, die Irland nun bei seiner Sanierung hilft. Bis in die 1990er basierte Irlands Geschäftsmodell auf Industriepolitik und der Nutzung von Kapitalzuschüssen, um ausländische

---

[20] Weltranglisten 2000/2001 des Weltwirtschaftsforums zur Wettbewerbsfähigkeit.

Investitionen in der Hochtechnologiefertigung anzulocken. Ab 1994 begann die EU, die Größe von Kapitalzuschüssen für die Industrie zu begrenzen. Als einer der Vorreiter hatte Irland begonnen, seine Politik zu ändern. Die Lissabon-Agenda von 2000 – aus der EU die weltweit „dynamischste und wettbewerbsfähigste wissensbasierte Ökonomie" zu machen - verlieh dieser Änderung zusätzlichen Schwung.

Irland ging von einer Industriestrategie zur Entwicklung einer weiter gefassten „Unternehmenspolitik" über. Dazu gehörte die Belebung einheimischer Branchen in Bereichen mit starkem Wachstum, besonders bei Dienstleistungen, einem Bereich mit enormem Wachstumspotenzial für Irlands kleine und offene Inselökonomie.

Wie das vorhergehende Kapitel schon andeutete und im Folgenden deutlicher werden wird, wurde dieser Übergang zwischen 2008 und 2012 durch eine deutliche Verbesserung der Wettbewerbsfähigkeit durch niedrigere Kosten unterstützt. Auch eine Anzahl gezielter Strategien, wie etwa der Aktionsplan für Arbeitsplätze („Action Plan for Jobs"), und verschiedene Haushaltsinitiativen, die Unternehmensgründungen, Innovationen und die Schaffung von Arbeitsplätzen unterstützten, haben zum Erfolg des irischen Geschäftsmodells beigetragen.

Doch Herausforderungen bleiben bestehen. So bleibt Irland trotz sich verbessernder Wettbewerbsfähigkeit ein Land mit relativ hohen Kosten für unternehmerische Tätigkeit. Das ist ein Ergebnis früherer Fehler in der Wirtschaftspolitik. Andere sind eher strukturbedingt. Beispielsweise fehlt dem irischen Mittelstand im Gegensatz zu seinem deutschen Pendant der Zugang zu einem inländischen Markt mit ausreichender Größe und Absatzmöglichkeit, um Exportkapazitäten zu entwickeln. Einige Probleme stehen eher im Zusammenhang mit der jüngsten Krise. Dazu gehört die mangelnde Kreditvergabe. Als dieser Artikel verfasst wurde, war Irlands Bankensystem immer noch auf dem Weg zur Normalisierung. Der für 2014 erwartete Stresstest irischer Banken durch die EZB wird eine entscheidende Schwelle sein.

Eine neue Herausforderung liegt darin, dass das produzierende Gewerbe nun einen geringeren Anteil an der Beschäftigung und Wirtschaft ausmacht als in den 1990er Jahren. Die hohe Produktivität multinationaler verarbeitender Unternehmen wird somit weniger gut in der Lage sein, Wirtschaftswachstumsraten wie in den 1990ern und 2000ern zu unterstützen. Andere Sektoren müssen sich stärker einbringen, wenn Irlands Wachstum die Höhen erreichen soll, die für die Rückkehr zur Prosperität nötig sind.

Glücklicherweise hat die Regierung bei der jüngsten Überarbeitung des irischen Geschäftsmodells innovative Strategien entworfen, die einen bedeutenden Schritt auf dem Weg zur Problemlösung darstellen. Sie werden im Weiteren erläutert. Doch zunächst lohnt sich ein Blick auf die Werte, die dem irischen Geschäftsmodell und seiner Fähigkeit zur Anpassung an Änderungen zugrunde liegen.

Werte, die das irische Geschäftsmodell stützen.

Die Wahrnehmung, das irische Geschäftsmodell beruhe allein auf seiner Steuerpolitik, ist völlig falsch. Eine Anzahl von Grundwerten dient als Unterbau für eine Reihe umfassender unternehmenspolitischer Ansätze, die auf die Unterstützung und kontinuierliche Entwicklung der Fertigungs- und Dienstleistungssektoren der Wirtschaft gerichtet sind.

Investitionen in die Ansiedlung ausländischer Unternehmen in Irland und in die Entwicklung der einheimischen Industrie waren grundlegend für Irlands Erfolg. Dabei lag der Schwerpunkt auf **Innovation** und auf der wachsenden **wechselseitigen Abhängigkeit** zwischen einheimischen und multinationalen Unternehmen. Die Schaffung von Branchen-**Clustern** ist ebenfalls ein Hauptmerkmal, das zunehmend deutlicher sichtbar wird, ebenso wie die Auswirkungen der **Kultur** und ein ausgeprägter Fokus auf **Wettbewerbsfähigkeit**.

Investitionen: Ausländische Direktinvestitionen

Nach Jahrzehnten schwachen Wachstums nach der Unabhängigkeit wurde dem jungen irischen Staat schnell die Bedeutung von Handelsinvestitionen aus dem Ausland für Irlands Entwicklung bewusst. Die große geografische Nähe machte Großbritannien zum wichtigsten Handelspartner, während enge historische Bande die USA zu einem naheliegenden Investitionsgeber machten. Die USA wurden schnell zu einer dominanten Kraft bei den ausländischen Direktinvestitionen. Mittlerweile sind diese Investitionen stärker diversifiziert, sowohl geografisch als auch im Hinblick auf die Branchen. In zunehmendem Maße zeigen nun international gehandelte Dienstleistungen das Potenzial, die Rolle zu ergänzen, die bisher verarbeitende Unternehmen der Hochtechnologie einnahmen. Ausländische Direktinvestitionen sind auch keine Einbahnstraße mehr: Irische Unternehmen investieren nun in einem Umfang im Ausland, der in keinem Verhältnis zu Irlands Größe als Nation steht.

Die 1949 gegründete Industrial Development Authority (IDA) ebnete den Weg für ausländische Investitionen in die irische Wirtschaft. Sie waren ein entscheidender Faktor bei der Umgestaltung des Landes. Viele andere kleine Nationen haben versucht, Irlands „Weltmeister"-Status in diesem Bereich nachzueifern.

Laut Daten des US-amerikanischen Bureau of Economic Analysis[21] stiegen die US-amerikanischen Investitionen in Irland 2011 um 20 Prozent auf 188,3 Mrd. US-Dollar. Dies bedeutet, dass Irland mehr multinationale Investitionen aus den USA erhält als Brasilien, Russland, Indien und China zusammen.

Dem IBM-Bericht über globale Standorttrends von 2012 („2012 Global Location Trends Report") zufolge liegt Irland weltweit auf Rang 1 bei Qualität und Wert von

---

[21] Zitat aus Quinlan, Joseph (2012). „The Irish-US Economic Relationship", Amerikanische Handelskammer Irland (American Chamber of Commerce Ireland).

Investitionen aus dem Ausland, auf Rang 1 in Europa bei der Schaffung von Arbeitsplätzen in Forschung und Entwicklung und auf Rang 2 in Europa bzw. Rang 4 weltweit bei der Anzahl von Investitionsjobs pro Kopf der Bevölkerung.

Investitionen: Einheimische Industrie

Neben der Förderung ausländischer Direktinvestitionen war die irische Regierung seit der Rezession auch darauf bedacht, Investitionen in einheimische kleine und mittelständische Unternehmen zu fördern. Mit Hilfe einer erfolgreichen staatlichen Agentur, der Enterprise Ireland, und einer Reihe staatlicher Strategien (die im Weiteren erörtert werden) hat eine eindrucksvolle Erholung der einheimischen Industrie begonnen.

Weitere Initiativen stärken diesen Trend. Zwar hat der Haushalt 2014 Irlands Finanzlage in geringerem Umfang verbessert als von der Troika verlangt[22], was – manch negative Kommentare provozierte. Doch die Differenz zwischen der von der Troika geforderten Anpassung und der erzielten Anpassung (etwas über 500 Mio Euro) floss in vollem Umfang direkt in ein Paket von Anreizen, mit denen der Mittelstand stimuliert werden soll.

Zu diesem Paket gehörten Initiativen zur Unterstützung der Handelsfinanzierung sowie Steuernachlässe für Unternehmensneugründungen. Mit verbesserten steuerlichen Anreizen sollen die Reinvestition von Kapitalzuwächsen und weitere Investitionen in Forschung und Entwicklung stimuliert werden.

Der Tourismus ist die älteste und bekannteste Quelle für Einkommen aus Dienstleistungen für Ausländer. Der Haushalt für 2014 sah eine Verringerung der Flughafengebühren vor und behielt eine verminderte Mehrwertsteuer für die Tourismusindustrie bei, um die Besucherzahlen nach oben zu treiben. Dies folgt der Initiative „Versammlung" („Gathering") von 2013. Sie zielte darauf ab, einer Reihe von Events für die ganze Familie Angehörige der weltweiten irischen Diaspora zu einem Besuch im Land zu bewegen. Initiativen wie das Programm Heimsanierung („Home Renovation") sind als Hilfe für kleine Baufirmen gedacht. Damit soll die Bauwirtschaft – ein anderer etablierter Wirtschaftszweig, der von der Misere schwer betroffen war – wiederbelebt und von spekulativen Aktivitäten wie vor der Krise weg gelenkt werden.

Wechselseitige Abhängigkeit

Man könnte Irlands Erfolg bei der Anwerbung ausländischer Direktinvestitionen als einen Fall übermäßiger Abhängigkeit von ausländischen Investoren sehen. Doch es verhält sich ganz anders. Irlands Position ist von wechselseitiger Abhängigkeit geprägt. Laut Recherchen der Amerikanischen Handelskammer in Irland

---

[22] Die Troika hatte eine Gesamtanpassung – einschließlich Steuererhöhungen und Ausgabenkürzungen – von 3,1 Mrd. Euro verlangt, der eine Anpassung von 2,6 Mrd. Euro am Tag der Haushaltsverabschiedung gegenübersteht.

beschäftigen irische Unternehmen in den USA mehr Mitarbeiter als Tochtergesellschaften von US-Unternehmen in Irland.

Das Gleiche gilt auch für Deutschland. So wie deutsche Unternehmen wichtige Arbeitgeber in Irland sind, sichern irische Unternehmen wie CRH, Glen Dimplex und Kingspan Tausende Jobs in Deutschland an.

Die wechselseitige Abhängigkeit zwischen multinationalen Unternehmen mit Sitz in Irland und einheimischen Unternehmen wird auf mehreren Ebenen deutlich, u. a. in Vereinbarungen zwischen Kunde und Anbieter, im Talentaustausch innerhalb des Landes und international sowie in der Entwicklung irischer multinationaler Unternehmen, die in den letzten 40 Jahren auf das europäische Festland und nach Übersee expandierten.

Zum Jahr 2012 waren international gehandelte Waren und Leistungen in der irischen Wirtschaft etwa 313 Mrd. Euro – oder ein Drittel einer Billion Euro – wert, was fast dem Doppelten des irischen BIP entspricht. Dies ist der bei weitem höchste Wert aller EU-Mitgliedsstaaten und macht Irland zur am stärksten globalisierten westlichen Volkswirtschaft und zur drittoffensten Volkswirtschaft der Welt nach Hong Kong und Singapur.

Eindrucksvollerweise verbesserte sich Irlands Exportbilanz und Anreiz für ausländische Investitionen sogar deutlich, während die Rezession die einheimische Wirtschaft noch fest im Griff hatte: 2010 lag das Exportwachstum sowohl bei multinationalen als auch bei einheimischen Unternehmen höher als die Quote des Rückgangs im Jahr zuvor.

Ganz gleich also, ob man den Index zur Wettbewerbsfähigkeit des Weltwirtschaftsforums, den Globalisierungsindex von Ernst & Young oder den IBM-Bericht über globale Standorttrends zu Grunde legt: Irland geht ohne Schaden an seinem Status als eine der führenden Nationen in der globalisierten Wirtschaft aus dieser Krise hervor.

Innovation

Seit seinem Beitritt zur EWG als Agrarland ist Irlands Wirtschaft stark gewachsen. Dies geht auf die eindrucksvolle Fähigkeit des Landes zurück, sich ständig zu erneuern. Der Welle produzierender Hochtechnologieunternehmen, die in den 1980er und frühen 1990er Jahren nach Irland kamen, folgte das Heranwachsen einer starken einheimischen Wirtschaft und Konsumkultur Ende der 1990er und Anfang der 2000er Jahre. Nun durchläuft das irische Geschäftsmodell seine vielleicht interessanteste Innovationsphase.

Das Aufkommen neuer Cluster in Bereichen wie der Nanotechnologie, Gesundheitsinformatik, Hochtechnologie, Nahrungsmittel, und der Internationalisierung von Knowhow im Bausektor, um nur einige zu nennen, ist nicht nur das Ergebnis der Arbeit der IDA. Es wurde auch durch diverse politische Initiativen auf den Gebieten Forschung und Entwicklung, Innovation und Anreizentwicklung für Investitionen gefördert.

Im Oktober 2007 räumte das nationalen Reformprogramm für eine intelligente Wirtschaft („Smart Economy Framework") innovationsbasierten Unternehmen und hochwertiger Beschäftigung Vorrang ein. Das Programm baute auf einem Sieben-Jahres-Plan („Strategy for Science, Technology and Innovation", 2006-2013) auf, der mittels staatlicher Zuschüsse für Forschung und Entwicklung die Umgestaltung Irlands zu einer Wissensgesellschaft anschieben sollte.

Zuletzt wurde 2012 der „Action Plan for Jobs" auf den Weg gebracht. Dadurch sollen Arbeitsplätze ersetzt werden, die während der Krise verloren gingen. Gefragt ist nachhaltige Beschäftigung, die auf Innovation, Unternehmergeist und Export basiert. Unter weit gefassten strategischen Zielsetzungen wie dem Ausbau von Wettbewerbsvorteilen, der Unterstützung des Wachstums der einheimischen Industrie, der Förderung von Unternehmensgründungen und der Vertiefung der Wirkung ausländischer Direktinvestitionen enthält der Plan Hunderte kleinerer Initiativen, die als pozentielle Jobmotoren gekennzeichnet sind. 2012, als der Plan eingeführt wurde, entstanden 12.000 Arbeitsplätze in der Privatwirtschaft. Mehr als 58.000 Arbeitsplätze wurden in den zwölf Monaten bis zum dritten Quartal 2013 geschaffen. Dieser positive Trend soll sich in den kommenden Jahren fortsetzen.

Die irische Wirtschaft hat ihre Innovationsfreude einmal mehr unter Beweis gestellt, indem sie erfolgreich auf dem Wachstumsmarkt neuartiger Dienstleistungen agiert. Demografische Trends wie das Wachstum der weltweiten Bevölkerung mit „mittlerem Einkommen" lassen diesem Markt weniger abhängig vom globalen Wirtschaftszyklus erscheinen. Er bietet einer kleinen vielseitigen Volkswirtschaft wie Irland die Möglichkeit, in Zukunft schneller zu wachsen. Zwischen 2003 und 2012 und trotz der Auswirkungen der Rezession auf andere Teile der Wirtschaft wuchsen die Dienstleistungsexporte aus Irland fast um das Dreifache von 35,3 Mrd. Euro auf 90,3 Mrd. Euro.[23] Im Gegensatz zu Warenexporten, wo der starke Einfluss der USA bis heute deutlich ist, sind Exporte bei Dienstleistungen stärker weltweit diversifiziert.[24]

Wettbewerbsfähigkeit
Ein auffälliges Merkmal seiner Wettbewerbsfähigkeit hat das irische Geschäftsmodell mit deutschen Autos gemein: die Fähigkeit, abrupt und schnell die Richtung zu wechseln!

Auf der Geschwindigkeit und Flexibilität zehntausender kleiner und mittelständischer Unternehmen beruhend, geht diese Fähigkeit, die „Straßenlage" zu halten, auf eine Kombination von Faktoren zurück, die eher mikroökonomischer

---

[23] Zentrales Statistikamt (Central Statistics Office), „Quarterly National Hosuehold Survey, Q3 2013".

[24] Newman, Carol (2012). ‚Manufacturing and Internationally Traded Services', *Carol von O'Hagan u.a. „The Economy of Ireland"*, Gill & Macmillan; Zentrales Statistikamt (Central Statistics Office), *„International Trade in Services Release 2012"*, 30. September 2013.

als makroökonomischer Natur sind. Zwischen dem Ausbruch der Krise 2008 und 2012 hat Irland einer Berechnung der EZB zufolge eine erstaunliche Verbesserung der Wettbewerbsfähigkeit um 40 Prozent erreicht (in **Illustration 2.1** unten dargestellt). Zwar folgte dies einem Zeitraum, in dem sich die Wettbewerbsfähigkeit verschlechtert hatte. Doch zeigt es Irlands Widerstandskraft und seine Fähigkeit, sich neuen Gegebenheiten schnell anzupassen. Eine fallende Linie beschreibt relativ fallende Kosten und damit eine Steigerung der Wettbewerbsfähigkeit. Irlands Verbesserung war grösser als der EU-Durchschnitt und lag erheblich vor anderen Staaten in Rettungsprogrammen.

Illustration 2.1: Irlands Steigerung der Wettbewerbsfähigkeit: eine drastische Verbesserung seit 2008

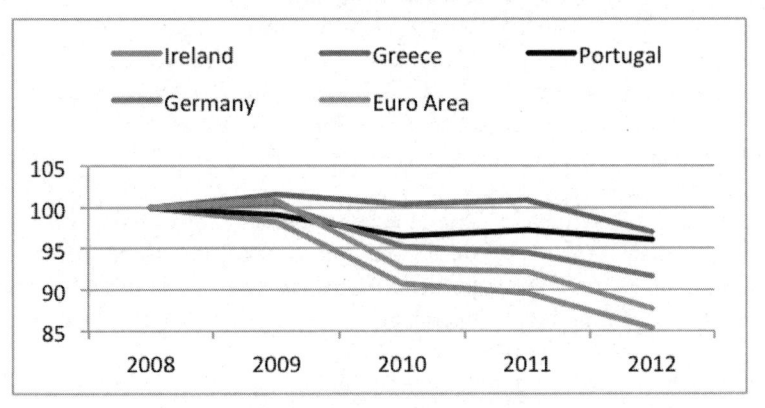

Ireland = Irland; Greece = Griechenland; Portugal = Portugal; Germany = Deutschland; Euro Area = Euroraum.
Quelle: EZB (index: 2008 = 100).

Diese Verbesserung war möglich, weil die Preise und Löhne im Verhältnis zum übrigen Europa fielen. Manche Wirtschaftswissenschaftler hatten argumentiert, Irland solle aus dem Euro austreten, um seine Währung abwerten zu können. Doch Irlands bisherige Erfahrung zeigt, dass eine echte Abwertung – eine Anpassung der Geschäftskosten im Vergleich zu seinen Peers – ohne das Opfer der Euro-Mitgliedschaft erreicht wurde. Darüber hinaus ist diese Anpassungsfähigkeit des irischen Geschäftsmodells durch einen starken Aufschwung des Exports belohnt worden, und das nach einem Jahr, 2009, in dem viele Länder des Euroraums, einschließlich Deutschland, starke Exportrückgänge verzeichneten.

Illustration 2.2 unten zeigt nicht nur, dass sich Irlands Export 2010 gut erholen konnte, sondern seither auch neue Höhen erklommen hat. Obwohl er über den Zeitraum nicht so stark war wie der deutsche Export, war er doch weniger unbeständig und übertraf den der anderen Troika-Länder.

Illustration 2.2: Irlands Exportwachstum in Prozent, 2008-2012

Land	Durchschnitt	2008	2009	2010	2011	2012
Irland	+1,7	-1,1	-3,8	6,4	5,4	1,6
Griechenland	-2,6	1,7	-19,4	5,2	0,3	-0,9
Portugal	-0,5	2,3	-11,9	0,8	8,1	-2,0
Deutschland	+3,2	2,8	-13,0	15,2	8,0	3,2
Euroraum	+1,6	0,6	-12,7	11,6	6,3	2,3

Quelle: IWF, *Weltwirtschaftsausblick*, Oktober 2013.

Obwohl die Exporte 2012 aufgrund internationaler Faktoren stockten, wird das Exportwachstum ein wichtiger Motor des Wiederaufschwungs sein. Die vom IWF in seinem jüngsten Weltwirtschaftsausblick prognostizierte Belebung des Wachstums ab 2014 beruht ganz klar auf einem anhaltenden Exportwachstum.

Mit dem 28. Platz im weltweiten Ranking des Weltwirtschaftsforums von 2013/2014 gehört Irland immer noch zu den 30 wettbewerbsfähigsten Volkswirtschaften der Welt. Wie in Kapitel 1 erwähnt, wird diese Gesamtleistung durch schwache Platzierungen hinsichtlich des makroökonomischen Umfelds (134.) und der Finanzmärkte (85.) beeinträchtigt, ein Erbe der Krise. Infolgedessen werden durch das Ranking die Vitalität und Erneuerungsfähigkeit des Landes unterbewertet. Diese beiden Qualitäten zeigen sich in Irlands Platzierungen in anderen Kategorien, wie etwa Technologisches Anpassungsvermögen (13.), Flexibilität des Warenmarktes (11.), Flexibilität des Arbeitsmarktes (16.) und Ausdifferenziertheit des Wirtschaftslebens (20.), um nur einige zu nennen. Irland kann es ganz klar wieder auf die Liste der 20 wettbewerbsfähigsten Länder der Welt schaffen, vielleicht sogar unter die Top 10. Die Tatsache, dass Intel seinen neuesten Mikrochip in Irland entwickeln will, ist ein ermutigendes Anzeichen dafür, dass das Land auf guten Weg ist.

Cluster

Einige Jahrzehnte nach der ersten Erprobung in Dänemark hat Irland Erfolge bei der Entwicklung von Branchen-Clustern erzielt. Sie haben das Potenzial, in der irischen Wirtschaft tiefere Wurzeln zu schlagen.

Von diesen ist der Informationstechnologie-Cluster, der weltweit renommierte Markennamen wie Microsoft, Dell, Hewlett Packard und Intel umfasst, der erste und bekannteste. Schon vor der Rezession wurde ein Teil der traditionellen Arbeitsprozesse in diesem Cluster aus Irland ausgelagert: Die Geschäftskosten waren gestiegen, Fertigungszentren im Osten konnten kostengünstiger produzieren. Während sich dies abzeichnete, entstanden dank der Regierungspolitik und der Umsicht der IDA Cluster der zweiten und dritten Generation. In der zweiten Welle sind Unternehmen der Pharmazeutik,

Gesundheitsfürsorge und der Biotechnologie sowie Dublins International Financial Services Centre (IFSC) zu nennen.

Wie in jeder dynamischen Wirtschaft ist die Veränderung eine Konstante. Während einige Branchen negative Entwicklungen durchlaufen – der pharmazeutische Bereich wird derzeit vom sogenannten „Patent cliff", den Umsatzeinbußen durch auslaufende Patente, beeinträchtigt –, erleben andere ein Wachstum. Die Ankündigung der Deutschen Bank im Jahr 2013, 700 Arbeitsplätze im IFSC schaffen zu wollen, ist ein Beispiel für solches Wachstum.

Eine dritte Generation von Clustern ist in den letzten Jahren in Bereichen wie Software-Entwicklung, Social Media, Umwelttechnik und Cloud Computing entstanden. Der „Action Plan for Jobs" von 2013 enthält die Absicht, Irland zum führenden Land in Europa für „Big Data" zu machen. Diesem Markt für Daten, die von Unternehmen und Regierungen erzeugt und gesammelt werden, wird schnelles Wachstum prognostiziert. Irland kann sich die neue Wirtschaftskraft zunutze machen, seine Trümpfe ausspielen und möglichen Bedenken entgegenwirken: Entsprechende Cluster – die Fachkräfte und Lieferketten für derartige Branchen – sind in Irland bereits vorhanden, wenn auch noch nicht in der erforderlichen Menge; Datenanalytik benötigt keinen Standort in Gebieten mit hoher Bevölkerungskonzentration, weshalb Irlands Lage an der Peripherie kein Hindernis für hohes Wachstum in diesem Sektor darstellt.

Indem es diese schnell wachsenden Wirtschaftszweige mit hohem Mehrwert ins Visier nimmt, kann Irland die Auswirkungen seiner relativ hohen Kostenbasis und des starken Euro ausgleichen.

Eine wichtige Herausforderung bleibt die Abstimmung der Leistungsfähigkeit des Bildungssektors auf die Bedürfnisse neuer Wirtschaftszweige. Nach den hochwertigen, doch generalisierten Bildungskompetenzen, die in früheren Entwicklungswellen gefragt waren, wird die Nachfrage nach Kompetenzen nun spezifischer. Zu den im „Action Plan for Jobs" von 2013 benannten strategischen Zielen gehörte beispielsweise die Bereitstellung von zusätzlich 2.000 Fachkräften mit Hochschulabschluss in der Informations- und Kommunikationstechnologie. Die Herausforderung, das irische Bildungssystem auf modernstem Stand zu halten, wird in **Kapitel 6** behandelt.

Kultur

Flexibilität und Pragmatismus sind Wesensmerkmale Irlands. Sie gehören zu den Hauptfaktoren, die dem irischen Geschäftsmodell die schnelle Anpassung an Änderungen im globalen Umfeld ermöglicht. Zudem sind Iren sehr gut darin, sich organisch und dynamisch zu vernetzen. Mängel des Regulierungssystems, die die Finanzkrise offenbart hatte, wurden ausgeräumt. Die Qualität der physischen Infrastruktur ist nun mit den anderen westlichen Industrienationen vergleichbar. Natürlich ist ein günstiges Körperschaftssteuersystem ein deutlicher Anreiz für Unternehmen. Doch spielen die kulturellen Vorteile der Offenheit, Flexibilität und eine einmalige Fähigkeit zur Vernetzung eine wichtige Rolle bei Irlands Erfolg, als

Brücke zwischen internationalen, insbesondere amerikanischen Unternehmen und dem europäischen Binnenmarkt zu fungieren.

Irland ist ein kleines Land. Familienleben und Gemeinschaft stellen wichtige Werte dar und werden durch eine lange Tradition intensiver verbaler Kommunikation gestärkt. Diese Eigenheiten und die Tatsache, dass Irland das einzige englischsprachige Land in der Eurozone ist, werden seit vielen Jahren erfolgreich in der Kommunikation zwischen Unternehmen genutzt. Netzwerkarbeit und Kommunikationsfähigkeit werden für die Entwicklung vieler aufsteigender und wachstumsstarker Wirtschaftszweige wie Social Media und Cloud Computing sogar noch wichtiger. Der Erfolg des Global Web Summit in Dublin 2013 hat verdeutlicht: Irlands Geschäftskultur kann die weitere Entwicklung dieser Branchen gut unterstützen.

In ihrer Arbeit hat die IDA die Dynamik und Flexibilität der irischen Geschäftskultur verkörpert. Die Regierungspolitik wurde so beeinflusst, dass sie kontinuierlich an die Bedürfnisse multinationaler Investoren angepasst wurde. Irland kann als weltweit führend auf diesem Gebiet gelten.

Herausforderungen für Irlands Geschäftsmodell

Kredit

Irlands Banken haben erhebliche Finanzspritzen von Steuergeldern erhalten, ihre Eigenkapitalquoten können sich im internationalen Vergleich sehen lassen, alle Anzeichen deuten auf eine wirtschaftliche Erholung hin. Dennoch bleibt die Wachstumsrate der Kreditvergabe an Unternehmen negativ. Die Regierung hat verschiedene Initiativen auf den Weg gebracht, um die Verfügbarkeit von Krediten für kleine Unternehmen zu verbessern. Ein neues Kreditprüfungsamt (Credit Review Office) ermöglicht es Kleinunternehmern, gegen die Kreditverweigerung bestimmter Banken vorzugehen. Ein Bürgschaftsprogramm (Credit Guarantee Scheme) garantiert zusätzliche 450 Mio Euro Bankkredite an existenzfähige Kleinst- , Klein- und Mittelstandsunternehmen zu. Außerdem wurde ein Mikrofinanzierungsfonds („Microfinance Fund") für Firmen mit maximal 10 Mitarbeitern geschaffen. Er stellt Kredite bis zu 25.000 Euro für kaufmännisch tragfähige Projekte zur Verfügung, die nicht den herkömmlichen, von Geschäftsbanken angewandten Risikokriterien entsprechen.

Die Zurückhaltung beschränkt sich jedoch nicht nur auf die Geberseite. Unternehmen gehen offenbar mit grösserer Vorsicht an die Kreditaufnahme heran. Viele Firmen haben seit 2008 schmerzhafte Umstrukturierungen durchlaufen und scheuen sich, neue Schulden aufzunehmen, so lange sie nicht überzeugt sind, dass das sich abzeichnende Wirtschaftswachstum nachhaltig bleibt. Laut Daten der irischen Zentralbank[25] fielen die Kredite an Kapitalgesellschaften außerhalb des

---

[25] Zentralbank Irland (Central Bank of Ireland), „Money and Banking Statistics", November 2013.

Finanzsektors zum September 2013 um 4,5 Prozent. Bei Krediten zwischen 1 und 5 Jahren – einer wichtigen Kategorie für kleine und mittlere Unternehmen – betrug der Rückgang 15 Prozent. Die Beschränkungen, mit denen die Regierung konfrontiert ist, und die Vorsicht der Banken vor dem Stresstest durch die Europäische Zentralbank stellen zusätzliche Faktoren dar. Die Kreditklemme sowie die mangelnde Risikobereitschaft seitens kleiner und mittelständischer Betriebe können bremsend auf das kurzfristige Wirtschaftswachstum wirken.

Internationalisierung
Die geringe Größe des irischen Binnenmarktes und Irlands Insellage bilden zusammen erhebliche Hindernisse für kleine und mittelständische irische Unternehmen auf dem Weg zur Internationalisierung ihrer Geschäftstätigkeit.

Für viele ist der Handel mit Großbritannien ein naheliegender erster Schritt zum Export. Dafür muss man neue Kompetenzen erwerben, Vertriebskanäle und Kreditlinien finden – ganz zu schweigen von der Entwicklung geeigneter logistischer Kapazitäten oder dem Zugriff darauf. Das kann auf kleinere Firmen abschreckend wirken.

Wieder hilft die Regierung: Als Teil der staatlichen Agentur Enterprise Ireland wurde der Bereich „Potential Exporters Division" eingerichtet. Dort wird potenziellen Exporteuren mit praktischer Beratung, Informationen und Marktwissen geholfen. Dazu gibt es ein bestimmtes Maß an Unterstützung für Aus- und Weiterbildung, Entwicklung und Finanzierung. Zwar verhindern EU-Beschränkungen aggressive Formen der Exportförderung. Doch sollten neue Strategien erkundet werden, um mehr irische KMU zu erfolgreichen Exportunternehmen umzugestalten. Schliesslich tun sich in der globalen Wirtschaft enorme Chancen auf.

Möglicherweise könnten spezialisierte Privatfirmen als „Exportbeschleunigungsdienste" den KMU beim Aufbau einer Basis für Produkte und Dienstleistungen in ausländischen Märkten helfen. Das Wachstum nicht-traditioneller Dienste, die online für den Kunden erbracht werden können, hat enormes Potenzial, allerdings ist der Wettbewerb in diesem Zweig extrem stark.

Besteuerung
Irlands Geschäftsmodell wurde durch das Kombinieren mehrerer Kernelemente aufgebaut und stützt sich daher nicht übermäßig auf einen einzigen Faktor. Allerdings ist Irlands günstiges Steuersystem von grundlegender Bedeutung für den Erfolg dieses Modells und war entscheidend für die Ansiedlung ausländischer Direktinvestitionen. Die OECD[26] hat es zu Recht als „zentrales Element in seinem Modell ausländischer Direktinvestitionen" bezeichnet und als „besten Weg, um für ausländische Direktinvestitionen, die für das Wirtschaftswachstum entscheidend sind, attraktiv zu bleiben". Irland hat konsequent mit einschlägigen internationalen

---

[26]   OECD, „Economic Survey: Ireland", September 2013.

Stellen zusammengearbeitet, damit sein Geschäftsmodell akzeptierter internationaler Praxis entspricht.

Die jüngste Kritik am irischen Steuersystem kam von Ländern, die um Steuereinnahmen von multinationalen Unternehmen konkurrieren. Sie beruht zum größten Teil auf fehlerhaften Informationen. 1956 führte Irland einen Steuersatz von null Prozent auf Einkommen aus Exportumsätzen ein. Dies stellte den Versuch dar, die stagnierende Wirtschaft wieder in Schwung zu bringen. Beim Eintritt in die damalige EWG 1973 vereinbarte Irland, diesen Steuernulltarif Schritt für Schritt abzuschaffen. Bis 1980 waren die Körperschaftssteuersätze in Irland für das produzierende Gewerbe auf 10 Prozent angehoben worden. 1987 wurde dieser Satz auf den sich entwickelnden Wirtschaftszweig der internationalen Finanzdienstleistungen ausgeweitet. In einem schrittweisen, mit den europäischen Partnern ausgehandelten Prozess hob Irland den Satz der Körperschaftssteuer bis 2003 auf den aktuell geltenden Satz von 12,5 Prozent an.

Irlands Kooperation mit anderen Partnern ist ebenfalls eng. Es betreibt über ein System von 69 Doppelbesteuerungsabkommen einen vollständigen Austausch von Steuerinformationen mit seinen Partnern. 2010 führte Irland gesetzlich vorgeschriebene Mitteilungspflichten ein. Sie sorgen für rechtzeitige Informationen über bestimmte Steuerprogramme und deren Nutzer. Programme, die als aggressiv betrachtet werden, können gestoppt werden. 2012 war Irland eines der ersten Länder, die das „Foreign Account Tax Compliance Act (FATCA)" mit den USA unterzeichneten.[27] FATCA ist inzwischen als aufkommender weltweiter Standard für den automatischen Austausch von Steuerinformationen anerkannt.

Die internationale Steuerzusammenarbeit war auch ein Hauptthema der erfolgreichen irischen EU-Präsidentschaft 2013. Irlands Präsidentschaft legte den Schwerpunkt auf die Bekämpfung von Steuerhinterziehung und Steuerflucht. Nach einem Treffen der Wirtschafts- und Finanzminister im April 2013 in Dublin legten der irische Finanzminister Michael Noonan und der EU-Kommissar für Steuern Algirdas Šemeta eine Liste von Maßnahmen zur Stärkung und Vertiefung der Zusammenarbeit auf europäischer Ebene gegen Steuerflucht und Steuerhinterziehung fest. Die am 22. Mai 2013 unterzeichneten Schlussfolgerungen des Europäischen Rates zum Thema Steuern forderten die Ausweitung des automatischen Informationsaustauschs auf die internationale Ebene. Zu diesem Zweck übernimmt Irland eine aktive Rolle in dem OECD-Projekt „Base Erosion Profit Shifting" (Aushöhlung der steuerlichen Bemessungsgrundlage und Gewinnverlagerung). Und schließlich soll ein symbolischer Punkt nicht unerwähnt bleiben: Die Erklärung des G8-Gipfels von Lough Erne, die eine Veröffentlichung der Steuern und Gewinne durch internationale Unternehmen unterstützt, wurde auf der irischen Insel unterzeichnet.

Regierungen unterschiedlicher Couleur sind bisher für die Aufrechterhaltung eines transparenten, internationalen Regeln entsprechenden und

---

[27] September 2012.

wettbewerbsfähigen Körperschaftssteuersystems eingetreten. Die Beibehaltung des Körperschaftssteuersatzes von 12,5 Prozent bleibt ein festes Ziel der Regierungs- wie auch der Oppositionsparteien.

Schlussfolgerungen

Irland hat wie wenige andere EU-Mitgliedsstaaten Anpassungsfähigkeit und Widerstandsfähigkeit bei der Aktualisierung und Erneuerung seines Geschäftsmodells bewiesen. Von einer kleinen Agrarwirtschaft, deren Exporte vom direkten Nachbarn dominiert wurden, ist Irland zu einer der weltweit offensten, flexibelsten, technisch höchstentwickelten und vielseitigsten Volkswirtschaften geworden. Die jeweilige Regierungspolitik – und die Flexibilität der Iren und der irischen Unternehmen – bei der Anpassung an Veränderungen und Herausforderungen waren in diesem Prozess unverzichtbar.

Irlands Geschäftsmodell ist an starken Werten orientiert:

- Innovation sowohl in der Geschäftspraktik als auch der Regierungspolitik.
- Wechselseitige Abhängigkeit zwischen Irland und seinen Partnern in Politik und Handel.
- Bekenntnis zu Investitionen in neue und aufkommende Technologien und Industriezweige.
- Konstante Aufmerksamkeit für die Aufrechterhaltung und Wiederherstellung der Wettbewerbsfähigkeit seiner Wirtschaft, seines Steuermodells und seiner Wirtschaftssektoren.
- Förderung von Branchen-Clustern sowohl im verarbeitenden Gewerbe als auch bei den Dienstleistungen, die Irlands individuelle Vorteile ausspielen und Wachstumschancen eröffnen.
- Eine Geschäftskultur, die Flexibilität, Anpassungsfähigkeit und Pragmatismus betont.

Das irische Geschäftsmodell steht vor wichtigen Herausforderungen. Der Zugang zu Krediten muss besser werden, es gilt Exporthindernisse, insbesondere für kleine und mittelständische Unternehmen, zu überwinden. Kleine, mittelständische und auch größere Firmen sollen sich auch weiterhin das transparente und günstige irische Steuersystem zunutze machen können.

KOMMENTAR: KAPITEL 2

Eine Fallstudie zu ausländischen Direktinvestitionen in Irland: Allianz Worldwide Care Limited

Frank Mee

Hauptaussagen

* Viele weltweit agierende Finanzdienstleister unterhalten heute Standorte in Irland aufgrund einer Kombination von Erfolgsfaktoren, von denen das irische Steuersystem nur einer ist. Die Allianz Gruppe, die 144.000 Mitarbeiter beschäftigt und 78 Millionen Kunden hat, ist ein gutes Beispiel dafür.
* Ein stabiles Geschäftsumfeld, unterstützende Regierungsbehörden und der Zugang zu gut ausgebildeten und unternehmerisch denkenden Mitarbeitern ermöglichten dem Finanzdienstleistungssektor ein starkes Wachstum und eine schnelle Erholung nach der Krise. Um Irlands Wettbewerbsfähigkeit aufrechtzuerhalten, müssen jedoch die nach wie vor hohen Kosten in Angriff genommen werden, die der Wirtschaft durch ihre geschützteren Sektoren auferlegt werden.

Einleitung

Die irische Körperschaftssteuer macht immer wieder Schlagzeilen als Hauptgrund für die Attraktivität des Landes für ausländische Direktinvestitionen. In Wirklichkeit ist sie nur einer der Gründe für den Erfolg des Landes in diesem Bereich, in vielen Fällen sogar nur ein untergeordneter Grund. Andere Faktoren, wie Irlands unternehmerfreundliches Umfeld, schlanke Bürokratie, der gut ausgestattete Arbeiterpool und ein vorteilhaftes Arbeitsgesetz sind ebenfalls wesentliche Faktoren. Irland ist in den Genuss eines bisher nicht gekannten Erfolges bei der Anwerbung ausländischer Direktinvestitionen gekommen, auch wenn einige der Vorteile während des wirtschaftlichen Zusammenbruchs im Zeitraum von 2008 bis 2012 eine Abschwächung erfuhren. Wenn es auch nach wie vor ein attraktiver Standort ist, so besteht doch die Notwendigkeit, dass die Regierung bestimmte Bereiche in den Fokus nimmt, wie z. B. Kosten und Personensteuer sowie die Beibehaltung des Körperschaftssteuersatzes von 12,5 Prozent, um diesen Vorteil aufrechtzuerhalten.

Jack Golden beschreibt in **Kapitel 2** („Irlands Geschäftsmodell") die Strategie irischer Regierungen bei der Schaffung eines Geschäftsmodells, das ein unternehmerfreundliches Umfeld bieten soll, um ausländische Direktinvestitionen in wichtigen Branchen anzuwerben. Einer dieser Sektoren waren internationale Finanzdienstleistungen. Die International Financial Services Centre-Initiative von 1987 bewirkte die Bildung eines Clusters von Firmen in Dublin, die im Besitz der wichtigsten weltweit agierenden Finanzinstitutionen im Banken-, Versicherungs- und Fondsverwaltungsbereich waren. Zurzeit gibt es mehr als 500 solcher internationaler Finanzdienstleistungsunternehmen in Irland, hauptsächlich in Dublin, mit mehr als 30.000 qualifizierten Mitarbeitern.

Hier folgt ein Beispiel aus der Praxis eines ausländischen Direktinvestors in Irland im Bereich der internationalen Finanzdienstleistungen. Die Allianz Gruppe mit Sitz in München ist mit 144.000 Beschäftigten und 78 Mio Versicherungskunden in mehr als 70 Ländern eines der weltgrößten Finanzinstitute. Ihr Geschäftsbereich Vermögensverwaltung managt Vermögen im Wert von mehr als 1,4 Bio Euro. Mitte 1999 entschied die Allianz Gruppe, ihr neues Geschäftsfeld im internationalen Gesundheitsbereich in Irland anzusiedeln. Diese Fallstudie beleuchtet den Hintergrund der Entscheidung sowie die Geschäftsentwicklung in Irland in den letzten 15 Jahren.

Allianz und Irland

In den späten 1990er Jahren hatte die deutsche Krankenversicherungstochter der Allianz Gruppe ermittelt, dass viele deutsche Firmen eine erhebliche Zahl von leitenden Angestellten im Ausland hatten. Diese im Ausland lebenden Mitarbeiter konnten nicht über eine einheimische deutsche Krankenversicherung versichert werden. Die Allianz rief eine Arbeitsgruppe ins Leben, um zu ergründen, ob die Gründung einer neuen Krankenversicherungsgesellschaft zur Abdeckung dieses Geschäftes tragfähig sein würde. Zu dieser Zeit war der Versicherungsmarkt innerhalb der EU gerade liberalisiert worden. Versicherern, die in einem EU-Land zugelassen (lizenziert) waren, war es also gestattet, gemäß den Bedingungen des Vertrages von Rom zur Dienstleistungsfreiheit Versicherungsprodukte in allen anderen EU-Ländern zu verkaufen. Die Arbeitsgruppe kam zu dem Ergebnis: Deutsche Firmen hatten nicht ausreichend Mitarbeiter im Ausland, um die Gründung einer neuen Gesellschaft zu rechtfertigen, die allein den deutschen Markt bedienen würde. Hingegen gab es ausreichend Geschäftsmöglichkeiten, wenn man den gesamten EU-Markt mit einbeziehen würde. Die Arbeitsgruppe empfahl die Gründung einer neuen Krankenversicherungsgesellschaft durch die Allianz. Ziel: Die im Ausland lebenden Mitarbeiter multinationaler Unternehmen aus EU-Ländern unter Nutzung der nach den EU-Versicherungsrichtlinien erlaubten Dienstleistungsfreiheit zu bedienen. Ihre vorläufige Empfehlung sah die Niederlande als Standort für diesen Geschäftsbereich vor. Nach einer Intervention durch das Management der Allianz Ireland zog die Arbeitsgruppe Irland als

potenziellen Standort in Erwägung. Hieraus entwickelte sich der Vorschlag an den Vorstand der Allianz, das neue Geschäft in Irland zu etablieren. Mitte 1999 wurde er vom Vorstand der Allianz gebilligt.

Eine ganze Reihe von Faktoren stützte 1999 die Entscheidung für eine Geschäftsansiedlung in Irland:

- Die Wahrnehmung von Irland als ein guter Standort für ausländische Investitionen mit einem guten Geschäftsmodell.
- Deutlich weniger Bürokratie bei der Gründung eines Geschäfts in Irland
- Geschäftsfreundliches unternehmerisches und regulatorisches Umfeld.
- Englischsprachiges Land (Englisch als Geschäftssprache der meisten multinationalen Konzerne).
- Ein gut zwischen Arbeitnehmer- und Arbeitgeberrechten ausbalanciertes Arbeitsrecht.
- Kostengünstiger Standort.
- Viele Arbeitnehmer mit Fremdsprachenkompetenz.
- Bereits bestehende Operation der Allianz Gruppe zur Unterstützung bei der Gründung.
- Niedrige Steuern (Körperschaftssteuersatz von damals 10 Prozent).

Der niedrigere Steuersatz war kein entscheidender Faktor, sondern eher das „Sahnehäubchen".

Die neue Gesellschaft, Allianz Worldwide Care Limited, brauchte 6 Monate, um ihr Geschäft zu etablieren und öffnete ihre Türen im April 2000 auf dem Park West Business Campus am Rande Dublins.

Wie ist es für die Allianz gelaufen? Momentan verzeichnet die Allianz Worldwide Care Prämieneinnahmen von etwa 500 Mio Euro und Jahresgewinne von mehr als 30 Mio Euro. Sie beschäftigt 825 Mitarbeiter, von denen 650 in Irland wohnen. Die Gesellschaft ist darüber hinaus auch in Dubai, Belgien, China, Libyen und Katar in wesentlichem Umfang operativ tätig. 42 Prozent der Beschäftigten sind irische Staatsbürger, zwei Drittel der Mitarbeiter sind weiblich, das Durchschnittsalter liegt bei 31 Jahren. Die Mitarbeiter kommen aus 58 unterschiedlichen Ländern und decken 27 unterschiedliche Sprachen ab. Damit ist dies die bei Weitem vielfältigste Gesellschaft der Allianz Gruppe. In jedem Jahr seit 2003 hat sie ihre Prämieneinnahmen- und Erfolgsziele mit großem Abstand übertroffen. Die Gesellschaft zeichnet in den meisten Ländern der Welt Geschäfte, wobei 60 Prozent ihrer Geschäfte außerhalb der EU gezeichnet werden. 90 Prozent der Geschäfte werden mit multinationalen Konzernen und großen Organisationen (wovon ein wesentlicher Teil Fortune 500-Unternehmen sind) und 10 Prozent mit im Ausland lebenden Einzelpersonen abgewickelt. Sie versichert über 350.000 im Ausland Lebende und hat 2013 in fast 200 Ländern Ansprüche ausgezahlt.

Während anfangs multinationale Unternehmen aus den EU-Ländern den Zielmarkt bildeten, erschloss sich die Gesellschaft schnell neue Märkte. Der nächstliegende Schritt war das Abzielen auf Unternehmen mit Sitz außerhalb der

EU, anschließend drang die Gesellschaft in neue Nischenmärkte vor, wie z. B. zwischenstaatliche Organisationen (IGOs), diplomatische Dienste, internationale Schulen und Reedereien. In jeder Hinsicht also eine echte Erfolgsgeschichte.

Die Tatsache, dass die Gesellschaft Teil der Allianz Gruppe ist und Allianz in ihrem Namen trägt, war ein wesentlicher Faktor für ihren Erfolg. Der Name Allianz öffnet alle Türen und vermittelt potenziellen Kunden einen Eindruck von Solidität und finanzieller Stärke. Außerdem unterstützte die Allianz ihre irische Tochtergesellschaft anfänglich mit Wissenstransfer und Einführungen bei großen Firmenkunden. Das Timing der Allianz zur Einrichtung dieser neuen Gesellschaft für weltweite Krankenversicherungen erwies sich als hervorragend. Es fiel mit mehreren wesentlichen Faktoren zusammen:

- Die rasante Globalisierung in den 2000er Jahren führte dazu, dass jährlich Zehntausende hochvermögende Personen aus ihren Heimatländern in ausländische Tochtergesellschaften und/oder übernommene Unternehmen entsandt wurden. Diese Entwicklung setzte sich während der für die westlichen Volkswirtschaften rückläufigen Jahre von 2008 bis 2012 schnell fort. Multinationale Konzerne investierten stark in Entwicklungs- und Schwellenländer, die noch hohe einstellige oder in manchen Fällen sogar zweistellige Wachstumsraten des BIP aufwiesen.
- Die Entwicklung des Internets ermöglichte die einfache Kommunikation mit Versicherten, die auf der ganzen Welt verstreut sind.
- Die EU-Versicherungsrichtlinie über die einheitliche Zulassung liberalisierte das Versicherungsrecht in der EU und ermöglichte Versicherern, auf Basis der Dienstleistungsfreiheit mit ihrer einheimischen Lizenz auch auf anderen europäischen Märkten zu agieren.

Aus meiner Sicht war der irische Standort ein wichtiger Faktor für den Erfolg von Allianz Worldwide Care. Woraus bestanden die Standortvorteile?

- Es stellte sich heraus, dass Irland hinsichtlich der Gründung eines Unternehmens im Vergleich zum europäischen Standard ein wesentlich weniger bürokratisches Land war. Der Betrieb wurde schnell und ohne viel Aufhebens eingerichtet. In den letzten Jahren musste die Gesellschaft mehrere kleinere Betriebe in anderen Ländern aufbauen. Das stellte sich bei allen als wesentlich komplizierter dar als seinerzeit in Irland. Die Erfahrung der Allianz Worldwide Care bestätigt Irlands sehr hohe Position auf dem Global Competitive Index des Weltwirtschaftsforums, der Ernst & Young Globalisierungsrangliste und dem IBM Global Location Trends-Jahresbericht.
- Die Allianz hat in Irland einen ausgezeichneten Arbeitsmarkt vorgefunden. Einerseits gab es hoch qualifizierte irische Staatsbürger mit fundiertem Wissen aus dem Versicherungs- und Geschäftsbereich. Hinzu kamen viele junge ausländische Staatsbürger, die nach Irland gezogen waren und die

notwendigen Fremdsprachkompetenzen mitbrachten, um mit medizinischen Anbietern aus der ganzen Welt und mit versicherten Mitgliedern in ihrer jeweiligen Muttersprache zu kommunizieren. Die erforderlichen Sprachen waren alle in Irland vorhanden, sogar während des wirtschaftlich schwierigen Zeitraums von 2008 bis 2013. Wie in allen englischsprachigen Ländern reicht die Sprachkompetenz der Einheimischen nicht an das Niveau der Kontinentaleuropäer heran. Multinationale Konzerne in Irland werden immer einige ausländische Staatsbürger anstellen müssen, um über die richtige Mischung an Fremdsprachen zu verfügen.

- In den ersten vier Jahren der Geschäftstätigkeit bot Irland der Gesellschaft noch einen Kostenvorteil gegenüber konkurrierenden europäischer Staaten. Dieser verschwand während des Booms Mitte der 2000er Jahre, und in manchen Bereichen, wie z. B. Infrastruktur und öffentliche Versorgung, stiegen die Kosten über den EU-Durchschnitt. Der wirtschaftliche Zusammenbruch brachte den Realitätssinn zurück. Seither sind die meisten, aber nicht alle Kosten auf ein Niveau gesunken, das Irland zu einem attraktiven Standort macht. Dies gilt insbesondere für neue oder wachsende Unternehmen, die ihre Belegschaft zu relativ niedrigen Gehältern vom Arbeitsmarkt rekrutieren können. Sogar während des Booms Mitte der 2000er Jahre konnte die Allianz Worldwide Care Mitarbeiter zu niedrigeren Gehältern beschäftigen als in konkurrierenden Volkswirtschaften. Die Allianz würde die allgemeinen Kosten in Irland jetzt als neutralen Faktor betrachten.

- Irland hat sein ausbalanciertes Arbeitsrecht aufrechterhalten, was der Gesellschaft das nötige Vertrauen gibt, ihre Geschäftsaktivitäten in Irland wachsen zu lassen. Während die Gesellschaft vornehmlich in Irland ansässig ist, beschäftigt sie inzwischen Mitarbeiter in vielen Ländern. Dabei wurde deutlich: Das irische Arbeitsrecht ist im Vergleich mit anderen Standorten deutlich unkomplizierter.

- Iren sind gute Geschäftsleute und kommen mit ausländischen Führungskräften gut zurecht. Die Angestellten der Gesellschaft sind im allgemeinen jung, gut ausgebildet (fast alle Mitarbeiter haben einen Universitätsabschluss und viele haben darüber hinaus ein abgeschlossenes Aufbaustudium oder eine berufliche Qualifikation) und denken sehr unternehmerisch. Dieser unternehmerische Geist, bei dem nichts unmöglich ist, war einer der Hauptgründe für das exponentielle Wachstum der Gesellschaft. Wir haben zum Beispiel Möglichkeiten gefunden, in schwierige, aber potenziell profitable Märkte wie Libyen, Algerien, Mosambik, Angola und nicht zuletzt China einzutreten.

- Trotz der jüngsten wirtschaftlichen Schwierigkeiten hat die irische Regierung ein stabiles wirtschaftliches Umfeld aufrechterhalten, nicht

zuletzt in der Steuerpolitik. Der Steuersatz von 10 Prozent für internationale Finanzdienstleister wurde Ende 2002 schrittweise abgebaut und durch einen Körperschaftssteuersatz von 12,5 Prozent ersetzt. Dieser gilt für alle irischen Unternehmen. Trotz beträchtlichem Druck seitens bestimmter Länder wird der Körperschaftssteuersatz von 12,5 Prozent von der Regierung angesichts seiner Bedeutung bei der Anwerbung ausländischer Direktinvestitionen nach Irland als unantastbare Grenze behandelt. Der niedrige Steuersatz war für die Allianz nicht der entscheidende Faktor für die Gründung ihrer internationalen Krankenversicherungsgesellschaft in Irland. Gleichwohl stellt er einen erheblichen Vorteil dar. Aufgrund des exponentiellen Wachstums der Gesellschaft bedurfte es in signifikantem Maße zusätzlichen Eigenkapitals. Der Großteil des zusätzlichen Eigenkapitals im Zeitraum von 2004 bis 2013 waren Gewinnrücklagen statt Kapitalspritzen. Der niedrige Steuersatz ermöglichte der Gesellschaft, das für die Finanzierung ihres Wachstums notwendige Kapital zu akkumulieren.

- Irische Ministerien und Behörden waren der Gesellschaft gegenüber stets sehr bemüht, Schwierigkeiten bei der Gründung und dem Wachstum ihres Geschäfts zu überwinden. Bei der IDA, im Finanzministerium, Gesundheitsministerium und im Ministerium für Arbeit, Unternehmen und Innovation standen stets leitende Angestellte zur Verfügung. Darüber hinaus verfügt Irland über eine ausgezeichnete Telekommunikation sowie über zahlreiche ausgezeichnete Unternehmens- , Rechts- und Finanzberater. Durch ihre langjährige Erfahrung im Umgang mit multinationalen Gesellschaften kommen sie mit allen rechtlichen, behördlichen, versicherungs- oder buchhaltungstechnischen Angelegenheiten zurecht.

- Internationale Versicherungsgesellschaften halten bei der Entscheidung über neue Standorte für ihre Geschäftsaktivitäten Ausschau nach fairer, vorhersehbarer und verhältnismäßiger Regulierung. Im Zeitraum von der ersten Zulassung bis 2008 machte die Gesellschaft hervorragende Erfahrungen mit der irischen Regulierung. Die Regulierungsbehörde war sehr behilflich durch das Ausstellen der notwendigen Genehmigungen zur Dienstleistungsfreiheit und bot eine sehr stabile regulatorische Grundlage. Der Zusammenbruch vieler irischer Banken im Zeitraum von 2008 bis 2009 führte zu einer erheblichen und nachvollziehbaren Verschärfung der Finanzregulierung in Irland. Diese schärfere Regulierung gilt für alle Finanzinstitute, einschließlich Versicherungsgesellschaften. Auch die Allianz Worldwide Care bekam diese verschärfte Regulierung zu spüren. Für einen bestimmten Zeitraum war die irische Finanzaufsicht, als unausweichliche Reaktion auf die weltweite (und irische) Finanzkrise, sicherlich schärfer als fast überall sonst. In den letzten zwei Jahren ist sie jedoch ausgereift und würde nun von internationalen Versicherern zwar

immer noch als streng, aber auch wieder als fair, verhältnismäßig und planbar angesehen werden.

Zusammenfassend war die Erfahrung der Allianz Worldwide Care als ausländischer Direktinvestor in Irland sehr positiv, einigen kleineren Hindernissen zum Trotz. Der Standort hat für die Gesellschaft bei der erfolgreichen Gründung und Entwicklung ihres Geschäfts eine wesentliche Rolle gespielt.

Blick in die Zukunft

Hinsichtlich der zukünftigen Aussichten für Projekte mit ausländischen Direktinvestitionen gibt es zwar viel Positives, jedoch ist nicht alles nur eitel Sonnenschein. Es kann davon ausgegangen werden, dass die Regierung ihre Politik des wirtschaftsfreundlichen Umfelds und der wirtschaftsfreundlichen Gesetze beibehalten wird. Die Aufrechterhaltung des niedrigen Körperschaftssteuersatzes ist unverzichtbar und stellt für alle politischen Parteien eine rote Linie dar. Die Regierung wird sich aber mit der als aggressiv empfundenen Ausnutzung der irischen Steuergesetze durch einige multinationale Konzerne auseinandersetzen müssen. Dazu zählt das „Double Irish With a Dutch Sandwich"-Arrangement (eine Strategie zur legalen Steuervermeidung). Wird dies nicht überarbeitet, dürfte es sehr schwierig werden, den Körperschaftssteuersatz von 12,5 Prozent aufrechtzuerhalten angesichts des Drucks durch andere westliche Länder und die OECD.

Ein weiteres Feld, das der Aufmerksamkeit der Regierung bedarf, ist die Kostenbasis. Der Boom hat Irland von einem kostengünstigen Standort in einen kostentechnisch weit über dem Durchschnitt liegenden Standort verwandelt. Das hat sich bereits stark verändert. Auch wenn das Lohnniveau und die Kosten im Privatsektor auf günstige Niveaus gefallen sind, gilt dies nicht für die Kosten im Staatssektor, zum Beispiel bezüglich der Versorgungsunternehmen. Hier muss noch mehr Arbeit geleistet werden.

Die Auflage an die Regierung, das Haushaltsdefizit auf unter 3 Prozent des BIP zurückzuführen, hat wesentliche Ausgabenkürzungen und Steuererhöhungen erforderlich gemacht. Aufgrund des Drucks von Interessenverbänden und der Gewerkschaft für den öffentlichen Dienst war es für die Regierung politisch einfacher, Steuern zu erhöhen statt Ausgaben zu kürzen. Die individuelle Steuerbelastung hat nun ein Niveau erreicht, bei dem sich jede weitere Erhöhung negativ auf ausländische Direktinvestitionen auswirken würde. Die irische Regierung und IDA wissen sehr genau: Irland hat kein gottgewolltes Recht auf ausländische Direktinvestitionen, multinationale Konzerne siedeln sich dort an, wo es für sie am besten passt. Angesichts der Erfolgsbilanz der IDA und der Regierungen sowie der Bedeutung ausländischer Direktinvestitionen für die irische Wirtschaft habe ich keine Zweifel daran, dass die notwendige Fokussierung und die entsprechenden Maßnahmen kommen werden. Denn darin sind wir wirklich gut!

KAPITEL 3

Reaktion auf die Krise und verbleibende Herausforderungen

Dr. Peter Breuer[28]

Hauptaussagen

- Zwar liegt Irlands Wachstumsrate unterhalb der anfänglichen Prognosen, doch hat sie den Durchschnitt des Euroraums übertroffen. Es gibt Anzeichen für eine Erholung. Nach einer deutlichen Erhöhung des Haushaltsdefizits und einem steilen Anstieg der Staatsverschuldung während der Krise hat eine schrittweise Konsolidierung die Finanzlage unter Erhaltung des sozialen Zusammenhalts deutlich verbessert. Reformen des Bankenwesens nach der Krise haben zur finanziellen Stabilität beigetragen.
- Eine weiterhin entschlossene Umsetzung politischer Entscheidungen an verschiedenen Fronten ist vonnöten, bevor die Einschätzung gestattet ist, Irland habe sich vollständig von der Krise erholt. Haushaltsdefizit und Staatsverschuldung liegen weiterhin hoch. In den nächsten Jahren ist eine weitere Konsolidierung notwendig, um bei den Schulden definitiv einen Abwärtstrend herbeizuführen und dafür zu sorgen, dass Irlands Rückkehr zur Marktfinanzierung von Dauer ist. Intensive Bemühungen müssen darauf abzielen, dass Banken und Hypothekenschuldner, die mit ihren Rückzahlungen im Rückstand sind, zu dauerhaften Lösungen kommen. Dann kann eine Neubelebung des Kreditgeschäfts zu einer nachhaltigen Erholung der Binnennachfrage beitragen.

Einleitung

Irland hat in den drei Jahren seit Beginn des EU/IWF-Programms im Dezember 2010 unglaublich viel erreicht. Irlands Dreijahresprogramm, das von der EU und dem IWF gestützt wird, folgte auf eine außergewöhnlich tiefe Bankenkrise, die mit dem Platzen der Immobilienblase einherging. Die irischen Behörden haben laut der letzten Quartalsprüfung unbeirrt an der Umsetzung der Programmgrundsätze

---

[28] Mein herzlicher Dank geht an das IWF-Team Irland für die Analysen, auf denen dieses Kapitel aufbaut.

festgehalten, es zeigen sich nun erste Anzeichen einer Erholung. Doch auch wenn sich Irland aus der tiefen Bankenkrise herausgearbeitet hat, steht das Land noch vor vielen Herausforderungen, wie es am Ende eines vom IWF gestützten Programms durchaus üblich ist.

Dieses Kapitel erörtert die Reaktion der öffentlichen Hand auf die Krise, insbesondere während des von EU und IWF gestützten Programms, und umreißt die verbleibenden Herausforderungen, die noch gemeistert werden müssen. Insbesondere wird Folgendes untersucht: (I) die Leistungsfähigkeit der Wirtschaft und die makroökonomischen Aussichten und Risiken, (II) die finanzpolitische Reaktion auf das Auftreten großer Defizite und die nach wie vor bestehende Notwendigkeit, bei der hohen Staatsverschuldung einen Abwärtstrend herbeizuführen, (III) die Bemühungen um Stabilisierung des Finanzsektors und die Notwendigkeit, die Qualität der Vermögenswerte sowie die Aussichten für die Wirtschaftlichkeit zu verbessern, und (IV) ausgewählte Strukturreformen.

Makroökonomie

Wachstum und Wettbewerbsfähigkeit

Illustration 3.1: Reales Wachstum des BIP

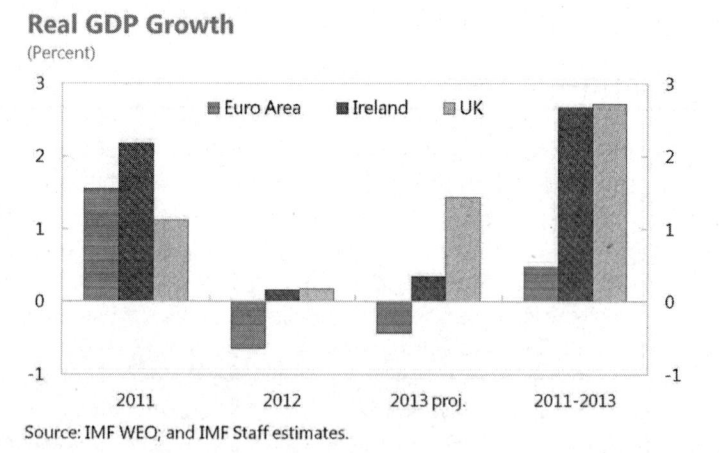

Source: IMF WEO; and IMF Staff estimates.

Quelle: IWF WEO und Schätzungen von IWF-Mitarbeitern.

Das Wirtschaftswachstum während des von EU und IWF gestützten Programms war langsamer als prognostiziert, auch wenn es über dem Durchschnitt des Euroraumes lag (siehe **Illustration 3.1**). Nach einem vom Export getriebenen Zuwachs von 2,2 Prozent im Jahr 2011 verlangsamte sich das Wachstum 2012 auf 0,2 Prozent und rutschte in der ersten Hälfte des Jahres 2013 in den negativen Bereich. Das hing teilweise mit dem Auslaufen pharmazeutischer Patente

zusammen, kam aber auch durch die nur langsame Erholung der Handelspartner. Das erwartete kumulative Wachstum für 2011–13 von etwa 2,75 Prozent bleibt hinter den ursprünglich prognostizierten 5,25 Prozent zurück. Das für den Euroraum für 2011–13 erwartete Wachstum von 0,5 Prozent liegt jedoch noch deutlicher hinter der Prognose vom Oktober 2010 von 5,2 Prozent. Das kumulative Wachstum Irlands für 2011–13 dürfte dem für Großbritannien entsprechen.

Die Wettbewerbsfähigkeit verbessert sich, auch wenn die Strukturreformen langsamer vorankommen als erhofft. Während des Booms bis 2007-8 verschlechterte sich die Wettbewerbsfähigkeit Irlands deutlich. Der anschließende Rückgang der Lohnstückkosten und die Konvergenz des Preisniveaus an den Euroraum führten letztlich dazu, dass Irland lediglich eine moderate Überbewertung des realen effektiven Wechselkurses (REER) im Bereich von 5–10 Prozent erlebte (siehe Artikel IV des Mitarbeiterberichts des IWF zu Irland von 2012). Gleichbleibende nominale Löhne und eine geringe Inflation deuten darauf hin, dass sich Verbesserungen der Wettbewerbsfähigkeit in den kommenden Jahren fortsetzen könnten. Bereits in Angriff genommene Strukturreformen sollen den Wettbewerb in den Sektoren der juristischen und medizinischen Dienstleistungen verbessern und die Wettbewerbsbehörden durch bessere Ausstattung stärken. Auf dem Arbeitsmarkt liegt der Fokus auf der Aus- und Weiterbildung von Arbeitslosen sowie die Überwindung von Strukturkrisen in einzelnen Branchen. Nicht alle Reformen sind schon gänzlich umgesetzt.

Schuldenlast der Privathaushalte

Die schwere Schuldenlast im privaten Sektor erschwert die Binnennachfrage. Durch höhere Ersparnisse haben die privaten Haushalte in den vergangenen viereinhalb Jahren ihre nominale Verschuldung um 16 Prozent verringert. Doch bleibt die Schuldenlast mit 198,3 Prozent des verfügbaren Einkommens Mitte 2013 hoch. Deshalb dürften die Ersparnisse für einige Zeit über dem normalen Niveau verharren. KMU können neue Investitionen und die Schaffung von Arbeitsplätzen nicht mit Krediten finanzieren, was häufig auf Schulden für vergangene Investitionen in Immobilien zurückzuführen ist.

Derzeit etwa 6 Prozent aller Haushalte sind so hoch verschuldet, dass sie mit der Rückzahlung ihrer Hypotheken im Rückstand sind. Nachhaltige Kreditumschichtungen werden in einigen Fällen zu Konsumverzicht führen, in anderen Fällen für Erleichterung sorgen. Doch werden diese direkten kurzfristigen Effekte auf den Konsum wahrscheinlich aufgewogen durch den umfangreicheren mittelfristigen Nutzen einer besseren Qualität der Vermögenswerte der Banken. Diese können dann billigere Finanzierungen finden und eine Wiederbelebung der Hypothekenvergabe einleiten. Die Anpassung notleidender Hypotheken wird auch die Ängste hinsichtlich des Schattenbestands an Immobilienobjekten aufgrund der Hypothekenfalle lindern. Dadurch könnte sich der Immobilienmarkt erholen, die Unsicherheit der Haushalte über ihre Vermögenswerte lindern und somit insgesamt die Erholung der Binnennachfrage stützen. Diese positiven

Entwicklungen könnten sich jedoch umkehren, wenn erneut massenhaft Hypothekenausfälle aufträten oder die Disziplin bei der Schuldenrückzahlung weiter nachließe.

Aussichten und Risiken für die Erholung

Ein höheres Wachstum der Handelspartner ist die wichtigste Antriebskraft für eine allmähliche Erholung Irlands, wobei der IWF für 2014 ein Wachstum von 1,7 Prozent im Vergleich zum Vorjahr vohersagt. Den jüngsten Prognosen des World Economic Outlook zufolge wird sich das Wachstum der Handelspartner Irlands von 0,4 Prozent 2013 im Vergleich zum Vorjahr auf 1,6 Prozent im Jahr 2014 beschleunigen. Dies würde eine Anhebung des irischen Wachstums um gut 1 Prozentpunkt durch die Nettoexporte ermöglichen. Das aktuelle Beschäftigungswachstum im 3. Quartal 2013 von 3,2 Prozent im Vergleich zum Vorjahr setzt sich offenbar fort, wodurch die Einkommen und das Vertrauen der Haushalte gestützt wird. Der Konsum der öffentlichen Hand wird in den kommenden Jahren weiter sinken, da die Politik die Zahl der Beschäftigten im öffentlichen Dienst verringern und andere Ausgaben kürzen will.

Irlands Wachstum wird sich laut Prognosen ab 2015 bei etwa 2,5 Prozent einpendeln, auch wenn hohe Schuldenlasten im privaten Sektor auf eine verzögerte Erholung der Binnennachfrage hindeuten. Verbesserungen des äußeren wirtschaftlichen Umfeldes, geringerer Widerstand aufgrund der finanziellen Konsolidierung und eine allmähliche Wiederbelebung der Kreditvergabe sind die wichtigsten Antriebskräfte. Diese Wachstumsrate lässt sich mittelfristig aufrechterhalten. Demografische Trends zeigen ein Wachstum der Bevölkerung im arbeitsfähigen Alter um etwa 1 Prozent in den nächsten zehn Jahren an. Ein Rückgang der Arbeitslosigkeit ermöglicht eine Phase des Beschäftigungswachstums in der Größenordnung von 1,5 Prozent ohne neuen Lohndruck. Zudem wächst Irlands Produktivität, auch aufgrund anhaltender ausländischer Direktinvestitionen, um etwa 1 Prozent pro Jahr.

Die Aussichten auf Erholung sind mit einer Anzahl von Unsicherheiten behaftet. Das kurzfristige Risiko stellt sich als beträchtlich dar, wird aber von positiven Faktoren ausgeglichen. Mittelfristig zeichnet sich das Risiko einer Verschlechterung ab:

- **Äußeres Umfeld:** Seine große Offenheit (Exporte machen rund 110 Prozent des BIP aus) macht Irland anfällig für Wachstumsschwankungen bei den Handelspartnern. Eine schwache wirtschaftliche Erholung im Ausland könnte über das Vertrauen der Verbraucher und der Unternehmen auch auf die Inlandsnachfrage durchschlagen. Nichtsdestoweniger sind die jüngsten Kennzahlen bei einigen von Irlands Haupthandelspartnern verhältnismäßig positiv, besonders im Vereinigten Königreich, was Raum für einen möglichen Aufwärtstrend lässt.
- **Binnennachfrage:** Die Konsumaussichten hängen wesentlich von einer Fortsetzung der jüngsten Beschäftigungszuwächse ab, die die Einkommen

stützen und Unsicherheiten verringern. Die andauernde Erholung der Hauspreise steht noch auf dem Prüfstand aufgrund der wertmindernden Auswirkungen eines potenziellen Anstiegs der Veräußerungen von Immobilien, die an die Gläubiger zurückfallen. Allerdings machen Häuser mit primären Wohnungshypotheken, deren Rückzahlung im Rückstand sind, nur 6 Prozent aller Immobilien aus. Die Erholung bei den Investitionen ist angesichts ihres niedrigen Standes (rund 11 Prozent des BIP) ein mögliches Aufwärtsrisiko.

- **Finanzwirtschaftliche Bedingungen:** Für eine anhaltende mittelfristige Erholung ist die Wiederbelebung von Kreditwachstum und Investitionen erforderlich. Dies wäre beeinträchtigt, wenn die derzeitigen Bemühungen, notleidende Kredite anzupassen und die Wirtschaftlichkeit der Banken zu verbessern, nicht den gewünschten Erfolg hätten. Falls sich eine spätere Verringerung der Wertpapierkäufe durch die US-Notenbank stärker auf die Peripherie des Euroraumes auswirken sollte, könnten negative Auswirkungen auf den Zugang der Banken zu Marktrefinanzierung und deren Kosten und somit auf die Verfügbarkeit von Krediten auftreten.

Finanzpolitik

Zwar hatte Irland beim Eintritt in die Krise einen ausgeglichenen Haushalt, doch verschleierten die boomenden Einnahmen eine deutliche Schwächung der zugrundeliegenden Finanzlage. Nach einem Zeitraum schnellen, vom Export getriebenen Wachstums in den 1990ern, als die Ausgaben und die Steuereinnahmen auf geringe Niveaus im Verhältnis zum BIP sanken, wurden die öffentlichen Finanzen zur Jahrtausendwende wieder auf die Verbesserung der sozialen Lage und die Ausweitung von Leistungen der öffentlichen Hand gerichtet. Die nominalen Primärausgaben stiegen von 2000 bis 2008 um 140 Prozent (strukturell 11 Prozentpunkte des BIP), wobei sich die Höhe der Sozialleistungen verdoppelte (im Falle des Kindergeldes verdreifachte), die Anzahl der Beschäftigten im öffentlichen Dienst sich um 35 Prozent erhöhte und die Gehälter im öffentlichen Dienst um 60 Prozent stiegen. Im Vergleich stieg das Pro-Kopf-BIP zwischen 2000 und 2008 um 45 Prozent und zwischen 2000 und 2011 um 24 Prozent.

Der steile Ausgabenanstieg ging mit strukturellen Steuersenkungen einher: Der bereits hohe Einstiegspunkt in die Einkommenssteuer (25 Prozent des Pro-Kopf-BIP im Jahr 2000) wurde bis 2009 verdoppelt, während die gesetzlichen Einkommenssteuersätze um 5 Prozentpunkte gesenkt wurden. Im Nachhinein schätzen IWF-Mitarbeiter, dass sich das strukturelle Primärdefizit im Jahr 2008 auf über 10 Prozent des BIP ausgedehnt hatte, dies aber durch eine Flut von Einnahmen aus dem Immobilienbereich während der Boomjahre 2003 bis 2007 verdeckt wurde.

Politische Reaktionen auf die Krise

Die Krise verlangte eine scharfe Kurskorrektur, mit einer substanziellen Konsolidierung in den vergangenen Jahren, die die finanzielle Lage erheblich verbessert hat. Noch vor Beginn des EU/IWF-Programms unternahm Irland eine erhebliche Konsolidierung, bei der das strukturelle Primärdefizit von 2009 bis 2010 um 5,25 Prozent des BIP gesenkt wurde. Eine stetige finanzielle Konsolidierung war dabei das Gütezeichen des Programms und der Schlüssel zur Wiederherstellung der politischen Glaubwürdigkeit Irlands, wobei während des EU/IWF-Programms jedes einzelne finanzielle Ziel erreicht wurde. Im Ergebnis wird erwartet, dass Irland sein strukturelles Primärdefizit 2013 auf 0,5 Prozent des BIP senkt, ein Rückgang von insgesamt 4,5 Prozentpunkten seit 2010 und von 10 Prozentpunkten seit Beginn der Krise. Die während des Programms umgesetzten Maßnahmen belaufen sich auf insgesamt über 13 Mrd. Euro oder 8 Prozent des BIP, zwei Drittel davon auf der Ausgabenseite.

Auch der finanzpolitische Rahmen wurde gestärkt. Im Rahmen des Gesetz über finanzpolitische Verantwortlichkeit („Fiscal Responsibility Act, 2012", FRA) wurden im Einklang mit dem Stabilitäts- und Wachstumspakt eine allgemeine Richtlinie für einen ausgeglichenen Staatshaushalt und eine allgemeine Richtlinie für die Staatsverschuldung verabschiedet. Der Haushalt 2012 führte eine 3-jährige Deckelung der Gesamt- und Ressortausgaben ein, die auf eine gesetzliche Grundlage gestellt wurde. Der FRA sorgte außerdem für die Unabhängigkeit und ausreichende Finanzierung des irischen Fiscal Advisory Council, des finanzpolitischen Beirates. Der Beirat ist verantwortlich für eine Vorabbestätigung der dem Haushalt zugrunde liegenden makroökonomischen Prognosen sowie für die Einschätzung der Fundiertheit der Haushaltsplanungen und der Finanzpolitik der Regierung. Maßnahmen zur Verbesserung der Transparenz sind u. a. der staatliche Maßnahmenplan zur Finanzberichterstattung, Prognostizierung und Risikoanalyse sowie die Einführung einer quartalsweisen Veröffentlichung der Government Finance Statistics, der Finanzstatistik der Regierung.

Verbleibende Herausforderungen

Es wird erwartet, dass die Staatsverschuldung 2013 124 Prozent des BIP erreicht, wenngleich dies teilweise hohe Kassenreserven widerspiegelt. Wenn man finanzielle Vermögenswerte aus der Staatsverschuldung herausrechnet, geht etwa die Hälfte des Anstiegs seit 2008 auf die Bankenstützung zurück, die sich auf 40 Prozent des BIP beläuft. Gemäß dem Basisszenario der IWF-Mitarbeiter geht das Verhältnis der Staatsverschuldung zum BIP bis 2018 auf 112 Prozent zurück, während die wirtschaftliche Erholung Tritt fasst. Die Nachhaltigkeit des Schuldenabbaus bleibt jedoch fraglich, da dieser prognostizierte Rückgang Risiken unterliegt: sowohl geringeres Wachstum wie Eventualverbindlichkeiten oder eine Kombination aus beiden.

Die Umsetzung des Haushaltsplanes war auch 2013 wieder solide, u. a. mit der reibungslosen Einführung der lokalen Immobiliensteuer und dem Zusammenhalt

der Sozialpartner, der sich im Abschluss des „Haddington Road Agreement" über Gehälter und Pensionen im öffentlichen Dienst zeigte. Für 2013 wird ein Defizit von etwa 7 Prozent des BIP erwartet, was locker unter der Deckelung des EU-Defizitverfahrens von 7,5 Prozent des BIP liegt. Dennoch bleibt das Haushaltsdefizit hoch. Zinszahlungen, die auf die Hochschuldenphase zurückgehen, werden die erheblichen primären Anpassungen teilweise aufheben.

Um bei der Staatsverschuldung definitiv einen Abwärtstrend herbeizuführen, bedarf es einer weiteren umfangreichen finanziellen Konsolidierung, während gleichzeitig Raum für die wirtschaftliche Erholung gelassen werden muss. Der Haushaltsplan für 2014 strebt primäre Ausgeglichenheit an. Bis 2015 soll das Haushaltsdefizit unter 3 Prozent des BIP fallen. Dieser Weg beinhaltet eine ausgewogene Geschwindigkeit des Sparkurses in den kommenden Jahren. Er soll die Staatsverschuldung auf eine Abwärtskurve setzen, auch wenn dies Risiken aus den Wachstumsaussichten und Eventualverbindlichkeiten unterliegt. Eine weiterhin solide Umsetzung der Konsolidierung wird entscheidend sein, um sicherzustellen, dass die Rückkehr Irlands zur Marktfinanzierung von Dauer ist.

Politik in Bezug auf den Finanzsektor

Die Integration des irischen Finanzsystems in die Eurozone, zusammen mit den vermeintlich soliden Staatsfinanzen, verschaffte irischen Banken während der Boomjahre uneingeschränkten Zugang zu den Geld- und Kapitalmärkten. Dies ermöglichte ihre turbogeladene Vermögensexpansion. In den fünf Jahren bis Mitte 2008 stiegen die Nettoauslandsverbindlichkeiten des irischen Bankensystems sprunghaft von etwa 20 Prozent auf etwa 70 Prozent des BIP an und die Finanzierung über die Geld- und Kapitalmärkte stieg auf 55 Prozent der Vermögenswerte.

Die Krise und die Reaktion der Politik vor dem Programm

Der Niedergang der irischen Immobilienpreise begann 2007. Nach schweren Verlusten bei immobilienbezogenen Vermögenswerten im Frühling 2008 stürzten die weltweiten Finanzturbulenzen nach der Lehman-Pleite das anfällige irische Bankensystem in eine tiefe Krise. Die Banken erlitten im Herbst 2008 einen Run auf Geld und Kapitalmarktkredite, was zu einem massiven Rückgriff auf Liquiditätshilfen des Eurosystems führte. Zu den staatlichen Maßnahmen gehörten eine weitreichende Bürgschaft ab September 2008, die Überführung von großen notleidenden Krediten für Immobilienentwicklungen und gewerbliche Immobilien von Banken zur National Asset Management Agency (NAMA) ab April 2009, umfangreiche Kapitalhilfen für zwei pleite gegangene Banken (die Bausparkassen Anglo Irish und Irish Nationwide Building Society) sowie große Finanzspritzen für andere Banken. Eine Zeit lang erhielten diese Maßnahmen die Stabilität aufrecht. Doch der Umfang der Kapitalhilfen und die Unsicherheit in Bezug auf weitere notwendige Hilfen trugen dazu bei, dass die Regierung ihren Marktzugang verlor,

und unterstützten eine Eskalation des Drucks auf die Finanzierung der Banken im Jahr 2010.

Die Reaktion der Politik während des Programms

Der Finanzsektor wurde mit Unterstützung des EU/IWF-Programms durch entschlossene Bemühungen um die Rekapitalisierung und die Umstrukturierung des Systems stabilisiert. Der Prudential Capital Assessment Review (PCAR) von 2011 unterzog die AIB, die BoI und die PTSB (zusammen die PCAR-Banken) einem Stresstest. Ihr Kapital wurde auf der Grundlage der Ergebnisse der Prüfung um 24 Mrd. Euro (15 Prozent des BIP) aufgestockt, gekoppelt an eine signifikante Umstrukturierung des Systems. Die PCAR-Banken meldeten zum Stichtag Mitte 2013 eine Kernkapitalquote von insgesamt 14,1 Prozent; zwischen Ende 2010 und Juni 2013 verdoppelten sich die Rückstellungen. Die Unterstützung der Banken ging jedoch mit einer schweren Belastung des öffentlichen Sektors einher, die Bruttokosten betrugen 64,1 Mrd. Euro (40 Prozent des BIP). Die Wiedereintreibung dieser Kosten steht erst am Anfang, macht jedoch mit der Veräußerung der Irish Life und den Vorzugsaktien und den Contingent Capital Notes (Bedingtes Kapital) an der Bank of Ireland Fortschritte.

Die inländischen Einlagen haben sich seit Mitte 2011 stabilisiert, wenn auch die Einlagenzinsen zurückgegangen sind. Unterstützt von einer erheblichen Entschuldung bei nicht zum Kern gehörenden Vermögenswerten ist das Kredit-Einlagen-Verhältnis von 190 Prozent Ende 2010 auf 117 Prozent im Juni 2013 gesunken. Die Hilfen des Eurosystems für PCAR-Banken sind von einem Höchstwert von über 90 Mrd. Euro auf etwa 31 Mrd. Euro zurückgegangen.

Die kürzliche Bilanzüberprüfung (Balance Sheet Assessment, BSA) analysierte die Hinlänglichkeit von Risikopuffern bei den drei PCAR-Banken. Sie prüfte vor allem die Angemessenheit der Rücklagen auf der Grundlage aufgelaufener Verluste und die Eignung intern generierter Risikogewichte gemäß den Basler Benchmarks, die in eine stichtagsbezogene Kapitalbewertung zum Juni 2013 einflossen. Wie vorgesehen, beauftragte die von der irischen Zentralbank (Central Bank of Ireland, CBI) geführte Untersuchung Privatunternehmen mit der Projektumsetzung sowie ein Beratungsunternehmen mit der Aufsicht und unabhängigen Einschätzung.

Diese Analyse befand angesichts der von der CBI im Mai 2013 aktualisierten Richtlinien für Risikovorsorge und Offenlegung („Impairment Provisioning and Disclosure Guidelines") eine weitere Erhöhung der Rückstellungen für angemessen, stellte jedoch keinen unmittelbaren Bedarf an zusätzlichem Kapital fest. Banken müssen nun anhand der BSA-Ergebnisse ihre Risikopuffer als Rückstellungen statt als Kapital in die Bilanzen einstellen, was auch eine rechtzeitigere Kreditanpassung fördert. Die BSA fließt in den fortgesetzten begleitenden Dialog der CBI mit den Banken über die adäquate Vorsorgehöhe am Jahresende ein.

Die finanzwirtschaftliche Regulierung und Aufsicht wurden radikal geändert, die Verbesserungen werden fortgesetzt. Im Oktober 2011 wurde ein spezielles Abwicklungssystem für Banken und Kreditgenossenschaften in Kraft gesetzt und im

Juli 2013 wurden die Aufsichtsbefugnisse der irischen Zentralbank gestärkt. Die CBI hat die Aufsicht über die Banken durch Erhöhung der Ressourcen und Operationalisierung ihres neuen, risikobasierten Aufsichtsansatzes verstärkt.

Verbleibende Herausforderungen: Notleidende Kredite und Wirtschaftlichkeit

Die Fortschritte der Banken bei der Abwicklung hoher notleidender Kredite sind sehr schleppend, eine schwache Wirtschaftlichkeit behindert die Wiederbelebung des Kreditgeschäfts. Notleidende Kredite bilden 26,5 Prozent der Kredite der PCAR-Banken, angeführt von Krediten für gewerblich genutzte Immobilien (41 Prozent), Wohnbauhypotheken (34 Prozent) sowie Unternehmens- und KMU-Krediten (19 Prozent). Dieser hohe Anteil von notleidenden Krediten treibt die Kosten der Marktrefinanzierung nach oben und zieht Managementressourcen ab, die für neue Kreditvergaben genutzt werden könnten. Die Fortschritte der Banken bei der Anpassung notleidender Kredite sind jedoch sehr schleppend, was die CBI veranlasste, Zielvorgaben für die Anpassung von Wohnbauhypotheken und KMU-Krediten festzulegen.

Bei den Hypotheken haben die hohe Arbeitslosigkeit und andere Probleme zu erheblichen Zahlungsrückständen, die länger als 90 Tage bestehen, geführt. Sie betreffen 17,4 Prozent des Gesamtwertes an ausstehenden Eigenheimhypotheken und von 29,3 Prozent an Hypotheken für Wohneigentum zur Vermietung. Dieser Anstieg der Zahlungsrückstände bei Hypotheken scheint sich in jüngerer Zeit abzuschwächen, da die verbesserten Beitreibungsbemühungen der Banken offenbar Fälle vorübergehender Zahlungsstörungen eindämmen. Auch die Stabilisierung der Hauspreise und der Rückgang der Arbeitslosigkeit haben wahrscheinlich dazu beigetragen. Ein erheblicher Hypothekenbestand muss jedoch entsorgt werden.

Die Banken melden Fortschritte gemäß den Zielvorgaben der CBI zur Behebung von Hypothekenzahlungsrückständen (Mortgage Arrears Resolution Targets, MART). Die CBI zitiert Bankberichte, wonach diese eine wichtige Zielvorgabe bis Ende September 2013 erfüllt haben: Für 30 Prozent der Hypotheken mit Zahlungsrückständen von über 90 Tagen wurden Lösungsvorschläge unterbreitet. Die verstärkten Bemühungen der Banken um die Einbringung der Kreditforderungen spiegeln sich in einem geringeren Anteil kurzfristiger Stundungen bei der Umschuldung von Hypotheken wider. Den Banken steht nun die Zielvorgabe bevor, bis Ende 2013 Lösungen für 15 Prozent aller Hypotheken mit Zahlungsrückständen zu vereinbaren; bis Ende Juni 2014 steigt dieser Wert auf 35 Prozent der Hypothekenzahlungsrückstände. Zur Unterstützung dieses Prozesses haben Reformen des Privatinsolvenzgesetzes („Personal Insolvency Act") drei neue, im Wesentlichen außergerichtliche Verfahren zur Schuldenbereinigung festgelegt und die Insolvenzdauer verkürzt.

Die Überwindung einer ungenügenden Interaktion zwischen Banken und Kreditnehmern ist entscheidend dafür, dass dieser Schritt von Vorschlägen hin zu Lösungen für die Zahlungsrückstände rechtzeitig getan wird. Auf Seiten der Banken

sollten Anreize verstärkt werden, belastbare Umschuldungen anzubieten. Dazu sollten klare Regeln zur Bilanzierung von Rückstellungen, Abschreibungen und das Auflaufen von Zinsen für nicht umgeschuldete Kredite mit lang andauerndem Zahlungsrückstand zum Ende 2014 eingeführt werden. Bleibt eine Bank erheblich hinter den Zielvorgaben zurück, ist eventuell eine stärkere Anleitung durch die Aufsicht bei der Kreditanpassung oder bei der Auslagerung der Einbringung der Kreditforderungen erforderlich. Schuldner sollten dazu ermutigt werden, ihre Suche nach nachhaltigen Lösungen zu verstärken. Wo ein Verlust des Eigentums unausweichlich ist, käme eine bessere Unterstützung für Lösungen, bei denen hypothekenbelastetes Wohneigentum in ein hypothekenfreies Mietverhältnis umgewandelt wird („Mortgage-to-rent"), in Frage. Die würde dazu beitragen, die sozialen Kosten abzufedern.

Bei den kleinen und mittleren Unternehmen (KMU) wird die Anpassung notleidender Kredite fortgeführt, wobei die beiden Banken, die das KMU-Kreditgeschäft dominieren, in den letzten Quartalen die Zielvorgaben der CBI hinsichtlich der Einbringung ihrer Kreditforderungen erfüllt haben. Die Anzahl der Kreditumschuldungen ist deutlich höher als die der Zwangsvollstreckungen. Die Behörden beschleunigen derzeit die Einführung neuer Vorschriften (Zusätze zum Companies Bill). Dadurch erhalten kleine Unternehmen die Möglichkeit, bei Circuit Courts, wo die Gerichtskosten in der Regel geringer sind, ein Überprüfungsverfahren (Examinership) – Umstrukturierung statt Abwicklung – zu beantragen. Dies ist ein willkommener Schritt nach vorn. Besser wäre es, wenn die Rolle der Gerichte im Überprüfungsverfahren optimiert würde, unter Rückgriff auf die Erfahrungen mit dem Insolvenzdienst (Insolvency Service) für Haushalte.

In der ersten Hälfte des Jahres 2013 verzeichneten die Banken deutlichen Gewinnzuwachs. Die Staatsgarantie für Bankenverbindlichkeiten (Eligible Liabilities Guarantee (ELG) Scheme) wurde aufgehoben, die Unternehmen bauten Personal ab und schlossen Filialen, die Einlagenquoten sanken. Die Profitabilität der Banken bleibt schwach. Das schränkt ihre Fähigkeit ein, Kapital zu generieren, das für die Aufrechterhaltung der Kreditvergabe erforderlich ist. Die Wirtschaftlichkeit reagiert besonders empfindlich auf Prognosen für Neugeschäftsvolumen, neue Kreditpreise und Finanzierungskosten – die jeweils vom makroökonomischen Umfeld und den Fortschritten bei den Bilanzsanierungen abhängen.

Eine Hauptherausforderung bleibt die Finanzierung von Hypotheken mit niedrigen Erträgen, die den Leitzinssätzen der Zentralbank folgen, zu einem angemessen niedrigen Satz. Insgesamt halten die PCAR-Banken in Irland für 48 Mrd. Euro zinsvariable Hypotheken mit einer geringen durchschnittlichen Gewinnspanne über den Leitzinsen der EZB. Die Leitzinsen waren stärker zurückgegangen als die Kosten der Bankenfinanzierung, was zu beträchtlichen Haltekosten für zinsvariable Hypotheken führte, wenn auch die schwache Wirtschaftlichkeit durch die jüngsten Rückgänge der Einlagen- und Marktrefinanzierungssätze ein wenig gelindert wurde. Das Einwerben von

Neukapital seitens privater Partner zu ausreichend geringen Sätzen wird schwierig bleiben.

Strukturreformen und Arbeitslosigkeit

Die Arbeitslosigkeit ist aufgrund einer Kombination aus der Schaffung von Arbeitsplätzen und Auswanderung von 15,1 Prozent zu Beginn des Jahres 2012 auf immer noch hohe 12,5 Prozent zum Ende des Jahres 2013 zurückgegangen. Langzeitarbeitslose machen allerdings etwa 56,4 Prozent aller Arbeitssuchenden aus, was die Teilhabe und die beruflichen Qualifikationen der Beschäftigten erodiert. Wird eine derart hohe Langzeitarbeitslosigkeit nicht bekämpft, so könnte dies auf Jahre das Wachstum dämpfen. Dann wäre eine Kombination aus Strukturreformen und Anreizen zur Arbeitsplatzschaffung erforderlich.

Eine intensive Interaktion mit Langzeitarbeitslosen ist wichtig. Dadurch wird gewährleistet, dass sie aktiv nach Arbeit suchen und sich neue Fähigkeiten aneignen. Nur so können sie im Wettbewerb um Arbeitsplätze erfolgreich sein, wenn sich das Jobwachstum weiter beschleunigt. Die kontinuierliche Eröffnung weiterer Intreo-Büros, die eine optimierte Rundum-Anlaufstelle für Arbeitssuchende bieten, und die vorgesehene Verdoppelung der an vorderster Front tätigen Fallbearbeiter werden in dieser Hinsicht hilfreich sein. Gleiches gilt auch für die ergebnisbasierten Zahlungen an private Arbeitsvermittlungen. Eine Studie zur Aus- und Weiterbildung ergab kürzlich, dass diese besser an den Bedürfnissen der Wirtschaft ausgerichtet werden muss. Neue Initiativen sind wichtig, um insbesondere zu gewährleisten, dass Langzeitarbeitslose Fähigkeiten erwerben, die ihnen die Rückkehr in Arbeit ermöglichen.

Mit Unterstützung europäischer Partner wie der EIB und der KfW sollen Krediten an KMU gefördert werden. Dies ist ein wichtiger Schritt für Investitionen und die Schaffung von Arbeitsplätzen. Der angekündigte irische Strategische Investmentfonds (Strategic Investment Fund) zeitigt bereits Wirkung: Der Nationale Pensionsrücklagenfonds (National Pension Reserve Fund) hat in Partnerschaft mit privaten Akteuren bis zu 950 Mio Euro für Investitionen zugesagt. Sie sind für die Eigenfinanzierung und neue Kredite für KMU vorgesehen. Eine große Anzahl potenzieller Transaktionen befindet sich derzeit in verschiedenen Phasen des Vortragsschlusses. Die Vorbereitungen für die Veräußerung von bis zu 3 Mrd. Euro Staatsvermögen gehen weiter, darunter mit jüngsten Ankündigungen zu Bord Gáis Energy. Diese Erlöse können zur Finanzierung von Projekten zur Schaffung von Arbeitsplätzen, u.a. von öffentlich-privaten Partnerschaften, beitragen.

Schlussfolgerung

Irland hat sich aus einer außerordentlich tiefen Bankenkrise herausgearbeitet, seine finanzielle Lage deutlich verbessert und wieder Zugang zu den

internationalen Finanzmärkten gefunden. Zwar liegt das Wirtschaftswachstum unter den anfänglichen Prognosen, doch hat es den Durchschnitt des Euroraums übertroffen. Eine Erholung zeichnet sich ab. Bankenreformen haben die finanzielle Stabilität unterstützt. Zwar führten die Krise und die Stützung der Banken zu einer deutlichen Erhöhung des Haushaltsdefizits und einem steilen Anstieg der Staatsverschuldung, doch hat eine schrittweise Konsolidierung – die vor dem EU/IWF-Programm begonnen und dann fortgeführt wurde – die finanzielle Lage unter Erhaltung des sozialen Zusammenhalts deutlich verbessert. Irland hat wieder Zugang zum Markt gewonnen. Dabei konnte es auch von der Verlängerung der EFSF/EFSM-Bonds, der Schuldverschreibungstransaktion und dem allgemeinen Nachlassen von Marktspannungen im Euroraum profitieren.

Die irischen Behörden wissen: Auch weiterhin ist eine solide Politik vonnöten, um Irlands Wachstum zu stützen. Dazu dient die vor Kurzem verabschiedete mittelfristige Wirtschaftsstrategie für den Zeitraum von 2014 bis 2020. Die Entschlossenheit, eine derartige Strategie zu formulieren und umzusetzen, ist ausgesprochen ermutigend. Die Politik muss weiterhin an vielen Fronten entschlossen neue Reformen umsetzen, ehe die Einschätzung gestattet ist, Irland habe sich vollständig von der Krise erholt. Da das Haushaltsdefizit und die Staatsverschuldung nach wie vor hoch sind, ist in den nächsten Jahren eine weitere umfangreiche Konsolidierung notwendig, um bei den Schulden definitiv einen Abwärtstrend herbeizuführen und dafür zu sorgen, dass Irlands Rückkehr zur Marktfinanzierung von Dauer ist.

Die langsamen Fortschritte bei der Bewältigung notleidender Hypotheken behindert eine allmähliche Wiederbelebung des Kreditgeschäfts, die erforderlich ist, damit die Erholung der Inlandsnachfrage nachhaltig wird. Deshalb braucht es intensive Bemühungen, um zu gewährleisten, dass Banken und Hypothekenschuldner, die mit ihren Rückzahlungen im Rückstand sind, zu dauerhaften Lösungen kommen. Auch müssen die Banken ihre Wirtschaftlichkeit wiederherstellen, obwohl sie angesichts niedriger EZB-Leitzinsen aufgrund der Struktur ihrer Vermögenswerte vor Herausforderungen stehen. Bemühungen zur Verbesserung der Beschäftigungsdienstleistungen sowie der Aus- und Weiterbildung sollten zügig fortgesetzt werden. Das Hauptziel dabei lautet: Langzeitarbeitslose sollen Teil der Erwerbsbevölkerung bleiben und markttaugliche Fähigkeiten erwerben.

KAPITEL 4

Ausgaben und Reform: Neuer Schwung

Marc Coleman

Hauptaussagen

- Irlands finanzpolitische Anpassungen waren eindrucksvoll und systematisch. Die Regierung hat versucht, schwächere Teile der Gesellschaft abzusichern. Gleichzeitig hat sie die Effizienz des öffentlichen Sektors verbessert und Senkungen bei den Gehältern im öffentlichen Dienst erreicht.
- Während sich der öffentliche Sektor Irlands im Hinblick auf seine Effizienz verbessert hat – es wird nun mit weniger Ressourcen mehr getan –, besteht die größte Herausforderung für Irland nun darin, die Wirksamkeit öffentlicher Ausgaben zu beurteilen. Auch liegen die öffentlichen Gehälter in Irland trotz erheblicher Kürzungen weiterhin deutlich über denen der Eurozone. Dafür ist eine eingehendere Analyse der Gründe und eine Rechtfertigung notwendig.
- Das neue Ministerium für öffentliche Ausgaben und Reform (Department of Public Expenditure and Reform) wirkt auf größere Effizienz und Wirksamkeit hin. Nach neuen Reformplänen, die 2014 veröffentlicht werden sollen, wird sich der Schwerpunkt von der Senkung der Kosten für die Bereitstellung öffentlicher Dienste hin zur Verbesserung der Qualität der öffentlichen Dienste verlagern.

Einleitung

Mit Schwerpunkt auf der Ausgabenseite und dem Reformprogramm untersucht dieses Kapitel Irlands Fortschritte auf dem Weg zur finanziellen Konsolidierung, und zwar in zweierlei Hinsicht: erstens in Bezug auf Irlands Erfolg bei seiner Annäherung an die Benchmarks des Fiskalpaktes, zweitens im Hinblick darauf, wie die Gestaltung dieser Konsolidierung (sowohl die allgemeine Balance zwischen Ausgabenkonsolidierung und Steuererhöhungen als auch die konkrete Ausgestaltung der Ausgabenreformen und Steuererhöhungen) die wirtschaftliche Erholung Irlands beeinflusst hat. Das Kapitel sucht nach operativen finanzpolitischen Leitlinien in Standards bei den Ausgaben und Steuern, wie sie in finanziell stabileren Ländern der Eurozone, wie beispielsweise Deutschland,

etabliert sind. Auf längere Sicht hin stellt sich die Frage, ob Irland diese Standards für sich übernehmen könnte. Die Diskussion profitiert von der vor kurzem erschienenen Veröffentlichung einer mittelfristigen Wirtschaftsstrategie durch die irische Regierung, die hilfreiche Richtwerte für die Zukunft enthält.

Der Erfolg der Regierung bei der Umsetzung ihres finanzpolitischen Konsolidierungsprogramms im Zuge des Troika-Programms ist nicht nur unbestritten, sondern auch eindrucksvoll. Laut Prognosen der Regierung – die auf vorsichtigen Annahmen beruhen und von unabhängiger Seite[29] untermauert wurden –, wird Irlands Haushaltsdefizit bis zum Jahr 2015 auf unter 3 Prozent des BIP fallen, sein Primärsaldo wird im Plus liegen und das Verhältnis seiner Verschuldung zum BIP wird eine Abwärtskurve beschreiben.

Doch ist die finanzielle Konsolidierung eine Sache, eine Finanzpolitik im Einklang mit Wachstumsmaximierung hingegen eine ganz andere. Die entscheidende Frage bei jeder finanziellen Konsolidierung ist: Wird sie durch Ausgabenkürzung und Kostenverringerung erreicht, durch Steuererhöhungen oder durch einen Mix aus beidem? Irlands Steuerlast war trotz gegenteiliger Behauptungen niemals gering. Im Gegenteil, ein junger neutraler Staat mit einem im Vergleich zu Deutschland relativ geringen altersbedingten Ausgabendruck und vergleichsweise wenigen militärischen Verpflichtungen sollte dazu in der Lage sein, mit geringerem Kostenaufwand ein ähnliches Niveau von sozialer Fürsorge und Sozialleistungen zu erreichen, wie es in Deutschland verfügbar ist. Wie eine Studie zeigt, lag der Anteil der Steuern an Irlands Wirtschaft, bereinigt um strukturelle und demografische Faktoren, im Jahr 2006, nur zwei Jahre vor der Krise, bereits über dem EU-Durchschnitt.[30] Daher war zwar eine gewisse Verbreiterung der Steuerbasis erforderlich – die übermäßige Abhängigkeit von stark fluktuierenden immobilienbezogenen Steuern musste überwunden werden. Doch gab es keinen Grund, die Höhe der Steuerlast insgesamt zu erhöhen. Wie aus jeder rationalen Analyse deutlich wird, wurde die finanzielle Nachhaltigkeitskrise Irlands durch eine Kombination zweier Faktoren auf der Ausgabenseite verursacht: erstens von den Auswirkungen einmaliger, aber umfangreicher Bankenrekapitalisierungsverpflichtungen zwischen 2009 und 2011, und zweitens von einem atemberaubenden Anstieg der öffentlichen Gesamtausgaben um jährlich 25 Mrd. Euro in den Jahren 2003 bis 2008. Letztere Entwicklung fand statt, bevor sich die Bankenkrise auf die öffentlichen Finanzen auswirkte, und anders als diese Auswirkungen stellt sie einen jährlichen, keinen einmaligen Anstieg dar.

---

[29] Der Finanzwirtschaftliche Beirat (Fiscal Advisory Council). Siehe IFAC, „Fiscal Assessment Report", 26. November 2013.

[30] De Butleir, Donal und Thornhill, Don (2008). „The Agenda for Tax Reform: Playing To and Developing Our Strengths", Dublin Economic Workshop.

Ausgaben der öffentlichen Hand in Irland 1997-2008

Wie kaum ein anderes Land in Europa, wie zu kaum einer anderen Epoche in der europäischen Geschichte erlebte Irland während seines verhängnisvollen Booms einen atemberaubenden Anstieg seiner öffentlichen Ausgaben. Waren sie anfangs noch gerechtfertigt, um die Bedürfnisse einer wachsenden Bevölkerung zu erfüllen, so stiegen die öffentlichen Ausgaben unkontrolliert auf eine Art und Weise, die Irland empfindlich exponierten, als die Krise 2008 ausbrach. Bis zu diesem Jahr wurde der entstandene Schaden an der Finanzlage Irlands durch das übermäßige Vertrauen auf Grundsteuern (Urkundensteuer) und andere Steuern auf Aktivitäten des Immobilienmarktes (Kapitalertragssteuer und Kapitalerwerbssteuer) verschleiert. Getragen von einem starken Kreditwachstum[31] stiegen die Einnahmen aus Urkundensteuer, Kapitalertragssteuer und Kapitalerwerbssteuer im Jahr 2005 um 30, 29 bzw. 31 Prozent und im Jahr 2006[32] um 38, 54 bzw. 37 Prozent. 2007 lagen die Zuwachsraten im moderaten positiven Bereich beziehungsweise im negativen Bereich mit starken Rückgängen von 2008 bis einschließlich 2011.

Damit einhergehend stiegen auch die Ausgaben stark an. Der offensichtliche Unterschied lag darin, dass die Steuereinnahmen während des Krisenzeitraums 2008 bis 2011 stark fielen, Ausgabenverringerungen hingegen politisch weniger leicht zu erreichen waren. Daraus ergibt sich der klare Schwerpunkt auf eine Erhöhung der Besteuerung während der frühen Jahre der im Weiteren erläuterten finanziellen Konsolidierung. **Illustration 4.1** zeigt das dramatische Ausmaß der Ausgabenanstiege in den fünf Jahren bis zur Krise 2008. Von 43 Mrd. Euro im Jahr 2003 stiegen die Ausgaben um atemberaubende 58 Prozent auf 68 Mrd. Euro im Jahr 2008.

---

[31]   Erörtert in **Kapitel 1**.

[32]   *Quelle:* Finanzministerium (Department of Finance), Daten der Monatsberichte.

Illustration 4.1: Ausgabenanstieg in Irland, 2003-2012

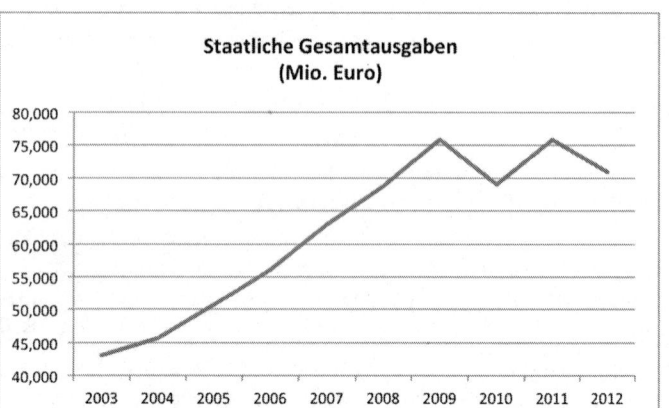

Quelle: Finanzministerium (Department of Finance).

Man sollte dabei nicht vergessen, dass diese Entwicklung nach einem Jahrzehnt kam, in dem man die irische Wirtschaft als hauptsächlich von einem gesunden, vom Export getragenen Wachstum angetrieben betrachten kann. In diesem Zeitraum gingen die öffentlichen Ausgaben von 18 Mrd. Euro im Jahr 1993 auf 43 Mrd. Euro im Jahr 2003 um mehr als das Doppelte nach Oben. Mit 36 Prozent des BNE und 31 Prozent des BIP (siehe Anmerkung am Ende dieses Kapitels zur Relevanz dieser beiden unterschiedlichen Messwerte) lagen die öffentlichen Ausgaben auf einem Niveau, das mit einem guten sozialen Schutz und guten öffentlichen Dienstleistungen vereinbar war. Wie im Vorangegangenen erläutert, lag die Steuerlast in Irland während dieses Zeitraums, bereinigt um Irlands relativ günstige aktuelle demografische Lage im Vergleich zu Deutschland und Frankreich und Italien (wo der altersbedingte Ausgabendruck viel höher ist), über dem EU-Durchschnitt und war somit für die Finanzierung öffentlicher Dienstleistungen und sozialer Absicherung gemäß dem europäischen Sozialmarktmodell angemessen.

Nach unabhängigen Schätzungen liegt die optimale Größe des Staates im Hinblick auf die Maximierung der sozialen Absicherung und des Wachstumspotenzials zwischen 30 und 35 Prozent der Wirtschaftsleistung.[33] Zwar kann eine größere Rolle für die öffentliche Hand hilfreich und mit hohem Wachstum und hoher Produktivität vereinbar sein. Doch ist dies stets – wie im Fall einiger nordischer Länder –mit viel Geduld über Jahrzehnte entwickelt worden. In

---

[33]   Siehe Tanzi (2000). „The Role of the State and the Quality of the Public Sector", IWF-Arbeitspapier WP/00/36; und auch Tanzi und Schuknecht (1995). „The Growth of Government and the Reform of the State in Industrial Countries", IWF-Arbeitspapier WP/95/130 und Tanzi (2004). „A Lower Tax Future? The Economic Role of the State in Industrial Countries", Politeia, Policy Series No.44.

Schweden stieg das Verhältnis der öffentlichen Ausgaben zum BIP beispielsweise von 31 Prozent im Jahr 1960 im Verlaufe zweier Jahrzehnte auf 60,1 Prozent[34]. Dabei stand im Vordergrund, zunächst einheimisches Wachstum in Industrien mit hoher Produktivität zu erreichen, das dann eine solide Grundlage für höheres Steueraufkommen und höhere Ausgaben bildete. Im Gegensatz dazu stiegen in Irland die öffentlichen Ausgaben von 35,9 Prozent des BNE im Jahr 2005 auf 51,0 Prozent im Jahr 2012, d. h. über einen Zeitraum von nur acht Jahren. Während der ersten Jahre dieses Zeitraums verringerte sich die Produktivität erheblich.

Das in **Illustration 4.2** dargestellte Ausgabenmuster zeigt deutlich, wie, im Gegensatz zum planvollen Anstieg in den nordischen Ländern, öffentliche Ausgaben in Irland im Vorfeld des Wahljahres 2007 schnell realisiert wurden.

Obwohl ein Ausgabenniveau erreicht wurde, das aus Sicht guter Sozialleistungen angemessen war, und obwohl sie sich in den vorangegangenen zehn Jahren verdoppelt hatten, wären einige der Ausgabenerhöhungen ab 2003 in den Folgejahren dennoch berechtigt gewesen. Aus **Illustration 4.2** wird jedoch ebenfalls klar, dass die Rate der Ausgabenerhöhung über das gerechtfertigte Maß hinausging. Im Jahr 2004 hätten eine (moderate) Inflationsrate von 2,1 Prozent und der Bevölkerungszuwachs von 1,6 Prozent zusammen eine Rate des Ausgabenzuwachses im Bereich von 4 Prozent gerechtfertigt. Die Bevölkerung wuchs im Zeitraum von 2004 bis 2007 durchschnittlich um rund 2 Prozent, doch die Inflation stieg aufgrund des in den vorangegangenen Kapiteln erläuterten Verlustes der Wettbewerbsfähigkeit unaufhaltsam. Dies, sowie das Anbrechen des Parlamentswahljahres 2007, trieb das Ausgabenwachstum auf eine Jahresrate von 12 Prozent im Jahr 2007, dem Wahljahr und dem Jahr vor Ausbruch der Krise. Erwähnenswert ist hier, dass auch Deutschland in einem Jahr, in dem Bundestagswahlen stattfanden, gegen den Stabilitätspakt verstieß (2002).

Illustration 4.2: Zuwachsraten der staatlichen Gesamtausgaben

% Änderung pro Jahr	2004	2005	2006	2007
Staatliche Gesamtausgaben	5,1	11,1	10,6	12,1
Inflation	2,1	2,5	3,9	4,9
Bevölkerungszuwachs	1,6	2,2	2,4	3,4

Quelle: Finanzministerium (Department of Finance).

Seit 2008 scheinen sich die öffentlichen Ausgaben stabilisiert, aber nicht verringert zu haben. In einem Land, dessen Bevölkerung seit Ausbruch der Krise um fast eine Drittelmillion gewachsen ist (d. h. um 8 Prozent) und in dem die Arbeitslosigkeit dramatisch zugenommen hat, bleibt diese Stabilisierung eine bemerkenswerte

---

[34] Tanzi und Schuknecht (2000). „The Role of the State and the Quality of the Public Sector", IWF-Arbeitspapier WP/00/36.

Leistung. Sie spiegelt unzureichend die erheblichen Anstrengungen wider, die unternommen wurden. Dabei ging es nicht nur um die Auswirkungen einer verantwortungslosen Politik vor 2008, sondern auch darum, den europaweit einzigartigen demografischen Druck im Rahmen zu halten, der die Ausgaben noch weiter nach oben hätte treiben können. Er wird später erläutert; zuerst jedoch soll die Art und Weise der finanzpolitischen Korrektur Irlands untersucht werden.

Bisherige finanzielle Konsolidierung 2008-2013

Die Balance zwischen Ausgabenkürzungen und Steuererhöhungen

Der Nationale Sanierungsplan (*National Recovery Plan*) 2011 bis 2014[35] verpflichtete die Regierung dazu, zwei Drittel der gesamten Haushaltsanpassungen durch Ausgabeneinsparungen und ein Drittel durch Maßnahmen zur Einnahmenerhöhung zu erreichen. Wie in **Illustration 4.3**[36] dargestellt, war die Gesamtsumme der Ausgabenkürzungen und der versuchten Steuererhöhungen[37] über die sieben Haushaltspläne des Korrekturzeitraums im Großen und Ganzen ausgewogen. Die letzte Spalte in der **Illustration 4.3** gibt das Verhältnis von Ausgabenkürzungen zu Steuererhöhungen an. Die Ausgewogenheit zwischen Ausgabenkürzungen und Steuererhöhungen spiegelt möglicherweise die Tatsache wider, dass sich in der Praxis gezeigt hat, dass Steuererhöhungen weniger lautstarken politischen Protest der Steuerzahler erregen, als Ausgabenkürzungen.

---

[35] Seite 9, „National Recovery Plan 2011-2014".

[36] Die angegebenen Zahlen sind Näherungswerte. Sie geben jedoch ein angemessenes Bild der Balance zwischen Ausgabenkürzungen und Steuererhöhungen, wie sie von aufeinanderfolgenden Regierungen während der Krise beabsichtigt war.

[37] Die Wirksamkeit von Ausgabenkürzungen hängt von der Umsetzung durch die Regierung ab, liegt also in deren Ermessen. Hingegen unterliegt die Wirksamkeit von Versuchen, die Steuern zu erhöhen, wirtschaftlichen und verhaltensbezogenen Reaktionen, auf die der Staat größtenteils keinen Einfluss hat.

Illustration 4.3: Balance zwischen Ausgabenkürzungen und Steuererhöhungen, 2008-2013

	Ausgaben-kürzungen (Mrd. Euro)	Steuer-erhöhungen (Mrd. Euro)	Verhältnis AK/StE (auf nächste Ganzzahl gerundet)
Oktober 2008	0,30	2,30	3/23
April 2009	1,20	2,70	4/9
Dezember 2009	3,10	0,10	31/1
Dezember 2010	2,20	2,40	11/12
Dezember 2011	1,60	1,60	1/1
Dezember 2012	1,85	1,65	37/33
Oktober 2013	1,60	0,90	16/9
Gesamt	11,85	11,65	1/1

Quelle: Berechnet aus Budgetdaten des Finanzministeriums (Department of Finance).

Die unterschiedlichen Auswirkungen einzelner Haushaltsplänen legen nahe: Trotz des stärkeren politischen Widerstandes haben Ausgabenkürzungen mehr bewirkt als Steuererhöhungen. Der Haushaltsplan vom Oktober 2008 sah pro 23 Euro angestrebter zusätzlicher Steuern eine Kürzung von 3 Euro vor. Der nachfolgende Nachtragshaushalt von 2009 erhöhte den Quotienten der Ausgabenkürzungen, hielt sich jedoch noch stark auf der Seite der Steuererhöhungen. Das Wachstum im Jahr 2009 war deutlich geringer als in jedem anderen Jahr der Krise. Dieses Ergebnis wurde zweifellos von der weltweiten Intensität der Krise beeinflusst, und Rückschlüsse zu den Auswirkungen der beiden ersten Krisenhaushalte auf die Wirtschaft sind durch Ungewissheiten getrübt. Dennoch ist eine Gegenüberstellung der beiden aufeinanderfolgenden Haushalte interessant.

Der erste, der Haushalt vom Oktober 2009, sah pro 1 Euro angestrebter zusätzlicher Steuern eine Kürzung von 31 Euro vor. Auf diese maßgebliche Verschiebung hin zur Vermeidung von Steuererhöhungen und zu radikalen Ausgabenkürzungen folgte eine kurze wirtschaftliche Erholung. In diesem Haushalt wurde nicht nur die Gesamthöhe der öffentlichen Gehälter um durchschnittlich 7,5 Prozent gekürzt; im Januar davor wurde auch eine Rentenabgabe[38] für Beamte eingeführt. Weitere Kürzungen bei den höheren Gehaltsklassen sollten folgen.

Nach einem Rückgang um 9,1 Prozent im Jahr 2009 stieg das BNE im Jahr 2010 um 0,5 Prozent, und während das BIP zwar in dem Jahr immer noch um 1,1 Prozent sank, war das Ergebnis des BIP im Jahr 2010 dennoch eine deutliche Verbesserung gegenüber 2009, als es um 6,4 Prozent gefallen war. Monate nach diesem Haushaltsplan begann die Zuversicht der Verbraucher zu steigen. Nach

---

[38] Die sog. Pensionskürzung für den öffentlichen Dienst (Public Service Pension Reduction).

einem Rückgang um eine Viertelmillion zwischen September 2008 und März 2010 stabilisierte sich die Zahl der Beschäftigten für einen Zeitraum von 6 Monaten bei 1,89 Mio. Im Vergleich zu einem Rückgang von 19 Prozent im Jahr 2009 fielen die Steuereinnahmen um sehr viel moderatere 4 Prozent und lagen am Jahresende mehr als eine halbe Milliarde Euro höher als die Prognose der Regierung.[39]

Im März 2010 verpflichtete sich die Regierung zum Schutz der öffentlichen Gehälter und Pensionen. Dabei zählten diese zu den höchsten in Europa und lagen unabhängigen Studien zufolge – bereinigt um verschiedene Faktoren – etwa 12,5 Prozent höher als die Durchschnittswerte im Privatsektor.[40] Diese Belege kamen nach der bereits erwähnten Pensionsabgabe, aber vor der Umsetzung von Gehaltskürzungen im Dezember 2009. Ein danach veröffentlichtes Papier[41] stellte jedoch fest, dass, mit Ausnahme von Portugal, Italien und Griechenland, der Unterschied zwischen den durchschnittlichen Gehältern im öffentlichen Sektor und denen im privaten Sektor in Irland deutlich höher ist als in anderen Ländern der Eurozone.

Im Mai 2013 verabschiedete die Regierung die „Stabilitätsvereinbarung für den öffentlichen Dienst 2013-2016" („Public Service Stability Agreement 2013-2016"), die weitere Gehaltskürzungen im öffentlichen Dienst für Gehälter von 65.000 Euro oder mehr im Jahr umsetzte.

Infolge dieser und weiterer ausgabenbezogener Maßnahmen hat der Haushalt vom Oktober 2013, obwohl nicht so positiv gegenüber Ausgabenkürzungen eingestellt wie der Haushalt vom Dezember 2009, die in dieser Hinsicht günstigste Balance aller Haushalte seit Beginn der Krise erzielt. Es weist alles darauf hin, dass dies Irlands wirtschaftliche Erholung und das Beschäftigungswachstum unterstützt.

Irlands frühere Konsolidierungen

Theoretiker sind sich uneins in der Frage, ob Ausgabenkürzungen oder Steuererhöhungen das wirksamste Mittel zur finanziellen Konsolidierung darstellen. Die Belege sprechen eher für den ersteren Ansatz. Zwar wurde das jüngste Papier *Expansionary Austerity: New International Evidence*[42] als Warnung vor den Wirkungen einer zu schnellen Korrektur interpretiert. Doch weist sein Urteil zu den Auswirkungen ausgabenbasierter Korrekturen auf das Wachstum im

---

[39] Finanzministerium, (Department of Finance), Daten der Monatsberichte für 2009, 2010 und 2011.

[40] Barrett, A., Kearney, I. & Goggin, J (2009). „Quarterly Economic Commentary, Herbst", ESRI.

[41] Guajardo, J., Leigh, D. & Pescatori, A. (2001). "The Public Sector Pay Gap in a Selection of Euro Area Countries", EZB-Arbeitspapier 1406.

[42] Guajardo, J., Leigh, D. & Pescatori, A. (2011). "Expansionary Austerity: New International Evidence", IWF-Arbeitspapier WP/11/158.

Vergleich zu steuerbasierten Korrekturen deutlich[43] in Richtung ausgabenbasierter Konsolidierung als den am wenigsten schädlichen Ansatz. In der Praxis bestätigen sowohl historische als auch jüngere Belege für Irland diese Ansicht deutlich.

Von 1982 bis 1986 reagierte die Regierung auf eine Finanzkrise mit der Erhöhung der staatlichen Gesamtausgaben von 10 Mrd. Euro auf über 13 Mrd. Euro, ein Anstieg von fast einem Drittel. Als Anteil am BIP bzw. am BNE ging der Umfang der Gesamtstaatsausgaben leicht zurück; dies lag hauptsächlich an den Auswirkungen einer hohen Inflation auf die Höhe der nominalen Produktionsleistung. Zur Finanzierung wurden die Bruttoeinkommensteuersätze auf bis zu 65 Prozent angehoben. In der Folge war Irland zu einer Zeit, als sich Europa und die USA von der Rezession der frühen 1980er Jahre erholten, durch ein schwaches Wachstum der einheimischen Wirtschaft gelähmt. Trotz eines gewissen vom Export getragenen Wachstums – das jährliche Wachstum des BIP lag in diesem Zeitraum bei durchschnittlich 1,3 Prozent – lag das Wachstum des BNE im Durchschnitt lediglich bei 0,4 Prozent. Das Haushaltsdefizit[44] blieb am Ende dieses Zeitraums aufgrund eines geringeren Wachstums in der Wirtschaft mit 11,4 Prozent hoch.

Der Kontrast zum nachfolgenden Fünf-Jahres-Zeitraum 1987 bis 1991 ist erhellend. Im Jahr 1986 wertete Irland seine Währung ab, was dem Export kurzfristig Auftrieb gab. Noch bemerkenswerter ist jedoch der krasse Unterschied zwischen den Ansätzen zur finanziellen Konsolidierung und insbesondere der Unterschied, der im Wachstum des BNE erzielt wurde (siehe die Anmerkung zu den Unterschieden zwischen BIP und BNE für Irland), zwischen den beiden Zeiträumen.

Zwischen 1987 und 1991 stiegen die Gesamtstaatsausgaben erneut, und zwar von 13,1 Mrd. Euro auf 15,4 Mrd. Euro. Im Vergleich zum Anstieg im vorangegangenen Zeitraum von etwa einem Drittel war dieser Anstieg von etwa 18 Prozent moderater und spiegelte eine stärkere Kontrolle sowohl über laufende als auch über Investitionsausgaben wider. Als Anteil am BNE fielen die Gesamtstaatsausgaben von 54,7 Prozent Ende 1986 auf 46 Prozent, was an erheblich höherem Wachstum lag. Von einer durchschnittlichen Jahresrate von 1,3 Prozent im Zeitraum von 1982 bis 1986 beschleunigte sich das Wachstum des BIP auf eine durchschnittliche Jahresrate von 4,3 Prozent im Zeitraum von 1987 bis 1991. In früheren Jahren war dies hauptsächlich auf die Geldabwertung zurückzuführen. Die starke Beschleunigung der durchschnittlichen jährlichen Wachstumsrate des BNE von nur 0,4 Prozent zwischen 1982 und 1986 auf 3,7 Prozent im darauffolgenden Zeitraum spiegelte eine Positivspirale aus Ausgabenkontrolle, sinkender Verschuldung und Steuern sowie Anstieg von

---

[43] Übersicht 9 auf Seite 25 in Guajardo, J., Leigh, D. & Pescatori, A. (2011). "Expansionary Austerity: New International Evidence", IWF-Arbeitspapier WP/11/158.

[44] Der Standardmesswert zum Messen der Haushaltsbilanz war damals die Bilanz des irischen Schatzamtes (die „Exchequer Balance").

Wachstum und Beschäftigung wider. Nur zu Anfang wurde dies in gewissem Umfang von der Abwertung unterstützt.

Warum sind die laufenden Ausgaben nicht zurückgegangen?

Angesichts dieser Belege – und angesichts des scharfen Anstiegs der öffentlichen Ausgaben zwischen 2003 und 2008 – stellt sich die Frage, warum die öffentlichen Ausgaben nicht stärker gekürzt wurden. Die **Illustration 4.4** und **Illustration 4.5** (siehe Anmerkung am Ende des Kapitels) zeigt, dass die laufenden Bruttoausgaben als Anteil am BNE seit Ausbruch der Krise nicht wesentlich zurückgegangen sind. Was sie jedoch nicht zeigt: Es gab erheblichen Aufwärtsdruck, der – wenn er nicht durch Maßnahmen und Reformen eingedämmt worden wäre – die öffentlichen Ausgaben deutlich nach oben getrieben hätte.

Illustration 4.4: Gesamtstaatsausgaben als Anteil am BNE (%)[45]

	2004	2005	2006	2007	2008	2009	2010	2011	2012
Gesamtstaatsausgaben	35,9	36,6	36,4	38,6	44,4	56,7	52,3	58,5	51,0
davon laufende	30,8	31,1	30,8	32,2	37,0	45,3	46,0	46,0	45,4
davon Investitionen	5,2	5,5	5,6	6,4	7,4	11,3	6,3	12,6	5,6

Quelle: Finanzministerium (Department of Finance).

Illustration 4.5: Gesamtstaatsausgaben als Anteil am BIP (%)[15]

	2004	2005	2006	2007	2008	2009	2010	2011	2012
Gesamtstaatsausgaben	30,5	31,2	31,6	33,2	38,1	46,8	43,6	47,0	41,3
davon laufende	26,1	26,5	26,8	27,7	31,8	37,4	38,4	36,9	36,8
davon Investitionen	4,4	4,7	4,9	5,5	6,3	9,3*	5,3*	10,1*	4,5

Quelle: Finanzministerium (Department of Finance).
* Durch staatliche Investitionen im Finanz-und Immobiliensektor beeinträchtigt.

Um es nochmal zu sagen: Seit Beginn der Krise ist die Bevölkerung des Landes um fast eine Drittelmillion Menschen angewachsen. Dies hat auf verschiedene Art und Weise den öffentlichen Ausgabendruck in den Bereichen Gesundheit, Bildung und Investitionen erhöht.

Abgesehen von diesem Bevölkerungswachstum machen Veränderungen im Altersprofil der Bevölkerung höhere Bildungsausgaben notwendig. Dies wäre

---

[45] Die Bankenrekapitalisierungsmaßnahmen haben sich in den Jahren 2009 bis 2011 auf die Zahlen für die Investitionsausgaben ausgewirkt.

ungeachtet des Zustandes der Wirtschaft der Fall. Die Anzahl der Schüler in Grund- und Sekundarstufe wird sich von 2007 um 75.000 auf voraussichtlich 889.300 im Jahr 2014 erhöhen. Mit anderen Worten: Ein Fünftel der irischen Bevölkerung ist im schulpflichtigen Alter, deutlich mehr als in vielen anderen EU Staaten. Zusätzlich hat sich über denselben Zeitraum die Anzahl der Studenten um 17.000 auf 165.000 erhöht. Ein Viertel der jungen und wachsenden Bevölkerung Irlands befindet sich in Ausbildung und verursacht Kosten für die Staatskasse, ihre Zahl steigt weiterhin deutlich an. Unter diesen Umständen ist es eine eindrucksvolle Leistung, dass die Ausgaben, die nicht für Gehälter getätigt werden, mehr oder weniger beibehalten wurden: Sie sind von 1,9 Mrd. Euro im Jahr 2007 auf voraussichtlich 2 Mrd. Euro im Jahr 2014 kaum gestiegen.

Gleichzeitig nahm die Zahl derer, die Leistungen für Arbeitslose in Anspruch nahmen, um eine Viertelmillion zu. Notwendigerweise stiegen daher die Ausgaben in diesem Bereich von 1,4 Mrd. Euro im Jahr 2007 auf voraussichtlich 3,3 Mrd. Euro im Jahr 2014.[46] Demografischer Druck hat außerdem zu einem Anstieg bei anderen Ausgaben der Sozialfürsorge von 13,8 Mrd. Euro im Jahr 2007 auf voraussichtlich 16 Mrd. Euro im Jahr 2014 beigetragen.

Effizienzreformen

In Irland wurden und werden starke Reformbemühungen – mit weniger Ressourcen mehr zu erreichen – unternommen. Eine Herausforderung bleibt es möglicherweise, eine Verlagerung des Schwerpunktes von „Effizienzreformen" zu „Wirksamkeitsreformen" ins Auge zu fassen. Effizienz betont das Erzielen der gleichen Ergebnisse und Leistungen mit weniger Ressourcen. Es ist kaum zu bezweifeln, dass dies derzeit stattfindet.

Von 17,5 Mrd. Euro im Jahr 2009 fielen die Kosten für die Gehälter im öffentlichen Dienst auf 14,5 Mrd. Euro im Jahr 2014, ein Rückgang um 17,5 Prozent. Ferner ist die Zahl der Beschäftigten im öffentlichen Dienst – die nach deutschen Standards nicht hoch ist[47] – zwischen 2007 und 2014 um 30.000 gefallen, ein Rückgang von 9 Prozent.

Diese Rückgänge wurden trotz des Gegenwindes durch den steigenden Druck, eine wachsende Bevölkerung mit Leistungen zu versorgen, erreicht. Sie sind ein deutliches Zeichen für einen allgemeinen Zuwachs an Effizienz.

Allerdings wäre die Konzentration darauf, die Kopfzahl der im öffentlichen Dienst Beschäftigten zu verringern, unnötig gewesen, wenn man nicht an der Höhe der Gehälter festgehalten hätte. Diese Gehälter bleiben trotz der genannten Gehaltskürzungen im EU-Vergleich großzügig. Daran hat sich starke Kritik entzündet. Tatsächlich erscheint ein Job-Abbau ungerechtfertigt, wenn die

---

[46] Schätzung zum Zeitpunkt des Verfassens des vorliegenden Artikels anhand der jüngsten verfügbaren (Oktober 2013) Haushaltsprognosen.

[47] Etwa ein Sechstel der Erwerbstätigen in Irland sind im öffentlichen Dienst beschäftigt.

öffentlichen Gehälter im Durchschnitt weiterhin über den Einkünften im Privatsektor bleiben. In Deutschland haben die Gewerkschaften der Erhaltung von Arbeitsplätzen Priorität eingeräumt, notfalls bei geringeren Gehältern. In Irland wurde hingegen eine erhebliche Anzahl von Arbeitsplätzen abgebaut, während die öffentlichen Gehälter durch die Vereinbarung von Croke Park geschützt blieben. Die Tatsache, dass der Anteil des öffentlichen Sektors in Irland an der Gesamterwerbstätigkeit im EU-Vergleich bescheiden bleibt, macht deutlich, dass mehr zur Sicherung von Arbeitsplätzen hätte getan werden können.

Neben den öffentlichen Gehältern betreffen die Konsolidierungsbemühungen bisher vor allem die Investitionsausgaben. Die Maßnahmen zur Bankenrekapitalisierung nicht mitgerechnet, sind Investitionen in die Infrastruktur von 9 Mrd. Euro im Jahr 2008 auf 3,3 Mrd. Euro im Jahr 2014 gefallen.[48] Dies könnte man insofern als Einschwenken auf einen relativ einfachen Weg der Ausgabenkürzungen kritisieren, als dass sich Investitionsausgaben gewöhnlich leichter kürzen lassen, aber langfristig produktiver für die Wirtschaft sind. Andererseits genoss Irland seit 1993 anderthalb Jahrzehnte lang umfangreiche und weitgehende „National Development Plans", mit denen die Infrastruktur des Landes radikal verbessert wurde. Dennoch werden Investitionsausgaben nun wichtiger, da sich Irland erneutem Wettbewerbsdruck ausgesetzt sieht und im Hinblick auf staatliche Investitionen in die Infrastruktur von der 4. Position innerhalb der EU auf die 21. zurückgefallen ist. Neue Impulse in diesem Bereich sind also gerechtfertigt.

Die Croke Park- und Haddington Road-Vereinbarungen
Die andere Dimension der Reform ist die Verbesserung der Effizienz im öffentlichen Sektor auf der Mikroebene. Im März 2010 stimmte Irlands Gewerkschaftsbewegung der Vereinbarung für den öffentlichen Dienst 2010-2014, dem „Public Service Agreement 2010-2014" (auch „Croke Park Agreement") zu. Im Gegenzug zur Verpflichtung der Regierung, Gehälter oder Pensionen nicht weiter zu kürzen und auch keine Entlassungen zu verordnen, erklärten die Arbeitnehmer ihren Verzicht auf Arbeitskämpfe und die Bereitschaft, an den Reformen zur Erhöhung der Effizienz mitzuwirken. Dazu gehören Versetzungen von Beschäftigten im öffentlichen Dienst, flexiblere Arbeitspraktiken und die Arbeitszeitverlängerung für Grund- und Sekundarstufenlehrer sowie für Hochschullehrer.

Im Juli 2013 wurde diese Vereinbarung von der Stabilitätsvereinbarung für den öffentlichen Dienst 2013-2016, dem „Public Service Stability Agreement 2013-2016" (auch „Haddington Road Agreement") abgelöst. Es sieht weitere Gehaltskürzungen zwischen 5,5 Prozent und 10 Prozent – je nach Gehalt – für Beschäftigte des öffentlichen Dienstes mit einem Gehalt von mehr als 65.000 Euro pro Jahr vor. Zusätzlich dazu wurden Pensionsminderungssätze für den

---

[48] Die Gesamtheit der Investitionsausgaben wurde durch staatliche Finanzspritzen für den Banken-und Immobiliensektor beeinflusst.

öffentlichen Dienst (Public Service Pension Reduction Rates) – im Jahr 2009 eingeführte Abgaben auf öffentliche Pensionen – erhöht. Die Regelarbeitszeit wurde ebenfalls verlängert, Überstundenvergütungen wurden reduziert und Gehaltserhöhungen für drei Jahre ausgesetzt.

Dennoch bleiben die öffentlichen Gehälter und Pensionen im Durchschnitt deutlich großzügiger als im privaten Sektor und auch als in vergleichbaren EU-Ländern. Jüngere Einkommensdaten[49] zeigen, dass die durchschnittlichen wöchentlichen Einkommen im öffentlichen Dienst weiterhin fast anderthalb mal so hoch sind wie die Einkommen im privaten Sektor. Trotz fehlender direkter Vergleichbarkeit verstärkt dieser Vergleich doch tendenziell die Botschaft, dass die in den erwähnten Studien zu dieser Frage benannten Probleme immer noch relevant sind. Auch steigen die Einkommen im öffentlichen Sektor schneller als die im privaten Sektor.

Fragen der Wirksamkeit

Die gleiche Aufgabe mit weniger Ressourcen zu erfüllen als bisher ist zweifellos eine Leistung im Hinblick auf Effizienz. Es ist jedoch nicht unbedingt eine Leistung im Hinblick auf Wirksamkeit. Wirksamkeit bedingt eine grundlegendere Frage: nicht, ob wir das Gleiche effizienter tun, sondern vielmehr, ob wir die gleiche Aufgabe überhaupt ausführen sollten.

Im Verlauf der irischen Geschichte hat der öffentliche Dienst dem Land gute Dienste geleistet, in vielen Bereichen gehören die Beschäftigten des öffentlichen Dienstes in Irland zu den besten in Europa. Dennoch hat der schnelle Anstieg der Gehälter und Pensionen zwischen 2003 und 2008 in der Öffentlichkeit Bedenken hervorgerufen. Dabei ging es um die Frage: Wie fair sind der Umfang öffentlicher Ausgaben und die damit einhergehende Belastung, und zwar besonders für jene in weniger abgesicherten Beschäftigungsformen?

In einigen Fällen haben diese Bedenken zu Groll und gesellschaftlicher Spaltung geführt. Ein konstruktiver Ansatz für diese Frage könnte sein, länderübergreifende Vergleiche der öffentlichen Gehälter vorzunehmen, unter Berücksichtigung der relativen Wirtschaftsleistung und der Lebenshaltungskosten. Statt einer Debatte, welche die Gegensätze verschärft, könnte ein konstruktiver internationaler Vergleich der Gehälter und Leistungen im öffentlichen Dienst bei der Klärung dieser Frage helfen und dafür sorgen, dass die öffentlichen Gehälter gerecht angesetzt sind und sich an transparenten und akzeptablen Richtwerten orientieren.

Ein derartiger Vergleich der Wirksamkeit und Produktivität des öffentlichen Dienstes würde nicht nur bei der Beurteilung der zukünftigen Gehaltspolitik helfen, sondern wäre auch für die Beurteilung der Finanzpolitik insgesamt hilfreich.

---

[49]   Zentrales Statistikamt (Central Statistics Office), „Earnings and Labour Costs Quarterly, Q3 2013".

Zum Beispiel wird häufig argumentiert – besonders von Vertretern der Beschäftigten im öffentlichen Dienst –, dass Irland sich an den hohen öffentlichen Ausgaben und Steuern in Skandinavien orientieren sollte, da diese Länder auch eine hohe Produktivität und hohe Lebensstandards hätten. Es ist jedoch keineswegs eine logische Schlussfolgerung, dass hohe öffentliche Ausgaben und Steuersätze automatisch zu hoher Produktivität und hohen Lebensstandards führen. In Wirklichkeit fanden die stärksten Anstiege der öffentlichen Ausgaben in Irland zu einer Zeit statt, als die Produktivität stark sank. Und tatsächlich weisen die Forschungen des Institute of Public Administration[50] auf einen interessanten Unterschied zwischen Irland und Skandinavien hin. In Skandinavien liegt der Unterschied zwischen den höchsten und den niedrigsten Gehältern in der öffentlichen Verwaltung bei einem Verhältnis von 3,8. In Irland beträgt dieses Verhältnis 7,7. Dies zeigt, dass es im öffentlichen Sektor in Irland deutlich mehr Ungleichheit in der Verteilung der Gehälter gibt. Studien sollten sich damit beschäftigen, ob diese größeren Unterschiede durch höhere Produktivität und Leistung an der Spitze des öffentlichen Dienstes in Irland gerechtfertigt sind. Dies wiederum könnte Licht auf die Frage werfen, ob es in der Tat angebracht ist, sich an skandinavischen Volkswirtschaften zu orientieren und den Umfang staatlicher Eingriffe in die Wirtschaft zu erhöhen, oder ob eine derartige Initiative lediglich zu höheren Kosten ohne jede Verbesserung der Wirtschaftsleistung führen würde.

Angesichts der in diesem Kapitel angeführten Veröffentlichungen, insbesondere der Autoren Vitor Tanzi und Ludger Schuknecht (zur optimalen Größe des Staates) sowie Don Thornhill und Donal De Butleir (zu einem korrekt angepassten und richtigen Maß für die Steuerlast in Irland als Anteil an der Wirtschaft), müssen außerdem zwei sehr unterschiedliche Schlussfolgerungen betrachtet werden: erstens, dass mit einem Anteil von 53,5 Prozent am BNE die Höhe der öffentlichen Ausgaben in Irland möglicherweise weit über dem liegen, was zur Erhaltung adäquater öffentlicher Dienstleistungen und Sozialleistungen auf optimaler Höhe oder zur Optimierung des Wachstums erforderlich ist. Zweitens, dass mit fast zwei Fünfteln der Wirtschaftsleistung – und mehr, wenn man diese Zahl um strukturelle und demografische Faktoren bereinigt – der Anteil der Steuereinnahmen aus der irischen Wirtschaftsleistung bereits ausreicht, um adäquate öffentliche Leistungen und Sozialleistungen zu finanzieren. In diesem Fall würde die Argumentation gestützt, dass sich Irland stark, wenn nicht gar ausschließlich auf die Ausgabenkonsolidierung statt auf Steuerverringerung konzentrieren sollte.

---

[50] Boyle, Richard (2011). „Public Sector Trends", Institute of Public Administration.

Eine technische Anmerkung zu BIP und BNE

Irlands Erfolg bei der Einwerbung direkter ausländischer Investitionen[51] hat einen statistischen Nebeneffekt, den berücksichtigen muss, wer BIP oder BNE als Bezugsgrößen für Finanzkennzahlen nutzt. Das Bruttoinlandsprodukt (BIP) umfasst die Leistung aller wirtschaftlichen Akteure, die in Irland angesiedelt sind, aber nicht unbedingt ihren Hauptsitz dort haben. Im Gegensatz dazu umfasst das Bruttonationaleinkommen die Leistung aller wirtschaftlichen Akteure, die ihren Hauptsitz in Irland haben, aber nicht unbedingt dort eine Niederlassung besitzen. Die starke Präsenz multinationaler Unternehmen bedeutet, dass das BIP dauerhaft um etwa ein Fünftel höher ist als das BNE. Der Anteil der irischen Wirtschaftsleistung, der dem BIP, aber nicht dem BNE zugeschrieben werden kann, ist sehr wichtig für die Wirtschaft, da er viele Arbeitsplätze und Lieferverbindungen unterstützt. Das günstige irische Steuersystem bedeutet jedoch, dass das BIP als Indikator für die Fähigkeit der Wirtschaft, Steuereinnahmen für notwendige Ausgaben zu generieren, weniger gut geeignet ist. Daher werden in diesem Kapitel zentrale finanztechnische Messwerte sowohl als Anteil am BIP (entsprechend internationaler Praxis) als auch am BNE dargestellt (was angesichts der Beschaffenheit der irischen Wirtschaft eine notwendige „Gegenprobe" ist). Das BNE ist auch insofern ein besseres Maß für die Gesundheit der einheimischen Wirtschaft, als dass Irland gelegentlich Zeiten mit einem gesunden, vom Export getragenen Wachstum des BIP erlebt hat, während das Wachstum des BNE schwach blieb. Während das BNE in Irland immer geringer sein wird als das BIP (zumindest in absehbarer Zukunft), ist eine gesunde Erholung durch ein starkes, reales Wachstum beider Größen gekennzeichnet.

Illustration 4.6: BIP und BNE in Irland, 2004-2012

Mio. Euro	2004	2005	2006	2007	2008	2009	2010	2011	2012	Durch-schnitt
BIP	150.024	162.897	177.573	189.655	180.249	162.284	158.097	162.600	163.938	
BNE	127.146	138.636	154.309	163.134	154.933	133.919	131.812	130.662	132.649	
Ratio	1,18	1,17	1,15	1,16	1,16	1,21	1,20	1,24	1,24	**1,19**

Quelle: Zentrales Statistikamt (Central Statistics Office).

---

[51] Siehe **Kapitel 1** und **2**.

KOMMENTAR: KAPITEL 4
Die Reformdividende

Brian Hayes

Hauptaussagen

- Der öffentliche Dienst in Irland steht vor der beispiellosen Herausforderung, Leistungen schneller, besser und kostengünstiger als bisher bereitzustellen. Zu diesem Zweck wurden Reformpläne in zwei Schritten veröffentlicht, der erste im November 2011 und der zweite im Januar 2014.
- Während der erste Plan bedingt war durch die Notwendigkeit, die öffentlichen Ausgaben im Zusammenspiel mit der finanziellen Konsolidierung zu reduzieren und dabei der Schwerpunkt klar auf Kosten und Effizienz lag, wird der zweite den Umfang der Reformen ausweiten und die Leistung und Effektivität des öffentlichen Dienstes verbessern.

Einleitung

Seit der Amtsübernahme 2011 sind und waren weitreichende Reformen des öffentlichen Dienstes ein wichtiger Teil der Regierungsstrategie, um die Herausforderungen zu meistern, denen wir in den vergangenen Jahren gegenübergestanden haben. Es war klar, dass der öffentliche Dienst radikal ändern musste, was er tut und wie er es tut.

Der öffentliche Dienst, den wir für unsere Bürger schaffen und bereitstellen, definiert deutlich das Bild, das wir als Land sowohl zu Hause als auch im Ausland abgeben. Nie zuvor war es dringender nötig, öffentliche Dienstleistungen wirksamer und effizienter zu erbringen als jetzt. Wir mussten und müssen die Ausgaben verringern, zu einer Zeit, in der angesichts des Zusammentreffens einer schwachen Wirtschaft mit einer starken Demografie der Bedarf an Leistungen größer ist als je zuvor. Nur durch nachhaltige radikale Reformen können wir weiterhin Leistungen bereitstellen, welche die schwachen Mitglieder unserer Gesellschaft schützen, die Schaffung von Arbeitsplätzen ankurbeln und unsere Wirtschaft erneuern.

Eine Vision für die Reform des öffentlichen Dienstes

Der öffentliche Dienst steht vor der beispiellosen Herausforderung, Leistungen schneller, besser und kostengünstiger bereitzustellen. Alle Elemente des

öffentlichen Dienstes müssen zusammenarbeiten, um kosteneffektive und hochwertige öffentliche Leistungen zu liefern. Unser Engagement für Reformen muss auf den Grundwerten Integrität, Gerechtigkeit, Verantwortlichkeit und Offenheit beruhen.

Wir müssen einen öffentlichen Dienst aufbauen, der die Flexibilität, Kapazität und Fähigkeit besitzt, um auf gegenwärtige und zukünftige Herausforderungen in einer sich ständig verändernden globalen und nationalen volks- und privatwirtschaftlichen Umgebung zu reagieren. Unsere Vision ist ein öffentlicher Dienst, der der bei der Erbringung bürgernaher Leistungen innovativ ist und ein gutes Preis-Leistungs-Verhältnis für den Steuerzahler bietet. Dazu müssen die Effizienz maximiert und Vergeudung beseitigt werden.

Die Reformbausteine

Der Erfolg des Reformprogramms der derzeitigen Regierung für den öffentlichen Dienst stützt sich auf einen starken Fokus auf Leistungserbringung und auf die Befähigung der Beschäftigten des öffentlichen Dienstes, vor Ort echte Reformen durchzusetzen. 2011 eingerichtet, stellte das Ministerium für öffentliche Ausgaben und Reform (Department of Public Expenditure and Reform) sowohl die Plattform als auch die Möglichkeit bereit, die vielen Elemente des Reformprogramms durch Integration unserer Ansätze zu Reformen und Ausgaben voranzutreiben. Die Rolle des Ministeriums besteht darin, die Reformen zu ermöglichen, zu unterstützen und voranzutreiben. Während die zentrale Administration die einzelnen Sektoren befähigt, die notwendigen Veränderungen durchzuführen, und sie dabei unterstützt, leitet das Department of Public Expenditure and Reform wichtige ressortübergreifende Initiativen und Unterstützungsangebote.

Die Selbstverpflichtung der Regierung zur Reform des öffentlichen Dienstes wurde durch die Entscheidung verdeutlicht, eigens einen Kabinettsminister für die Durchsetzung der Reformagenda einzusetzen. Dies rückt die Reformen ins Zentrum der Regierungsarbeit und zementiert die Beziehung zwischen den Reform- und den Ausgabenfunktionen der öffentlichen Hand.

Es wurde ein eigenes Amt für Reformen und deren Durchsetzung (Reform and Delivery Office) eingerichtet, um die verschiedenen Reforminitiativen im gesamten öffentlichen Dienst zu koordinieren und ein strategisches und abgestimmtes Umsetzungsprogramm zu gewährleisten. Dieses Amt wird von einem Programmdirektor angeführt, der Erfahrungen aus dem privaten Sektor bei der Umsetzung größerer Veränderungen und Umstrukturierungen mitbringt. Außerdem hat jedes Ministerium und jedes größere Amt sog. Änderungsdurchsetzungsteams (Change Delivery Teams). Sie sind dafür bestimmt, den Reformprozess in ihren Organisationen und Sektoren sowie in den verschiedenen Stellen und Behörden zu leiten und voranzubringen.

Die Schaltstelle in dem Reformprozess ist der Kabinettsausschuss für die Reform des öffentlichen Dienstes (Cabinet Committee on Public Service Reform),

der die Reformen politisch führt und verantwortet. Der Ausschuss, dem ich angehöre, steht unter der Leitung des irischen Premierministers (Taoiseach). Er kommt regelmäßig zusammen, um wichtige Fragen zu erörtern und zu gewährleisten, dass insgesamt Fortschritte erzielt werden. Außerdem bietet eine auf Staatssekretärebene (Secretary General) angesiedelte Beratungsgruppe Unterstützung und Rat für das Kabinettsgremium zu strategischen Fragen.

Regelmäßig trifft sich ein Reformdurchsetzungsstab (Reform Delivery Board), um die Durchsetzung der Reform des öffentlichen Dienstes auf Organisations- und Sektorebene zu beaufsichtigen und zu überwachen; dieses Gremium besteht aus Unterstaatssekretären (Assistant Secretaries), die für die Leitung der Reformen in jedem Ministerium und größeren Amt verantwortlich sind. Es ist dem Reform and Delivery Office und dem Kabinettsausschuss gegenüber dafür verantwortlich, dass die Reform des öffentlichen Dienstes erfolgreich durchgesetzt wird.

Schaffung der Grundlagen – der Plan zur Reform des öffentlichen Dienstes (Public Service Reform Plan)

Im November 2011 brachte die irische Regierung einen umfassenden Plan zur Reform des öffentlichen Dienstes (Public Service Reform Plan) auf den Weg. Er umriss die wichtigsten Maßnahmen zu den geplanten Veränderungen im gesamten öffentlichen Dienst. Der Reformplan beschrieb fünf zentrale Reformthemen:

- Den Kundenservice zum Mittelpunkt all dessen machen, was wir tun;
- Neue und innovative Kanäle für die Erbringung von Dienstleistungen maximieren;
- Unsere Kosten radikal reduzieren, um ein besseres Preis-Leistungs-Verhältnis zu erzielen;
- Auf neue Art und Weise führen, organisieren und arbeiten
- Starke Orientierung auf Umsetzung und Ergebnisse.

Der Reformplan enthielt rund 70 Empfehlungen und mehr als 200 Maßnahmen, unter die folgenden 14 Hauptpunkte gruppiert: Umsetzung, eGovernment, Informations- und Kommunikationstechnologie, Informationsaustausch und Kundenservice, ressortübergreifende Dienste, Verbesserung der Geschäftsprozesse, Reform der öffentlichen Auftragsvergabe, Management der Vermögenswerte, externe Bereitstellung von Dienstleistungen, Rationalisierung und Neuorganisation, Reform der öffentlichen Ausgaben, Leistungsmanagement auf Regierungsebene; Organisatorische Effizienz, Führungskompetenz und individuelle Leistung, Beschäftigungszahlen im öffentlichen Dienst, Personalplanung und Versetzung sowie legislative und politische Reformen.

Abgestimmte Maßnahmen

Zur Untermauerung dieses integrierten Ansatzes wurden von jedem Ministerium und größeren Amt auf Leitungsebene Reformdurchsetzungspläne (Reform Delivery Plans) erstellt. Dies ermöglicht ein klares Verständnis der vorrangigen Reforminitiativen, die sowohl ressortübergreifend als auch auf Ebene der Organisationen im gesamten öffentlichen Dienst ablaufen. Diese Pläne der Ministerien sind am zentralen Public Service Reform Plan ausgerichtet und erfassen gegebenenfalls auch die Reformen für den dazugehörigen Sektor.

Voranschreiten an mehreren Fronten

Irland hat offenkundig eine Regierung, die sich für Reformen engagiert. In der Folge der Wirtschafts- und Finanzkrisen wurde eine ganze Reihe von Maßnahmen umgesetzt, mit denen fast 30 Mrd. Euro eingespart werden sollen. Mehr als zwei Drittel dieser Anpassungen wurden auf der Ausgabenseite vorgenommen. Die parlamentarisch beschlossenen Ausgaben wurden von ihrem Höchstwert von 63,1 Mrd. Euro im Jahr 2009 auf 54,6 Mrd. Euro im Jahr 2013 verringert. Dies stellt eine Kürzung von etwa 13,5 Prozent dar.

Die Zahl der Beschäftigten im öffentlichen Dienst wurde von einem Höchstwert von 320.000 im Jahr 2008 um über 30.000 auf derzeit weniger als 290.000 reduziert. Dieses Ziel zu erreichen, erfordert weiterhin die Mitwirkung vieler, doch bin ich überzeugt, dass die Bereitschaft da ist, in dieser Hinsicht voranzuschreiten.

Den Beschäftigten des öffentlichen Dienstes wurden nun bereits zweimal die Gehälter gekürzt, um insgesamt durchschnittlich 14 Prozent. Außerdem haben diejenigen mit einem Gehalt über 65.000 Euro seit Juli 2013 eine weitere Kürzung erlebt. Die Gehälter des öffentlichen Dienstes wurden von ihrem Höchstwert von 17,5 Mrd. Euro im Jahr 2009 auf 14,1 Mrd. Euro in diesem Jahr gekürzt, den pensionsbezogenen Abzug (Pension Related Deduction) mitgerechnet. Dies ist eine Kürzung um fast 17,7 Prozent. Außerdem ist die Zahl der Beschäftigten im öffentlichen Dienst um fast 10 Prozent gefallen.

Der Reformplan hat die Führung der Beschäftigten durch Einführung einer größeren Beschäftigtenflexibilität und neuer Arbeitsregelungen verändert; gleichzeitig wurden die höheren Führungsebenen und die Führungskompetenzen gestärkt.

Der Service am Kunden bleibt trotz sinkender Personalzahlen geschützt. Neue Regelungen ermöglichen die Versetzung von Personal in die Bereiche mit dem größten Bedarf. Derzeit setzen wir einen Rahmenplan für alle Sektoren um, mit dem eine strategische Personalplanung aufgebaut werden soll. Sie soll gewährleisten, dass wir die richtigen Leute zur richtigen Zeit am richtigen Ort haben. Das „Public Service Stability Agreement-2013-2016", das als „Haddington Road Agreement" bekannt ist, regelt die Grundlage für den Beitrag von 1 Milliarde Euro aus den Gehältern und Pensionen des öffentlichen Dienstes zu unserer finanziellen Sanierung. Dazu gehören eine Reihe vernünftiger und nachhaltiger

Maßnahmen, die die Schaffung eines schlankeren und kompakteren öffentlichen Dienstes ermöglichen.

Außerdem wurden neue Arbeitsregelungen eingeführt, darunter längere Arbeitszeiten, neue Dienstpläne, standardisierte Regelungen für den Jahresurlaub und ein verbesserter Rahmen für Leistungsmanagement. Die neue integrierte Pensionskasse, die am 1. Januar 2013 startete, wird für deutliche, langfristige Einsparungen bei der Pensionsverwaltung für den öffentlichen Dienst sorgen. Dies sind nur einige Beispiele dafür, wie wir unseren öffentlichen Dienst reformieren.

Deutliche Fortschritte wurden bei den ressortübergreifenden Diensten erzielt. Beispielsweise ist *PeoplePoint*, das ressortübergreifende Servicezentrum für Personal und Pensionen des öffentlichen Dienstes (Civil Service HR & Pensions Shared Service Centre), in Dienst genommen worden. Sobald es voll einsatzfähig ist, soll es Einsparungen von geschätzten 12,5 Mio Euro pro Jahr bringen. Die Regierung hat auch die Einrichtung eines einzigen, ressortübergreifenden Servicezentrums für die Gehaltsabrechnung im öffentlichen Dienst (Civil Service Payroll Shared Service Centre) gebilligt. Diese Initiative wird schätzungsweise Einsparungen von 5,6 Mio Euro pro Jahr erzielen, sobald sie voll funktionsfähig ist.

Wir haben darüber hinaus die Einrichtung eines Amtes für nationale, ressortübergreifende Dienste (National Shared Services Office) genehmigt. Es soll die ressortübergreifenden Dienste des öffentlichen Dienstes für Beamte und Tarifangestellte führen und eine integrierte Vorgehensweise fürs ganze Land vorgeben.

Derzeit wird nach Möglichkeiten für neue Wege bei der Leistungserbringung gesucht. Das Ziel lautet: Kosten verringern, die Effizienz verbessern und eine größere Konzentration auf entscheidende Mehrwertaktivitäten ermöglichen. Vom Amt für Reformen und deren Durchsetzung wurde ein Programm zur Kompetenzentwicklung aufgelegt, um die Kompetenzen und Fähigkeiten von Führungskräften des öffentlichen Dienstes zu verbessern.

Die eGovernment-Strategie 2012-2015 der Regierung gewährleistet den besseren und innovativeren Einsatz von Technik, damit die Bürger sich den öffentlichen Dienst besser zu Nutze machen können. Mehr als 400 öffentliche Dienstleistungen sind über unser zentrales Portal www.gov.ie zugänglich. Im Lauf der Jahre sollen laut eGovernment-Strategie weitere hinzukommen.

Das Management der öffentlichen Ausgaben wird durch die Einführung einer leistungsorientierten Haushaltsführung, mittelfristiger Ausgabenrahmen sowie eines neuen Kodex für öffentliche Ausgaben reformiert. Die leistungsorientierte Haushaltsführung hat zu einer radikalen Umgestaltung der Dokumentation von Kalkulationen geführt, sodass diese nun auch Ergebnisinformationen zusammen mit den bereitgestellten Ressourcen enthält. Darüber hinaus veröffentlichen nun alle Ministerien und staatlichen Ämter quartalsweise alle Einkäufe über 20.000 Euro. Auch mit der Veröffentlichung von Bilanzen wurde begonnen.

2013 fand ein großer Umbruch in der öffentlichen Auftragsvergabe für Waren und Leistungen statt, die etwa 9 Mrd. Euro der Staatsausgaben ausmacht. Ein

nationales Amt für die öffentliche Auftragsvergabe (National Procurement Office) wurde eingerichtet, das von einem Hauptverantwortlichen für die Auftragsvergabe (Chief Procurement Officer) durch den öffentlichen Dienst geleitet wird. Dieses neue Amt integriert Richtlinien, Strategien und Abläufe der Auftragsvergabe. Es wird die Analyse der Ausgaben und die Datenpflege stärken und – mit einer viel stärkeren Konzentration von Auftragsvorgängen aus allen öffentlichen Stellen – ein viel besseres Preis-Leistungs-Verhältnis erzielen. Angestrebt sind Einsparungen von 500 Mio Euro über drei Jahre.

Arbeitsfrieden zum Wohle aller

Wenn wir betrachten, wie weit wir bei der Reform des öffentlichen Dienstes gekommen sind, müssen wir die Rolle des „Public Service Stability Agreement 2013-2016" hervorheben. Dazu gehören die Gehaltskürzungen, die das Gesetz über finanzielle Notfallmaßnahmen im öffentlichen Interesse von 2013 („Financial Emergency Measures in the Public Interest Act, 2013") vorgibt.

Das Erreichen eines Haushaltdefizits von unter 3 Prozent des BIP bis 2015 bleibt ein anspruchsvolles Hauptziel unserer Wirtschaftspolitik. Gehälter und Pensionen bilden 36 Prozent der parlamentarisch beschlossenen Ausgaben. Deshalb müssen bis 2015 die Gehälter und Pensionen im öffentlichen Dienst einen anteiligen Beitrag von 1 Milliarde Euro zu den Einsparungen leisten.

Zu diesem Betrag von 1 Milliarde Euro steuern die Gehaltskürzungen bei den höheren Gehaltsklassen – Gehälter über 65.000 Euro – etwa 210 Mio Euro bei. Andere zentrale Maßnahmen, darunter Pensionskürzungen, erbringen etwas über 130 Mio Euro.

Zusätzlich zu den offensichtlichen Kostenvorteilen verschafft uns diese Vereinbarung den Raum, zur nächsten Phase der ehrgeizigen Reformagenda der Regierung überzugehen und bisher ungekannte Produktivitätszuwächse im gesamten öffentlichen Dienst zu erzielen. Die Vereinbarung sieht zum Beispiel fast 15 Mio zusätzliche Arbeitsstunden im öffentlichen Dienst vor, die für erheblich höhere Effizienz sorgen werden.

Neben diesen grundsätzlichen Veränderungen gab es zahlreiche spezifische Maßnahmen, die auf Sektorebene vereinbart wurden. Diese Maßnahmen werden dazu beitragen, den größten Gewinn für jeden Sektor im Hinblick auf sowohl Kosteneinsparungen als auch Effizienzzuwachs zu erzielen.

Den Schwung beibehalten

Zwei Jahre nach Veröffentlichung des Public Service Reform Plan durch die Regierung wurde eine neue Reformphase ausgestaltet. Sie baut auf den Fortschritten bei der Umsetzung des ersten Reformplans auf und schreibt eine neue ehrgeizige Phase im Reformprogramm fest.

Dieser neue, im Januar 2014 veröffentlichte Plan umreißt die wichtigsten ressortübergreifenden und sektorspezifischen Reforminitiativen, die innerhalb der nächsten drei Jahre umgesetzt werden. Er blickt auch weiter nach vorn auf die Reformzielsetzungen bis zum Jahr 2020.

Bessere Leistungen erbringen

Die bisherige Reformphase konzentrierte sich notwendigerweise stark auf die Verringerung der Kosten für die Erbringung öffentlicher Dienstleistungen. Die nächste Reformphase wird diese Arbeit fortführen, jedoch mit stärkerem Schwerpunkt auf der Erzielung besserer Ergebnisse für die Nutzer der Dienste. Dazu gehören alternative Vorgehensweisen der Dienstleistungserbringung , etwa die Auftragsvergabe anhand klar vorgegebener Ergebnisse; umfangreichere Dienstleistungen über das Internet; und eine Reihe organisatorischer Veränderungen zur Bereitstellung von Dienstleistungen.

Die Reformdividende sichern

In den vergangenen Jahren hat es große Effizienz- und Produktivitätszuwächse im öffentlichen Dienst gegeben, und auf diesen werden wir aufbauen und noch mehr liefern. Gemäß dem neuen Plan dreht sich die neue Reformagenda um den Schutz und die Verbesserung öffentlicher Leistungen, und somit wird über die Laufzeit dieses Plans ein Schwerpunkt auf „Einsparungen zwecks Investition" liegen. Der Staat beabsichtigt, Ressourcen freizusetzen, indem die existierenden Prozesse kostengünstiger und effizienter gestaltet werden, und die Einsparungen in neue oder verbesserte Leistungen zu investieren.

Mehr und mehr offene Daten

Die Technik lässt die Welt schrumpfen und erhöht die Erwartungen der Menschen. Anfang 2014 wird eine neue Regierungsstrategie zur Informations- und Kommunikationstechnik (ICT Strategy) veröffentlicht. Sie befasst sich mit der Anwendung neuer und gerade erst aufkommender Technologien. Damit soll gewährleistet werden, dass das eGovernment auf echte Bedürfnisse ausgerichtet ist. Ausserdem soll sich die Akzeptanz des eGovernment verbessern.

Offenheit gleich Verantwortlichkeit

Die Bürger müssen eindeutig nachvollziehen können, dass der öffentliche Dienst in seiner Entscheidungsfindung, bei der Umsetzung von Richtlinien und bei der Bereitstellung von öffentlichen Dienstleistungen fair arbeitet. Das politische Reformprogramm der Regierung wird sich auf die Schaffung größerer Offenheit, Transparenz und Verantwortlichkeit konzentrieren, um das Vertrauen in die Regierung, die Verwaltung und ihre öffentlichen Dienste zu stärken.

Der neue Reformplan für den öffentlichen Dienst befasst sich auch mit vielen anderen Fragen. Dazu gehören beispielsweise die Umsetzung von Modellen für ressortübergreifende Dienste, die Beurteilung neuer Geschäftsmodelle für die

Bereitstellung von Leistungen, die nicht zu den Kernleistungen gehören, die Reform der öffentlichen Auftragsvergabe, die Vermögensrationalisierung, die Stärkung der Führung sowie Reformen im Personalmanagement.

Schlussfolgerung

Irlands Reformprogramm ist dynamisch und reaktiv. Das muss es auch weiterhin sein. Irlands Schwierigkeiten waren weltweit Gegenstand von Berichten und Betrachtungen. Ich glaube, dass wir in unseren bisherigen Lösungen radikal sind. Die Welt hat die Vorteile gesehen, die eine reformfreudige Regierung hervorbringen kann.

Wir haben uns aus einer düsteren wirtschaftlichen und finanziellen Lage herausgearbeitet und sind entschlossen, die Bedingungen für nachhaltiges Wachstum zu schaffen. Zu diesem Zweck muss Irland anpassungsfähig sein, um die vor uns liegenden neuen Herausforderungen und Möglichkeiten zu meistern. An diesem Punkt überlasse ich das Wort Lewis Carroll, in dessen Meisterwerk die Königin zu Alice sagt: *„... Du musst so schnell laufen, wie Du kannst, um nur an Ort und Stelle zu bleiben. Wenn Du weiterkommen willst, must Du mindestens doppelt so schnell laufen!"*.

KAPITEL 5

Banken und Finanzen: Zurück zur Stabilität[52]

Dr. Stefan Gerlach

Hauptaussagen

- Der irische Bankensektor sieht heute deutlich anders aus als vor der Krise. Nachdem er während der Krise enorme Verluste verzeichnete, wurde der Sektor rekapitalisiert und verkleinert. Er hat eine erhebliche Konsolidierung erfahren und in mehreren Fällen auch die Verstaatlichung.
- Die Schwierigkeiten, vor denen der irische Bankensektor während der Finanzkrise stand, offenbarten die Notwendigkeit von Reformen und Verbesserungen in verschiedenen Bereichen der Geschäftstätigkeit und bei der Finanzaufsicht. Sowohl die internationale als auch die einheimische Politik spielten eine wichtige Rolle bei der Gestaltung dieser Veränderungen. Die wichtigste Maßnahme war das Unterstützungsprogramm von IWF und EU, welches die Umsetzung einer großen Anzahl struktureller, steuerrechtlicher und finanzieller Reformen vorschrieb.
- Obwohl große Fortschritte erzielt wurden, bleiben immer noch einige Probleme bei der Wiederherstellung der vollen Lebensfähigkeit staatlich gestützter Banken und ihrer Rückkehr in private Hand bestehen.

Einleitung

Sechs Jahre nach Ausbruch der globalen Finanzkrise sieht der irische Bankensektor deutlich anders aus als in den Jahren vor der Krise. Während des Booms war der Sektor durch schnelles Wachstum, hohe Gewinne, vernachlässigbare Kreditausfälle und zunehmenden Wettbewerb gekennzeichnet. Nach enormen Verlusten während der Krise wurde der Sektor rekapitalisiert, verkleinert und hat eine erhebliche Konsolidierung erfahren. Mehrere Banken mussten verstaatlicht werden. Der Sektor leidet noch immer unter hohen Zahlungsrückständen und einer großen Anzahl fauler Kredite. Zwischenzeitlich hat sich auch die Finanzaufsicht

---

[52] Mein herzlicher Dank geht an Lars Frisell und insbesondere Yvonne McCarthy für ihre Arbeit an dem Kapitel.

drastisch verändert, mit einer neu entwickelten Aufsicht und Regulierung auf einheimischer wie auch auf europäischer Ebene. Dies hat tiefgreifende Auswirkungen auf das Umfeld, in dem die Banken operieren.

Der irische Bankensektor umfasst drei Hauptgruppen – Privatkundenbanken in irischer Hand, nicht-irische Privatkundenbanken und Banken im Zentrum für internationale Finanzdienstleistungen (International Financial Services Centre, IFSC). Während die Privatkundenbanken hauptsächlich Finanzdienstleistungen für einheimische Privathaushalte und Unternehmen bereitstellen, machen die Institute des IFSC ihr Geschäft hauptsächlich mit Geschäftspartnern außerhalb von Irland.[53] Dieses Kapitel untersucht einige der entscheidenden Veränderungen, die seit Beginn der Finanzkrise im irischen Bankensektor stattgefunden haben, und gibt eine Einschätzung des derzeitigen Ausblicks für den Sektor. In der Diskussion spezifischer Entwicklungen im Bankensektor liegt das Hauptaugenmerk größtenteils auf den irischen Privatkundenbanken, die am stärksten von der Krise betroffen waren. Das übrige Kapitel ist wie folgt gegliedert: Der nächste Abschnitt gibt eine kurze Zusammenfassung des Hintergrundes der Bankenkrise und der ersten politischen Reaktionen. Der darauf folgende Abschnitt stellt detailliert wichtige Änderungen in der Bankenaufsichts- und -regulierungslandschaft seit Ausbruch der Krise dar. Der letzte Abschnitt schließt mit einer Einschätzung des Bankensektors in Irland und einer Illustration über die wichtigsten Herausforderungen ab, vor denen die Branche mit großer Wahrscheinlichkeit in den kommenden Jahren stehen wird.

Hintergrund der Krise

In den Jahren vor der Krise gab es im irischen Bankensektor mehrere unhaltbare Trends zu beobachten, die ihn besonders anfällig machten, als die Finanzkrise und der wirtschaftliche Abschwung kamen.[54] Vor dem Hintergrund aufkommender Ungleichgewichte in der einheimischen Wirtschaft erlebten die Banken ein drastisches Bilanzwachstum, das überwiegend durch Immobilienkredite zustande kam. Zwischen 2000 und 2008 wuchs die Kreditvergabe an Privatkunden um über 400 Prozent, wobei immobilienbezogene Darlehen (Geschäfts- und Privatkunden) 80 Prozent dieses Wachstums ausmachten.[55] In gewissem Umfang beruhte dies auf einem Volumenwachstum, das wiederum von einem sehr deutlichen Bevölkerungszuwachs herrührte. Gleichzeitig stiegen jedoch auch die

---

[53] Zu einer ausführlichen Darstellung der Entwicklungen in diesen drei Gruppen für den Zeitraum 2003 bis 2012 siehe Box 1 im „Quarterly Bulletin 3, 2013", der irischen Zentralbank.

[54] Zu einer vollständigen Erklärung dieser Fragen siehe **Kapitel 2** des Berichts der Untersuchungskommission zum Bankensektor in Irland (2011).

[55] Diese Zahlen basieren auf internen Daten der irischen Zentralbank, die so bereinigt wurden, dass sie nicht-kreditbezogene Transaktionen wie Neubewertungen, Forderungsabsicherungen und Übernahmen durch die NAMA widerspiegeln.

Immobilienpreise sehr deutlich; die Preise für neue Häuser stiegen beispielsweise zwischen 2000 und 2007, als die Hauspreise einen Höchststand erreichten, um 88 Prozent. Die **Illustration 5.1** zeigt die sektorale Zusammensetzung der Kreditvergabe durch Banken über den Zeitraum von 2002 bis 2008.

Um das Wachstum in ihren Bilanzen zu finanzieren, stützten sich die Banken zunehmend auf Finanzierungen am Kapitalmarkt, größtenteils in Form von Kreditaufnahmen im Ausland. Die **Illustration 5.2** zeigt die wachsende Finanzierungslücke, die Differenz zwischen Kreditvergabe im Inland und den Einlagen der Privatkundenbanken, die sich über diesen Zeitraum im irischen Finanzsystem auftat. Die Nachfrage der Banken nach Finanzierung, bei der es sich nicht um Einlagen handelt, wuchs im Zeitraum von 2004 bis 2007 besonders schnell. Dieser Anstieg an nicht über Einlagen laufenden Finanzierungen setzte die Banken einer hohen Gefährdung durch Fluktuationen der internationalen Zinssätze und Änderungen der Marktstimmung aus.

Illustration 5.1: Sektorale Zusammensetzung der Kreditvergabe durch Banken (ohne Finanzintermediation)

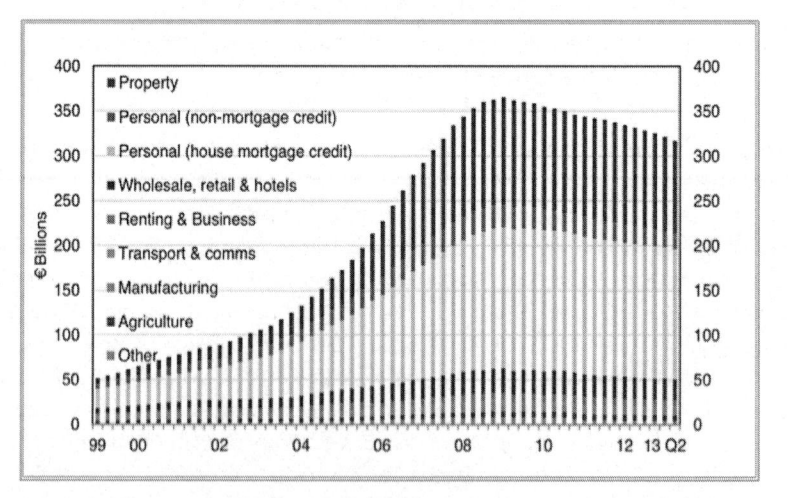

€ billions = Mrd. Euro; Property = Immobilien; Personal (non...) = Privat (nicht durch; Hypotheken abgesicherte Darlehen); Personal (house ...) = Privat (durch Hypotheken abgesicherte Hausdarlehen); Wholesale ... = Groß- und Einzelhandel, Hotellerie; Renting ...= = Vermietung und Geschäfte; Transport ... = Transport und Kommunikation; Manufacturing = Verarbeitendes Gewerbe; Agriculture = Landwirtschaft; Other = Andere.
Quelle: Irische Zentralbank (Central Bank of Ireland).
Hinweis: Daten sind so bereinigt, dass sie nicht-kreditbezogene Transaktionen wie Neubewertungen, Forderungsabsicherungen und Übernahmen durch die NAMA widerspiegeln.

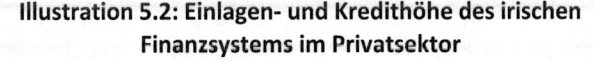

Illustration 5.2: Einlagen- und Kredithöhe des irischen Finanzsystems im Privatsektor

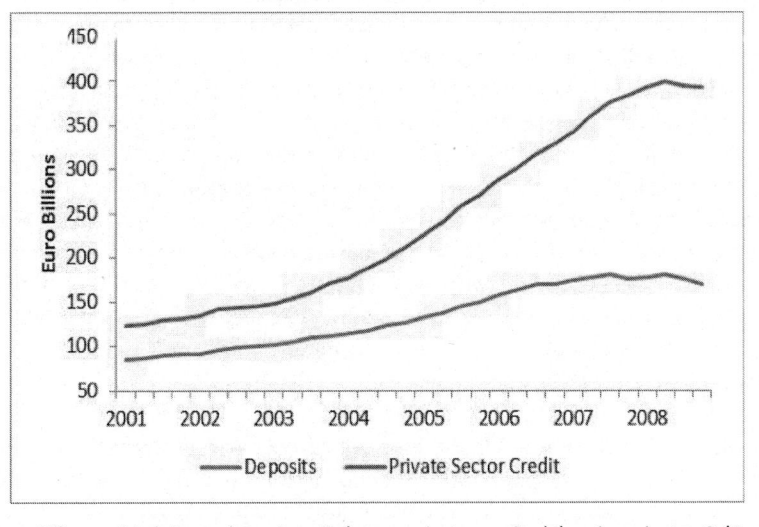

Euro Billions = Mrd. Euro; deposits = Einlagen; private ... = Darlehen im privaten Sektor.
Quelle: Irische Zentralbank (Central Bank of Ireland).

In den Jahren vor der Krise trat eine Reihe ausländischer Banken in den irischen Bankensektor ein.[56] Dies erhöhte den Wettbewerb und führte zu einer Lockerung der Risikostandards sowie zu neuen Hypothekenprodukten wie beispielsweise endfällige Darlehen, hypothekarisch gesicherte Verbraucherkredite (Equity Release) und Hypotheken mit beweglichen Sätzen. Die ersten beiden Produkte führten zu Beleihungsausläufen von bis zu 100 Prozent und mehr. Dies setzte Kreditnehmer wie auch Banken den Gefahren eines Abschwungs des Wohnimmobilienmarktes aus, während Hypotheken mit beweglichen Sätzen auf der Annahme beruhten, dass auch weiterhin ausreichend Finanzierung fast zu EZB-Sätzen verfügbar sein würde. Auch der Erwerb von Investitionen mit höherem Risiko oder von Immobilien zum Zweck der Vermietung durch Privatkunden stieg in diesem Zeitraum, während auch der ausländische Wettbewerb auf dem Sektor der Kreditvergabe für gewerbliche Immobilien zunahm.

Als sich das finanzielle und wirtschaftliche Klima Mitte 2007 zu verschlechtern begann, fielen die Mieten und Immobilienwerte in Irland rapide. Dies führte zu einem Anstieg der Beleihungsausläufe und zu einer Erosion des Eigenkapitalpolsters bei Immobiliendarlehen. Gekoppelt mit der erheblichen Belastung durch immobilienbezogene Kreditaufnahme und die potentiellen

---

[56]   Die Bank of Scotland trat 1999 in den irischen Markt ein. Die Ulster Bank, eine Tochter der Royal Bank of Scotland (RBS), übernahm 2004 First Active, wodurch sie einen großen Anteil am Hypothekenmarkt für Wohnimmobilien erhielt.

Darlehensausfälle in einem geschwächten wirtschaftlichen Umfeld verschlechterte sich das Vertrauen der Investoren in die Banken im irischen Markt rapide. 2007 stiegen die Finanzierungskosten für irische Banken deutlich über den EZB-Zinssatz. Nach der Pleite der Lehman Brothers im September 2008 verschloss sich für irische Banken schnell der Zugang zur Marktfinanzierung.

Reaktion der Politik

Honohan u. a. (2010)[57] und Honohan (2012)[58] bieten eine ausführliche Beschreibung der ersten Reaktion politischer Entscheidungsträger Irlands auf die Finanzkrise. Als Antwort auf den Druck im Bankensektor gab die irische Regierung im September 2008 eine umfassende Garantie für alle irischen Bankenschulden ab. Seit dieser Garantie war die Regierung darum bemüht, die Bankbilanzen von faulen Vermögenswerten zu befreien und die Finanzhäuser ausreichend zu rekapitalisieren. Um den Sektor zu stabilisieren, kam es zu folgenden Bemühungen: mehrere Kapitalaufstockungen der wichtigsten irischen Banken ab Ende 2008, die Verstaatlichung der Anglo Irish Bank im Januar 2009, die Ausgabe von Schuldverschreibungen (promissory notes) zur Stärkung der Kapitallage der Anglo Irish Bank seit Anfang 2010, die Einführung der Liquiditätsunterstützung in Sonderfällen (Exceptional Liquidity Assistance, ELA) 2009 und die Einrichtung einer Vermögensverwaltungsgesellschaft (NAMA) Ende 2009 zur Verwaltung von Immobiliendarlehen.[59]

Die NAMA wurde zu dem Zweck eingerichtet, die großen Immobiliendarlehen der irischen Banken zu einem „langfristigen wirtschaftlichen Wert" zu kaufen, so dass sich die erwarteten Verluste der Banken in Bezug auf diese Darlehen zeigen würden. Ferner führte die Central Bank eine Bewertung der zukünftigen Kapitalanforderungen irischer Banken durch (bekannt als „Prudential Capital Assessment Review (PCAR)"), deren Einzelheiten im März 2010 veröffentlicht wurden.[60] Das Ergebnis war ein Bedarf von weiteren 11 Mrd. Euro an frischem Kapital für die Allied Irish Bank (AIB), die Bank of Ireland (BOI) und die Educational Building Society sowie von etwa 20 Mrd. Euro für die Anglo Irish Bank und die Irish Nationwide Building Society (INBS). Ende August 2010 wurde klar, dass die bis dato

---

[57] Honohan, P., Donovan, D., Gorecki, P. & Mottiar, R. (2010). "The Irish Banking Crisis: Regulatory and Financial Stability Policy", Irische Zentralbank (Central Bank of Ireland).

[58] Honohan, P. (2012). "Recapitalisation of Failed Banks – Some Lessons from the Irish Experience", Rede auf der 44. Annual Money, Macro and Finance Conference, Trinity College, Dublin, 7 September.

[59] Der erste Kapitalisierungsplan wurde im Dezember 2008 bekanntgegeben, als je 2 Mrd. Euro in die AIB und die BOI (plus eine Zusicherung, für je eine weitere Milliarde Euro an neu auszugebendem Kapital zu garantieren) und 1,5 Mrd. Euro in die Anglo Irish Bank fließen sollten. Diese Ankündigung wurde von den Ereignissen überholt und im Januar 2009 wurde die Anglo Irish Bank verstaatlicht. Ferner wurden die anfänglichen Kapitalspritzen in die AIB und die BOI auf je 3,5 Mrd. erhöht.

[60] Weitere Einzelheiten dazu unter: http://www.centralbank.ie.

geschätzten Verluste bei NAMA-Übertragungen höher als erwartet sein würden. Weitere Kapitalspritzen waren erforderlich und es wurde entschieden, die Anglo Irish Bank abzuwickeln.[61]

Im November 2010 wurde ein Unterstützungsprogramm von EU/IWF für Irland im Gesamtwert von 85 Mrd. Euro bekanntgegeben (einschließlich eines Beitrags von 17,5 Mrd. Euro aus Irlands eigenen Ressourcen). Das Hauptziel des Programms war die Wiederherstellung des internationalen Vertrauens in die irische Wirtschaft und das irische Bankensystem. Dieses Programm stellte ein stabiles Fundament für einen reformierten und umstrukturierten Bankensektor dar. Es brachte eine Verpflichtung zu einer Anzahl von Reformen mit sich, die entscheidend bei der Gestaltung des irischen Bankensektors sein würden.[62] Diese Verpflichtungen richteten sich hauptsächlich auf die Verkleinerung und Neugestaltung des irischen Bankensystems zu einer nachhaltigen Struktur. Zum Beispiel verlangte das Programm den Abbau nicht zum Kern gehörender Vermögenswerte irischer Banken, eine Erhöhung der Ressourcen für die Bankenaufsicht, eine Reform des Privatinsolvenzsystems,   Maßnahmen   zum   Umgang   mit Hypothekenzahlungsrückständen sowie die Gewährleistung eines ausreichenden Angebots an Darlehen für lebensfähige Unternehmen.

Reform – Wie sich die Dinge verändert haben

Die Schwierigkeiten, vor denen der irische Bankensektor während der Finanzkrise stand, offenbarten die Notwendigkeit von Reformen und Verbesserungen in verschiedenen Bereichen der Geschäftstätigkeiten und bei der Finanzaufsicht. Sowohl die internationale als auch die einheimische Politik spielten eine wichtige Rolle bei der Gestaltung dieser Veränderungen. Die wichtigste Maßnahme war das Unterstützungsprogramm von IWF und EU, das eine große Anzahl struktureller, steuerrechtlicher und finanzieller Reformen vorschrieb. Dieser Abschnitt gibt einen Überblick über die wichtigsten Änderungen, die jetzt die Struktur des Banken- und Finanzwesens in Irland prägen.

---

[61]   Die neuen Kapitalanforderungen wurden am 30. September 2010 bekanntgegeben. Für die AIB wurde ein Bedarf von weiteren 3 Mrd. an frischem Kapital festgestellt, für die Anglo Irish Bank ein Bedarf von weiteren 12 Mrd. Euro und für die INBS ein Bedarf von fast 3 Mrd. an zusätzlichem Kapital.

[62]   Alle Einzelheiten dieser Verpflichtungen in Bezug auf den Finanzsektor sind im „Memorandum of Economic and Financial Policies" (http://www.finance.gov.ie/documents/ publications/reports/2010/EUIMFmemo.pdf) verfügbar, während die Details zu den Fortschritten bei deren Umsetzung in den IWF-Länderberichten und den IWF-Prüfberichten zur erweiterten Kreditfaszilität zu entnehmen sind. Der jüngste Prüfbericht ist verfügbar unter: http://www.imf.org/external/pubs/cat/longres.aspx?sk=40978.0.

Europäische Ebene

Die Krise hatte gezeigt: Risiken im Finanzsektor wurden in der EU falsch und ungleich eingeschätzt. Um dies zu ändern, stellte die Europäische Union einen neuen Finanzaufsichtsrahmen für Europa auf.[63] Die Richtlinie trat am 16. Dezember 2010 in Kraft. Das Herzstück dieses Rahmenwerks war die Schaffung des Europäischen Ausschusses für Systemrisiken (European Systemic Risk Board, ESRB). Diesem wurde die Aufgabe übertragen, einen Beitrag zur „Abwendung oder Eindämmung von Systemrisiken für die Finanzstabilität in der Union zu leisten, die aus Entwicklungen innerhalb des Finanzsystems erwachsen, wobei er den makroökonomischen Entwicklungen Rechnung trägt, damit Phasen weit verbreiteter finanzieller Notlagen vorgebeugt werden kann".[64] Zu diesem Zweck sollte der ESRB Warnungen und Empfehlungen herausgeben, die einem Mechanismus „handeln oder rechtfertigen" unterliegen sollten. Der Ausschuss besitzt auch beratende Funktion in diversen Bereichen. Zum Zeitpunkt seiner Einsetzung besaß der ESRB jedoch keinerlei rechtliche Handhabe zur Durchsetzung von Empfehlungen; diese Verantwortung verblieb bei den nationalen Behörden.

Kurz- bis mittelfristig wird die bedeutsamste Entwicklung auf europäischer Ebene erhebliche Auswirkungen auf das irische Bankenumfeld haben: Es handelt sich um den Einheitlichen Bankenaufsichtsmechanismus (Single Supervisory Mechanism, SSM). Ab 2014 übernimmt die EZB die Aufsicht über alle Kreditinstitute im Euroraum, mit einem dezentralen Ansatz für die weniger wichtigen Institute und einer Teilnahmeoption für EU-Mitgliedsstaaten außerhalb der Eurozone.

Schließlich wurde im Januar 2014 mit der Eigenkapitalverordnung und -richtlinie ein neuer Regulierungsrahmen für Banken eingeführt, der die sogenannten Basel-III-Vorgaben umsetzt.[65] Demzufolge gelten schrittweise deutlich strengere Vorgaben für Eigenkapital und Liquidität. Die Richtlinie behandelt außerdem Fragen im Zusammenhang mit Geschäftsführungs- und Vergütungspraktiken. Die neuen Vorgaben werden zukünftig zu stabileren Bankensystemen beitragen. Kurzfristig bereiten sie irischen Banken aber auch

---

[63] Im November 2008 wurde eine hochrangige Gruppe unter Leitung von Jacques De Larosière von der EU-Kommission damit beauftragt, Vorschläge zur Stärkung der europäischen Finanzaufsicht zu unterbreiten. Der Bericht der Gruppe, der im Allgemeinen als „De-Larosière-Bericht" bezeichnet wird, wurde im Februar 2009 veröffentlicht.

[64] ESRB (2013). "The Consequences of the Single Supervisory Mechanism for Europe's Macro-prudential Policy Framework", Berichte des Beratenden Wissenschaftlichen Ausschusses, September.

[65] Basel III: *A global regulatory framework for more resilient banks and banking systems* (Originalversion: Dezember 2010, überarbeitete Version: Juni 2011) und Basel III: *International framework for liquidity risk management, standards and monitoring* (Originalversion: Dezember 2010, überarbeitete Version: Januar 2013).

Probleme, da diese immer noch grösstenteils von kurzfristigen Finanzierungen abhängig und bisher nicht profitabel sind.[66]

Nationale Ebene

Nach dem „Central Bank Reform Act, 2010" ist nun die Zentralbank (Central Bank of Ireland) sowohl für Zentralbankaktivitäten als auch für die Finanzregulierung zuständig.[67] Mit der Verabschiedung des „Central Bank (Supervision and Enforcement) Act, 2013" wurden die Befugnisse der Zentralbank noch erweitert. Dieses Gesetz sorgt dafür, dass viele der Befugnisse der Zentralbank (beispielsweise Weisungsberechtigungen) für alle regulierten Finanzdienstleister vereinheitlicht werden und nicht nur für eine Branche allein gelten. Vor Verabschiedung des Gesetzes war die Situation umgekehrt: Die rechtlichen Befugnisse der Zentralbank zur Ausübung ihrer Funktion in einem bestimmten Branchensektor wurde üblicherweise von der betreffenden sektorspezifischen Gesetzgebung bestimmt.

Die Vorgehensweise und Ziele der Finanzregulierung wurden für die integrierte Behörde neu formuliert, und zwar sowohl in Bezug auf die Beaufsichtigung auf der Ebene des einzelnen Kreditinstituts (Mikro-Aufsicht) als auch in Bezug auf die systemweite Finanzstabilität (Makro-Aufsicht). Die Zentralbank hat auch verbesserte Standards der Geschäftsführung, Eignung und Seriosität in Finanzinstituten in Irland angemahnt. In den Grundsätzen der Unternehmensführung für Kreditinstitute und Versicherungsunternehmen („Corporate Governance for Credit Institutions and Insurance Undertakings") wurden klare Vorgaben für Direktoren und Vorstände von Banken und anderen Finanzunternehmen festgelegt. Die gesetzlichen Standards für Eignung und Seriosität („Fitness and Probity Standards") stärken die Rolle der Zentralbank bei der Besetzung hoher Posten in den regulierten Finanzunternehmen.

Im Hinblick auf die Aufsicht wurde festgestellt: Die Aufseher in Irland und anderen Ländern agierten in der Zeit vor der Krise zu rücksichtsvoll gegenüber der Bankenindustrie. Honohan u. a. (2010)[68] analysieren die Schwachstellen der irischen Finanzaufsicht vor der Krise: für die Aufsicht wurden zu wenige Ressourcen abgestellt; die Aufsichtspraxis war zu stark auf die Überprüfung der Geschäftsführungs- und Risikomanagementmodelle der Finanzinstitute

---

[66]　Wie für andere europäische Banken auch ist die Frage der latenten Steueransprüche (Deferred Tax Assets, DTA) von besonderem Interesse. Nach mehreren Jahren mit deutlichen Verlusten besitzen die irischen Banken nun beträchtliche Eventualansprüche auf Steuern an den Staat, gegen die sie unter Umständen zukünftige Körperschaftssteuern aufrechnen können. Gemäß den neuen Vorgaben zählen DTA nicht mehr zum Mindesteigenkapital.

[67]　Die neue Struktur ersetzte die entsprechenden bisherigen Stellen, die Central Bank und die Financial Services Authority of Ireland sowie den Financial Regulator. Das Gesetz trat am 1. Oktober 2010 in Kraft.

[68]　Honohan, P., Donovan, D., Gorecki, P. & Mottiar, R. (2010). "The Irish Banking Crisis: Regulatory and Financial Stability Policy", Irische Zentralbank (Central Bank of Ireland).

konzentriert, statt eine unabhängige Risikobewertung zu versuchen; die erwarteten Ergebnisse scheinbar gut geführter Banken führten zu einer Nachlässigkeit, die sich als nicht gerechtfertigt herausstellte.

Die Krise brachte die Erkenntnis, dass erhebliche Veränderungen notwendig waren. Als Reaktion darauf gestaltete die Zentralbank ihre Herangehensweise bei der Bankenaufsicht neu, erweiterte ihre Ressourcen und verstärkte ihren Fokus auf quantitative und finanzielle Analysen, setzte einen neuen Risikoausschuss ein, der externe Risikoberater umfasst, und führte ein spezielles Maßnahmendurchsetzungsteam ein (Central Bank of Ireland, 2010, 2011)[69]. Das Herzstück dieser Veränderungen war eine grundlegende Änderung der Aufsichtskultur; die Zentralbank konzentriert sich nunmehr auf die Umsetzung eines durchsetzungsstarken, risikobasierten und anspruchsvollen Ansatzes bei der Bankenaufsicht, dem ein glaubwürdiges Abschreckungsmittel in Form der Maßnahmendurchsetzung zugrunde liegt.

Zur Unterstützung ihres geänderten Vorgehens bei der Aufsicht entwickelte die Zentralbank einen neuen Risikobewertungsrahmen, das Prudential Risk and Impact System (PRISM). Der Rahmen wurde 2011 mit der Absicht eingeführt, ein strukturiertes Rahmenwerk für die Aufsicht über Finanzinstitute zu schaffen und die Fähigkeit der Zentralbank zu einer urteilsbasierten, ergebnisorientierten Regulierung zu erweitern. Das System verlangt, dass die Kontrolleure sich ein Urteil über die Risiken bilden, die jedes Finanzinstitut darstellt, und dann geeignete Risikoabschwächungsprogramme entwickeln, um untragbare Risiken auf ein akzeptables Niveau zu verringern.

Das PRISM-System bedingt die Einteilung regulierter Institutionen in verschiedene Relevanzkategorien, wobei diese Kategorien auf der Grundlage quantitativer Daten festgelegt werden. Es gibt vier Relevanzkategorien, die die relative Bedeutung eines Finanzinstituts zeigen und u. a. auf seiner Größe, seinem Umsatz und seinem Kundenstamm basieren, und es gibt vier Aufsichtsmodelle passend zu diesen Relevanzkriterien. Die Institute mit der höchsten Relevanz erhalten die höchste Aufsichtsstufe, bei der spezielle Aufsichtsteams ein proaktives Aufsichtsprogramm verfolgen. Die vorausschauende Bewertung von Risiken, die Rücklagen und das Kapital, die zu deren Absicherung vorgehalten werden, und die Überprüfung der Liquidität und Finanzierung stehen im Mittelpunkt des Aufsichtsprozesses der Zentralbank. Dies wird durch eine Auswertung von Analysen zu Eignung und Seriosität, zur Geschäftsführung, zum Geschäftsmodell und zur Wirtschaftlichkeit ergänzt.

Im Herbst 2013 führte die Zentralbank eine umfassende Bilanzbeurteilung und eine Prüfung der Qualität der Vermögenswerte der drei wichtigsten einheimischen

---

[69] Irische Zentralbank (Central Bank of Ireland), "Banking Supervision: Our New Approach" (June 2010); Irische Zentralbank (Central Bank of Ireland), "Banking Supervision: Our Approach 2011 Update" (June 2011).

Privatkundenbanken (AIB, BOI und PTSB) durch, um Darlehensklassifizierungen, Rückstellungen und aufsichtlich vorgegebene Risikogewichte zu prüfen.

Zur Bewältigung der Bankenkrise hat die Zentralbank weitere, nicht vom Gesetzgeber untermauerte Richtlinien herausgegeben. So legt beispielsweise der Kundenschutzkodex („Consumer Protection Code") Vorgaben für die Führung der Geschäfte fest, die für viele verschiedene, in Irland angebotene Finanzdienstleistungen gelten. Im Frühjahr 2013 stellte die Bank quantitative Zielvorgaben für die Auflösung von in Zahlungsrückstand geratenen Hypotheken auf.

Aktuelle Bewertung und wichtige Herausforderungen

Der irische Bankensektor sieht heute nach der Krise deutlich anders aus. Gemäß den Vorgaben des EU/IWF-Unterstützungsprogramms wurden sowohl die Größe des Sektors deutlich verringert als auch die Geschäftätigkeiten erheblich dahingehend umstrukturiert, dass der Schwerpunkt nun auf Aktivitäten im Inland liegt. Im Jahr 2008 beliefen sich die Vermögenswerte des irischen Bankensektors (Privatkunden- und IFSC-Banken) auf insgesamt über 1.400 Mrd. Euro (789 Prozent des BIP). Dabei machten Privatkundenbanken in irischer Hand einen Anteil von etwa 44 Prozent aus. Bis 2012 waren die Vermögenswerte des ortsansässigen Bankensystems auf insgesamt 859 Mrd. Euro (525 Prozent des BIP) gefallen, wovon Privatkundenbanken in irischer Hand 51 Prozent ausmachten.

Im Sektor der Privatkundenbanken, der die einheimische Wirtschaft bedient, hat eine umfangreiche Umstrukturierung stattgefunden. Drei der größten Banken des Privatkundensektors, die sich in irischer Hand befanden, existieren nicht mehr (Anglo Irish Bank, INBS und EBS). Zu den verbleibenden bedeutenden inländischen Instituten gehören die AIB und die BOI. Nach umfangreichen Rekapitalisierungen und der Übertragung ausfallgefährdeter Immobiliendarlehen auf die NAMA sind diese Banken nun in einer viel stärkeren Position als bei Ausbruch der Krise.

In den vergangenen Monaten hat sich das Vertrauen internationaler Anleger in irische Banken erheblich verbessert. Einheimische Banken haben einige besicherte Anleihen ausgegeben und ihre Abhängigkeit von der Finanzierung durch die Zentralbank verringert. Der Schuldenabbau der Banken wurde fortgesetzt, die Kapitalquoten liegen derzeit komfortabel über den Vorgaben der Aufsehörs. Es hat also Fortschritte gegeben. Erhebliche Herausforderungen bleiben bestehen, bis die staatlich gestützten Banken wieder überlebensfähig sind und privatisiert werden können. Dazu gehören:

- **Wirtschaftlichkeit:** Die Profitabilität wurde durch eine Reihe von Faktoren beeinträchtigt, u. a. durch faule Kredite, eine schwächelnde einheimische wie europäische Wirtschaft, das geringe Niveau neuer Kreditvergaben, ein hoher Anteil ertragsschwacher Hypotheken mit beweglichen Sätzen und relativ hohe Finanzierungskosten. Zwar wurden Verbesserungen erzielt, doch bleibt die zukünftige Ertragsfähigkeit einheimischer Banken

schwierig; die Banken planen weitere Kostenminderungen, die die
Margen verbessern sollten. Bestimmte Aspekte liegen jedoch außerhalb
ihres Einflussbereichs. Beispielsweise hängen die Kosten für die
zukünftige Ausgabe von Anleihen von der positiven Haltung der Anleger
ab. Des Weiteren bringen die bevorstehende Bilanzbewertung und der
Stresstest 2014 Ungewissheit über die zukünftigen Kreditrückstellungen
mit sich.

- **Zahlungsverzug bei Darlehensrückzahlungen und Kreditrisiko:** Dass sich
  immer mehr Kredite als faul herausstellen, bleibt weiterhin eine
  Herausforderung für Irlands Banken. Der Bestand an ausfallgefährdeten
  Krediten erreichte im zweiten Quartal 2013 eine Höhe von 57 Mrd. Euro
  oder 27 Prozent aller ausstehender Darlehen. Zwar hat sich die
  Verschlechterung gegenüber den vergangenen Quartalen verlangsamt,
  doch haben sich die Bemühungen im Umgang mit notleidenden Krediten
  bisher als unzureichend erwiesen. Im Falle von Hypotheken
  beispielsweise bevorzugten die Banken bisher eher
  Stundungsmaßnahmen. Regierung und Zentralbank haben eine Reihe von
  Maßnahmen zur Behebung von Zahlungsrückständen eingeführt.[70] Im
  März 2013 folgte ein neuer, auf Zielvorgaben basierender Rahmen für den
  Umgang mit Zahlungsrückständen bei Hypotheken, „Mortgage Arrears
  Resolution Targets (MART)" genannt. Erste Anzeichen lassen auf
  Fortschritte gemäß dem MART-Rahmen hoffen, wenn sie auch auf
  ungeprüften Daten basieren.[71]
- **Finanzierungsrisiken:** Die einheimischen Banken haben seit der Krise
  große Fortschritte im Umgang mit den Finanzierungsproblemen gemacht.
  Dazu gehören eine Verringerung der offiziellen Sektorunterstützung,
  neuere Anleiheausgaben und Verringerungen bei den Einlagen. Die
  Finanzierungsbedingungen sind jedoch nach wie vor anfällig für
  Umschwünge des Marktvertrauens und die Banken sind immer noch
  größtenteils von kurzfristigen Finanzierungen abhängig.

---

[70] Beispielsweise wurde der Verhaltenskodex für Hypothekenzahlungsrückstände („Code of
Conduct on Mortgage Arrears") überarbeitet, neue Gesetze zur Privatinsolvenz wurden
in Kraft gesetzt, der irische Insolvenzdienst (Insolvency Service of Ireland) wurde
eingerichtet und bisherige rechtliche Hürden für die Aufnahme von Verfahren zur
Wiederinbesitznahme beseitigt.

[71] Bei seiner Einführung verpflichtete der MART die Banken, bis Ende 2013 umsetzbare
Lösungen für 50 Prozent der Hypothekenschuldner vorzuschlagen, deren Zahlungen
mehr als 90 Tage im Rückstand lagen. Weitere Zielvorgaben wurden September 2013
bekanntgegeben, mit denen die Hypothekengläubiger verpflichtet wurden, vor
Jahresende mit mindestens 15 Prozent der Schuldner mit Zahlungsrückständen von
mehr als 90 Tagen zu nachhaltigen Lösungen zu kommen und mit 25 Prozent bis März
2014.

Vor diesem Hintergrund arbeiten die irischen Behörden weiterhin an der Umstrukturierung und Stärkung des irischen Bankensektors. Hauptziel dieser Bemühungen ist es, die einheimischen Banken in eine Lage zu bringen, in der sie die wirtschaftliche Erholung in Irland durch Bereitstellung der notwendigen Kredite an Verbraucher und Unternehmen unterstützen können. In dieser Hinsicht ruht ein Hauptaugenmerk weiterhin auf der Kreditvergabe an kleine und mittelständische Unternehmen, einem entscheidenden Sektor für die Schaffung von Arbeitsplätzen.[72]

KOMMENTAR: KAPITEL 5

Das International Financial Services Centre während der Bankenkrise: Perspektive einer IFSC-Bank[73]

Werner Schwanberg

Hauptaussagen

- Obwohl es eine große Vielfalt internationaler Finanzdienstleister beherbergt, war das International Financial Servies Centre (IFSC) von Irlands Finanzkrise nicht betroffen. Nur wenige Firmen im IFSC gerieten durch die Krise in Schwierigkeiten, und auch diese nahmen keine Hilfe aus dem Rettungsprogramm in Anspruch.
- Dennoch ist das IFSC jetzt der verbesserten Finanzaufsicht unterworfen, die als Reaktion auf die Krise eingeführt wurde. Das neue Regime stützt sich auf einen risikobasierten Ansatz, bei dem die Verhältnismäßigkeit

---

[72] Beispielsweise wurde im April 2010 ein unabhängiges Credit Review Office (Kreditprüfungsamt) eingerichtet, um KMU zu unterstützen, denen Kredite von den großen Banken verweigert wurden. Die irische Regierung hat außerdem ein Credit Guarantee Scheme (Kreditgarantieprogramm) und ein Micro-finance Scheme (Mikrofinanzierungsprogramm) eingeführt, um die Verfügbarkeit von Darlehen für lebensfähige Unternehmen zu verbessern.

[73] Mein Dank gilt John Wright und Christine Pisch für ihre wertvolle Hilfe beim Verfassen dieses Kapitels.

gewahrt bleibt. Es hat die Vertrauenswürdigkeit der Finanzbranche in Irland wiederhergestellt, wie sich unter anderem an Irlands Aufwertung durch die Ratingsagenturen zeigt.

Einleitung

- In seinem Kapitel **Banken und Finanzen – Zurück zur Stabilität** bezieht sich Stefan Gerlach, der stellvertretende Präsident der irischen Zentralbank, auf die drei Hauptgruppen im irischen Bankensektor, nämlich Privatkundenbanken in irischem Besitz, Privatkundenbanken, die nicht in irischem Besitz sind, sowie im International Financial Services Centre IFSC angesiedelte Banken. Angesichts meines Hintergrunds werde ich mich auf letztere konzentrieren, d. h. auf IFSC-Banken und dabei insbesondere auf solche, die in deutschem Besitz sind.

- Ich kam 1991 zur Dresdner Bank in Irland und arbeitete als Kundenbetreuer für ihre Assetmanagement-Tochter, dem ersten deutschen Finanzinstitut, das unter IFSC-Führung gegründet wurde. In der Folgezeit weitete sich die Präsenz der Dresdner Bank in Dublin auf insgesamt drei Unternehmen aus, von denen eines eine vollkonzessionierte Bank war. Ich leitete diese Bank bis 2003, als die Gruppe im Zuge einer internen Neustrukturierung ihre weltweite internationale Präsenz reduzierte und sich auch aus Irland zurückzog. 2006 wurde ich CEO der WGZ Bank Ireland plc, einer weiteren deutschen Bank in Dublin, und habe diese Position nach wie vor inne. Neben dieser Vorstandsfunktion gehöre ich dem Aufsichtsrat anderer irischer Finanzdienstleister an.

Die Geschichte des IFSC

Um die Motivation für die Gründung eines internationalen Finanzdienstleistungszentrums nachzuvollziehen, muss man den Blick auf die Probleme der irischen Wirtschaft Mitte der 80er Jahre richten. Bedingt durch zu hohe Ausgaben, überhöhte Darlehensvergaben und eine an den Wechselkursmechanismus (WKM) gebundene, überbewertete Währung kämpfte das Land mit einer schwachen Konjunktur, hohen Zinsen, hoher Arbeitslosigkeit, Massenauswanderung und Unruhen auf dem Arbeitsmarkt, die zu schweren Arbeitskämpfen führten. Im Jahr 1986 wurde das Punt, die irische Währung, abgewertet.

Aufeinanderfolgende Regierungen versuchten, die vielfältigen Herausforderungen anzugehen. Durch Reformen in der Wirtschaft und im Sozialsystem, durch Steuersenkungen und ähnliches wurden Verbesserungen erzielt. Auf der Suche nach weiteren Anreizen traten die Politiker mit irischen Unternehmern in Dialog. Dabei kam die Idee auf, ein internationales

Finanzdienstleistungszentrum zu gründen. Es sollte ausländische Investitionen ins Land bringen, Arbeitsplätze schaffen und die Infrastruktur in vernachlässigten Stadtteilen Dublins verbessern.

Die Idee des IFSC (International Financial Services Centre) war geboren. Das grundlegende Konzept war recht einfach und vergleichbar mit früheren Projekten wie beispielsweise der 1959 gegründeten Freihandelszone Shannon. Diese hatte eine Reihe multinationaler Konzerne aus unterschiedlichen Branchen nach Irland geführt. Das IFSC zielte ausschließlich auf Unternehmen aus dem Finanzdienstleistungsbereich. Sie sollten sich dazu verpflichten, aktiv in Dublin zu handeln, in Übereinstimmung mit den gebilligten Businessplänen eine Mindestanzahl an Mitarbeitern zu beschäftigen und mit ihren Büros in die Dubliner Docklands umzuziehen. Im Gegenzug erhielten die erfolgreichen Bewerber einen Sonderkörperschaftssteuersatz von 10 Prozent (der allgemeine Satz in Irland lag damals bei 40 Prozent) sowie bestimmte Mietzuschüsse. Sämtliche Bedingungen wurden in einem so genannten „Steuerzertifikat" des Finanzministeriums festgehalten. Bedenken des heimischen Finanzsektors wurden durch ein Verbot auf Geschäfte mit irischen Gegenparteien aus der Welt geschafft. Zudem war auch das Privatkundengeschäft verboten.

Hauptförderer dieses Projekts waren der bekannte irische Unternehmer Dermot Desmond, dem nachgesagt wird, das Konzept entwickelt zu haben, sowie der damalige Premierminister (Taoiseach) Charles Haughey. Dieser erkannte das Potenzial des Projekts, machte es sich zueigen und verteidigte es gegen die Skepsis und die Opposition aus Teilen des öffentlichen Dienstes und der inländischen irischen Banken, die einen massiven Wettbewerb aus dem Ausland befürchteten. Auf EU-Ebene gab es keine Einwände unter der Voraussetzung, dass die Steuerzugeständnisse einer zeitlichen Befristung bis zum Jahr 2000 unterliegen würden. Die Frist wurde später unter bestimmten Umständen auf 2005 erweitert.

Neben den Steuervorteilen bot Irland auch gut ausgebildete Arbeitskräfte, die teilweise bereits internationale Erfahrungen insbesondere in den Vereinigten Staaten und im Vereinigten Königreich gesammelt hatten. Sie wollten gern heimkehren und in einem Bereich arbeiten, in dem sie ihre im Ausland erworbenen Fachkenntnisse einbringen konnten.

Das IFSC heute

Nachfolgende Regierungen haben das IFSC seit seiner Gründung unterstützt, und zwar unabhängig von ihrer jeweiligen politischen Ausrichtung. 27 Jahre später hat es sich als großer Erfolg erwiesen, der einen Anschub für die irische Wirtschaft darstellte. Mehr als 500 Firmen wurden gegründet: Banken, Versicherungen, Fonds- und Vermögensverwalter, Leasingunternehmen, Spezialisten in Wertpapierverbriefung, Inkasso- und Geldtransfer sowie Corporate Treasury. Sie stellen 33.000 direkte Arbeitsplätze, sorgen darüber hinaus für 6.000 Beschäftigte in heimischen Unternehmen und sind in ganz Irland tätig. Die IFSC-Unternehmen

tragen 7,4 Prozent zum irischen BIP bei.[74] Der Sondersatz der Körperschaftssteuer von 10 Prozent gehört der Vergangenheit an; er wurde von einer allgemeinen Körperschaftssteuer von 12,5 Prozent für Gewinne aus Handelsgeschäften abgelöst. Auch die mit dem Steuerzertifikat einhergehenden Bedingungen – und sogar das Steuerzertifikat selbst – waren nicht länger notwendig.

Die Auswirkungen der jüngsten Finanzkrisen auf IFSC-Banken

Das globale Geschehen

Wie viele andere, waren auch die IFSC-Banken oder ihre Muttergesellschaften ab 2007 in verschiedener Weise und in unterschiedlichem Ausmaß von Problemen betroffen. Diese ergaben sich aus Ereignissen wie der Subprime-Krise in den USA, dem Zusammenbruch der isländischen Banken, dem Untergang der Lehman Brothers und, erst kürzlich, der Eurokrise.

Die Auswirkungen auf die IFSC-Banken waren häufig von der Situation der Muttergesellschaften abhängig. Erhielt die Muttergesellschaft beispielsweise Kapitalhilfe durch den Staat, in dem sie ansässig war, so war sie oft dem Druck ausgesetzt, ihre Geschäfte zu konsolidieren, Randaktivitäten einzustellen und die Konzernstruktur zu straffen. Buchhalterische Faktoren, wie Verlustvorträge auf Konzernebene, die zuweilen die Begeisterung für Unternehmungen an Standorten wie Irland schmälerten, spielten ebenfalls eine Rolle. Einige europäische Banken überdachten ihre Position und begannen ihre Gesellschaften in Irland abzuwickeln. Das betraf vor allem Europäer; US-amerikanische Banken waren nicht in gleichem Ausmaß betroffen.

Unter dem Strich bedeutete dies, dass

- IFSC-Banken in gravierenden finanziellen Schwierigkeiten aufgrund der Finanzkrise eine absolute Ausnahme blieben. In Fällen, in denen Probleme auftauchten, halfen die Muttergesellschaften aus der Klemme.
- Keine der IFSC-Banken den irischen Steuerzahler auch nur einen Euro kostete.

Die irische Bankenkrise

Die aus dem Immobilienboom in Irland hervorgegangenen Probleme und die Schwäche der inländischen Banken hatten keine direkten Auswirkungen auf die Gemeinschaft der internationalen Finanzdienstleister im IFSC. Jedoch wurden bald indirekte Nebenwirkungen spürbar, die sich aus der Krise ergaben.

Erstens nahm Irlands internationaler Ruf erheblichen Schaden sowohl aufgrund der finanziellen Schwierigkeiten, die das Land erlebte, als auch aufgrund der Notwendigkeit, den durch IWF und EU bereitgestellten Rettungsschirm von

---

[74] http://www.ifscireland.ie/facts-figures.

67,5 Mrd. Euro in Anspruch nehmen zu müssen.[75] Die Rufschädigung wurde noch verschärft durch zuweilen irreführende oder übertriebene Medienberichte sowohl in Irland selbst als auch im Ausland. In den Jahren 2009 und 2010 waren diese besonders beunruhigend und hatten ganz sicher Einfluss auf die Entscheidungsprozesse bei global agierenden Finanzinstituten, wenn es um die Frage ging, Dublin als Standort für Kapitalanlagen zu nutzen.

Die Iren reagierten darauf, indem sie vollständig mit den internationalen Geldgebern und den Bedingungen des Rettungsschirms kooperierten und ein großes Aufgebot an Maßnahmen zur Verringerung der öffentlichen Ausgaben und zur Aufbesserung der Steuereinkommen implementierten. Dies war und ist ein schmerzhafter Prozess, der der Allgemeinheit erhebliche Belastungen aufgebürdet hat. Darüber hinaus starteten die Regierung und diplomatische Vertreter zusammen mit Organisationen wie der IDA (irische Wirtschaftsförderungsagentur) und der Deutsch-Irischen Handelskammer eine umfangreiche Informationskampagne innerhalb und außerhalb Irlands. Es ging darum zu verdeutlichen, welche Anstrengungen das Land unternahm, um die Krise zu meistern, und warum die Grundlagen seiner Wirtschaft in viel besserem Zustand waren als die anderer, in Schwierigkeiten geratener Volkswirtschaften.

Die Ergebnisse sind allgemein bekannt. Irland ist erfolgreich auf den Kapitalmarkt zurückgekehrt, ist kapitalgedeckt bis 2015 und hat den Rettungsschirm im Dezember 2013 verlassen. 2014 gab der Staat eine Benchmarkanleihe über 10 Jahre zu 3,4 Prozent aus, was 3,75 Mrd. Euro von den für das Jahr angestrebten 8 Mrd. Euro brachte (2011 hatte der entsprechende Zinssatz einen Gipfel von 15 Prozent erreicht). Anfang 2014 wurde Irland zudem von der Ratingagentur Moody's auf Investment-Grade-Rating mit positiven Aussichten hochgestuft. Zweifelsohne bleiben große Herausforderungen bestehen, nicht zuletzt die Altlasten aus der Banken- und Immobilienkrise. Doch der Ruf des Landes ist im Zuge dieses erstaunlichen Comebacks wiederhergestellt. Das spiegelt sich auch in den aktuellen Medienberichten und Kommentaren seiner europäischen Partner wider.

Ein zweiter Nebeneffekt, den die IFSC-Unternehmen aufgrund der irischen Bankenkrise zu spüren bekamen, war die Finazregulierung im Land. Die schwachen irischen Banken zogen massive Kritik seitens der irischen Regulierungsbehörde und der irischen Zentralbank (Central Bank of Ireland, CBI) auf sich. Infolgedessen kam die Forderung nach strengerer Regulierung auf. Dies erforderte eine erhebliche Erweiterung der Ressourcen und Beschäftigtenzahlen. Zusätzlich wurde Know-How aus anderen Ländern hinzugezogen. Die regelbasierte Regulierung löste die prinzipienbasierte Regulierung ab. Die Zentralbank führte für Banken und

---

[75] Das Gesamtprogramm von 85 Mrd. Euro beinhaltete 17,5 Mrd. Euro Barreserven und Pensionsrückstellungen.

Versicherungsunternehmen den verbindlichen „Corporate Governance Kodex"[76] ein, zusätzlich zu anderen Maßnahmen.

Obgleich dies eine verständliche und notwendige Reaktion auf die inländische Bankenkrise war, stellte es doch für die internationalen Finanzdienstleister im IFSC ein Ärgernis dar. Die Vorgehensweise der Regulierungsbehörde zeigte anfangs wenig Verhältnismäßigkeit, so dass eine IFSC-Bank aus dem Bereich des Großkundengeschäfts mit 20 Mitarbeitern plötzlich vor den gleichen Aufgaben wie die inländischen Banken stand. Für internationale Banken und Versicherer ergab sich ein Dilemma: Einerseits wollten sie eine durchdachte Regulierung angewandt wissen, andererseits sollte aber auch die Verhältnismäßigkeit gelten. Auch hier hatten global agierende Finanzinstitute Bedenken hinsichtlich der aus ihrer Sicht unverhältnismäßigen regulatorischen Belastungen ihrer irischen Tochtergesellschaften. In einigen Fällen wird dies Eingang in die strategische Planung gefunden haben. Inzwischen hat die CBI jedoch einen risikobasierten Ansatz übernommen, indem sie Institutionen in Risikoklassen einordnet, nach denen die Intensität der Überwachungsaktivitäten entschieden wird. Dies hat meines Erachtens den notwendigen Grad der Verhältnismäßigkeit in die Überwachung der irischen Banken gebracht.

Fazit

Die sowohl global generierte als auch hausgemachte Finanzkrise hat das „IFSC-Boot" zwar leicht ins Schlingern gebracht, jedoch keine wesentlichen Schäden angerichtet, wie sie etwa andere Teile des Marktes erlebten. Irland bietet noch immer die gleichen Vorteile für internationale Finanzdienstleister und Investoren wie zuvor:

- Ein starkes Finanzdienstleistungszentrum mit Präsenz wichtiger internationaler Akteure.
- Ein stabiles politisches Umfeld.
- Ein transparentes und attraktives Körperschaftssteuersystem.
- Ein Pool gut ausgebildeter Fachkräfte.
- Regulierung nach EU-Normen.
- Eine wirtschaftliche Verbindung zwischen den USA und der EU als einziges englischsprachiges Land in der Eurozone.

In meinen Augen haben Irland und das IFSC auch weiterhin viel zu bieten für international aufgestellte Finanzdienstleistungskonzerne mit vernünftigen Business-Plänen, einer soliden Risikostrategie und einem Fokus auf Rentabilität.

---

[76] Irische Zentralbank (Central Bank of Ireland), "Corporate Governance Code for Credit Institutions and Insurance Undertakings 2010".

KAPITEL 6
Die Dynamik des irischen Arbeitsmarktes

Christoph Müller[77]

Hauptaussagen

- Nach vier Jahren im Land kann ich sagen: Irland ist ein hervorragender Wirtschaftsstandort. Premierminister (Taoiseach) Enda Kenny und die irische Regierung planen den nächsten Schritt: Sie wollen Irland zum weltweit besten kleinen Land der Welt für Unternehmer machen.
- Um dieses Ziel zu erreichen, müssen wir in Ausbildung und Fachkräfteentwicklung investieren. Diese Investitionen sollten sich auf die zukünftigen Bedürfnisse des Arbeitsmarktes konzentrieren, doch sind jetzt schon Maßnahmen erforderlich.

Einleitung

Die irische Wirtschaft hat in den letzten Jahren eine beispiellos verheerende Zeit durchlitten. Den meisten Volkswirtschaften in Europa hat die Krise zugesetzt. Irlands kleine und offene Wirtschaft bekam die Auswirkungen sehr viel härter zu spüren als die Staaten in Europas Mitte. Die Wellen nahmen bei ihrer Ausbreitung vom Kern an Größe zu, und Irland als kleine offene Ökonomie bekam ihre volle Wucht ab.

Während manche Länder auf dem europäischen Kontinent bereits 2010 wieder auf die Beine kamen, einige sogar in eine zweite Krise gerieten, ist Irland nach seinem monumentalen Rückschlag noch nicht zu seiner Wirtschaftsleistung zurückgekehrt.

Dies soll nicht heißen, dass es in Irland nicht ganz eigene Faktoren gab, die zur Wirtschaftskrise beitrugen, sie vielleicht sogar verstärkten. Das Versagen der Regierung, des Gemeinwesens, der Entscheidungsträger in der Wirtschaft, der Regulierungsbehörden, der Finanzinstitute, großer Teile der Wirtschaft und zahlloser Interessengruppen wurde im Verlauf der Krise ausführlich diskutiert und dokumentiert. Ich habe nicht die Absicht, dieses gut beackerte Feld nochmals zu bearbeiten. Vielmehr möchte ich spezifisch betrachten, was ich als das

[77] Der Autor möchte insbesondere Ernst & Young, Goodbody und Davy für die Unterstützung bei diesem Kapitel danken.

bedeutsamste Ergebnis des wirtschaftlichen Zusammenbruchs und die größte Herausforderung für unsere Wirtschaft betrachte: die Arbeitsplatzkrise.

Die gegenwärtige Situation

Bevor wir die Einzelheiten der gegenwärtigen Situation betrachten, ist es wichtig, einige grundlegende Fakten zu würdigen:

- Die Wachstumsrate der irischen Bevölkerung ist die höchste unter den EU-Mitgliedsstaaten. Wenn sich die Schaffung neuer Jobs nicht beschleunigt, wird die Kluft zwischen Angebot und Nachfrage weiter wachsen.
- Diese wachsende Kluft bedeutet: Wer die Arbeitslosigkeit insgesamt beseitigen will, muss den Schwerpunkt entschlossen auf die Beseitigung der Jugendarbeitslosigkeit legen.
- Es reicht nicht aus, die gegenwärtige Situation mit den Vorkrisenjahren des sogenannten „Keltischen Tigers" zu vergleichen. Aber insbesondere die Zeit der 1990er Jahre kann als Blaupause für die kommenden Jahre dienen und bedarf deshalb besonderer Aufmerksamkeit. Diese frühen Jahre des Keltischen Tigers legten ein unternehmerisches Fundament für Irlands wachsenden Wohlstand und seine Wettbewerbsfähigkeit. Die meisten der Faktoren, die zu diesem Wohlstand führten, stehen uns heute immer noch zur Verfügung.

Unter Fachleuten besteht Konsens darüber, dass der irische Arbeitsmarkt stabiler geworden ist. Zwar hat sich die Gesamtbeschäftigung 2013 bis zum 2. Quartal um 33.800 erhöht, doch ist die Arbeitslosigkeit mit 300.700 Menschen ohne Arbeit, was einer Arbeitslosenquote von 13,9 Prozent im Jahr 2013 bis zum 2. Quartal[78] entspricht, weiterhin extrem hoch. Zum jetzigen Zeitpunkt scheint eine leichte Verbesserung der Statistik im 3. Quartal möglich, von Vollbeschäftigung ist man immer noch weit entfernt.

Dem bescheidenen Beschäftigungswachstum liegt ein moderates Wirtschaftswachstum zugrunde, das zwar gering, aber höher als in den meisten EU-Ländern ist.

---

[78] Zentrales Statistikamt (Central Statistics Office), „Quarterly Household Survey, Q2 2013".

Illustration 6.1: BIP, BNE und Arbeitslosigkeit in Irland, 2003 - 2012

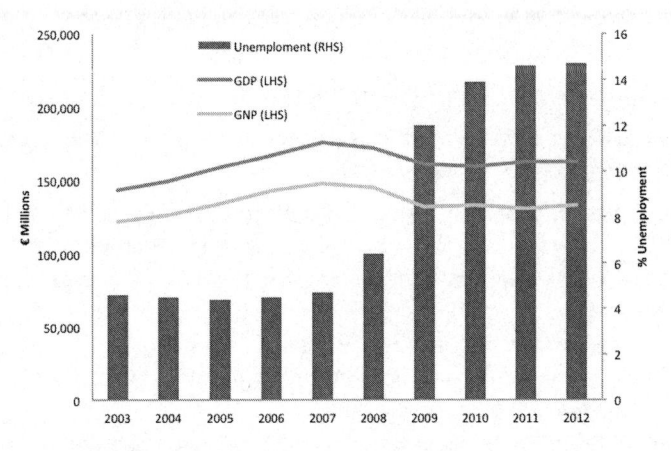

Unemployment (RHS) = Arbeitslosigkeit (RS); GDP (LHS) = BIP (LS); GNP = BNE (LS).
Quelle: Zentrales Statistikamt (Central Statistics Office).

Die Beschäftigung insgesamt setzt sich jedoch aus vielen, mitunter gegenläufigen Trends zusammen. Das folgende Diagramm zeigt die Größenordnung der unterschiedlichen Entwicklungen.

Illustration 6.2: Beschäftigungswachstum in Irland, 2005-2013

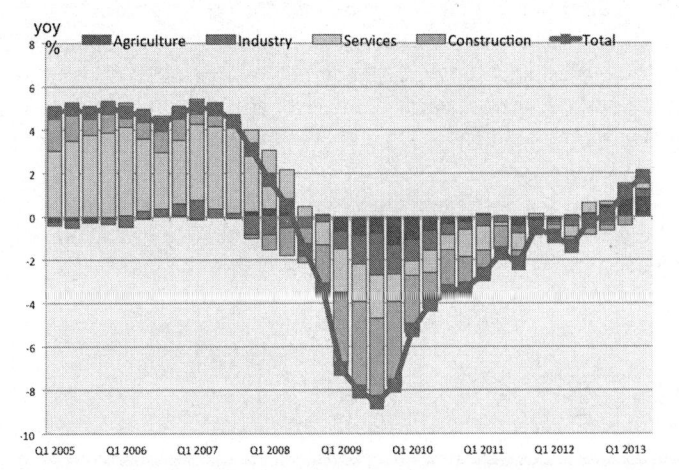

yoy % = % i. Jahres-vergleich; Agriculture = Landwirtschaft; Industry = Industrie;
Services = Dienstleistungen; Construction = Bau; Total = Gesamt.
Quelle: Zentrales Statistikamt (Central Statistics Office).

Den stärksten Abschwung hat das Baugewerbe erlitten. Dies hat nicht nur zum höchsten Anstieg der Arbeitslosigkeit geführt. Auch der Zustrom von Wanderbauarbeitern auf den irischen Arbeitsmarkt ist versiegt.

Im Dienstleistungssektor gibt es Zeichen der Erholung. Vor allem deutet das Wachstum im Hotel- und Gaststättengewerbe sowie im Einzelhandel darauf hin, dass die einheimische Wirtschaft und der Arbeitsmarkt sich stabilisieren. **Illustration 6.3** verdeutlicht die prognostizierten Arbeitsplatzzuwächse und -verluste in Irland von 2013 – 2014.

Illustration 6.3: Arbeitsplatzzuwächse und -verluste in Irland, 2013 – 2014

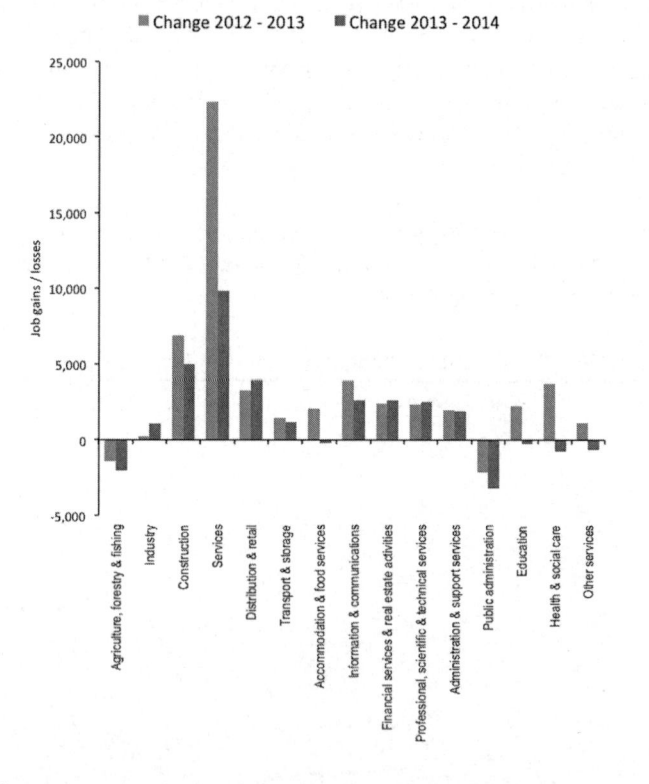

Change = Änderung; Agriculture ... = Land- und Forstwirtschaft, Fischereiwesen; Industry = Industrie; Construction = Bau; Services = Dienstleistungen; Distribution ...= Groß- und Einzelhandel; Transport .. = Transport und Lagerung; Accommodations ... = Hotel- und Gaststättengewerbe; Information ... = Information und Kommunikation; Financial ... = Finanzdienstleistungen und Immobiliengewerbe; Professional, ... = Akademische, wissenschaftliche und technische Dienstleistungen; Administration ... = Verwaltung und unterstützende Dienstleistungen; Public ... = Öffentliche Verwaltung; Education = Bildung; Health ... = Gesundheit und soziale Dienste; Other = Andere Dienstleistungen.
Quelle: Zentrales Statistikamt (Central Statistics Office).

Es sieht so aus, als würde die Beschäftigung erstmals seit Ausbruch der Krise 2008 im Jahr 2013 tatsächlich zunehmen.

Größere Flexibilität

Ebenfalls positiv festzustellen ist, dass der irische Arbeitsmarkt offenbar flexibler geworden ist.

Im Jahr 2012 gab es mehr als 250.000 Wechsel auf dem Arbeitsmarkt: 130.000 Menschen schafften den Sprung von der Arbeitslosigkeit in ein Erwerbsverhältnis, 120.000 erging es umgekehrt. Eine weitere Viertelmillion Menschen wechselten in diesem Zeitraum die Art ihrer Erwerbstätigkeit, ihren Arbeitgeber oder beides. Diese Flexibilität ist zwar willkommen, scheint jedoch auf der geringer qualifizierten Seite des Marktes stattzufinden. Das stellt die Möglichkeiten des Einzelnen, dauerhafte Beschäftigung zu finden, ebenso in Frage wie die bestehenden Systeme zur Angleichung von Angebot und Nachfrage an beruflichen Fähigkeiten.

Eine weitere positive Entwicklung ist der Rückgang der Langzeitarbeitslosigkeit: Sie fiel im Verlauf des Jahres 2013 bis zum Ende des 2. Quartals von 9,2 Prozent auf 8,1 Prozent.[79]

Während die Arbeitslosigkeit insgesamt abnimmt, bleiben die Quoten in drei Gruppen hoch: bei jungen Leuten unter 25 Jahren, im Bausektor sowie bei jenen mit den geringsten Qualifikationen.

Illustration 6.4: Arbeitslosigkeit in Irland nach Altersgruppe, 1998-2013

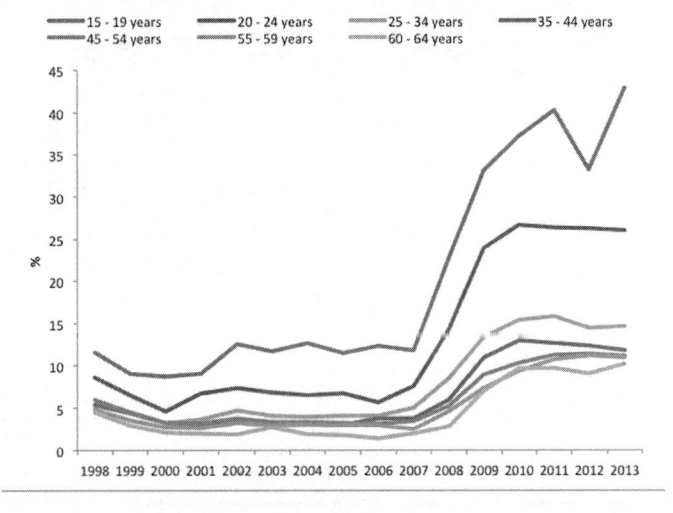

years = Jahre.

Quelle: Zentrales Statistikamt (Central Statistics Office).

---

[79]   Zentrales Statistikamt (Central Statistics Office), „Quarterly Household Survey, Q2 2013".

Illustration 6.5: Arbeitslosigkeit und Bildungsabschluss in Irland, 2013

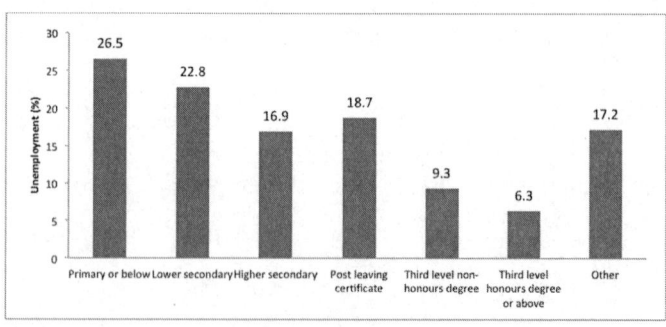

Primary ... = Primär oder geringer; Lower ... = Sekundar I; Higher ... = Sekundar II; Post ... = Abitur; Third level non ...= einfacher Uni-Abschluss; Third level ... = höherer Uni-Abschluss, Doktorgrad u.ä.; Other = Andere. *Quelle:* Ernst & Young.

Dass die Arbeitslosigkeit im Bausektor am höchsten ist, wird angesichts der übermäßig großen Aktivität in diesem Bereich bis 2007 wohl kaum jemanden überraschen. Nicht sonderlich bemerkenswert ist auch die niedrige Arbeitslosigkeit im Dienstleistungssektor, insbesondere in den Bereichen IT, Wissenschaft und Technik. Dass unser Arbeitsmarkt weiterhin an deutlichem Fachkräftemangel leidet, ist hingegen erstaunlich.

Laut nationalem Fachkräftebericht 2013, dem National Skills Bulletin, besteht bei uns ein Arbeitskräftemangel im Bereich Informations- und Kommunikationstechnologie sowie bei Berufen in den Bereichen Wissenschaft, Ingenieurswesen, Finanzen, Gesundheitswesen, Kundendienst (fremdsprachenbezogen) und Fachvertrieb.

Dieser Mangel verursacht eine neue Welle extrem hochqualifizierter Einwanderung nach Irland mit einigen klaren Auswirkungen auf die Wirtschaft. Die Einwanderung findet selbstredend zum größten Teil in urbane Gebiete statt, ist jedoch im Großraum Dublin ganz besonders hoch. Dort treibt die Nachfrage nach Wohnungen die Preise nach oben, was erhebliche Auswirkungen auf die Lebenshaltungskosten mit sich bringt.

Während der Abwärtsdruck auf die Nominallöhne fortbestehen muss, um den Export attraktiver zu machen, bewirkt diese neue Migration von Angestellten in urbanen Gebieten einen Aufwärtsdruck auf die Nominallöhne im Dienstleistungssektor.

Illustration 6.6: Nettomigration nach Altersgruppe in Irland

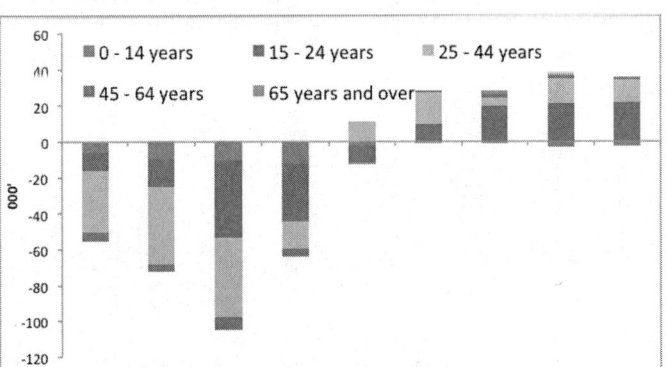

years = Jahre; years and over = Jahre und älter
Quelle: Zentrales Statistikamt (Central Statistics Office).

Auch wenn der Vergleich ein wenig hinken mag, lohnt es sich doch festzuhalten: Die massenhafte Migration von Ost- nach Westdeutschland in den letzten zwanzig Jahren konnte durch staatliche Eingriffe und künstliche Arbeitsplatzbeschaffung weder gestoppt noch wenigstens verlangsamt werden. Wirklich dauerhafte Arbeitsplätze wurden auf der Basis verfügbarer Fachkräfte geschaffen. Weder einheimische noch ausländische Investoren können sich viele Jahre Vorlaufzeit ohne Ertragsfluss leisten, bis die notwendige Fachkräftebasis aufgebaut ist.

Irland und Deutschland: Das gleiche Problem, zu unterschiedlichen Zeiten - gleiche Lösung?

Während der Zeit des Wirtschaftsbooms bis 2008 schien sich die Beschäftigungspolitik der irischen Regierung darauf zu konzentrieren, auf starke Wirtschaftsaktivität hinzuarbeiten, die dann schon für neue Jobs sorgen würde. Die irische Wirtschaft verdoppelte sich im Verlaufe der 1990er Jahre, die Arbeitslosigkeit fiel von einem Höchststand von 17 Prozent gegen Ende der 1980er Jahre auf nur 4,7 Prozent im Jahr 2007. Die 1990er Jahre werden oft als „die echte Hälfte" des Keltischen Tigers bezeichnet. In dieser Zeit stieg die Produktivität und der Unternehmergeist, die internationale Wettbewerbsfähigkeit Irlands nahm zu. Diese Phase war durch Produktionssteigerungen und höhere inländische Investitionen gekennzeichnet statt durch steigenden Konsum, welcher die Zeit von 2000 bis 2007 prägte.

Irland konnte erhebliche ausländische Investitionen anziehen. Das lag zum Teil am Anreiz der niedrigen Körperschaftssteuer, hauptsächlich jedoch an dem sehr attraktiven Lohnunterschied zwischen Irland und den Ländern des europäischen Kontinents. So wurden beispielsweise in den arbeitsintensiven Bereichen der

Flugzeugwartung und der Callcenter viele Jobs geschaffen, und zwar nicht nur eng auf Dublin begrenzt, sondern auch in anderen Gebieten des Landes.

Im gleichen Zeitraum verursachten nicht wettbewerbsfähige hohe Lohnstückkosten in Deutschland Rekord-Arbeitslosenzahlen, was dazu führte, dass Deutschland zum sprichwörtlichen „kranken Mann Europas" wurde. Deutschland hatte seine Wettbewerbsfähigkeit verloren, als Folge davon lagen Jugend- und Langzeitarbeitslosigkeit auf Rekordhöhe. Die Kluft zwischen Ost- und Westdeutschland vertiefte sich weiter, die Wirtschaft schritt mit zwei unterschiedlichen Geschwindigkeiten voran.

Da Deutschlands damalige Lage dem derzeitigen irischen Profil nicht unähnlich war, stellt sich die Frage, ob Irland für seine Gesundung die gleiche Medizin braucht.

Zweifellos hat die fast zehn Jahre anhaltende deutsche Lohnmäßigung, gekoppelt mit geringen Inflationsraten, die Wettbewerbsfähigkeit Deutschlands gesteigert. Ein scharfer Anstieg der Produktivität bei konstanten Nominallöhnen über einen Zeitraum von 15 Jahren hat die Lohnstückkosten auf sehr geringe Werte gedrückt.

Im Rückblick war die Wiederherstellung der Wettbewerbsfähigkeit Deutschlands innerhalb von 10 Jahren nach der Wiedervereinigung eine Herkulesaufgabe. Dies war nur möglich, indem die Verbraucherpreise fast konstant gehalten wurden. Stärkerer Wettbewerb im Einzelhandel und Preissenkungen im Bereich der Telekommunikation bewirkten, dass der Preis des Warenkorbs im Verhältnis zu den meisten anderen europäischen Ländern fiel.

In Irland haben die jüngsten Maßnahmen zur Lohnmäßigung zu einer Senkung der Nominallöhne geführt. Jedoch passen die allgemeinen Lebenshaltungskosten (Verbraucherpreisindex) bisher nicht zu einer Lohnmäßigung, da die realen Lebenshaltungskosten weiterhin steigen. Der Teil des Lebenshaltungskosten-Warenkorbs, der dem privaten Sektor zugeordnet wird, ist tatsächlich zurückgegangen, doch der staatlich kontrollierte Teil ist gestiegen, was zu weniger verfügbarem Einkommen führt.

Öffentliche Gebühren, wie beispielsweise Fernsehgebühren, Abfallgebühren, Kfz-Steuern und Grundsteuern, sind stark angestiegen. Ermessensausgaben wurden insbesondere von den Geringverdienern zurückgehalten. Insgesamt sind die Lebenshaltungskosten in Irland höher als in Deutschland und liegen sehr nahe bei denen der nordischen Länder mit ihren teuren Sozialsystemen.

Illustration 6.7: Preisindex Endverbraucherausgaben der Haushalte, 2011 (EU27=100)

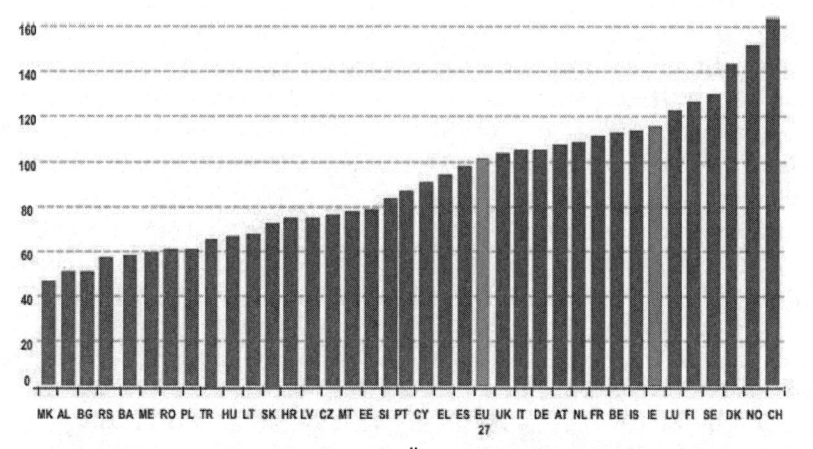

Länderabkürzungen: AL = Albanien; AT = Österreich; BE = Belgien; BA = Bosnien und Herzegowina; BG = Bulgarien; HR = Kroatien; CY = Zypern; CZ = Tschechische Republik; DK = Dänemark; EE = Estland ; EU27 = Europäische Union; DE = Deutschland; FI = Finnland; FR = Frankreich; EL = Griechenland; HU = Ungarn; IS = Island; IE = Irland; IT = Italien; LV = Lettland; LT = Litauen; MK = Ehem. jugoslawische Republik Mazedonien; MT = Malta; ME = Montenegro; NL = Niederlande; LU = Luxemburg; NO = Norwegen; PL = Polen; PT = Portugal; RO = Rumänien; RS = Serbien; SK = Slowakei; SI = Slowenien; ES = Spanien; SE = Schweden; CH = Schweiz; TR = Türkei; UK = Vereinigtes Königreich. *Quelle:* Eurostat (Europäische Kommission).

**Illustration 6.8: Preisentwicklungen in Irland – öffentlicher Sektor
im Vergleich zum privaten Sektor**

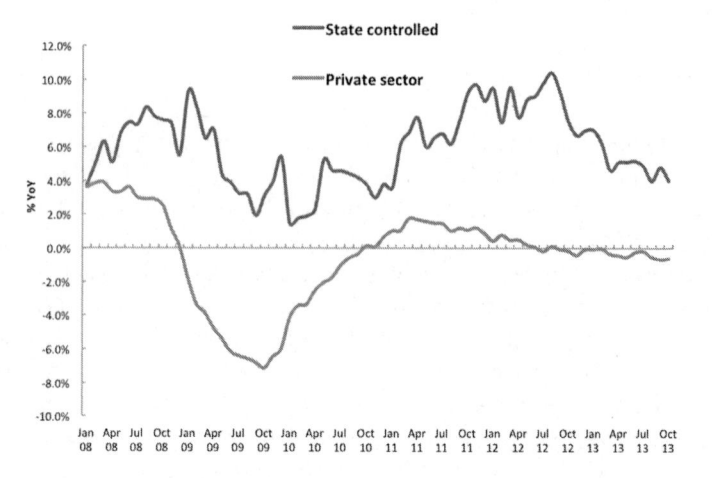

State controlled = Staatlich kontrolliert; Private sector = Privatsektor.
Quelle: Zentrales Statistikamt (Central Statistics Office).

Steigende Lebenshaltungskosten bedrohen die Wettbewerbsfähigkeit des irischen Exportsektors und unsere Fähigkeit, ausländische Investoren zu gewinnen. Außerdem mindern sie unsere Fähigkeit, durch höheren privaten Konsum wirtschaftliche Anreize zu schaffen. Das Problem wurde erkannt, die verbraucherbezogenen Gebühren sinken nun in bestimmten Bereichen. Die Aussetzung der Flughafengebühr und die Senkung der Mehrwertsteuer für Hotels und Restaurants sind gute Beispiele für Anreizmaßnahmen, die zu einer Erhöhung der Konsumausgaben führen.

In der Zeit des Booms erfreute sich der irische Fiskus ansehnlicher Überschüsse, die Regierung liess die Sozialleistungen steil ansteigen. Diese erreichten eine mit den nordischen Ländern vergleichbare Höhe. Doch ein Bericht der Organisation für wirtschaftliche Zusammenarbeit und Entwicklung (OECD) hat 2009 festgestellt: In den nordischen Ländern wurde deutlich mehr in Aktivierungsmaßnahmen zur Verringerung der Arbeitslosigkeit investiert. Es wurden dort also mehr Ressourcen darauf verwandt, Arbeitslose zurück in Arbeit zu bringen, als im irischen System.

Die derzeitige öffentliche Debatte über eine Senkung der Transferleistungen insgesamt und auch über eine Senkung der Zahl der Leistungsempfänger sowie über steigende Lebenshaltungskosten in urbanen Gebieten kommt zur richtigen Zeit.

Die Arbeitslosigkeitsfalle

Bei der Bewertung dieses Phänomens ist es wichtig, die beiden potenziellen Probleme und Lösungen zu betrachten.

Wenn sich ein Privathaushalt für Sozialhilfe entscheidet, weil diese mehr einbringt als bezahlte Arbeit, handelt er wirtschaftlich vollkommen vernünftig. Deshalb könnte man einerseits der Ansicht sein, dass die Sozialleistungen zu hoch sind. Zu dieser Schlussfolgerung ist die Regierung offenbar gelangt, was sich an ihrer jüngsten Kürzung der Sozialhilfe für die Altersgruppe der unter 25-Jährigen zeigt. Einige Ökonomen haben dies als die Ursache für den jüngsten Rückgang der Jugendarbeitslosigkeit ausgemacht.

Andererseits kann man argumentieren, dass die Löhne für ungelernte Arbeit zu niedrig sind, was den Eintritt in den Arbeitsmarkt unattraktiv macht. Diejenigen, die diese Ansicht unterstützen, bringen die hohe Jugendarbeitslosigkeit mit der geringen Marktnachfrage in Verbindung. Sie argumentieren daher damit, dass eine Senkung der Sozialhilfesätze für die Jugend letztere nicht dazu ermuntere, Jobs anzunehmen, da diese Jobs schlicht nicht existierten. Die Senkung würde es unserer Jugend einfach nur noch schwerer machen.

Es besteht kein Zweifel, dass die relativ hohen Sozialhilfesätze in Irland in gewissem Umfang eine Gefahr für die Arbeitsmoral darstellen. Immer wieder hören wir Einzelfälle über Menschen, die nicht arbeiten wollen, weil sie mit Sozialhilfe besser dran sind. Auch gibt es zahlreiche Geschichten über Leute, die vom großzügigen Sozialhilfesystem profitieren, während sie außerhalb des Landes leben, und über solche, die schwarz arbeiten und gleichzeitig Sozialleistungen empfangen.

Zweifellos existieren solche Beispiele, doch ist es fast unmöglich festzustellen, in welchem Umfang. Die beste Lösung für die Arbeitslosigkeitsfalle liegt darin, attraktive Wege aus der Arbeitslosigkeit zu schaffen. Wo keine direkten Arbeitsplätze zur Verfügung stehen, sind Aktivierungsmaßnahmen von staatlichen Agenturen erforderlich. Dadurch können Menschen eine Fachausbildung bekommen, die auf die Bereiche in der Wirtschaft mit echter und steigender Nachfrage ausgerichtet ist. Aktivierungsmaßnahmen sind auch erforderlich, um die Menschen im Kontakt zum Arbeitsmarkt zu halten. Für Leute, die langzeitarbeitslos werden, rückt die Aussicht auf eine Rückkehr in die Erwerbstätigkeit in weite Ferne. Viele Forschungsarbeiten zeigen, dass junge Menschen, die die Erfahrung der Arbeitslosigkeit machen, für den Rest ihres Lebens unter Einkommensbenachteiligungen zu leiden haben. Dies führt zu einem klaren Dominoeffekt für die Gesellschaft und die Wirtschaft.

Wie bereits erwähnt, fällt am irischen Sozialsystem insbesondere seine eigenartige Kombination aus hohen Sozialhilfesätzen und geringen Aktivierungsmaßnahmen auf. Dies trägt wahrscheinlich am meisten zur Arbeitslosigkeitsfalle bei und bedarf einer Lösung.

Die Jugendarbeitslosigkeit hat sich verdreifacht

Das Hauptaugenmerk in Irland ist nun auf die Jugendarbeitslosigkeit gerichtet. 30 Prozent unserer Jugendlichen sind arbeitslos. Das sind 65.000 junge Menschen ohne Arbeit, eine unhaltbare Situation.

Illustration 6.9: Jugendarbeitslosigkeit, Quote und Anteil, 2004-2013

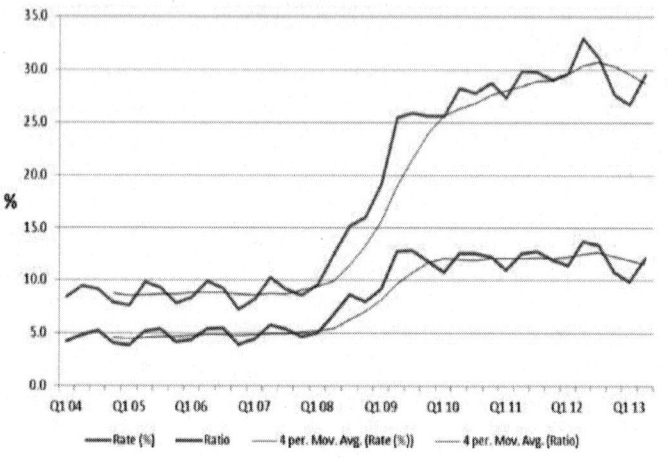

Youth unemployment ... = Jugendarbeitslosigkeit, Quote und Anteil; rate = Quote (%); ratio = Anteil; 4 per. ...(Rate) = Gleitender Durchschnitt über 4 Punkte (Quote %); 4 per. ... (ratio) = Gleitender Durchschnitt über 4 Punkte (Anteil).
Quelle: Zentrales Statistikamt (Central Statistics Office).

Der scharfe Anstieg der Jugendarbeitslosigkeit während der Rezession stand dem Rückgang der Anzahl junger Menschen mit Jobs spiegelbildlich gegenüber. Die Lage bessert sich inzwischen. Laut Daten des Zentrales Statistikamt (Central Statistics Office) vom 2. Quartal 2013 ist die Zahl junger Arbeitsloser auf 64.700 zurückgegangen, ein Rückgang von fast 12.000 im Vergleich zum gleichen Zeitpunkt 2012. Dies ist zwar ermutigend, es muss aber noch viel mehr getan werden. Schliesslich ist demografisch belegt, dass der Arbeitsmarkt weiter durch junge Menschen, die ins Arbeitsleben eintreten, unter Druck bleiben wird.

Die hohe Quote der Jugendarbeitslosigkeit ist natürlich hauptsächlich das Ergebnis der Wirtschaftskrise und des damit einhergehenden Nachlassens der allgemeinen Nachfrage. Doch meiner Meinung nach ist sie auch das Ergebnis einer fehlenden Übereinstimmung zwischen Angebot und Nachfrage nach bestimmten Fachkräften.

Seit ich nach Irland gekommen bin, stelle ich fest: Hier wird alles, was keine Universitätsausbildung ist, als minderwertig betrachtet. Das ist weltweit ziemlich einmalig und war auch in Irland nicht immer so.

Ich möchte anmerken, dass dies kürzlich auch von der City and Guilds, der internationalen Organisation für berufliche Aus- und Weiterbildung, festgestellt wurde. Die Organisation untersuchte in einer Umfrage unter mehr als 500 jungen Menschen In Irland deren Haltung zur Berufsausbildung und kam zu folgendem Ergebnis: *„Es besteht ein offensichtlicher Mangel an Wissen darüber, was eine Berufsausbildung tatsächlich bedeutet und welche Chancen sie bietet. Eine grundlegende Einstellungsänderung ist erforderlich, um der Berufsausbildung den Status zu verleihen, den sie verdient, nämlich den eines lohnenswerten Berufsweges für junge Menschen".*

Außerdem stellte der Bericht fest, dass: *„junge Leute eine Berufsausbildung typischerweise für weniger anspruchsvoll und weniger prestigeträchtig als eine akademische Ausbildung hielten; 32 Prozent sahen sie als einen Weg für weniger Begabte, und 26 Prozent betrachteten eine Berufsausbildung als eine Option mit geringem Status".*

Ich bin der festen Überzeugung: Wir können eine Volkswirtschaft nicht allein mit Universitätsabsolventen unterhalten, die hauptsächlich für die in Dublin ansässige Finanz- und IT-Branche ausgebildet wurden. Vielmehr brauchen wir eine gesunde Pyramide aus Kompetenzen und Qualifikationen, die nicht nur Arbeiter, sondern auch das Handwerk und eher praktische Kompetenzen umfasst, jedoch mit praktischen und anerkannten Qualifikationen in allen Bereichen wirtschaftlicher Aktivität.

Um dies zu erreichen, muss eine Reihe von Aufgaben in Angriff genommen werden:

- Um Angebot und Nachfrage auf dem Arbeitsmarkt wieder ins Gleichgewicht zu bringen, müssen wir die Familien, die Lehrer und die gesamte Gesellschaft darüber aufklären, dass die nichtakademische Ausbildung als mindestens ebenbürtig zu einer akademischen Ausbildung anzusehen ist. Auf allen Ebenen des irischen Arbeitsmarktes besteht ein Ungleichgewicht. Der Bedarf an Menschen, die Qualifikationen in Mathematik, Informations- und Kommunikationstechnologie oder den Wissenschaften erworben haben, kann nicht gedeckt werden. Hingegen verlassen voll qualifizierte Buchhalter, Steuerberater und Rechtsanwälte das Land, um sich in Großbritannien, Kanada und Australien nach Arbeit umzusehen.
- Wir brauchen eine Runderneuerung unseres dualen Ausbildungssystems. Der Ruf der nicht-akademischen Fachabschlüsse muss neu aufgebaut werden. Derzeit ist ihr Ruf geschädigt, da sie fälschlicherweise als nur für diejenigen geeignet betrachtet werden, die „es nicht an die Uni geschafft haben". In Deutschland durchlaufen jedes Jahr über 60 Prozent der Abiturienten dieses System. Das heißt, Schulabgänger, die das Äquivalent zum irischen Leaving Certificate erworben haben, gehen nicht automatisch an eine Universität oder ein anderes Institut des

Tertiärbereichs, sondern beginnen eine Berufsausbildung. Die Chancen auf einen Arbeitsplatz nach erfolgreichem Abschluss einer Lehre oder später als Meister werden als gleichwertig oder höher eingestuft. Tatsächlich werden die meisten KMU in Deutschland von Absolventen des dualen Ausbildungssystems gegründet.

- Wir müssen uns darauf konzentrieren, dass unsere jungen Leute mehr praktische Kompetenzen erwerben. Wer von der Universität kommt, dem fehlen häufig die praktischen Erfahrungen, mit denen man auf dem Arbeitsmarkt Fuß fassen kann. Universitätsstudenten müssen keine praktische Ausbildung absolvieren. In den meisten EU-Ländern ist dies fast zu einem Pflichtbestandteil des Curriculums geworden, und zwar nicht durch ein Gesetz, sondern durch die Gewohnheit. Wenn Arbeitgeber Hochschulabsolventen rekrutieren, suchen sie nach zukünftigen Mitarbeitern, die neben ihren akademischen Kompetenzen eine gute praktische Ausbildung genossen haben.

- Wir müssen den Umfang nicht-akademischer Qualifikationen, die unserer Erwerbsbevölkerung zur Verfügung stehen, vergrößern. Wenn wir das deutsche System der dualen Ausbildung als Beispiel nehmen, so übersteigen die 350 verschiedenen Lehr- und Ausbildungsberufe, die über die deutschen Handelskammern verfügbar sind, das Angebot in Irland um das Vierfache. Dies stellt sich in anderen europäischen Ländern mit einer ähnlichen Geschichte der Produktion wie Deutschland ähnlich dar.

- Die Organisation und Verwaltung der praktischen und beruflichen Ausbildung sollte nicht vollständig dem Staat überlassen werden. Es ist von fundamentaler Bedeutung, dass die Privatwirtschaft und die Unternehmen voll in die Abstimmung von Nachfrage und Angebot an Fachkräften eingebunden sind. Auf Mitgliedschaft gründende Organisationen wie die Handelskammern sind in der besten Ausgangsposition, um diese Lücke zu füllen, da sie in direkter Verbindung zu ihren Mitgliedern stehen und deren Herausforderungen in Bezug auf Arbeitskräfte am besten kennen.

- Wir müssen die Arbeitgeber ermuntern und Anreize schaffen, Ausbildungsplätze sowie Lehr- und Praktikumsstellen zu schaffen. Dies duldet keinen Aufschub. Zwar sind nicht alle Arbeitgeber in der Lage, Lehrstellen anzubieten, doch könnten Partnerschaften als Alternative in Betracht gezogen werden. Bei Aer Lingus arbeiten wir derzeit an einem Pilotprojekt. Wir wollen ausgebildete Mechaniker nicht nur für unser eigenes Unternehmen bereitstellen, sondern auch für kleine und mittlere Firmen, die zu klein sind, um ihre eigenen Arbeitskräfte auszubilden. In unserer jüngsten Einstellungsrunde erhielten wir für 20 Lehrstellen im Bereich Flugzeugmechanik und Flugzeugelektronik mehr als 2.000 Bewerbungen, 100 Bewerber auf jede freie Stelle!

- Die in praktischen oder beruflichen Ausbildungen erworbene Qualifikation muss in irgendeiner Form ein international anerkanntes Zeugnis werden, um als Währung auf dem internationalen Arbeitsmarkt dienen zu können. Die weltweit verstreute irische Diaspora ist ein eindrucksvoller Beleg nicht nur dafür, dass irische Fachkräfte weltweit stark gefragt sind. Sie spricht auch dafür, dass die irische Arbeitsmoral und die Fähigkeit irischer Mitarbeiter, sich schnell in fremde Umgebungen zu integrieren, **„Trained in Ireland"** zu einer erfolgreichen Marke machen könnten.

- Eine ordentliche Berufsausbildung bedient nicht nur den unmittelbaren Arbeitsmarkt, sondern fördert auch das Unternehmertum. Während meiner Arbeit und meiner Reisen rund um den Globus war ich immer wieder beeindruckt, wie viele ehemalige Auszubildende aus Deutschland aufgrund einer international anerkannten Berufsqualifikation schließlich zu Unternehmern wurden. Nicht nur der sprichwörtliche deutsche Braumeister, Bäcker oder Zimmermann, sondern auch Mechaniker und Labortechniker. Ähnliches gilt für Hotelfachleute aus der Schweiz, Wasserwirtschaftsingenieure aus den Niederlanden und Chefköche aus Frankreich. In unserer Branche, der Luftfahrt, basieren die Qualifikationen häufig auf internationalen Sicherheits- und Zertifizierungsnormen, die vorherrschende Sprache ist Englisch. Da kann es nicht überraschen, dass Fluggesellschaften, Flugzeugwartungsunternehmen und Flugzeugleasinggesellschaften weltweit von Managern und Inhabern übersät sind, die ihr Handwerk in Irland gelernt haben. Dies könnte auch in vielen anderen Bereichen der Wirtschaft so sein.

Derzeitige Politik der Regierung

Die Politik der Regierung passt sich der Krise an. Sie konzentriert sich darauf, die Rückkehr zu Wirtschaftswachstum, größere Wettbewerbsfähigkeit und verbesserte Produktivität als Mittel zur Schaffung von Arbeitsplätzen zu fördern. Gleichzeitig , ist ihr bewusst, dass Systeme geschaffen werden müssen, um Arbeitslose im Kontakt zum Arbeitsmarkt zu halten. Dazu gehören neue Programme zur Unterstützung der Arbeitsplatzsuche, Sanktionen gegen diejenigen, die die angebotenen Leistungen nicht annehmen und gegen diejenigen, die nicht schnell in Arbeit zurückkehren können, sowie das Angebot von allgemeiner und beruflicher Bildung.

Allgemeine und berufliche Bildung: Angebot und Nachfrage auf einander abstimmen

Eine Reihe von Programmen der irischen Regierung zielt darauf ab, jungen Arbeitslosen einen Zugang zur allgemeinen und beruflichen Bildung zu ermöglichen:

- Das Programm „Youthreach" stellt 6.000 integrierte Ausbildungsplätze für Schulabgänger im Alter von 15 bis 20 Jahren bereit, die keine Abschlüsse oder Berufsausbildung haben. Fast alle Teilnehmer sind unter 25, etwa zwei Drittel sind 18 Jahre alt oder jünger.

- Das Programm „Vocational Training Opportunities Scheme" umfasst 5.000 Plätze in verschiedenen Kursen, um die allgemeinen und beruflichen Bildungslücken von Langzeitarbeitslosen über 21 zu schliessen. Es richtet sich besonders an Arbeitslose, die die Schule vorzeitig verlassen haben. Etwa ein Fünftel der Teilnehmer ist unter 25 Jahre alt.

- Die Beihilfe „Back to Education Allowance" ermöglicht es Arbeitslosen, zum Vollzeitunterricht in anerkannten Kursen zurückzukehren und gleichzeitig weiter Einkommensbeihilfen zu erhalten.

- Von ungefähr 27.000 Personen, die 2012 an einem Ausbildungskurs der irischen Ausbildungs- und Beschäftigungsbehörde FÁS teilnahmen (Lehrstellen, Abendkurse und Youthreach nicht mitgerechnet), waren fast 10.000 unter 25 Jahre alt.

- Das von der FÁS gesteuerte Programm „MOMENTUM" bietet 6.500 Plätze für langjährige Arbeitssuchende an. Die Kurse schulen Fachkompetenz in solchen Bereichen, in denen es Chancen auf Arbeitsplätze gibt. Das Programm beinhaltet eine praktische Ausbildung und die Entwicklung von Kompetenzen am Arbeitsplatz. Über 1.250 dieser Plätze sind an Unter-25-Jährige vergeben.

Diese Programme werden von staatlichen Agenturen geleitet und zielen auf die Entwicklung von Kompetenzen ab, um die Arbeitslosigkeit zu bekämpfen. Sie müssen sich aber besser an den aktuellen und zukünftigen Anforderungen von Arbeitgebern am Markt ausrichten.

Die Arbeitgeber wiederum müssen eine aktivere Rolle bei der Entwicklung von beruflicher Kompetenz und von Qualifikationen spielen, als es gegenwärtig der Fall ist. Lehrverhältnisse im irischen System schienen bisher darauf konzentriert zu sein, ein „Handwerk" zu erlernen, statt anerkannte Qualifikationen für eine breitere Palette von Tätigkeiten zu ermöglichen.

Die Unternehmen müssen ihren zukünftigen Arbeitskräftebedarf ermitteln und dann bei der Bereitstellung der Fachkräfte, die zur Deckung dieses Bedarfs erforderlich sind, eine Partnerschaft mit den staatlichen Agenturen eingehen. In Deutschland bestimmen die Arbeitgeber die Ausbildungsinhalte in der

Berufsbildung. Auch die Zugangsqualifikationen und -kriterien für die Aufnahme der Bewerber, die Qualifikation der Ausbilder und natürlich Inhalt und Mindestanforderungen für die Zwischen- und Abschlussprüfungen sowie die Zeugnisausstellung – alles Sache der Arbeitgeber. Staatliche Eingriffe erfolgen in minimalem Umfang, um zu gewährleisten, dass die kurzfristigen Bedürfnisse der Arbeitgeber nicht größeren Bildungs- und Wirtschaftszielen entgegenstehen.

Volkswirtschaften mit zwei Geschwindigkeiten. Die Herausforderung der Schaffung von Arbeitsplätzen in ländlichen Gebieten

Sowohl Irland als auch Deutschland stehen vor besonderen Problemen hinsichtlich der geografischen Verteilung der Arbeit.

Die folgenden Heatmaps der beiden Volkswirtschaften veranschaulichen auf beeindruckende Weise die langsame Reaktion der nationalen Arbeitsmärkte auf eine veränderte Nachfrage.

Illustration 6.10: Registrierte Arbeitslosenquoten in Prozent in Deutschland nach Bezirken, Oktober 2013

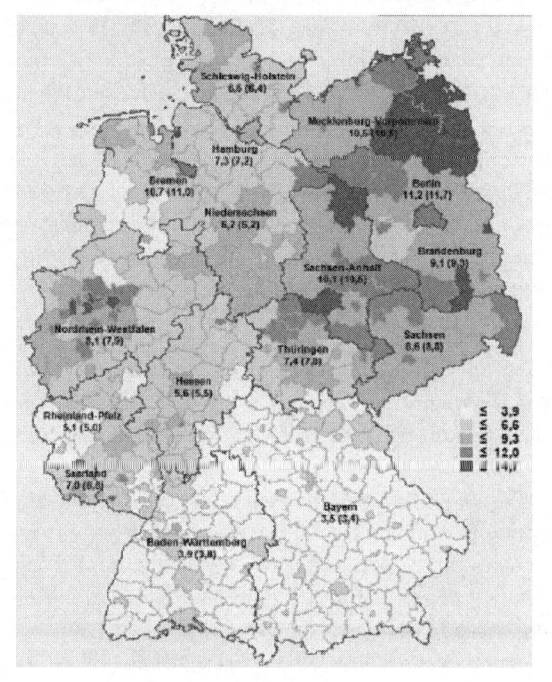

Quelle: Bundesamt für Statistik.

Deutschland hat die strukturelle Herausforderung des Arbeitsmarktes nach der Wiedervereinigung nicht gemeistert. Die Abbildung zeigt, dass die ländlichen Gebiete in Ostdeutschland unter einer deutlich höheren Arbeitslosigkeit leiden - ein Bild, das Irland sehr ähnelt. In den neuen Bundesländern, wo die Arbeitslosigkeit am höchsten ist, ist die Schaffung von Arbeitsplätzen in urbanen Gebieten deutlich höher als im ländlichen Raum.

In Süddeutschland ist das genaue Gegenteil der Fall. Bayern und Baden-Württemberg haben Vollbeschäftigung hauptsächlich im ländlichen Raum. Als ich kürzlich im Süden auf dem Land unterwegs war, ähnelte sich das Bild über Hunderte von Kilometern: ein typisches mittelständisches Unternehmen in einer Kleinstadt mit großen Plakatwänden, die qualifizierte Arbeitsplätze in allen Arbeitsfeldern und auf allen Ebenen, von Ingenieur/innen bis zu Mechaniker/innen, von Ärzt/innen bis zu Geschäftsführungsassistent/innen anboten.

In Irland unterscheiden sich die beiden Geschwindigkeiten stark zwischen Dublin/Cork und dem Rest des Landes. Wie ich bereits erläutert habe, birgt ein Boom im Raum Dublin immer das akute Risiko der Überhitzung. Die wichtigste Frage bleibt, wie eine ausreichende Anzahl von Arbeitsplätzen im Rest des Landes geschaffen werden kann.

Illustration 6.11: Regionale Arbeitslosenquoten in Irland, 2013

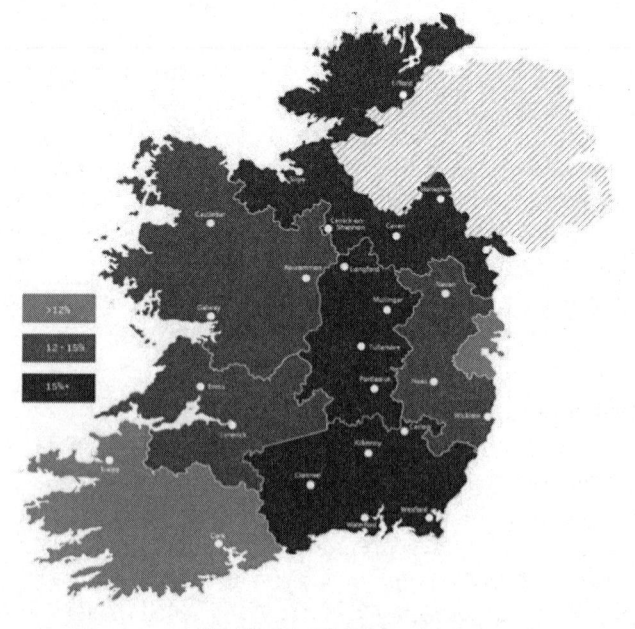

Quelle: Ernst & Young.

Illustration 6.12: Regionale Arbeitslosigkeit in Irland, 2007-2013

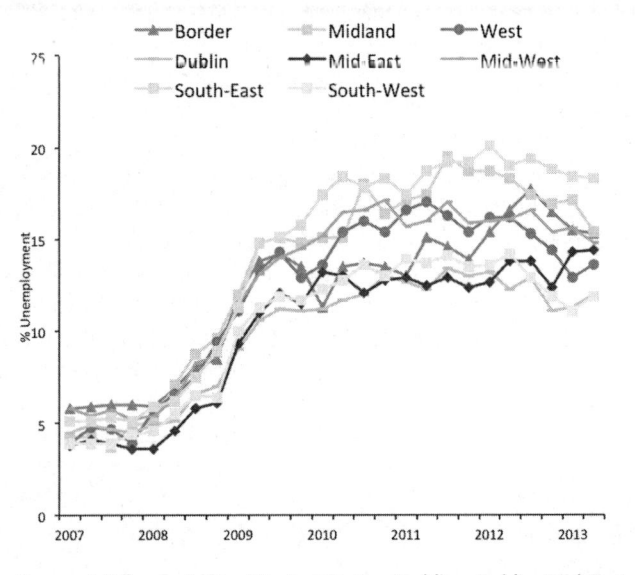

Border = Grenze; Midland = Mitte; West = Westen; Dublin = Dublin; Mid-East = Östliche Mitte; Mid- West = Westliche Mitte; South-East = Südosten; South-West = Südwesten. *Quelle:* Ernst & Young.

Die Werbung für Irland als Touristenziel hat erfreuliche Wirkung gezeigt, allerdings mit zwei erheblichen Wermutstropfen: Erstens sind Dienstleistungsjobs im unteren Einkommenssegment hauptsächlich mit Nicht-Iren besetzt. Diese Besonderheit gilt nicht für Nordirland. Zweitens sorgt die starke Saisonabhängigkeit auf das Jahr gesehen nicht für Vollzeitbeschäftigung. Ein ähnliches Problem führte in der Schweiz vor einigen Jahrzehnten zum Aufbau eines Hotelschulgeschäfts, das die Nebensaison für die Aus- und Weiterbildung nutzte.

Der Aufbau einer mehr mittelständischen Wirtschaft erfordert eine langfristige Perspektive mit einer Reihe fortlaufender Maßnahmen.

Unternehmerschaft

In den letzten Jahren wurde die große Mehrheit der Arbeitsplätze im Angestelltenbereich von großen multinationalen Konzernen, ausländischen Investoren geschaffen. Fast 1.000 multinationale Gesellschaften haben Irland als Standort für ihre Niederlassung in Europa ausgewählt. Diese Gesellschaften mögen die zupackende Geschäftskultur in Irland und fühlen sich nicht nur von der Körperschaftssteuer angezogen, wie es häufig von außen wahrgenommen wird. Sie sehen auch die Erfolge bisheriger ausländischer Direktinvestoren und die Fähigkeiten unserer Beschäftigten als wichtige Anziehungspunkte.

Die Mehrheit dieser Investoren kommt aus den Vereinigten Staaten. Was bei dieser Beziehung häufig außer Acht gelassen wird, ist die Tatsache, dass die Investitionen in beide Richtungen fließen. Laut jüngsten Forschungen der Amerikanischen Handelskammer begünstigt die Beschäftigungsbilanz eher die USA als Irland, d. h. irische Firmen beschäftigen direkt 136.100 US-Mitarbeiter in Amerika, während US-Firmen in Irland 115.000 irische Mitarbeiter haben.

Die Zahl der Neugründungen von Unternehmen in Irland liegt hingegen unter dem europäischen Durchschnitt. Man könnte über den wahren Grund dafür spekulieren – Risikoscheu, mangelnder Ehrgeiz usw., doch ist eines gewiss: Spitzentalente aus den Universitäten werden in Irland fast vollständig von den Grosskonzernen aufgesaugt.

Der klassische Weg zur Firmengründung liegt ohnehin meist in nicht-akademischen Lebensläufen. Ein junger Mensch mit abgeschlossener IT-Ausbildung nach der Sekundarschule hat im Alter von etwa 21 eine Arbeit. Er oder sie ist dann nicht nur in der Lage, eine geschätzte Dienstleistung zu erbringen, sondern besitzt auch die nachweislichen Kompetenzen und den Ruf, um einen Kredit zu erhalten und eigene Mitarbeiter zu beschäftigen und auszubilden.

Die wichtigste Antriebskraft ist meines Erachtens das Vertrauen eines jungen Menschen in die eigene Fähigkeit, etwas herzustellen, anzubieten und zu verkaufen, das ganz und gar von ihm oder ihr selbst in den frühen Jahren der beruflichen Laufbahn geschaffen wurde.

Der Spielraum studierter Betriebswirtschaftler und Rechtsanwälte für die Gründung eigener Unternehmen ist in der heutigen Welt der Konzerne recht begrenzt, im Gegensatz zu neueren Berufsbildern wie den Fachleuten für landwirtschaftliche Dienstleistungen, Technikern für audiovisuelle Medien, Biologielaboranten usw. Einer meiner eigenen Schulkameraden absolvierte nach der Schule eine Ausbildung zum Uhrmacher und Goldschmied und hatte im Alter von 25 Jahren seine eigene Firma mit 10 Mitarbeitern.

In Irland wird zu häufig nach dem Staat gefragt, um den Arbeitsmarkt zu regulieren. Aber auf diesem bestimmten Gebiet braucht es offenbar einen Katalysator, um das Henne-Ei-Problem zu überwinden. Es ist zu spät, die Unternehmer von heute auszubilden, aber wir müssen damit anfangen, die Unternehmer von morgen auszubilden. Und wir müssen so früh wie möglich damit beginnen, noch während ihrer Schulausbildung. Dies ist nicht nur nötig, um den Hunger nach Karrieren in neuen Branchen zu wecken. Es geht auch um Sommerpraktika in kleinen oder großen Unternehmen, im Dienstleistungsgewerbe, im Handwerk oder in der industriellen Produktion, vielleicht sogar im Ausland.

Wir haben nicht genügend KMU in neuen Berufsfeldern, um die kritische Masse von Absolventen aus unseren eigenen Ressourcen auszubilden. Hier wird unser Pilotprojekt ansetzen und Möglichkeiten ausloten, um eine Basis für ein „Train-the-Trainer"-Konzept zu entwickeln.

Sprachen

Die Wichtigkeit von Sprachen in der allgemeinen und beruflichen Bildung ist zu einem modernen Merkmal der globalen Wirtschaft geworden. Während die Bürger kleinerer Länder wie die Niederlande, Belgien und Luxemburg berühmt sind für ihre seit früher Kindheit entwickelten, hervorragenden Sprachkenntnisse, haben sich weder Irland noch Deutschland in diesem Bereich hervorgetan.

Irische Auswanderer konzentrierten sich auf die englischsprachige Welt, heute immer noch das wichtigste Kennzeichen der irischen Diaspora. Der Schwerpunkt des irischen Exportmarktes verlagert sich immer mehr nach Europa und in die BRIC-Staaten. Es wäre ratsam, die Sprachkompetenzen daran anzupassen.

Deutschland und Frankreich sind traditionell auf ihre eigene Muttersprache fokussiert, doch wurden in den letzten Jahren einige wichtige Fortschritte erzielt.

Irland und Deutschland starten von ähnlichen Ausgangspunkten. Ein stärkeres Gewicht auf Fremdsprachen wird die Fähigkeit beider Länder fördern, Fachkräfte miteinander auszutauschen und, wichtiger noch, miteinander Handel zu treiben.

Für Irland sind an dieser Stelle zwei kurzfristige Chancen auf dem Arbeitsmarkt zu nennen.

Für Arbeitsuchende mit Fremdsprachenkenntnissen bestehen gute Beschäftigungschancen in Irland. Ein Callcenter in der Nähe von Dublin hat über 1.000 Mitarbeiter, aber weniger als 10 von ihnen haben einen irischen Pass. Diese Chancen werden vollständig von ausländischen Arbeitskräften und ausländischen Studenten, die Teilzeitarbeit suchen, wahrgenommen. Man könnte fast sagen, dass die flüssige Beherrschung einer anderen Sprache als das Englische in Irland beinahe die Garantie für eine Beschäftigung mit sich bringt.

Außerdem gibt es eine kurzfristige Chance im Ausland. Auf dem deutschen Arbeitsmarkt herrscht derzeit und wohl auch in absehbarer Zukunft eine starke Nachfrage nach qualifizierten Arbeitskräften. Die demografischen Entwicklungen in Deutschland und Irland ergänzen einander, und die kulturelle Übereinstimmung ist sehr groß. Junge Iren, die Deutsch sprechen oder bereit sind, es zu lernen, haben gute Beschäftigungsmöglichkeiten in der deutschen Wirtschaft, entweder für einen zeitweiligen Aufenthalt zur Erweiterung des eigenen Horizonts oder auf Dauer, um zum gegenseitigen Verständnis beizutragen.

Derzeit tritt eine erhebliche Anzahl junger Spanier mit Deutschkenntnissen in den deutschen Arbeitsmarkt ein, was von der lokalen Industrie sehr begrüßt wird.

Schlussfolgerung

Der irische Arbeitsmarkt beschäftigt sich hauptsächlich mit bestehenden Problemen. Es wurden einige Fortschritte erzielt, doch die endgültige Struktur, auf die wir hinarbeiten, ist immer noch etwas unklar. Es wird eine weitere Konzentration auf den Dienstleistungssektor mit Finanzdienstleistungen, IT und Pharmazeutik prognostiziert.

Doch aus dem kritischen Blickwinkel des Risikomanagements unterliegen diese Jobkategorien einem permanenten Druck aus Ländern mit niedrigeren Kosten. Wir haben große weltweite Umwälzungen der Finanzdienstleistungsbranche infolge geringfügiger Änderungen bei der Besteuerung oder anderen Anreizen erlebt. Um dieses Risiko auszugleichen, muss die irische Wirtschaft ein zweites Standbein in der industriellen Produktion oder einer echten Fachkräftespezialisierung aufbauen und auch einheimische Investitionen fördern.

Ernst & Young „Economic Eye" prognostiziert die folgenden Arbeitsplatzzuwächse (und -verluste) in Irland von heute bis 2020:

Illustration 6.13: Arbeitsplatzverluste und -zuwächse in Irland, 2013-2020

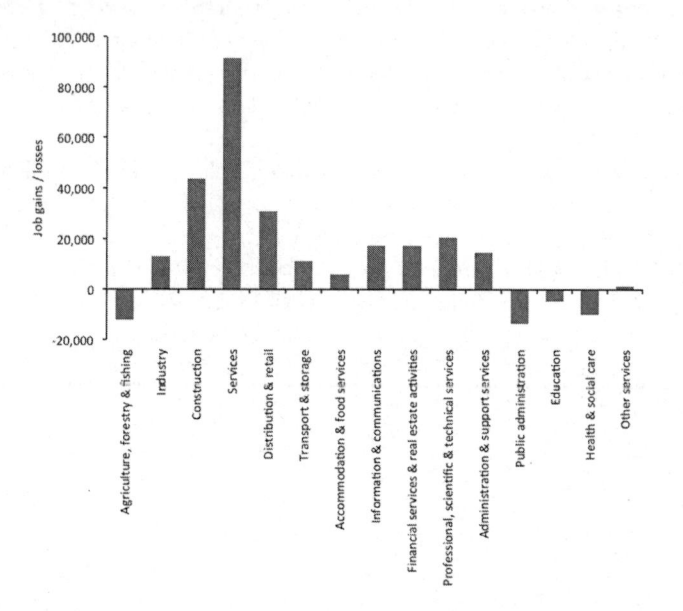

Change = Änderung; Agriculture ... = Land- und Forstwirtschaft, Fischereiwesen; Industry = Industrie; Construction = Bau; Services = Dienstleistungen; Distribution ...= Groß- und Einzelhandel; Transport .. = Transport und Lagerung; Accommodations ... = Hotel- und Gaststättengewerbe; Information ... = Information und Kommunikation; Financial ... = Finanzdienstleistungen und Immobiliengewerbe; Professional, ... = Akademische, wissenschaftliche und technische Dienstleistungen; Administration ... = Verwaltung und unterstützende Dienstleistungen; Public ... = Öffentliche Verwaltung; Education = Bildung; Health ... = Gesundheit und soziale Dienste; Other = Andere Dienstleistungen.
Quelle: Zentrales Statistikamt (Central Statistics Office).

Der Landwirtschaftssektor war in den Jahren des Keltischen Tigers fast zur Bedeutungslosigkeit verkommen. Ein sprunghafter globaler Anstieg des Handels mit Nahrungsmitteln und landwirtschaftlichen Erzeugnissen hat nun dieses

Wirtschaftssegment derart beflügelt, dass es zu einem wichtigen Wachstumsmotor geworden ist. Dies sollte als Beispiel der erforderlichen Strukturveränderungen dienen.

Das romantische Bild des irischen Farmers, der für den Touristen mit seinen Schafen für ein Foto posiert, ist passé. Stattdessen bricht die Zeit einer völlig neuen Hightech-Branche an. Nun sind Doktorgrade in der Nahrungsmittelverarbeitung, IT-Spezialisten für Precision Farming, Robotik und Herstellung von Melkrobotern, Chemieingenieure für Hygienekontrolle und viele weitere handwerkliche Qualifikationen wie beispielsweise in der Mechanik erforderlich, um Irlands Position in dieser schnell wachsenden Branche zu verteidigen.

Es bestehen Chancen für Irland, seinen Handelsumfang mit EU-Partnern auf dem Kontinent zu vergrößern. Neben dem unmittelbaren wirtschaftlichen Effekt würde dies die Möglichkeit eröffnen, Arbeitsplatzqualifikationen anzubieten, die in ganz Europa anerkannt sind. Dies könnte entweder die Vision „Trained in Ireland" oder die langfristige Investition in Ausbildungen im Ausland sein: „Learn and Return".

Migrationsbewegungen in eine kleine offene Volkswirtschaft wie Irland hinein und aus ihr heraus sind unvermeidlich. Wenn die Qualifikationen in ganz Europa einheitlicher wären, würde dies die Möglichkeiten fördern, auf dem Kontinent zu arbeiten, Erfahrungen zu sammeln und nach Irland zurückzukehren.

Entscheidend für alle Teile der irischen Wirtschaft ist es, Arbeitsplätze in allen Einkommenssegmenten und auf allen Qualifikationsstufen anzubieten. Dafür müssen alle Beteiligten – Familien, Firmenmitarbeiter, Gewerkschaften und Regierung – zusammenarbeiten und an einem Strang ziehen.

Deutscher Mittelstand: sieben Säulen des Erfolges

Dr. Eric Schweitzer

Hauptaussagen

- Der Erfolg der deutschen Wirtschaft in den vergangenen Jahren ist zu einem großen Teil den großen Anstrengungen der Wirtschaftsunternehmen des Landes zu verdanken. Interne Umstrukturierungen, gekoppelt an eine zunehmende internationale Ausrichtung und Investitionen in Forschung und Entwicklung bildeten den Grundstein hierfür. Der Prozess wurde seitens der Regierung außerdem durch Arbeitsmarktreformen und das Körperschaftssteuersystem unterstützt.
- Deutschland ist ein starker Standort mit einer ungewöhnlichen Mischung an Unternehmen. Es ist die Heimat von erfolgreichen, großen, öffentlich notierten Firmen, unzähligen hochengagierten kleinen Geschäften – und einem breiten Mittelstand. Diese Firmen, in vielen Fällen im Familienbesitz, stehen nicht immer im Rampenlicht. Sie sind dennoch hoch innovativ und – als „hidden Champions" – erfolgreich auf den Weltmärkten.

Vom „kranken Mann" Europas zum Vorbild?

„The real sick man of Europe", so titelte im Mai 2005 der *Economist*. Gemeint war der Wirtschaftsstandort Deutschland. Hohe Arbeitslosigkeit und niedrige Wachstumsraten prägten das Bild. Manches von dem, was derzeit Irland und andere Staaten der Europäischen Union in der Staatsschuldenkrise durchmachen müssen, war in der ersten Hälfte der vergangenen Dekade auch in Deutschland zu bewältigen.

Sieben Jahre später hat sich das Deutschland-Bild deutlich gewandelt. Nun lautet die Titelschlagzeile „Germany's economic model – what it offers to the world". Geringe Arbeitslosigkeit, eine starke Industrie, ein breiter Mittelstand – mit diesen Attributen verbindet man dieser Tage den Standort Deutschland.

Sicherlich sind beide Bilder überzeichnet. Doch wahr ist: Hinter uns liegt eine Zeit harter Veränderungen, die uns gleichwohl nach vorne gebracht hat. Die

Unternehmen haben neue Märkte erschlossen, gerade in Osteuropa und vielen Schwellenländern weltweit. Sie haben in ihren Betrieben einschneidende Restrukturierungen vorgenommen. Sie haben geforscht und entwickelt und damit Produkte platziert. Das verlangte Unternehmenslenkern und Mitarbeitern viel ab. Die Politik hat z. B. im Jahr 2003 die „Agenda 2010" initiiert und damit den Kurs flankiert. Der Arbeitsmarkt wurde flexibler, Steuern für Unternehmen wurden gesenkt, moderate Tarifabschlüsse verbessern die Wettbewerbsfähigkeit der Unternehmen auf den Weltmärkten.

Starker Mittelstand

Eine bedeutende Rolle in der wirtschaftlichen Erfolgsgeschichte Deutschlands spielt der Mittelstand. Der Zuwachs an Beschäftigung zwischen 2005 und 2010 – das waren 1,8 Mio Erwerbstätige – ging fast vollständig auf mittelständische Unternehmen zurück. In der angelsächsischen Wirtschaftspresse wird der deutsche Begriff „Mittelstand" heute schon gar nicht mehr übersetzt. Er ist zu einem Synonym für ein erfolgreiches Wirtschaftsmodell geworden. Als Präsident des DIHK werde ich von vielen ausländischen Delegationen gefragt: Was ist das Geheimnis des „German Mittelstand"?

So geheimnisvoll ist es aber dann doch nicht. Denn viele Länder verfügen über mittelständische Unternehmen. Neben der ausgeprägten Regionalität und Eigenwilligkeit der Familienunternehmer kommt aber hierzulande ein weiterer Aspekt hinzu: Viele Familienunternehmen sind über Generationen gewachsen, fast muss man sagen zu „Familien-Konzernen" geworden. Dabei haben sie sich die mittelständische Denke, die unmittelbare Verantwortlichkeit und das Engagement der Familie bewahrt.

Ein weiterer Erfolgsfaktor des deutschen Mittelstandes ist seine internationale Präsenz. Exportorientierte Mittelständler, die einen Jahresumsatz zwischen 10 und 50 Mio Euro erwirtschaften, sind im Schnitt auf 16 Auslandsmärkten aktiv. Selbst kleine Unternehmen mit einem Jahresumsatz von unter 500.000 Euro bearbeiten durchschnittlich sechs Märkte. Das macht die Betriebe robust – Einbrüche hier können durch Erfolge dort kompensiert werden. 98 Prozent der rund 350.000 deutschen Exporteure sind mittelständische Unternehmen. Im Blickpunkt sind dabei neben den europäischen Märkten auch immer mehr weiter entfernte, aufstrebende Regionen wie z.B. China, Indien und Indonesien.

Ein weiterer Erfolgsfaktor: Der deutsche Mittelstand treibt Innovationen voran. 30.000 deutsche Unternehmen – ein Großteil davon Mittelständler – haben eigene Forschungsabteilungen.

Viele mittelständische Betriebe haben sich auf diese Weise mit mutigen Ideen und Beharrlichkeit Marktnischen erobert. Dort sind sie mit spezialisierten Angeboten erfolgreich. Ein passgenauer After-Sales-Service auch auf ausländischen Märkten rundet das Bild ab. Damit sind diese Unternehmen trotz überschaubarer Größe weltweit vorne. Teilweise handelt es sich hierbei um Betriebe mit 200, 100

oder noch weniger Mitarbeitern. Dafür hat sich der Begriff „Hidden Champions" eingebürgert. In Deutschland gibt es etwa 1.300 Unternehmen dieser Kategorie, so viel wie in keinem anderen Land. Mit weitem Abstand dahinter liegen die USA mit etwa 350.

Warum gibt es diese „Hidden Champions" gerade in Deutschland so zahlreich? Ein erster Erklärungsansatz sind strukturelle Besonderheiten: Mittelständische Unternehmen in Deutschland sind größer als in anderen Ländern. Sie beschäftigen im Schnitt sieben Mitarbeiter, doppelt so viel wie in Frankreich, Italien oder Spanien. Der Grund: Deutschland verfügt über eine starke Industrie. Und Industrieunternehmen sind zumeist größer als etwa Dienstleistungs- oder Handelsbetriebe. Fast ein Viertel des Bruttoinlandsprodukts kommt aus diesem industriellen Mittelstand. In Spanien und Großbritannien sind es knapp 16 Prozent, in Frankreich sogar nur 13 Prozent.

Die sieben Säulen des Erfolges

Doch viel wichtiger als Zahlen ist das ganz besondere Selbstverständnis, die Kultur des deutschen Mittelstandes. Das „Geschäftsmodell Mittelstand" gründet auf sieben Säulen:

- **Erstens:** Eigentum und Leitung liegen in einer Hand. Mehr als 90 Prozent aller deutschen Unternehmen werden mehrheitlich von Inhabern und deren Familienmitgliedern geleitet. Das für eine Marktwirtschaft so wichtige Prinzip der Haftung erhält auf diese Weise volle Geltung. Der Handelnde erntet den Erfolg seiner Entscheidungen. Er muss aber auch für den Misserfolg gerade stehen.

- **Zweitens:** Langfristorientierung. Ein Familienunternehmer wäre schlecht beraten, sich vornehmlich an kurzfristigen Kennziffern und Quartalsbilanzen zu orientieren. Vielmehr steht bei seinen Geschäftsentscheidungen die Frage im Vordergrund: Was bedeutet das für meine Kinder bzw. meinen Nachfolger? Das lässt einen Mittelständler auch so manche Durststrecke aushalten, in denen die Renditen niedriger sind. Unterstützt wird der lange Atem durch das spezifische deutsche Bankensystem: das Drei-Säulen-Modell aus privaten Banken, Sparkassen und genossenschaftlichen Kreditinstituten. Es bietet den Unternehmen eine große Bandbreite, um Finanzierung auch in der langen Frist zu sichern. Der Mittelstand hat es nicht weit zu einem Finanzierungspartner, der auch nachhaltige Unternehmensstrategien unterstützt. Dieses Modell wird durch öffentliche Förderbanken komplettiert: auf Bundesebene durch die KfW-Bankengruppe, auf Ebene der Länder durch Landesförderbanken und auch durch die Bürgschaftsbanken, die dort in die Bresche springen, wo es mittelständischen Unternehmen an Kreditsicherheiten fehlt.

- **Drittens:** Kundennähe. Viele erfolgreiche Mittelständler reüssieren mit spezialisierten, Produkten in Marktnischen. Das erfordert Service auch nach Vertragsabschluss. Flexibilität und kurze Entscheidungswege runden die Kundenorientierung ab. Die Unternehmen setzen zudem auf internationale Präsenz vor Ort. DIHK-Umfragen zeigen, immer mehr Betriebe investieren zunehmend in von Deutschland weit entfernten Regionen.
- **Viertens:** Enge Bindung zu Mitarbeitern. „Die Firma muss sich anfühlen wie Familie", sagen viele Chefs im Mittelstand. Sie setzen auf ihr angestammtes qualifiziertes Personal. Die niedrige Fluktuation fördert über ein hohes Teamgefühl die Produktivität. Auch der hierzulande zunehmende Mangel an Fachkräften – bedingt durch die demografische Entwicklung – verstärkt diese Haltung. Begünstigt wird die hohe Mitarbeiterbindung durch das deutsche System der dualen Ausbildung. Jugendliche werden bereits früh in den Betrieb integriert und passgenau für die betrieblichen Erfordernisse und den Arbeitsmarkt ausgebildet. Der Erfolg dieses Modells wird nicht zuletzt an der vergleichsweise geringen Jugendarbeitslosigkeit in Deutschland sichtbar.
- **Fünftens:** Eine enge Bindung zur Stammregion. Ein Engagement über das rein geschäftliche und gesetzlich geforderte hinaus fördert das Ansehen des Unternehmens am Ort. Mittelständische Unternehmen nehmen bürgerschaftliche Verantwortung für ihre Regionen wahr. Das neue Label „Corporate Social Responsibility" beschreibt eine hierzulande seit Jahrzehnten gelebte Realität. Unternehmen unterstützen Kultur und Bildung in der Region, fördern Projekte für benachteiligte Jugendliche, engagieren sich für Kindergärten, Schulen, Sportstätten, um nur einige Beispiele zu nennen.
- **Sechstens:** Keine selektive, sondern eine breite Mittelstandspolitik. Die deutsche Mittelstandsförderung ist nicht auf die Förderung einzelner Branchen oder Unternehmen ausgerichtet. Eine ausgewogene Branchenstruktur macht die Wirtschaft krisenrobust. Trotz aller Kritik im Detail: In Deutschland gibt es ein Grundverständnis dafür, dass der Mittelstand im Wettbewerb Chancengleichheit braucht – oder man ihm zumindest keine Knüppel zwischen die Beine wirft.
- **Siebtens:** Unterstützung vor Ort und weltweit. „Germany is often singled out as having the most effective and integrated business support infrastructure."[80] So vertreten die Industrie- und Handelskammern (IHKs) vor Ort die Interessen des gewerblichen Mittelstandes gegenüber der lokalen Politik. Ihr Dachverband, der Deutsche Industrie- und Handelskammertag (DIHK), tut dies auf dem politischen Parkett in Berlin

---

[80] Lord Heseltine of Thenford, „No Stone Unturned in Pursuit of Growth", Anhörung im Wirtschaftsausschuss des Unterhauses, Oktober 2012.

und Brüssel. Die Präsenz der IHK-Organisation vor Ort macht es möglich, zu jedem Thema auch kleinere Mittelständler mit der Politik an einen Tisch zu bringen. Zudem bieten die IHKs Serviceleistungen wie Unterstützung bei der Existenzgründung, Beratung zur Energieeffizienz und Finanzierung. Sie übernehmen unbürokratisch Aufgaben vom Staat für die Unternehmen, wie etwa das Ausstellen von Ursprungszeugnissen für den Export. An erster Stelle aber sind sie der Kümmerer für die duale Ausbildung.

Über das Netz der Auslandshandelskammern – AHKs – an mehr als 120 Standorten in 85 Ländern schlägt die IHK-Organisation Brücken zu den internationalen Märkten. Für erste Sondierungen des Marktumfeldes in Asien etwa muss ein Mittelständler nicht selbst dorthin reisen. Hier kann eine AHK vor Ort unterstützen. Damit ersparen die Vertretungen dem Mittelstand in ganz erheblichem Maße Transaktionskosten und sind damit eine wichtige Stütze des deutschen Exporterfolges.

Ich möchte aber nicht verhehlen, dass auch ein wenig Glück den Erfolg des deutschen Mittelstands beflügelt. Deutschland liegt in der Mitte Europas. Wir können jeden Markt der EU in 48 Stunden mit dem Zug, in 24 Stunden mit dem Auto und in drei Stunden mit dem Flugzeug erreichen.

Was Kann Man Lernen?

Kann man den „German Mittelstand" kopieren? Nein! Die deutsche Mittelstandskultur ist auch Produkt der deutschen Geschichte. Lange Zeit gab es auf dem Gebiet des heutigen Deutschland hunderte von Klein- und Kleinststaaten mit eng abgegrenzten lokalen Märkten. Diese kleinen Wirtschaftsräume erhielten erst spät einen Nationalstaat und dann Europa als Rahmen. Seit Jahrhunderten haben deutsche Unternehmen und ihre Vorläufer gelernt, sich zu spezialisieren, grenzüberschreitend zu handeln und dabei eng mit der Stammregion in Verbindung zu bleiben. Der regionale Aspekt war und ist ein ganz erheblicher Faktor in Deutschland, auch in der Wirtschaft.

Aber es gibt einige Voraussetzungen, die heute auch anderswo geschaffen werden können. Viele Länder interessieren sich für das System der dualen Ausbildung – nicht zuletzt angesichts hoher Jugendarbeitslosigkeit im Zuge der Euro-Staatsschuldenkrise. Hier engagieren sich die IHKs und AHKs sehr stark mit eigenen Initiativen. Auch Teile des bewährten Fördersystems der staatlichen Förderbank Kreditanstalt für Wiederaufbau (KfW), von Förderinstituten der Bundesländer oder die Bürgschaftsbanken und Mittelständischen Beteiligungsgesellschaften können interessant für andere Länder sein. Dazu zählen nicht nur Kreditprogramme, sondern auch Beratungsunterstützung. Beispiel sind die „Runden Tische" der KfW für Unternehmen in Schwierigkeiten: Unter Moderation der IHK loten Unternehmer, Banken und Gläubiger Wege aus dem

Engpass aus. Fast 70 Prozent finden nach einem Runden Tisch die Spur zurück in den Markt, die Unternehmen werden aus der Schieflage gerettet.

Als große Herausforderung für den deutschen Mittelstand sehe ich in den kommenden Jahren den zunehmenden Fachkräftemangel. Die demografische Entwicklung trifft Deutschland hart. Auf dem deutschen Arbeitsmarkt werden 2025 sechs Mio Menschen fehlen. Unsere duale Berufsausbildung schafft gute Voraussetzungen, doch das allein wird nicht reichen. Wir müssen alle Potenziale erschließen. Das betrifft die Weiterbildung ebenso wie die Beschäftigung Älterer, eine bessere Vereinbarkeit von Beruf und Familie sowie eine Willkommenskultur für ausländische Fachkräfte. Denn eins ist sicher: Ohne kluge Köpfe funktioniert kein Geschäftsmodell, erst recht nicht das „Geschäftsmodell deutscher Mittelstand".

KOMMENTAR: KAPITEL 7

Ist ein irischer Mittelstand möglich?

Marc Coleman und Ralf Lissek

Hauptaussagen

- Die geringe Größe des Landes war bisher ein Hindernis, wenn es darum ging, die kleinen und mittleren Unternehmen in Irland auf ein angemessenes Maß zu führen. Dies wiederum beeinträchtigte die Exportkapazitäten dieses Sektors. Immerhin hat ein florierender KMU-Sektor die Krise überlebt. Er zeigt viele Charakteristika, die auch für den deutschen Mittelstand typisch sind. Dazu gehört eine starke Ausfuhrleistung in einigen Teilsektoren.

- Der Sektor wird durch eine dynamische Regierungspolitik unterstützt, jedoch gibt es weiterhin große Herausforderungen. Dazu gehören der Zugang zu Krediten sowie das Erreichen einer für den Export notwendigen Größe. Unter den richtigen Bedingungen könnten irische Unternehmen mit der Zeit für den Dienstleistungssektor den Erfolg nachbilden, den der deutsche Mittelstand im verarbeitenden Sektor erreicht hat. In ihrer mittelfristigen Wirtschaftsstrategie ("Medium Term Economic Strategy") schaut die Regierung auf andere Länder, insbesondere auf Deutschland, und sucht nach Anregungen, wie sie KMU besser helfen kann. Für beide

Länder erschließen sich viele Möglichkeiten zum Austausch bewährter Konzepte und Verfahren. Insbesondere die deutsche Langfristorientierung und damit zusammenhängend die Unterstützung durch ein starkes Bank- und Ausbildungssystem könnten dem irischen KMU-Sektor zur Ausschöpfung seines Potenzials dienlich sein.

Irland und Deutschland: Ein „Sieben Säulen"- Vergleich

Den deutschen Mittelstand direkt auf die irische Wirtschaft zu übertragen ist nicht möglich. Aber der Vergleich zwischen Irland und Deutschland hinsichtlich der „Sieben Säulen" aus dem vorangegangenen Kapitel kann aufschlussreich sein.

Diese im vorangegangenen Kapitel ausgearbeiteten „Sieben Säulen" sind:

- Inhaberführung.
- Langfristorientierung.
- Kundennähe und die Fähigkeit, Kundenbindung durch innovative Kundenorientierung zu erzielen.
- Enge Bindung zwischen Management und Mitarbeitern.
- Enge Bindung zur Stammregion.
- Ein breiter Konsens in Deutschland darüber, dass das Mittelstandsmodell geschützt und gefördert werden sollte.
- Weltweite Unterstützung durch das starke Kammernetzwerk.

Es zeigen sich sowohl auffällige Unterschiede als auch subtile Ähnlichkeiten. Beides eröffnet die Möglichkeit für eine Geschäftskultur, die zwar auf einzigartigen irischen Werten basiert, jedoch an relevanten Stellen auf bewährte und übertragbare Stärken des deutschen Systems zurückgreift: Dauerhaftigkeit, eine langfristige Orientierung und die zuverlässige Unterstützung eines gut gestalteten Ausbildungs- und Kreditsystems. Umgekehrt kann die Flexibilität und Anpassungsfähigkeit des irischen Geschäftsmodells mit seiner Verschmelzung europäischer und amerikanischer Elemente, wie in **Kapitel 2** besprochen, deutschen Unternehmen als Anregung dienen.

Ein Vergleich der beiden Modelle sollte zwei offenkundige – und bereits angedeutete – Unterschiede beachten: Irlands geringere Größe und seine Lage an Europas Peripherie. Irlands kleinere Größe bedeutet, dass für Beschäftigten- und Umsatzzahlen eine andere Messlatte gilt. In Deutschland gelten Unternehmen mit bis zu 500 Beschäftigten als Teil des Mittelstands. Für Irland ist es sinnvoller, den von der EU-Kommission[81] angewandten Standard für die Definition von „Small and Medium-sized Enterprise (SME)" anzusetzen. Dieser korreliert eng mit dem deutschen Konzept der KMU (Kleinere und Mittlere Unternehmungen).

---

[81] Empfehlung der Kommission 2003/361/EC veröffentlicht am 20. Mai 2003.

Als Insel am Rande Europas gelegen, behindert Irlands Lage seinen KMU-Sektor in erheblichem Maße dabei, Firmen in einer Größenordnung zu generieren, die in Deutschland Standard ist. Wer dies bedenkt, versteht auch die verhältnismäßig wichtige Rolle, die das Firmensteuersystem für Irland spielt. Es wird hier als ausgleichender Faktor bei der Überwindung starker Standortvorteile von Ländern wie Frankreich, Deutschland, Belgien und den Niederlanden wahrgenommen.

Was die erste Säule betrifft, gab es in Irland im Jahr 2012 einer Studie zufolge etwa 242.000 inhabergeführte Unternehmen[82]. In ihrer aktuellen mittelfristigen Wirtschaftsstrategie 2014-2020 setzt die Regierung diese Zahl bei 180.000 an.

Die zweite Säule beschreibt die Langfristorientierung und Beständigkeit, die den deutschen Mittelstand charakterisiert. Hierzu einige Beobachtungen: Erstens ist die Quote der Geschäftsinhaber in Irland trotz vierjähriger Krise gemessen an OECD-Standards recht hoch geblieben. Es gibt also ein Potenzial für den Aufbau und die Nachhaltigkeit eines irischen Mittelstands, vorausgesetzt, weitere Bedingungen lassen dies zu. Allerdings hat es jüngst auch Hinweise darauf gegeben, dass ein über dem üblichen OECD- sowie EU-Durchschnitt liegender Anteil irischer Unternehmer sich mangels anderer Beschäftigungsalternativen für das Unternehmertum entscheidet.[83]

Der irische KMU-Sektor hat insbesondere in den Immobilien-bezogenen Branchen viele Arbeitskräfte verloren. Der deutsche Mittelstand scheint also stabiler zu sein als irische KMU. Dies kann jedoch zum Teil als Überbleibsel der Krise betrachtet werden; mittlerweile sind Irlands KMU hoffentlich auf dem Weg in eine stabilere und langfristiger orientierte Phase. Allerdings fehlt ihnen bisher die Stärke und Stabilität des Finanzsystems. Dies bildet, wie oben angemerkt, einen Hauptfaktor bei der Unterstützung der Langfristorientierung des deutschen Mittelstands. Wie in **Kapitel 2** besprochen, hat die irische Regierung bereits mehrere Schritte eingeleitet, um die Verfügbarkeit von Krediten für irische Firmen zu verbessern. Bei diesem Thema kann Deutschland möglicherweise helfen und auf staatlich finanzierte Investitionsbanken in Deutschland, wie beispielsweise die KfW, als mögliche Idee für neue Kapitalquellen hinweisen.

Die mittelfristige Wirtschaftsstrategie vermerkt die Schwierigkeit irischer KMU, angesichts der Änderungen im System der Finanzregulierung Zugang zu langfristigen Finanzierungen zu erhalten. Sie schlägt zudem eine erhöhte Anwendung kurzfristiger Eigenfinanzierungen vor, eine Vorgehensweise, die im Vergleich zu den Vereinigten Staaten in Europa relativ selten vorkommt. Der Regierungsplan sieht – nach Vorbild der deutschen KfW – die Etablierung eines Strategischen Investmentfonds für Irland (Irish Strategic Investment Fund) vor. Ausserdem sollen Mittel aus dem Nationalen Pensionsrücklagenfonds (National

---

[82] Tabelle 1, Seite 29, Fitzsimons, Paula und O'Gorman, Colm (2013). "Entrepreneurship in Ireland" (Global Entrepreneurship Monitor).

[83] Seite 28, Fitzsimons, Paula und O'Gorman, Colm (2013). "Entrepreneurship in Ireland" (Global Entrepreneurship Monitor).

Pension Reserve Fund) genutzt werden, um irischen KMU den Zugang zu Kapital zu erleichtern. Es muss genau überlegt werden, wie die Arten und Fälligkeiten der zur Verfügung gestellten Finanzierung mit den Unternehmens- und Sektorenstrategien der Regierung in Einklang gebracht werden können.

Die dritte Säule des deutschen Mittelstands bezieht sich auf die Kundennähe und die Fähigkeit der Spezialisierung. Auch hier hat Irlands vergleichsweise geringe Größe eine Rolle bei der Entwicklung des KMU-Sektors gespielt.

Illustration 7.1 zeigt Daten aus dem Dienstleistungssektor. Die Mehrheit der Firmen (21,2 Prozent) fällt in die Kategorie „Wissenschaftliche und technische Dienstleistungen". Dies umfasst viele kleine Firmen aus den Bereichen der Rechts- und Steuerberatung sowie den medizinischen Diensten. Sie spiegeln wider, dass Irlands Städte und Dörfer relativ klein sind und dass solche Dienstleistungen auch auf dem Land gebraucht werden. Die beiden nächstgrößeren Sektoren sind mit 17,1 Prozent der Einzelhandel, gefolgt von Tourismus mit 12,4 Prozent.

Illustration 7.1: Anzahl der KMU aus dem Dienstleistungssektor nach Bereichen[84]

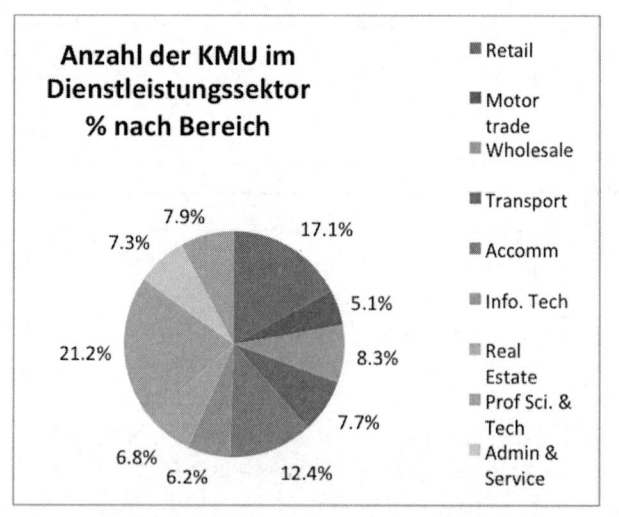

Retail = Einzelhandel; Info Tech = Informationstechnologie; Motor trade = KFZ-Handel; Real Estate = Immobilien; Wholesale: = Großhandel; Prof Sci. & Tech = Wissenschaftliche und technische Dienstleistungen; Transport = Transport; Admin & Service = Verwaltung und Dienstleistungen; Accomm = Unterkunft (Tourismus). *Quelle:* Zentrales Statistikamt (Central Statistics Office), "2011 Annual Services Inquiry".

---

[84] Die aktuellsten Daten liegen für 2011 vor. Sie sind der jährlichen Umfrage im Dienstleistungssektor des Zentralen Statistikamtes (Central Statistics Office) entnommen.

Der irische KMU-Sektor: Gesamtgröße und Ausgewogenheit zwischen verarbeitender Industrie und Dienstleistung

Die Daten für den Bereich der verarbeitenden Industrie[85] sind nachfolgend in der **Illustration 7.2** zusammengefasst.[86] Hier stand der KMU-Sektor für mehr als 90.000 Arbeitsplätze.

Illustration 7.2: Produzierende KMU in Irland

	<€200.000	€200.000 - €1 Million	€1 Million - €5 Million	€5 Million - €10 Million	€10 Million - €50 Million	Gesamt
Zahl der Unternehmen	584	2.097	1432	337	450	**4.900**
Besitzer/ Familienbeschäftigt	658	1.611	656	79	99	**3.103**
Gesamt beschäftigt	1.742	11.793	22.964	13.557	41.910	**91.966**
Lohnkosten €m	32,2	316,6	721,3	485,8	1.555,4	**3.111,3**
Umsatz €m	69,2	1105,0	3.127,5	2.383,8	9.481,8	**16.167,3**
% Ums. exportiert	27,2	23,4	24,9	34,4	44,8	**38,0**
Industriesteuer €m	0,4	9,5	29,3	19,2	64,0	**122,4**
Durchschn. beschäftigt	*4,1*	*6,4*	*16,5*	*40,5*	*93,4*	***19,4***

Quelle: Zentrales Statistikamt (Central Statistics Office), "Erhebung über die Industrielle Produktion 2011".

Die Illustration verdeutlicht eine solide Exportausrichtung quer durch den Sektor: Immerhin 27 Prozent sehr kleiner Unternehmen (mit Schwellenbeträgen von 200.000 Euro oder weniger) produzieren für den Export, der Durchschnitt aller KMU beträgt 38,0 Prozent. Ein direkter Vergleich mit der Statistik, die für den Anteil mittelständischer[87] Unternehmen an den deutschen Exporten herangezogen wird, lässt sich nicht anstellen. In jedem Fall ist der Anteil irischer KMU am Export erfreulich. Allerdings bezieht sich dies auf einen im Vergleich zu Deutschland

---

[85] Daten von 2011. Sie sind der Erhebung über die Industrielle Produktion des Zentralen Statistikamtes (Central Statistics Office) entnommen.

[86] Eine Zusammenführung der Daten aus den Bereichen industrielle Produktion und Dienstleistung ist schwierig, da die Daten auf unterschiedliche Weise erhoben werden.

[87] Wonach 98 Prozent aller deutschen Exporte auf den Mittelstand entfällt.

deutlich kleineren produzierenden Sektor, was den Anteil an Beschäftigung und Gesamtumsatz angeht.

Wie steht es um die Exporte der KMU aus dem irischen Dienstleistungssektor? Nach neuesten Erhebungen rechnet eine Mehrheit von 66 Prozent derjenigen, die 2012 ein Unternehmen in Irland gegründet haben, zumindest mit einigen Exportaktivitäten[88] - das ist eine gute Nachricht.

Nach der obigen Aufschlüsselung des **Dienstleistungs**sektors (**Illustration 7.1**) zu urteilen, ist es jedoch unwahrscheinlich, dass die dienstleistenden KMU bereits von Exportfirmen dominiert werden.

Die nachfolgende **Illustration 7.3** zeigt die Vielfalt der KMU im Dienstleistungshandel: 122.136 Firmen beschäftigen gut 600.000 Personen, davon fast eine Drittelmillion in Vollzeit, und generieren 111 Mrd. Euro Umsatz. Hier könnte die in **Kapitel 2** behandelte Strategie zur Förderung des Dienstleistungsexports von weiterem großen Nutzen für die irische Wirtschaft sein. Möglicherweise kann Irland – wenn auch in kleinerem Maßstab – in Bezug auf seinen Dienstleistungshandel das erreichen, was Deutschland in Bezug auf seine verarbeitende Industrie bereits geschafft hat: ein Exzellenzzentrum für den weltweiten Export zu werden.

Exhibit 7.3: KMU im Dienstleistungsbereich in Irland

	Retail	Motor trade	Wholesale	Tran-sport	Accom	Info. Tech	Real Estate	Prof Sci. & Tech	Admin & Service	Other	Total
Anzahl der Unternehmen	20.942	6.205	10.111	9.366	15.184	7.533	8.290	25.907	8.971	9.660	122.169
Umsatz (Mio. €)	15.755	6.693	48.140	6.943	7.143	5.564	1.461	9.007	7.508	2.814	111.032
Personen	107.807	24.883	73.021	39.903	131.757	26.725	19.214	85.127	49.919	46.026	604.382
davon in Vollzeit	49.158	16.548	55.887	25.130	57.519	17.185	5.088	47.180	30.803	21.215	325.713

Retail = Einzelhandel; Info Tech = Informationstechnologie; Motor trade = KFZ-Handel; Real Estate = Immobilien; Wholesale: = Großhandel; Prof Sci. & Tech = Wissenschaftliche und technische Dienstleistungen; Transport = Transport; Admin & Service = Verwaltung und Dienstleistungen; Accomm = Unterkunft (Tourismus); Other: andere; restl.
Quelle: Zentral Statistikamt (Central Statistics Office), "2011 Annual Services Inquiry".

---

[88] Seite 43, Fitzsimons, Paula und O'Gorman, Colm (2013). "Entrepreneurship in Ireland" (Global Entrepreneurship Monitor).

Illustration 7.4: Tabellarische Zusammenfassung

	Produktion	Dienstleistungen	Gesamt
Umsatz (Mio. Euro)	16.167	111.032	127.199
Beschäftigung	91.966	604.382 (325.713 Vollzeit)	696.348 (Teilzeit anrechnend)

Quelle: Zentrales Statistikamt (Central Statistics Office), "2011 Annual Services Inquiry";
"Erhebung über die Industrielle Produktion 2011".

Eine Zusammenfassung der Lage des irischen KMU-Sektors anhand jüngster offizieller Statistiken wird oben in **Illustration 7.4** dargestellt. Auch wenn sie nicht ganz vergleichbar ist, bietet die tabellarische Zusammenfassung eine grobe Orientierungshilfe bezüglich des Beschäftigungsniveaus (etwa 700.000) und des Umsatzes (etwa 120 Mrd. Euro) insgesamt. Die in der mittelfristigen Wirtschaftsstrategie der Regierung enthaltenen Schätzungen erscheinen als ein wenig hochgegriffen.

Qualitative Aspekte

Aber wie lassen sich diese Zahlen über den irischen KMU-Sektor in Beziehung setzen mit anderen qualitativen Eigenschaften des deutschen Mittelstands?

Die vierte Eigenschaft des deutschen Mittelstands – die enge Bindung zwischen Management und Mitarbeitern – vermengt den persönlichen Aspekt (das „Familiengefühl") mit strategischen Überlegungen (duales System der Berufsausbildung). In dieser Hinsicht ist das Verhältnis zwischen Management und Mitarbeitern in Deutschland ein sehr besonderes. Das heißt aber keineswegs, dass es nicht auch außerhalb Deutschlands nachgebildet werden könnte. Selbst wenn sich Deutschlands duales System der Berufsausbildung vielleicht nicht direkt kopieren lässt, findet doch in Irland derzeit eine spannende Diskussion über die Zukunft seines tertiären Bildungssektors statt. Irland bringt eine beeindruckende Zahl von Uni-Absolventen hervor. Die jetzige Erholungsphase nach der Krise bietet eine Chance, die Verbindungen zwischen Industrie und tertiärem Bildungssystem zu stärken und zu vertiefen. Das gilt nicht nur für die Ebene der Hochtechnologieforschung und –entwicklung, sondern auch für andere Sektoren. Viele von ihnen haben eine wesentliche Bedeutung für die Schaffung von Arbeitsplätzen, insbesondere in kleineren Städten und ländlichen Gegenden, profitieren zumindest zum jetzigen Zeitpunkt aber weniger von Beschäftigten der Hochtechnologie.

Die fünfte Eigenschaft des deutschen Mittelstands lässt sich angesichts der niedrigen Bevölkerungszahl und der Insellage nur schwer auf Irland übertragen. Bevor sie überhaupt in andere Gebiete Deutschlands expandieren, verfügen viele deutsche Mittelständler in ihren Stammregionen bereits über ein Einzugsgebiet,

dessen Bevölkerung oft grösser ist als der gesamte irische Binnenmarkt. Die Internationalisierung des irischen KMU-Sektors bringt erhebliche Schwierigkeiten mit sich. Immerhin gibt es auch Pluspunkte: einerseits die oben angeführte Bereitschaft junger irischer Unternehmer, sich am Export zu beteiligen, andererseits Irlands stolze Stellung als eine der weltweit am meisten globalisierten Ökonomien. Zweifellos steht das Land gleichermassen vor einer Herausforderung wie vor einer Chance, wenn es den KMU-Sektor genau so erfolgreich machen will wie seinen Hochtechnologiesektor. Irische Firmen werden schon bisher durch Enterprise Ireland auf starke und beeindruckende Weise unterstützt. Als erhebliche Herausforderungen für KMU bleiben logistische Probleme und der Mangel an grössenbedingten Kostenvorteilen.

In dieser Hinsicht könnte die sechste Eigenschaft des deutschen Mittelstands hilfreich sein. Irland erfreut sich bereits eines starken politischen Konsenses zugunsten seines günstigen Steuersystems, der Erfolg der IDA (irische Wirtschaftsförderungsagentur) als weltweit führende Akteurin bei der Gewinnung ausländischer Direktinvestitionen spiegelt dies wider. Jüngste politische Initiativen in Irland – der „Action Plan for Jobs" und der Haushalt 2014, der mehrere Anreize für kleine Unternehmen schuf – legen nahe, dass Irland auch bezüglich einer erfolgreichen Unternehmensförderung einen Konsens anstrebt. Eine solche Politik bedarf einer Vielzahl von Ideen und großer Geduld, um sich zu entwickeln. Multinationale Unternehmen – eine wesentliche (aber bei weitem nicht die einzige) Quelle für den bisherigen irischen Exporterfolg – sind groß und kapitalstark genug, um qualifizierte Mitarbeiter zu rekrutieren und Forschung und Entwicklung zu betreiben. Irlands KMU-Sektor wird Fachwissen und den Zugang zu Krediten benötigen, um ebenso zu agieren. Der Erfolg der irischen Politik bei der bisherigen Förderung von Export und Jobs durch den KMU-Sektor zeigt – trotz bedeutender Herausforderungen -, dass Bemühungen in diesem Bereich oft reich belohnt werden. Enterprise Ireland - beim Aufbau einheimischer KMU – wie IDA beim Anwerben großer multinationaler Unternehmen haben schon bisher Erfolge vorzuweisen. Eine verstärkte Zusammenarbeit der beiden sowie eine grössere Rolle der einheimischen KMU als Zulieferer multinationaler Unternehmen verdient größtmöglichen Einsatz.

Bezüglich der siebten Säule des deutschen Mittelstands – Unterstützung für familiengeführte Unternehmen – ist die weltweit verfügbare Unterstützung für deutsche Firmen durch die IHK und das AHK-Netzwerk gewährleistet. Im irischen Fall machen Enterprise Ireland und Irlands hochqualifizierter diplomatischer Dienst ausgezeichnete Arbeit im Interesse irischer Firmen auf der ganzen Welt. Die Fortentwicklung, Integration und kontinuierliche Umorientierung dieses Netzwerks auf neue Prioritäten und neue Chancen hin kann nur zu Irlands Vorteil gereichen.

Abschließend lohnt sich ein Blick auf Bereiche, in denen irische KMU überraschende Ähnlichkeiten mit ihren deutschen Pendants aufweisen.

Dem Monitorbericht zum weltweiten Unternehmertum (Global Entrepreneurship Monitor report[89]) (Tabelle N, Seite 68; Tabelle O, Seite 69) zufolge sind irische Unternehmensgründer um einiges jünger sind als ihre deutschen Pendants. Etablierte Unternehmen kommen tendenziell eher aus Industriezweigen wie der Landwirtschaft und der Fischerei (Tabelle V, Seite 76) als das in Deutschland der Fall ist (3 Prozent). Dies läßt sich negativ bewerten, ist es aber keineswegs. Weltweit gehören Hunderte Millionen von Konsumenten zur Mittelschicht. Irlands Image als Produzent exzellenter Nahrungsmittel stellt einen riesigen Vorteil dar. Dies zielt auf den Kern der Frage, ob Irland einen Mittelstand entwickeln sollte. Die Herausforderung besteht darin, Deutschland nicht einfach zu kopieren. Irland sollte sich Aspekte des deutschen Erfolgs zunutze machen und damit seine ureigenen Vorteile ausschöpfen.

Weitere Details aus dem Bericht lassen darauf schließen: Dies ist auf jeden Fall möglich. Die internationale Ausrichtung (Tabelle R, Seite 72) irischer und deutscher Unternehmer ähnelt sich weitgehend. Der höhere Prozentsatz deutscher Firmen ohne Kunden außerhalb des eigenen Landes (46 Prozent im Vergleich zu 34 Prozent für Irland) spiegelt den größeren Binnenmarkt wider, von dem deutsche KMU profitieren. Regierungspolitik kann helfen, den entsprechenden Nachteil für Irland zu überwinden. Auch macht die irische Fokussierung auf den Sektor des Dienstleistungshandels (in **Kapitel 2** erörtert) den kleinen irischen Binnenmarkt weniger bedeutend. Ohnehin wiegen beim Export von Dienstleistungen die Hindernisse weniger schwer als bei Gütern; und selbst wo es Probleme gibt, haben sie seltener mit der Herausforderung zu tun, zur Kostenerparnis eine bestimmte Größe erreichen zu müssen.

Das vielleicht hoffnungsvollste Zeichen für das Potenzial des irischen KMU-Sektors besteht darin, dass sich irische und deutsche Unternehmer in ihrer Haltung zur Innovation sehr ähneln (Tabelle T, Seite 74). Im Vergleich zu den deutschen Pendants (60 Prozent) bieten weniger der irischen Unternehmer (51 Prozent) nicht schon im Frühstadium ihres Unternehmens ein neues Produkt an. Irische Jungunternehmer (23 Prozent) wenden häufiger als die deutsche Vergleichsgruppe (15 Prozent) neue Technik an. Nur wenn es um die allerneueste Technologie geht, haben die Deutschen (14 Prozent) die Nase knapp vorn (Irland: 8 Prozent).

Kein Wirtschaftsmodell eines Landes lässt sich direkt einem anderen Land überstülpen, ohne dass dabei die nationalen Bedingungen berücksichtigt werden. Davon einmal abgesehen, bieten die übertragbaren Aspekte des deutschen Mittelstands gewaltige Möglichkeiten. Insbesondere die deutsche Langfristorientierung und die damit zusammenhängende Unterstützung durch starke Finanz- und Ausbildungssysteme könnten irischen KMU dienlich sein. Dieser Sektor ist mit logistischen Nachteilen konfrontiert, die deutschen Firmen – mit ihren großen regionalen und nationalen Märkten und ihrem unkomplizierten

---

[89]　Fitzsimons, Paula und O'Gorman, Colm (2013). "Entrepreneurship in Ireland" (Global Entrepreneurship Monitor).

Zugang zu Exportmärkten über Landgrenzen – nicht entstehen. Irland entwickelt jedoch Potenzial im Bereich des Dienstleistungshandels. Mit kontinuierlicher Unterstützung durch staatliche Behörden und gezielten Strategien kann Irland seine eigene Mittelstand-Marke entwickeln, die zu seinen einzigartigen Vorteilen und nationalen Eigenschaften passt.

KAPITEL 8

Irland und Deutschland: Partner im Europäischen Aufschwung

Dr. Joachim Pfeiffer

Hauptaussagen

- Die europäische Schuldenkrise kann zum wichtigen Wendepunkt in der Geschichte Europas werden. Wenn die Europäer aus ihren Fehlern lernen, können der Integrationsprozess und die Bildung einer stabileren Union beschleunigt werden. Nur als Verbund kann Europa seiner Stimme in internationalen Angelegenheiten Geltung verschaffen.
- Wie Irlands erfolgreicher Anpassungsprozess anschaulich zeigt, zeitigen die Reformbemühungen Erfolge. Die europäische Erholung ist insgesamt auf dem richtigen Weg. Angesichts der beträchtlichen, noch verbleibenden Herausforderungen ist es entscheidend, den Reformprozess schwungvoll weiterzuführen. Die fortdauernde Konsolidierung der öffentlichen Finanzen und die Umsetzung von Strukturreformen sind erforderlich, um die Wettbewerbsfähigkeit zu erhöhen und ein anhaltendes Wachstum der Eurozone zu gewährleisten.

Ein Wendepunkt für Europa

Im Rückblick wird man möglicherweise die derzeitige Krise als Wendepunkt auf Europas Weg zur Bildung einer stabileren Union und zu tieferer Integration betrachten. Hoffentlich wird man sich an diesen Moment erinnern als den Zeitpunkt, zu dem Europa seine Kräfte vereinte und die Stärke fand, mit einer Stimme zu sprechen.

Die europäische Schuldenkrise hat Lücken in unserer Wirtschafts- und Währungsunion aufgezeigt. Die Stabilität der Europäischen Union und der Einheitswährung wurde einer ernsten Belastung ausgesetzt. Es ist jedoch Aufgabe aller Mitgliedsstaaten der Eurozone, unsere Union aufrechtzuerhalten und den Herausforderungen entgegenzusehen, die die Zukunft für uns bereithält. Die Schuldenkrise könnte unsere Chance sein, die Widerstandsfähigkeit der Einheitswährung zu erhöhen und einen stärkeren Verbund aufzubauen. Hoffen wir, dass die Bewältigung der Krise uns hilft, unsere Fehler einzusehen und aus ihnen zu lernen. Angesichts der ernsten Probleme in einigen Ländern des Euroraums, die

durch die Krise zutage traten, stehen die Entscheidungsträger in Politik, Wirtschaft und Finanzen vor der Aufgabe, schmerzhafte Reformen und einen fortgesetzten Konsolidierungsprozess voranzutreiben. Dazu gehört auch, insbesondere den Bürgern krisengeschüttelter Länder deutlich zu machen, dass sich ihre Opfer und ihre Geduld während des notwendigen Anpassungsprozesses am Ende auszahlen. Alle Bürger müssen zu den Reformbemühungen beitragen und dabei helfen, einen stabileren Rahmen für Europas Zukunft zu schaffen.

Zunehmend wird deutlich: Europa befindet sich auf dem richtigen Weg und erlebt einen starken Wiederaufschwung nach der schweren Krise, die einige Euromitgliedsstaaten hart getroffen hat. Irlands hat eine eindrucksvolle Entwicklung hinter sich: Als ersten Land erhielt es Hilfe aus der europäischen Finanzstabilitätsfazilität, als erstes Land war es stark genug, das Rettungsprogramm wieder zu verlassen. Irland hat bewiesen, dass die schnelle Umsetzung umfassender Reformen zu Erholung und nachfolgender finanzieller Unabhängigkeit führt. Das Land dient als unverzichtbares Vorbild für den Wiederaufschwung und hat sich in entscheidenden Momenten bei der Führung Europas bewährt, etwa kürzlich während der EU-Ratspräsidentschaft. So spielt Irland eine maßgebliche Rolle bei der Gewährleistung der Stabilität der Union. Darüber hinaus gibt Irlands erfolgreiche Reaktion auf die Krise den Ländern Hoffnung, die derzeit aufgrund grundlegender Strukturprobleme in schwerer Bedrängnis sind. Zum insgesamt positiven Ausblick hat Spaniens Ankündigung beigetragen, in Irlands Fußstapfen zu treten und den Rettungsschirm 2014 zu verlassen. Spaniens und Irlands Ausstieg aus dem Rettungsprogramm ohne weitere Unterstützung beweist, dass die Strategie der Eurogruppe allmählich Ergebnisse zeitigt.

Deutschland hingegen findet sich in der Position eines etwas zögerlichen Anführers in europäischen Wirtschafts- und Finanzfragen wieder, da seine Wirtschaft während der Krise recht stark war. Mit seiner wachstumsorientierten Beschäftigungspolitik, die den einheimischen Konsum stärkte, hoher industrieller Wettbewerbsfähigkeit und seiner Exportstärke war Deutschland in der Lage, die Auswirkungen der Krise auf seine eigene Wirtschaft abzuschwächen. Gleichzeitig hat Deutschland durch sein Angebot außergewöhnlicher Unterstützung für seine europäischen Partner Solidarität gezeigt. Um den Euro zu stärken, hat Deutschland auf Reformen in den von der Krise betroffenen Ländern gedrängt. Manche haben Deutschland dafür kritisiert, andere baten um mehr finanzielle Unterstützung. Freilich darf die deutsche Wirtschaft nicht übermäßig belastet werden, weil dadurch die Stabilität des gesamten Euroraums gefährdet wäre.

Eine stabile deutsche Wirtschaft ist eng an die Stabilität der Europäischen Union geknüpft und umgekehrt. Bei aller wirtschaftlichen Stärke gilt es zu bedenken, dass Deutschland bereits einen Prozess schmerzhafter Reformen hinter sich hat. Er ähnlich jenem, den derzeit einige Länder der Eurozone durchlaufen. Auch Deutschland steht zukünftig vor einer Reihe schwieriger Herausforderungen, nicht zuletzt aufgrund seiner alternden Bevölkerung und seines föderalen Systems.

Um wettbewerbsfähig zu bleiben, wird auch Deutschland zu Strukturreformen gezwungen sein.

In der gesamten Eurozone bleiben noch Herausforderungen zu bewältigen. Um Europas Stärke zu bewahren, muss der Anpassungsprozess, der derzeit in mehreren Ländern abläuft, fortgesetzt werden. Entscheidende Reformen müssen umgesetzt werden und die Bemühungen um finanzielle Konsolidierung müssen fortgeführt werden. Um uns zu vergewissern, dass wir auf dem richtigen Weg sind, sollten wir einen Schritt zurücktreten und zusammenfassen, was bislang erreicht wurde. Dazu gehören die erneute Einschätzung der Ursachen für die Schuldenkrise, die Neubewertung der Maßnahmen zum Anstoß des Anpassungsprozesses und die Identifizierung der verbleibenden Aufgaben. Da sowohl Irland als auch Deutschland effektive Mittel zum Umgang mit der Krise entwickelt haben, können wir bei unserer Analyse auf die jeweiligen Erfahrungen zurückgreifen. Wenn Irland und Deutschland ihre Erkenntnisse teilen, tragen sie dadurch erheblich zur Lösung der Schuldenkrise bei. Angesichts des bereits hohen Grades gegenseitiger Abhängigkeit bieten die aktuellen Herausforderungen eine Reihe von Chancen für eine engere politische Zusammenarbeit in der Zukunft.

Mehrere Fragen sollten uns durch den Prozess des europäischen Wiederaufschwungs führen: Was können wir jeweils aus den deutschen und irischen Erfahrungen während der europäischen Schuldenkrise lernen? Welchen Beitrag können Irland und Deutschland zum europäischen Wiederaufschwung leisten? Was bleibt noch zu tun? Bevor wir uns jedoch der deutschen und der irischen Reaktion auf die Krise zuwenden, ist es wichtig, noch einmal die Ursachen zu betrachten, die zur Krise geführt haben. Dabei müssen wir auch überprüfen, welche Rolle der Euro in der nach ihm benannten Krise wirklich spielte.

Der Euro und die Europäische Schuldenkrise

Europas gegenwärtige Schwierigkeiten werden häufig mit einer Krise seiner Währung gleichgesetzt. Dies zeigt sich in dem häufig verwendeten Begriff der „Eurokrise". Dieser Ausdruck ist irreführend und stellt fälschlicherweise einen Zusammenhang zwischen dem Euro und dem Verlauf der Krise her. Der Euro ist nicht der Ursprung der Krise. Vielmehr wirkte die Währungsunion als Verstärker, der bestehende Strukturprobleme in einigen europäischen Ländern offenlegte und uns daran erinnerte, dass wir über unsere Verhältnisse gelebt hatten.

Tatsächlich hat sich der Euro mehr als ein Jahrzehnt lang – sowohl intern als auch extern – als stabiler erwiesen, als es die D-Mark je war. In der gesamten Geschichte der D-Mark von 1948 bis 2001 stiegen die Preise im Durchschnitt mit einer jährlichen Rate von 2,6 Prozent. Während der ersten zehn Jahre nach Einführung des Euro betrug die Jahresinflation im Euroraum lediglich 1,6 Prozent. Mit seiner Einführung brachte der Euro eine neue Dynamik in den Binnenmarkt, hauptsächlich, indem er ihn effizienter machte. Unter anderem erhöhte er die Preistransparenz, beseitigte Währungsumtauschkosten, senkte die Barrieren für internationalen Handel deutlich

und erhöhte die Mobilität des Arbeitsmarktes. Für Unternehmen hat der Euro Unwägbarkeiten erheblich verringert. Vor Einführung des Euro mussten sich paneuropäische Unternehmen gegen Währungsschwankungen absichern. In einer Währungsunion wurde dies überflüssig, was allein der deutschen Wirtschaft 10 Mrd. Euro pro Jahr spart. Eine Abwertung von Währungen ist unmöglich geworden, was Strukturunterschiede zwischen Ländern der Eurozone klar aufzeigt. Außerdem garantiert der Euro stabile Wechselkurse mit anderen Währungen, wie beispielsweise dem US-Dollar. Wegen seiner starken Wertentwicklung ist der Euro zur zweitwichtigsten Reservewährung nach dem US-Dollar geworden (**Illustrationen 8.1 und 8.2**).

Illustration 8.1: Der Euro-Dollar-Wechselkurs

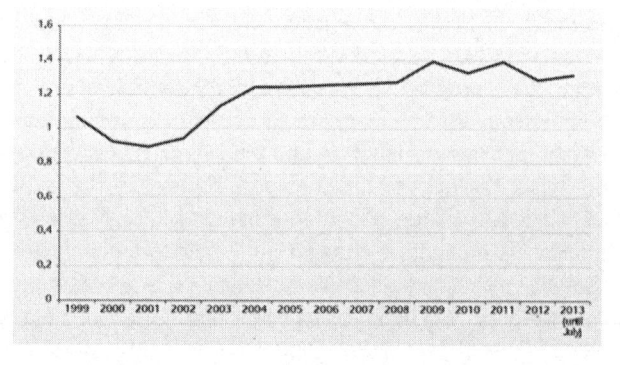

Quelle: Bundesfinanzministerium, 2013, "Auf dem Weg zur Stabilitätsunion".

Illustration 8.2: Der Euro als Weltreservewährung

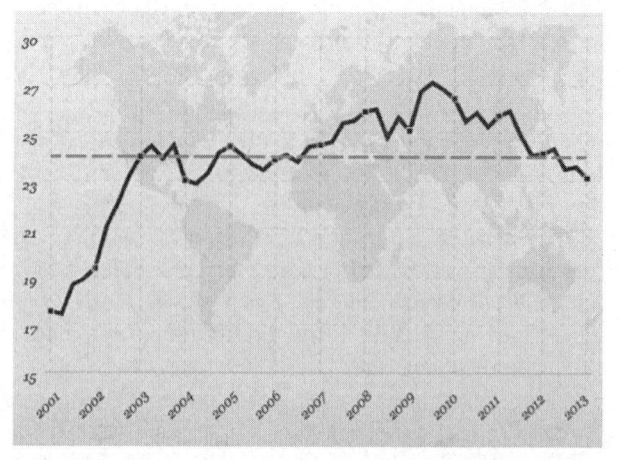

Quelle: Bundesfinanzministerium, "Die Vorteile des Euro".

Die Euroschuldenkrise rührt nicht vom Euro an sich her, sondern hat vielfältige Ursachen. Die wichtigsten davon waren Fehler in der Wirtschafts- und Finanzpolitik und allgemein mangelnde Abstimmung in der Finanzpolitik. Dieses Umfeld gestattete es Staaten im Euroraum, über ihre Verhältnisse zu leben. Wiederholte Haushaltsdefizite, stetig steigende Staatsverschuldung und hohe öffentliche Ausgaben waren das Ergebnis einer relativ laxen Aufsicht. Diese grundlegenden Defizite wurden durch den globalen finanziellen und wirtschaftlichen Abschwung verschlimmert. Die globale Finanz- und Wirtschaftskrise entwickelte sich in vier Phasen bis zur europäischen Schuldenkrise. Zuerst offenbarte die Hypothekenkrise des US-Immobilienmarktes die gefährliche Verknüpfung des Immobilienmarktes mit Finanzprodukten. Hypotheken auf US-amerikanische Wohnhäuser waren in Finanzprodukte verpackt und international gehandelt worden. Der Vertrauensverlust in das internationale Finanzsystem, der aus der Pleite der Lehmann Brothers resultierte, kennzeichnete die zweite Phase der Krise. Als sich dies auf die Realwirtschaft auswirkte, führte dies zur dritten Phase, der globalen Wirtschaftskrise. Die europäische Staatsschuldenkrise stellt die vierte Phase der Krise dar. Zwar hatte diese Schuldenkrise schon zuvor bestanden, doch wurde sie durch das Platzen der Immobilienblase und die Finanzkrise enorm verschlimmert. Wenn dieser Kreislauf nicht unterbrochen wird, könnte die Staatsschuldenkrise zu einer neuen Finanzkrise werden und einen weiteren Teufelskreis in Gang setzen.

Die hohen Staatsschulden, die von einigen Mitgliedern der Eurozone angehäuft wurden, können nicht auf die Einführung der gemeinsamen Währung zurückgeführt werden. Vielmehr resultierten die hohen Schuldenstände aus falschen Prioritäten in der jeweiligen nationalen Wirtschafts- und Finanzpolitik. Die Einführung des Euro verschaffte den heute von der Krise betroffenen Ländern sogar einen gewissen Spielraum. Ab 1995 führte die bloße Ankündigung der neuen Währung zu einer erheblichen Verringerung der Zinssätze, den südliche Länder im Vergleich zu Deutschland auf Staatsanleihen zahlten. Griechenland beispielsweise gab 2005 nur 4,7 Prozent seines Bruttoinlandsproduktes (BIP) für Zinszahlungen aus, im Vergleich zu mehr als 11 Prozent Mitte der 1990er Jahre. Doch statt eine Politik zur Erhöhung ihrer Wettbewerbsfähigkeit zu verfolgen, erhöhten Länder wie Griechenland und Portugal ihre Staatsausgaben deutlich, und das schon vor der jüngsten Eskalation der Krise. Der öffentliche Sektor wurde aufgebläht, die Sozialausgaben wurden massiv ausgeweitet – im Falle Griechenlands von etwa 19 Prozent des BIP im Jahr 1995 auf mehr als 25 Prozent im Jahr 2007. In Portugal war der Anstieg der Sozialausgaben ähnlich drastisch. Gleichzeitig verlor die Wirtschaft dieser Länder an Wettbewerbsfähigkeit. Das Ergebnis dieser Politik sind hohe Staatsschulden und mangelnde Strukturreformen, aufgrund dessen die Wettbewerbsfähigkeit der Wirtschaft massiv geschwächt ist.

Der Euro ist nicht an der europäischen Schuldenkrise schuld – diese Erkenntnis stellt den ersten Schritt dar auf dem Weg zu einer europäischen Stabilitätsunion. Als Europäer müssen wir das enorme Potenzial erkennen, das uns auf dem Weg der Integration in Aussicht steht. Bereits jetzt vereint der Euro einen der weltweit

größten Handelsblöcke. Um jedoch Europas ganzes wirtschaftliches Potenzial umzusetzen, müssen wir mehrere Fehler ausmerzen, die dem Aufbau unserer Währungsunion innewohnen. Dieser Prozess struktureller und finanzieller Anpassungen beinhaltet eine deutliche Verringerung hoher Schuldenstände.

Europäisches Krisenmanagement

Die Ausbreitung der Krise hätte die Stabilität der Eurozone und der Einheitswährung beeinträchtigt. Um dies zu verhindern, haben wir in einer gemeinsamen europäischen Anstrengung verschiedene Maßnahmen umgesetzt, die auf europäischer und auf nationaler Ebene ansetzen und die Hauptsäulen einer nachhaltigen Wirtschafts- und Finanzarchitektur für die Eurozone bilden. Dadurch haben wir den Weg geebnet, damit die Eurozone ihre Wettbewerbsfähigkeit verbessern und ihre Wachstumsraten erhöhen kann.

Die europäische Ebene

Maßgebliche Fortschritte wurden dabei erzielt, die europäische Wirtschafts- und Währungsunion auf ein stärkeres institutionelles Fundament zu setzen. Da dem Maastricht-Vertrag ein wirksamer Durchsetzungsmechanismus fehlte, war es Frankreich und Deutschland möglich, gegen die im Vertrag festgelegten Defizitkriterien zu verstoßen und damit schon frühzeitig zu einer Verwässerung des Vertragsrahmens beizutragen. Im Jahr nach der Eurobargeldumstellung setzte dieses Verhalten frühzeitig in der Geschichte von Europas Einheitswährung falsche Maßstäbe. Als Folge der Krise haben die Regierungschefs der Eurozone mehrere Instrumente und Maßnahmen vereinbart, mit denen eine stabilere, wettbewerbsfähige und zukunftsfähige Eurozone aufgebaut werden soll. Diese umfassen unter anderem eine verschärfte EU-Haushaltsüberwachung mit Hilfe des Europäischen Fiskalpaktes; einen stärkeren Stabilitäts- und Wachstumspakt; die verbesserte Abstimmung im Bereich der Wirtschaftspolitik, beispielsweise durch den Euro-Plus-Pakt und das Europäische Semester; und höhere Standards für die Regulierung der Finanzmärkte. Am 22. November 2013 wertete die Eurogruppe erstmalig die Stellungnahmen der Kommission zu nationalen Haushaltsentwürfen und den finanziellen Ausblick für die Eurozone insgesamt aus.

Die Bankenunion ist unter den verbleibenden Aufgaben von höchster Wichtigkeit, da sie dabei hilft, das Vertrauen der Märkte in den Euro wiederherzustellen. Durch den Aufbau einer gemeinsamen europäischen Bankenaufsicht bei der Europäischen Zentralbank EZB stehen wirksame Instrumente zur Verfügung, damit nationale Bankenkrisen nicht auf die Realwirtschaft durchschlagen. So wie Banken immer stärker europäisiert werden, müssen sich auch die Aufsichtsstrukturen an das sich veränderte Umfeld anpassen. Als zweite Säule der Bankenunion dient der Mechanismus zur Bankenabwicklung (SRM) mit einem Bankenabwicklungsfonds (SRF) als Mittel, um weitere

Bankenrettungen durch den Steuerzahler zu verhindern. Der von den europäischen Finanzministern am 18. Dezember 2013 erzielte Kompromiss wird gewährleisten, dass die Kosten zur Abwicklung zuerst den Anteilseignern und Gläubigern auferlegt werden. Nur wenn dies nicht ausreicht, wird der von den Banken gespeiste SRF zur Abdeckung zusätzlicher Kosten herangezogen. Wir brauchen eindeutige Regeln für die Gläubigerbeteiligung im Krisenfall. Es muß klar sein, wer die Kosten eines Mangels an Eigenkapital trägt, den der Stresstest von 2014 möglicherweise offenbart. Außerdem ist der im Europäischen Stabilitätsmechanismus (ESM) enthaltene Krisenbewältigungsmechanismus ein weiteres Merkmal der verbesserten institutionellen Architektur der Eurozone.

Über die Rettungsfonds wurde den von der Krise betroffenen Ländern umfangreiche finanzielle Unterstützung gewährt. Darüber hinaus war die Erhöhung des Kapitals der Europäischen Investitionsbank ein Schritt in die richtige Richtung, mit dem private Investitionen gefördert werden und die europäische Wachstumsagenda unterstützt wird. Im Kampf gegen die hohe Jugendarbeitslosigkeit in Europa – sie betrug im Oktober 2013 im Euroraum 24,4 Prozent – wurden mehrere europäische und nationale Initiativen auf den Weg gebracht, weil sich Europa keine „verlorene Generation" leisten kann. Auf dem Gipfel zur Jugendarbeitslosigkeit in Paris im November 2013 haben die europäischen Regierungschefs Strategien entwickelt, um jungen Menschen in ganz Europa Sicherheit zu bieten. Die finanziellen Instrumente, die zur Lösung dieses äußerst wichtigen Problems erforderlich sind, stehen ab Januar 2014 durch den 6 Mrd. Euro starken EU-Fonds für junge Menschen bereit. Unterdessen müssen wir uns auf die Schaffung größerer Flexibilität und Mobilität auf dem Arbeitsmarkt konzentrieren, da das Angebot einer tragfähigen Perspektive für Europas junge Generation entscheidend für Europas Zukunft ist.

Zusätzlich zu den Maßnahmen auf europäischer Ebene musste jedes Land seine eigene Strategie im Umgang mit der Krise entwickeln. Im Angesicht schwerwiegender einheimischer Ungleichgewichte beschloss Irland ein ehrgeiziges Anpassungsprogramm. Der Blick auf Irlands Erfahrungen hilft uns, die Wirksamkeit der bisherigen Politik zu bewerten.

Irlands rasche und umfassende Rückkehr in die Märkte - vom Keltischen Tiger zum europäischen Vorreiter

Als erstes Land, das das EU/IWF-Hilfsprogramm in Anspruch genommen hatte, kehrte Irland im Dezember 2013 in die Märkte zurück. Irlands Beispiel verdeutlicht: Die Kombination aus finanzieller Konsolidierung und der Umsetzung von Strukturreformen zahlt sich am Ende aus. Nach drei Quartalen mit negativen Raten hat das Wachstum im September 2013 wieder zugenommen. Für 2014 wird ein Wachstum des BIP um 2 Prozent prognostiziert. Die Ankündigung der irischen Regierung, dass kein Nachfolgeprogramm erforderlich sein wird, ist ein weiterer Beleg für Irlands wiedergewonnene Stärke. Mit der Erfüllung aller vom Anpassungsprogramm festgelegten Zielvorgaben ist Irland in den letzten drei

Jahren zum Vorbild für andere von der Krise betroffene Länder geworden. Irlands Entscheidung gibt den Märkten und den internationalen Kreditgebern die Sicherheit, dass die umfangreichen Austeritätsmaßnahmen ihr Vertrauen verdienen. Irland ist nun in der Lage, eine tragfähige Rückkehr in die Märkte vorzunehmen, und benötigt dafür keine weiteren Darlehen.

Bei der Analyse der irischen Wirtschaftsleistung müssen wir die spezifischen Umstände berücksichtigen, die zum Ausbruch der Schuldenkrise in Irland geführt haben. Im Gegensatz zu anderen Ländern war die Krise in Irland vornehmlich eine Bankenkrise. Bevor Irland 2008 von der Finanzkrise getroffen wurde, hatte das Land einen soliden Haushalt, die Staatsschulden waren gering. Anders als in Griechenland gab es im Falle Irlands keine Misswirtschaft der öffentlichen Hand, der man die Schuld an der Krise geben könnte. Stattdessen führten niedrige Zinssätze und eine Bankenaufsicht, die sich im Nachhinein als zu lax herausstellte, zu einer ungehinderten Ausweitung der Bankendarlehen. Dies feuerte eine Zunahme des Konsums an und nährte eine wachsende Immobilienblase, wobei der Immobilienmarkt 2007/2008 seinen Höhepunkt erlebte. Das Platzen der Blase machte Abschreibungen von Eigenheimkrediten erforderlich, was wiederum die Bankenkrise verursachte. Infolgedessen sah sich die irische Regierung gezwungen, für die Verbindlichkeiten der Banken zu garantieren und die Banken mit frischem Kapital auszustatten. Um Irlands schwer belasteten Haushalt zu entlasten, sorgte das EU/IWF-Rettungsprogramm für finanzielle Hilfen in Höhe von etwa 68 Mrd. Euro.

Was Irland von anderen Krisenstaaten unterscheidet, ist die ebenso schnelle wie umfassende Reaktion auf die Krise. Im Gegenzug für die finanzielle Hilfe willigte Irland in eine Verkleinerung und Umstrukturierung seines Bankensystems sowie die Konsolidierung seiner öffentlichen Finanzen ein und gelobte ferner, die erforderlichen Maßnahmen für mehr Wachstum zu ergreifen. Durch nachhaltige Bemühungen um die Kürzung von Ausgaben und Erhöhung der Einnahmen hat Irland stetige Fortschritte bei der kontinuierlichen Verringerung seines Defizits gemacht. Seit Ausbruch der Krise in Irland im Jahr 2008 sind Ausgabenkürzungen und Steuererhöhungen von insgesamt 28 Mrd. Euro aufgelaufen, was 17 Prozent des heutigen BIP entspricht. Der jüngste Haushalt von Finanzminister Michael Noonan enthielt weitere Ausgabenkürzungen von 2,5 Mrd. Euro. Es wird erwartet, dass das Haushaltsdefizit 2014 mit 4,8 Prozent des BIP unter der Grenze von 5,1 Prozent bleiben wird, die das gemäß dem Stabilitäts- und Wachstumspakt eingeführte Defizitverfahren (EDP) vorgibt. Ferner will die irische Regierung das Defizit im Jahr 2015 auf weniger als 3 Prozent senken. Angesichts des Defizithöchststandes von fast 31 Prozent des BIP im Jahr 2010 sind diese Zahlen bemerkenswert.

Neben der Konsolidierung der öffentlichen Finanzen hat Irland Strukturreformen durchgeführt, die zur Ankurbelung der Wirtschaft dienen. Als Stütze für Irlands zunehmende Wettbewerbsfähigkeit sind die Lohnstückkosten

erheblich gesunken. Genauer gesagt sind die nominalen Lohnstückkosten im Zeitraum von 2009 bis 2013 um geschätzte zehn Prozent zurückgegangen.

In Kombination mit der Verkleinerung und Umstrukturierung seines Bankensystems hat Irland bedeutende Fortschritte in seiner wirtschaftlichen Erholung erzielt und alle von der Troika der internationalen Geldgeber festgelegten Zielvorgaben erfüllt. Der insgesamt positive Ausblick macht sich an mehreren ermutigenden Indikatoren fest. Die Warenexporte, der Einzelhandel und die Zuversicht der Verbraucher wachsen. Da sein Wachstum zum großen Teil vom Außenhandel getragen wird, hat Irland seit 2010 einen Leistungsbilanzüberschuss erwirtschaftet. Der Immobilienmarkt setzt seine Erholung fort. Darüber hinaus werden Irlands Entschlossenheit und harte Austeritätsmaßnahmen durch das Vertrauen der Märkte belohnt, das sich verbessert hat und sich auch weiterhin verbessern wird. Die Renditen auf irische Staatsanleihen mit einer Laufzeit von 10 Jahren sind von zweistelligen Zahlen auf unter 4 Prozent erheblich zurückgegangen.

Deutschland – ein starker Partner in der Krise

Deutschland ist bisher recht erfolgreich mit der Krise umgegangen. Die deutsche Wirtschaft ist von 2009 bis 2013 mit einer geschätzten Rate von 8,5 Prozent kontinuierlich gewachsen. Für die Analyse, warum Deutschland der Krise im Großen und Ganzen getrotzt hat, lassen sich mehrere entscheidende Faktoren nennen.

Die Konsolidierung unserer öffentlichen Finanzen hat es der deutschen Regierung ermöglicht, einen strukturell ausgeglichenen Haushalt für 2014 vorzulegen. Seit 2010 hat Deutschland sein strukturelles Defizit von etwa 46 Mrd. Euro auf Null reduziert. Die Neuverschuldung wurde auf 6,4 Mrd. Euro verringert, der geringste Betrag seit 40 Jahren. Wie im Stabilitäts- und Wachstumspakt festgelegt, müssen die Staaten des Euroraums ihre Verschuldung auf unter 60 Prozent ihrer Wirtschaftsleistung verringern. Deutschlands neue Große Koalition hat vereinbart, die Schuldenquote innerhalb von 10 Jahren von 81 Prozent Ende 2012 auf weniger als 60 Prozent des BIP zu senken.

Neben der finanziellen Konsolidierung sind eine starke Industrie wie auch der Mittelstand entscheidende Standbeine unserer Wirtschaft. Mit seiner hohen Flexibilität und seinem Angebot einer breiten Produktpalette ist der deutsche Mittelstand außergewöhnlich wettbewerbsfähig. Da die anderen Erfolgsfaktoren des deutschen Mittelstandes ausführlich in **Kapitel 7** behandelt werden, verzichte ich hier auf weitere Einzelheiten.

Die Arbeitsmarktreformen, die wir vor einigen Jahren durchgeführt haben, bilden einen weiteren Eckpfeiler unserer heutigen relativen Stärke. Insgesamt erhöhten diese Reformen die Flexibilität des Arbeitsmarktes mit Hilfe mehrerer grundlegender Instrumente. Zunächst wurde die Niedriglohnbeschäftigung ausgebaut, insbesondere mit Hilfe der sogenannten Minijobs. Sie brachten nicht nur viele Menschen in Arbeit, sondern verringerten auch die Anreize für illegale

Arbeit. Darüber hinaus bewirkten die Reformen der Agenda 2010 auch eine Ausweitung der Zeitarbeit. Indem es Unternehmen Spielraum bei der Anpassung an Veränderungen der Nachfrage gibt, ist Zeitarbeit ein wirksames Instrument, um den Menschen die Rückkehr in Arbeit zu ermöglichen. Zusätzlich wurde während der Krise Kurzarbeit eingeführt, um Arbeitslosigkeit zu verhindern. Im Ergebnis dieser Reformen hat sich der deutsche Arbeitsmarkt als außerordentlich widerstandsfähig erwiesen. Mit Ausnahme eines leichten Anstiegs während des finanziellen und wirtschaftlichen Abschwungs 2008-2009 ist die Arbeitslosigkeit seit 2005 deutlich zurückgegangen. Im September 2013 betrug die Arbeitslosenquote in Deutschland 5,2 Prozent. Dies macht Deutschland nach Österreich (4,9 Prozent) zu dem Land mit der zweitniedrigsten Arbeitslosenquote unter den 28 EU-Mitgliedsstaaten. Mit mehr als 42 Mio Menschen in Beschäftigung haben wir einen historischen Höchststand erreicht. Die Stärke unseres Arbeitsmarktes wird sogar noch deutlicher, wenn man sie in einem größeren Zusammenhang betrachtet. Entgegen dem allgemeinen OECD-Trend ist die Arbeitslosigkeit in Deutschland während der Rezession 2008-2009 kaum gestiegen und seit 2009 stetig gefallen (**Illustration 8.3**). Allerdings war unsere Wirtschaft nicht immer so stark. Vor einem Jahrzehnt, als wir immer noch mit den Kosten der Wiedervereinigung zu kämpfen hatten, wurde Deutschland der „kranke Mann Europas" genannt. Der Wiederaufschwung kam nicht über Nacht und erforderte, dass Deutschland einen Weg harter Strukturreformen ging.

Illustration 8.3: Arbeitslosigkeit in Deutschland

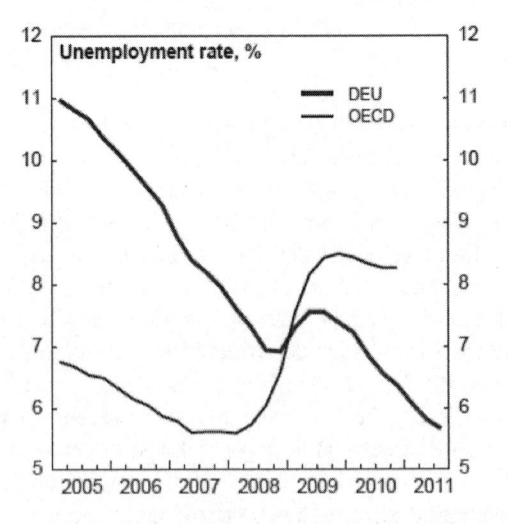

Unemployment rate = Arbeitslosenquote
Quelle: OECD, Better Life, *Datensammlungen „Economic Outlook" und „National Accounts".*

Zu den von der deutschen Wirtschaftspolitik erkannten Hauptthemen gehören die Bereiche Bildung sowie Forschung, Entwicklung und Innovation. Sie bilden die Grundlage für langfristigen wirtschaftlichen Erfolg und Wohlstand in Deutschland. Mit zusätzlichen Investitionen von mehr als 13 Mrd. Euro in die Bildung und Forschung während der vorherigen Legislaturperiode haben wir einen entscheidenden Impuls gesetzt, der das zukünftige Wachstum fördert. Als eine der Hauptsäulen des deutschen Bildungssystems hat uns das duale System der Berufsausbildung zur niedrigsten Jugendarbeitslosenquote in Europa verholfen. Andere Länder wie Österreich, Dänemark und die Schweiz haben ebenfalls sehr von diesem System profitiert. Die Förderung der Ausbildung hochqualifizierter Arbeitskräfte ist äußerst wichtig, wenn wir die allgemeine Stärke der deutschen Wirtschaft aufrechterhalten wollen, besonders die der deutschen Industrie und des Mittelstandes. So lautet eine vitale Erkenntnis: Ausgebildete Facharbeiter sind für unsere Wirtschaft ebenso wichtig wie akademische Bildung.

Als größte Volkswirtschaft der Europäischen Union hat Deutschland geholfen, den umfassenden Reformprozess in der Eurozone in Gang zu setzen. Gestützt auf seine robuste Wirtschaft hat es seine Solidarität mit Ländern gezeigt, die unter der Krise leiden. Deutschland hat stark von der politischen und ökonomischen Stabilität profitiert, welche die Europäische Union bietet, und erkennt seine große Verantwortung für die Zukunft der Union und der Einheitswährung an. Kurz gesagt: Europas Einigkeit ist lebenswichtig für Deutschland.

Anpassungsprozesse ähnlich dem in Deutschland sind in einer Reihe von Ländern der Eurozone zu beobachten. Zwar erfordern diese Prozesse weiterhin ein hohes Maß an Ausdauer und Engagement von vielen Bürgern in krisengeschüttelten Ländern, doch ist es wichtig zu bedenken, dass die Reformen einige Zeit brauchen, um zu greifen.

Strukturreformen und Konsolidierung zeitigen Ergebnisse

Im Einklang mit dem von Irland erzielten Erfolg beginnt auch der Anpassungsprozess in ganz Europa Ergebnisse zu zeigen. Die Kombination aus institutionellen Reformen auf europäischer Ebene und Strukturreformen sowie die Konsolidierung der öffentlichen Finanzen auf nationaler Ebene haben sich als wirksam erwiesen. Insgesamt haben wir festgestellt, dass die Ungewissheiten, die im Zusammenhang mit der Staatsschuldenkrise aufgetreten sind, größtenteils überwunden wurden. Es wurde eine deutliche Verringerung der öffentlichen Haushaltsdefizite in Ländern des Euroraums erreicht. Mit einem Durchschnittswert von 3,7 Prozent des BIP im zweiten Quartal 2013 sind die Defizite im Vergleich zu 6,4 Prozent im Jahr 2009 deutlich geschrumpft. Das US-Haushaltsdefizit dagegen beläuft sich 2013 laut Congressional Budget Office auf 4,1 Prozent des BIP. Mit deutlich sinkenden Lohnstückkosten in den von der Krise betroffenen europäischen Ländern sind die einzelnen Volkswirtschaften wettbewerbsfähiger geworden. Dementsprechend nehmen die Exporte zu, und die nationalen Leistungsbilanzen in der Eurozone haben sich verbessert. Krisenländer haben deutliche Senkungen ihrer Leistungsbilanzdefizite erreicht. Griechenlands

Defizit ist beispielsweise drastisch von 18 Prozent des BIP auf geschätzte 2,8 Prozent im Jahr 2013 zurückgegangen (**Illustration 8.4**).

Illustration 8.4: Leistungsbilanzen

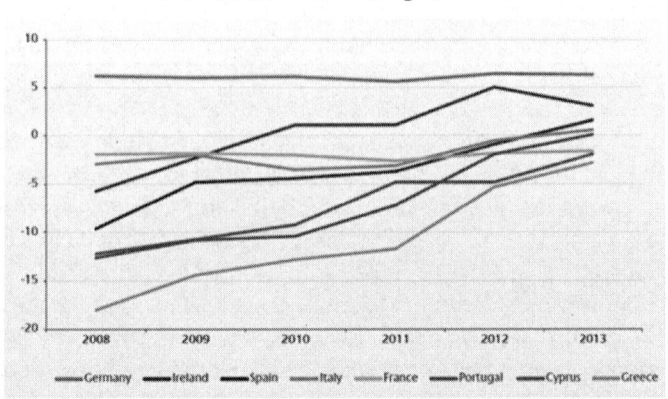

Länder: Germany = Deutschland; Ireland = Irland; Spain = Spanien; Italy = Italien; France = Frankreich; Portugal = Portugal; Cyprus = Zypern; Greece = Griechenland.
Quelle: Bundesfinanzministerium, 2013: *Auf dem Weg zur Stabilitätsunion.*

Dem positiven Trend entsprechend wuchs die Wirtschaft in der Eurozone im zweiten Quartal 2013 im Vergleich zum vorherigen Quartal um 0,3 Prozent. Es wird erwartet, dass das Wachstum im Verlaufe des Jahres 2014 allmählich mehr von der Binnennachfrage getragen und robuster sein wird.

Der Weg vor uns

Im Hinblick auf Irlands Zukunft hat Premierminister (Taoiseach) Enda Kenny korrekt festgestellt, dass trotz der enormen Fortschritte immer noch „schwierige ökonomische Entscheidungen" vor Irland liegen. Unter den verbleibenden Herausforderungen sind Arbeitslosigkeit und Abwanderung die dringlichsten Probleme. Im September 2013 betrug die Arbeitslosenquote in Irland 13,6 Prozent. Immer noch verlassen jeden Monat etwa 3.000 Menschen das Land. Außerdem erzeugt Irlands exportorientierte Wirtschaft eine starke Abhängigkeit vom globalen Wirtschaftswachstum. Langfristig muss die Inlandsnachfrage gestärkt werden, die Bedingungen für Investitionen sollten noch besser werden. Dies ist ein kritischer Moment in Irlands Erholung ebenso wie ein wichtiger Moment für Europas Zukunft. Mit der Hilfe seiner europäischen Partner muss Irland den erfolgreichen Reformprozess fortsetzen. Die neue mittelfristige Wirtschaftsstrategie („Medium Term Economic Strategy") wie auch das erneute Bekenntnisses zur Verringerung der Kreditaufnahme der öffentlichen Hand unterstreichen die Entschlossenheit der Regierung, den Reformeifer beizubehalten.

Obwohl Deutschland in der Krise beträchtliche Widerstandskraft gezeigt hat, liegen auch vor uns große Herausforderungen. Das Land kann es sich nicht leisten, die Reformbemühungen zu stoppen. Stattdessen müssen wir eine ehrgeizige Agenda 2030 erarbeiten, um unsere zukünftige Wettbewerbsfähigkeit und dauerhafte Wachstumsraten zu gewährleisten. Deutschland muss wie alle anderen Länder der Eurozone weitere Reformen anpacken. Erstens müssen die Einschränkungen durch das derzeitige System des deutschen Föderalismus gelockert werden; zweitens müssen wir einen ständigen Prozess der Innovation fördern, beispielsweise durch steuerliche Anreize im Bereich der Forschung; drittens müssen wir erheblich in Infrastruktur investieren. Vor allem brauchen wir Rezepte gegen die rasche Überalterung der Bevölkerung, die sich zunehmend auf den Arbeitsmarkt auswirkt. Dabei spielen wirksame Instrumente gegen den Fachkräftemangel eine wichtige Rolle. Um qualifizierte Arbeitskräfte aus dem Ausland anzuwerben, wurde eine Fachkräftekampagne gestartet; das Berufsbildungsprogramm sorgt für unsere zukünftigen Facharbeiter; schliesslich streben wir an, die Erfahrungen und das Potenzial unserer älteren Arbeitnehmer effektiver zu nutzen. Darüber hinaus wollen wir mit einer Fachkräfte-Initiative die Aufmerksamkeit der Entscheidungsträger in Politik, Wirtschaft und den Gewerkschaften auf die Wichtigkeit dieser Frage lenken und zur Zusammenarbeit in diesem Bereich ermuntern.

Vor dem Hintergrund der fundamentalen Herausforderungen, vor denen Europa steht, brauchen wir eine starke Partnerschaft für Konsolidierung und Erholung. Sowohl Irlands gutes Beispiel – das sich in Opferbereitschaft und schnellen Anpassungen zeigt – als auch Deutschlands Stärke bei der Unterstützung des Euro sind Beispiele dieser europäischen Partnerschaft. Die Lösung der Krise bietet sogar neue Möglichkeiten für intensivere Zusammenarbeit. Deutschland und Irland haben eine gemeinsame Initiative vereinbart, um die Finanzierung der Realwirtschaft zu verbessern und den Zugang zu Finanzmitteln für Irlands KMU zu vereinfachen. Zu diesem Zweck soll in Kürze eine Zusammenarbeit zwischen KfW und den irischen Behörden beginnen.

Im Hinblick auf die gesamte Eurozone gibt es mehrere Kernprobleme. In vielen Ländern ist sowohl die private wie auch die öffentliche Verschuldung nach wie vor hoch. Angesichts einer Arbeitslosenquote von 12,1 Prozent in der Eurozone im Oktober 2013 muss noch mehr getan werden, um eine höhere Arbeitsmarktflexibilität und -mobilität zu erzeugen (**Illustration 8.5**).

Illustration 8.5: Arbeitslosenquoten in der EU (Oktober 2013, saisonbereinigt)

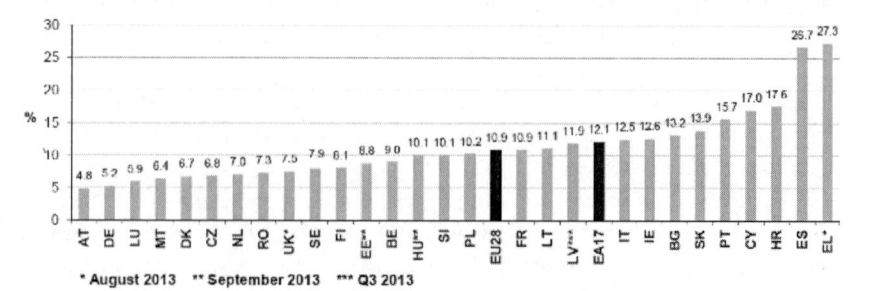

* August 2013 ** September 2013 *** Q3 2013

Quelle: Eurostat-Pressemitteilung *euroindicators,* November 2013.

Um zukünftige Krisen zu vermeiden, muss die Bankenregulierung vorangetrieben werden. Denn die derzeitige bevorzugte aufsichtstechnische Behandlung von staatlichen Risiken reicht nicht aus und ermuntert die Finanzinstitute dazu, in Staatsanleihen zu investieren. Diese potenziell gefährliche Verflechtung zwischen Staaten und Banken muss aufgelöst werden. Banken sollten ihre Bestände an Staatsanleihen durch Eigenkapital absichern müssen. Anderenfalls ist ihre Solvenz durch einen staatlichen Zahlungsausfall direkt gefährdet, was zu einer weiteren Finanzkrise führen könnte. Gleichzeitig setzt dies falsche Anreize, da in Staatsanleihen investiertes Kapital nicht für Investitionen in kleine und mittelständische Unternehmen zur Verfügung steht.

Wie die Eurogruppe zum Ausdruck brachte, müssen die von der Krise betroffenen Länder ihre Reformdynamik aufrechterhalten, um die verbleibenden Herausforderungen zu meistern und einen nachhaltigen Wiederaufschwung zu gewährleisten. Deutschland wird seine Partner in ihren fortgesetzten Reformbemühungen unterstützen. Ähnlich dem Prozess, den Deutschland und Irland durchlaufen haben, ist es wichtig, dass jedes einzelne Mitglied der Eurozone seinen Beitrag leistet und Probleme zuerst auf der nationalen Ebene zu lösen versucht. Damit die Währungsunion funktioniert, ist es unerlässlich, dass jeder seine Hausaufgaben macht. Insbesondere die irischen Erfahrungen zeigen uns, dass es keine Alternative zur Konsolidierung der öffentlichen Finanzen und zu Strukturreformen gibt.

Schlussfolgerungen

Trotz aller Unkenrufe haben der Euro und die EU überlebt, sie konsolidieren und erholen sich. Nun ist es äußerst wichtig, dass die Eurozone weitergeht auf dem Weg zu einer Union der Stabilität, mit gemeinsamen Werten, glaubwürdigen Regeln und klaren Sanktionen. Wir können es uns nicht leisten, die notwendige zukünftige Konsolidierung aus dem Auge zu verlieren. Es ist unerlässlich, dass wir

unsere Währungsunion auf eine solide finanzielle Basis gründen und weiterhin stetig das institutionelle Fundament unserer Wirtschafts- und Währungsunion verbessern. Unterdessen müssen wir den Reformprozess in Gang halten und hart daran arbeiten, unseren Anspruch, ein respektierter Partner in der Weltwirtschaft zu sein, zu untermauern. Als Schlüssel zu Wachstum und Beschäftigung ist die Wettbewerbsfähigkeit der ausschlaggebende Faktor bei der Sicherung von Europas zukünftigem Wohlstand.

Europas Zukunft wird nicht durch die Handlungen einzelner Staaten wie Griechenland, Irland oder Deutschland bestimmt. Vielmehr hängt sie davon ab, was wir als Union zu erreichen in der Lage sind. Es geht um Europa als Wirtschaftsmacht, die sich in einem ständigen Prozess der Zusammenarbeit und des Wettbewerbs mit anderen Mächten befindet. Wenn Europa eine signifikante Rolle neben anderen Großmächten wie den USA oder China spielen soll, müssen die europäischen Staaten ihre Kräfte vereinen. Der zukünftige europäische Integrationsprozess sollte sich über ein breites Spektrum politischer Bereiche erstrecken, darunter auch die Außen- und Sicherheitspolitik. Unterdessen bietet die Krise die Chance für eine weitere Integration des Arbeitsmarktes, da sie eine größere Flexibilität und Mobilität erfordert. Die Staatsschuldenkrise hat nicht nur Lücken in unserer monetären Union aufgezeigt, sondern auch unsere Schritte zu einer tiefgreifenderen Integration beschleunigt. Wie der Binnenmarkt ist der Euro gleichzeitig ein unverzichtbares Instrument für die europäische Integration wie auch ein Bekenntnis zu ihr. Nun liegt es an uns allen, den Weg zur Bildung eines vereinigten Europas weiterzugehen. Kurz gesagt: Eine stabile Einheitswährung bildet die Grundlage für ein stärkeres Europa. Die Gewährleistung der europäischen Währungsunion wird auch in Zukunft weiterhin eine Reihe mutiger politischer Entscheidungen erfordern. Durch Partnerschaft und Engagement können Irland und Deutschland dazu beitragen, die europäische Integration auf die nächste Stufe zu heben.

Die erheblichen Fortschritte der krisenbetroffenen Länder, allen voran Irland, sollten uns dazu ermutigen, die derzeitige Krise als Wendepunkt zu sehen, der zu einer nachhaltigen europäischen Wirtschafts- und Finanzpolitik führt. Wir müssen uns unserer Optionen und des immensen Wertes Europas und unserer gemeinsamen Währung bewusster werden. Ohne den Euro würde sich Europas Macht, auf die internationale Politik Einfluss nehmen und seine Interessen durchsetzen zu können, dramatisch vermindern. Die Einheitswährung stärkt Europas Wachstumspotenzial und seine Wirtschaftskraft insgesamt. Der Euro ist im Grunde eine permanente Erinnerung an die Notwendigkeit unserer Zusammenarbeit und ein Vorbote der zukünftigen Stärke eines vereinten Europas.

Was haben europäische Staaten getan, um zur Stabilität zurückzukehren?

Dr. Volker Treier

Hauptaussagen

- Die Wirtschaftskrise spiegelt nicht nur systemische Probleme der globalen und europäischen Volkswirtschaften wider, sondern auch Fehler in den einzelnen Mitgliedsstaaten. Eine Mischung aus europaweiter Aktion und nationalen Reformen überwindet die Krise schrittweise. Ein zunehmend stabiler Euro, sich bessernde Finanzsalden der Regierungen und steigende Exporte sind Zeichen dafür, dass die Lage in Europa besser ist, als sie scheint.
- Ein Vergleich der irischen Leistung mit anderen Anpassungsprogrammen zeigt, dass Irland seine Sache gut gemacht hat, aber auch, wie viele große Herausforderungen auf europäischer und auf nationaler Ebene weiterhin bestehen, Herausforderungen, die trotz seiner heilsamen Leistungen in mancher Hinsicht auch für Irland gelten.

Einleitung

Der amerikanische Schriftsteller Mark Twain hat einst gesagt: "Wagners Musik ist besser, als sie klingt". Treffender lässt sich die Situation in Europa derzeit kaum beschreiben. Europa steht fundamental betrachtet heute schon wieder besser dar, als vielfach gedacht.

Bevor der Blick auf die erzielten Fortschritte fällt, ist es wichtig, sich die zentralen Ursachen der Krise vor Augen zu führen:

- **Das billige Geld**: Kredite gab es bis 2009 gerade in den USA für jeden – auch ohne Sicherheiten. Europäische Banken und Anleger haben Verbriefungen daraus gekauft – und das ungeprüft! Aber nicht nur die Häuslebauer in den USA, auch die Immobilienmärkte in Europa haben vom billigen Geld profitiert.
- **„Politik auf Pump"**: Die Politik versprach und der Wähler – auch die Wirtschaft – hat gefordert, die Versprechungen einzulösen. Man hat sich daran gewöhnt, dem Staat mehr Leistungen abzuverlangen, als auf Basis von laufenden Einnahmen möglich war. Oder einfacher: Politik hat mit

Rabatt verkauft und die Schnäppchen wurden mitgenommen. Und dieses Spiel galt nicht nur in Euroland: In Japan, den USA oder England ist die Schuldenquote zum Teil noch viel höher gestiegen als in den Ländern der Eurozone.

- **Die Kultur des „Nichthinsehens":** Jeder hätte wissen können, wie hoch die Staatsverschuldung in Griechenland wirklich war. Das Ausmaß der Immobilienkredite der spanischen Banken war kein Staatsgeheimnis. Und wie schlecht die Jugendlichen in vielen Mitgliedsstaaten tatsächlich ausgebildet sind, ist auch bekannt. Es wurde nicht genau hingeschaut oder die Daten nicht ernst genommen. Jetzt kann keiner mehr an den Realitäten vorbei!

Ein Geburtsfehler der Währungsunion war ganz sicher zudem, dass die Koordination der Wirtschafts- und Finanzpolitik in Europa untereinander unzureichend war. Und dass ausgerechnet die europäischen Schwergewichte Frankreich und Deutschland den Stabilitäts- und Wachstumspakt im Jahr 2005 aufgeweicht haben, war nicht hilfreich.

Europa hat durch die Krise an Ansehen verloren. Zum Wiederaufbau von Vertrauen gehört, dass die europäische Politik jetzt konsequent auf Wachstum und Beschäftigung sowie auf die Solidität von Staatshaushalten und Finanzmärkten ausgerichtet wird. Ein „Weiter so!" darf es nicht geben und gibt es auch nicht.

Die EU und die Euro-Staaten haben seit Beginn der Schuldenkrise wichtige Schritte unternommen, um die Eurostaaten zu mehr Disziplin zu motivieren und ein konsequenteres Monitoring aufzubauen. Eine Reihe von Maßnahmen wurde in die Wege geleitet. Wichtige Reformschritte lassen sich dabei herausheben:

- Der „Fiskalpakt" mit der Verpflichtung zur Einführung nationaler Schuldenbremsen.
- Der Europäische Stabilitätsmechanismus mit harten Reform-Auflagen für das Empfängerland von Zahlungen aus dem Europäischen Stabilitätsmechanismus.
- Eine verbindlichere wirtschaftspolitische Koordinierung auf europäischer Ebene.

Alle Maßnahmen zielen darauf, der „Politik auf Pump" sowie der „Kultur des Nichthinsehens" einen Riegel vorzuschieben. Und das ist auch richtig so.

Hinzu kommt die nötige Stärkung der Wettbewerbsfähigkeit. Hier sind natürlich vor allem die Mitgliedsstaaten selbst gefordert. Es ist richtig, dass es Hilfe nur für Selbsthilfe gibt. Letztlich sind die Anstrengungen nötig, um die Staaten wieder in die Spur zu bringen – um langfristiges Wachstum möglich zu machen. Es geht um eine Verbesserung der Standortbedingungen, um die Verbesserung der Wettbewerbsfähigkeit. So abgedroschen das auch mittlerweile klingen mag.

Die Bestandsaufnahme der Reformen, die wir als DIHK durchführen, beeindruckt:

- Spanien hat z. B. ein Paket von über 30 Reformen geschnürt – von der Schuldenbremse bis zu Erleichterungen von Unternehmensgründungen.
- In Portugal wurden unter anderem vier Feiertage gestrichen und umfangreiche Privatisierungen vorangetrieben.
- Auch Irland hat Maßnahmen hinterfragt. Im öffentlichen Dienst wurden Einsparungen bei Gehältern durchgesetzt, Wettbewerbsbeschränkungen bei der Rechtsberatung oder bei Apotheken aufgehoben.

Bemerkenswert ist die „Entziehungskur", die jetzt in Europa stattfindet, auf jeden Fall. Allein die Einsparungen im griechischen Haushalt in den letzten beiden Jahren lägen, auf Deutschland umgerechnet, bei fast 180 Mrd. Euro! Das würde den Wegfall sämtlicher Verwaltungsausgaben in Deutschland bedeuten! Das nötigt unglaublich viel Respekt ab.

Es lohnt sich, genau hinzuschauen. Da werden in einem enormen Tempo umfangreiche Maßnahmen eingeführt. Europa beschreitet derzeit nicht den einfachen Weg. Es ist eben nicht damit getan, mit billigem Geld der Zentralbanken neue Ausgabenprogramme zu implementieren. Strohfeuer sind das Letzte, was Europa derzeit braucht. Sie würden nur den Blick verstellen, und am Ende wäre es noch schwieriger, sich aus der Krise zu befreien. Es geht darum, Strukturen anzupassen.

Keine Frage: Die Reformen sind schmerzhaft – und Zeit brauchen sie allemal. Aber sie werden sich auszahlen. Das wissen wir aus Deutschland von der „Agenda 2010". Im Jahr 2003 eingeführt, konnten die Früchte erst ab 2006 geerntet werden. Damit wird auch klar, dass das politische Umsteuern in den Krisenländern hart an die Grenzen der Akzeptanz der Bürger geht. Daher ist es umso wichtiger, die Notwendigkeit der Maßnahmen immer wieder zu erklären. Und es ist genauso wichtig, nicht in Schwarzmalerei zu verfallen, sondern bei den Ergebnissen genau hinzusehen.

Denn, erste Erfolge sind sichtbar: Die Eurozone hat sich im 2. Quartal 2013 aus der Rezession befreit. Die Leistungsbilanz- und Haushaltsdefizite der Krisenländer schmelzen, die Exporte steigen. Für 2014 erwartet die DIHK sowohl in der EU wie auch in der Eurozone wieder ein Wachstum. Beides könnte knapp 1 Prozent erreichen. Es bewegt sich also etwas – auch wenn man in die Länder selbst blickt.

Fortschritte in anderen Ländern der Eurozone

Portugal

In Portugal ist die Wirtschaft im zweiten Quartal 2013 sogar um 1,1 Prozent im Vergleich zum Vorquartal gewachsen.[90] Damit hat das Land in ganz Europa die Nase bei den Wachstumsraten vorn. Und: Portugal zeigt sich als Musterknabe. Die mit der Troika ausgehandelten Vereinbarungen werden trotz Rückschlägen

---

[90] *Eurostat*, Oktober 2013.

eingehalten. Im Jahr 2014 wird das Land wohl einen Primärüberschuss im Staatshaushalt erzielen.

Das Wachstum in Portugal wird 2014 eine durchschnittliche positive Rate von 0,8 Prozent[91] erreichen und 2015 noch einmal auf 1,5 Prozent anziehen. Im Einklang mit diesem verbesserten Wachstumstrend wird für das Haushaltsdefizit ein Rückgang von 5,9 Prozent des BIP für 2013 auf 4 Prozent für 2014 und 2,5 Prozent für 2015 – damit komfortabel unterhalb der 3 Prozent des Defizitkriteriums – prognostiziert. Nach mehreren Jahren im Defizit ist auch Portugals Leistungsbilanz nun positiv, von einem 1,9-prozentigen Defizit 2013 auf einen für 2013 geschätzten 0,9-prozentigen Überschuss und für 2014 bzw. 2015 prognostizierte Überschüsse von 0,9 Prozent bzw. 1,0 Prozent.

Das wirtschaftliche Anpassungsprogramm für Portugal wurde im Mai 2011 nach der Bitte um Unterstützung aus dem Vormonat verhandelt. Es beinhaltet ein gemeinsames Finanzierungspaket in Höhe von 78 Mrd. Euro für den Zeitraum bis Mitte 2014, dessen Last zu gleichen Teilen von der EU[92] und der Eurozone[93] getragen wird und das zum Zeitpunkt des Verfassens fast komplett ausgezahlt ist.

Wie auch für Irland, bedingt dieses Paket nicht nur eine strenge fiskalische Konsolidierung, sondern auch eine Reihe von Strukturreformen, die darauf abzielen, das Wachstum zu fördern, Arbeitsplätze zu schaffen und die Wettbewerbsfähigkeit zu verbessern sowie eine Rekapitalisierung und den Schuldenabbau für das Bankensystem zu ermöglichen. Im Gegensatz zu Irland gibt es jedoch in Portugal zum Zeitpunkt des Verfassens keine Anzeichen dafür, dass die Arbeitslosigkeit sinkt. Für 2014 wird ein Anstieg auf 17,7 prognostiziert, bevor die Zahlen 2015 leicht zurückgehen.

In ihrem aktuellsten Quartalsbericht des Anpassungsprogramms bemerkt die EU-Kommission,[94] dass die „Umsetzung des Programms weitgehend auf Kurs ist", trotz anspruchsvoller Umstände. Sie stellt auch Anzeichen für einen Aufschwung fest, der sich in den Wachstumszahlen für das zweite Quartal 2013 zeigt.

Vorgesehen ist, dass Portugal das Anpassungsprogramm 2014 verlässt. Es ist abzuwarten, ob Portugal wie Irland das Programm verlassen kann, ohne eine Notkreditfazilität in Anspruch nehmen zu müssen, eine Fazilität, für die sich die irischen Behörden nicht entschieden haben. Schließlich wird die Last der Staatsverschuldung für Portugal mit 126,7 Prozent als Anteil am BIP für 2014 nahe derjenigen Irlands prognostiziert.

---

[91]   EU-Kommission, „Herbstprognose", Oktober 2013.

[92]   *Über* den Europäischen Finanzstabilisierungsmechanismus (EFSM) (siehe **Anhang II: Glossar).**

[93]   *Über* die Europäische Finanzstabilisierungsfazilität (EFSF) (siehe **Anhang II: Glossar).**

[94]   EU-Kommission, EZB, IWF, „Das wirtschaftliche Anpassungsprogramm für Portugal, Achter und neunter Bericht", November 2013.

Griechenland

In Griechenland bleiben die Wachstumsaussichten deutlich herausfordernder als in Irland, Portugal oder Spanien. Während andernorts das Wirtschaftswachstum entweder zurückkehrte oder die Geschwindigkeit des Konjunkturrückgangs moderat blieb, sank das BIP in Griechenland in signifikanten, wenn auch mäßigenden Raten, bis das BIP dann im Jahr 2013, nach Schätzungen zum Zeitpunkt des Verfassens,[95] um 4 Prozent fiel. Nach diesen Schätzungen war ein moderates Wachstum von 0,6 Prozent für 2014 vorhergesagt, jedoch mit einer deutlichen Beschleunigung auf 2,9 Prozent für 2015.

Die Situation des Haushaltsdefizits zeigt jedoch mehr Anzeichen für Fortschritt, und es wird erwartet, dass Griechenlands Haushaltssaldo 2014 das 3 Prozent-Ziel erreicht, bei einem Defizit von nur 2 Prozent des BIP. Griechenland weist bereits einen „Primärüberschuss" auf.

Griechenlands bessere Leistung hinsichtlich seines Haushaltssaldos spiegelt höchstwahrscheinlich die Tatsache wider, dass es quasi keine andere Option hat, als sich in diesem Bereich zu übertreffen: Sogar im Vergleich mit Irland und Portugal – deren beider Staatsschuldenquote 120 Prozent des BIP überschreiten wird – ist die griechische Staatsschuldenlast deutlich höher und wird ihren Höchststand schätzungsweise bei 176,2 Prozent in 2013 erreichen, bevor sie dann 2014 leicht auf 175,9 Prozent und dann 2015 auf 170,9 Prozent fallen wird. Anders als für Irland, Portugal und Spanien, bleibt Griechenlands Leistungsbilanz ebenfalls negativ.

Im Gegensatz zu Irland war Griechenlands Erfahrung mit der finanziellen Anpassung viel turbulenter. Das wirtschaftliche Anpassungsprogramm für Griechenland stammt aus dem Mai 2010 und beläuft sich auf ein Gesamtpaket in Höhe von 164,5 Mrd. Euro bis 2014, wovon der größte Betrag von der Eurozone gestellt wird.

Im Juli 2011 wurde auf Einladung der griechischen Regierung eine Sonderarbeitsgruppe für Griechenland installiert, um sowohl die fachliche Unterstützung für Griechenland zu koordinieren, als auch die griechischen Behörden bei der Bestimmung der legislativen, regulatorischen und administrativen Aspekte zu unterstützen.

Anders als Irland, erhielt Griechenland im November 2012 eine zweijährige Verlängerung für seinen Weg der finanziellen Anpassung. Zur gleichen Zeit hat ein Paket besonderer Maßnahmen – einschließlich einer freiwilligen Abschreibung einiger Staatsschulden, Zinssatzsenkungen auf Rettungsdarlehen und einer Fristverlängerung für Kreditfälligkeiten – zum Ziel, die griechische Staatsverschuldung bis 2020 auf ein kontrollierbareres Niveau von 124 Prozent zu senken.

Trotz der Turbulenzen der vorangegangenen drei Jahre in Hinblick auf Griechenland, stellte die Eurogruppe im Juli 2013 mit Befriedigung fest, dass das

---

[95]   EU-Kommission, „Herbstprognose", Oktober 2013.

griechische Programm weitgehend auf Kurs war.[96] Fortschritte bei wichtigen Strukturreformen wurden aufgezeichnet, ebenso wie eine sich bessernde Wettbewerbsfähigkeit in Bezug auf Lohnkosten. Die Themen, die Griechenland in Zukunft angehen muss, sind jedoch zahlreich und vielfältig und beinhalten den sozialen Zusammenhalt, Arbeitsmarktreformen, eine Verbesserung der wirtschaftlichen Rahmenbedingungen und eine Reform der Verwaltung staatlicher Einnahmen. Die größte Herausforderung aus wirtschaftlicher Sicht bleibt die Arbeitslosenquote in Griechenland, die mit einem Viertel der Erwerbsbevölkerung weit höher ist als die in Irland oder Portugal, und die auf absehbare Zeit so bleiben wird.

Spanien

In Spanien ist der Anstieg der Arbeitslosigkeit im dritten Quartal 2013 zum Stillstand gekommen. Die Wirtschaft ist nach zwei Jahren zum ersten Mal wieder leicht gewachsen. Und für 2014 und 2015 gibt es Grund für noch mehr Optimismus. Von einer negativen durchschnittlichen Wachstumsrate 2013 wird für das BIP zum Zeitpunkt des Verfassens für 2014 und 2015 von einem Wachstum von 0,5 Prozent bzw. 1,7 Prozent ausgegangen.[97]

Spanien bat im Juni 2012 um Unterstützung, in erster Linie bei der Stabilisierung seines Bankensektors. Dies war später als Irland, Griechenland oder Portugal, und in Spaniens Fall ist die Anpassung stärker auf das Bankwesen fokussiert und aus Sicht der Troika von kürzerer Dauer.

Der Haushaltssaldo scheint einen langsameren Fortschritt in Richtung Konsolidierung vorzulegen und die EU-Kommission erwartet für 2014 ein Defizit von 5,9 Prozent und für 2015 ein Defizit von 6,6 Prozent. Die spanische Staatsverschuldung ist hoch, jedoch nicht ganz so hoch wie die irische oder portugiesische (für 2015 wird erwartet, dass sie 104,3 Prozent erreicht). Wie Portugal, aber später als Irland, hat Spanien den Wandel von einer negativen zu einer positiven Leistungsbilanz geschafft, was auf eine verbesserte Wettbewerbsfähigkeit hindeutet.

In ihrem Bericht für Spanien[98] hält die EU-Kommission fest, dass die Stabilisierung und Sanierung des spanischen Finanzsektors „weiter vorangeschritten" ist und drückt ihr Vertrauen in die verbesserte Solvenz der spanischen Banken aus. Sie betont jedoch auch, dass die Haushaltslage weiterhin „schwierig" sei. Im Gegensatz zu Irland, Portugal und Griechenland könnten Aspekte hinsichtlich der finanzpolitischen Belastungen durch die spanischen Regionen ein einschränkender Faktor für die Fähigkeit der Zentralregierung sein,

---

[96]   EU-Kommission, EZB, IWF, „Das zweite wirtschaftliche Anpassungsprogramm für Griechenland, Dritter Bericht", Juli 2013.

[97]   EU-Kommission, „Herbstprognosen", Oktober 2013.

[98]   EU-Kommission, EZB, IWF, „Finanzhilfeprogramm für die Rekapitalisierung von Finanzinstituten in Spanien, Vierter Bericht", November 2013.

eine Haushaltskonsolidierung mit der gleichen Geschwindigkeit zu erreichen, wie es für kleinere, finanzpolitisch zentralistischer geordnete Länder möglich ist.

Auch wenn Spanien hier Erwähnung findet, ist doch festzuhalten, dass die Möglichkeiten für einen Vergleich mit Irland angesichts des enormen Größenunterschieds zwischen der irischen und der spanischen Volkswirtschaft einigermaßen begrenzt sind. In einer Hinsicht ist jedoch eine Gegenüberstellung erwähnenswert: Wie Griechenland, hat auch Spanien eine der höchsten Arbeitslosenquote in der EU, mit einem Viertel der Bevölkerung ohne Arbeit und einem viel höheren Anteil an jungen Menschen ohne Arbeit. Der Gegensatz zu Irland ist umso krasser, angesichts der Art und Weise, wie sich Irland dem Druck einer wachsenden jungen Bevölkerungen gestellt hat. In dieser Hinsicht könnten sowohl Griechenland als auch Spanien, und in gewissem Umfang auch Portugal, mit Fug und Recht auf Irland und natürlich Deutschland schauen, um Anregungen für eine Lösung des Problems der Jugendarbeitslosigkeit zu finden.

Lettland
Lettland ist aus mehreren Gründen ein interessantes Vergleichsland. Erstens ist es die im Durchschnitt am schnellsten wachsende Volkswirtschaft in der Eurozone – sein BIP-Wachstum erreichte 5 Prozent in 2012, 4,2 Prozent in 2013 und wird nach Erwartungen in den folgenden Jahren im Durchschnitt bei 4 Prozent liegen. Zweitens ist Lettland ab dem 1. Januar 2014 der neueste Mitgliedsstaat in der Eurozone. Drittens durchlitt Lettland ähnlich wie Irland eine Bankenkrise, mit einem von Auslandskrediten abhängigen, aufgeblähten Bankensektor. Viertens ist es wie Irland eine kleine, offene Volkswirtschaft mit wichtigen Wirtschaftsbeziehungen mit einem großen Nachbarland, das nicht zur Eurozone gehört (Russland). Fünftens, obschon kein Mitglied der Eurozone, war Lettlands Währung an den Euro gekoppelt, und trotz großen Drucks, seine Währung abzuwerten und die Kursstützung aufzugeben, lehnte Lettland dies ab und konzentrierte sich stattdessen darauf, eine so genannte „innere Abwertung" seiner Währung zu erreichen, wobei die Wettbewerbsfähigkeit durch Senkung der Preise und Gehälter in der Binnenwirtschaft wiederhergestellt wurde. Dies erforderte eine große Disziplin seitens der Planungsbehörden. Als letzter Punkt sei genannt, dass, während die meisten EU-Staaten ihre finanzpolitische Konsolidierung auf viele Jahre streckten, Lettland seine finanzpolitische Konsolidierung auf einen viel kürzeren Zeitraum, von 2008 bis 2010, konzentrierte.

Die wesentlich beeindruckenderen Wachstumsraten der lettischen Volkswirtschaft legen nahe, dass der Anpassungsprozess hier nach wirtschaftlichen Kriterien vorbildhaft war – die sozialen Konsequenzen waren jedoch nicht unumstritten.

Die globale Liquiditätskrise im September 2008 führte zum Zusammenbruch der Parex Bank, Lettlands zweitgrößter Bank. Konfrontiert mit den beträchtlichen Kosten für die Rekapitalisierung der Bank, wandte sich Lettland für Unterstützung

an den IWF und die EU-Kommission.[99] Als Teil einer koordinierten internationalen Anstrengung unter Mitwirkung der EU und des IWF wurde ein Hilfspaket in Höhe von 7,5 Mrd. Euro geschnürt.

Im Juni 2009 einigten sich die lettische Regierung, die Gewerkschaften und die Arbeitgeber auf tiefgreifende Kürzungen der öffentlichen Ausgaben, deren Größe und Umfang insofern beachtlich sind, als dass das Haushaltsdefizit innerhalb eines einzigen Haushaltes um 4 Prozent des BIP gesenkt wurde. In manchen Fällen wurden die Verwaltungshaushalte für einige Regierungsorgane um bis zu 50 Prozent gekürzt. Öffentliche Gehälter wurden deutlich und sogar in größerem Maß als in Irland gekürzt und die Raten für die Kernfürsorge wurden etwas mäßiger gekürzt.

So beachtlich wie das Ausmaß dieser Anpassung ist auch die Tatsache, dass sie in einem Monat durchgeführt wurde, in dem sowohl Europa- als auch Kommunalwahlen stattfanden. Ein im Dezember nachfolgender Haushalt führte dazu, dass die größte Koalitionspartei die Regierung verließ, und doch verfasste der IWF im Juli desselben Jahres trotz alledem seinen dritten Bericht zur lettischen Wirtschaft im Rahmen des Hilfsprogramms und befand Lettlands Fortschritt darin für ausreichend, um einer weiteren Auszahlung an das Land zuzustimmen. Trotz der Tiefe der Kürzungen und des Umfangs der politischen Veränderungen endeten die im darauffolgenden Oktober durchgeführten Wahlen mit der Wiederwahl des amtierenden Premierministers.

Wie in Griechenland führte Austerität auch in Lettland zu politischen Reaktionen. Aber anders als in Griechenland und näher an der irischen Erfahrung, drehte sich die politische Debatte in Lettland nicht darum, ob, sondern wie Austerität umzusetzen sei. Darüber hinaus wurde die Notwendigkeit einer finanzpolitischen Disziplin – und insbesondere die Notwendigkeit, eine Währungsdisziplin aufrechtzuerhalten – durch einen öffentlichen Konsens getragen, der stark genug war, um die Veränderungen in der politischen Zusammensetzung der Regierung zu überleben.

Während sich Lettland den aus der Krise geborenen, nicht unerheblichen gesellschaftlichen Fragen und Spannungen stellen muss, ist sein Erfolg bei der Überwindung der massiven finanzpolitischen und wechselkursbedingten Belastungen und dem Wandel nicht nur zu einem der Wachstumsspitzenreiter Europas, sondern auch zum neuesten Mitglied der Eurozone beeindruckend.

Zu einer Zeit, als viele davon ausgingen, dass Länder wie Irland und Griechenland den Euro verlassen müssten und dies die Zerschlagung der Währung herbeiführen würde, geschah genau das Gegenteil: Irland und Griechenland bleiben zum Zeitpunkt des Verfassens im Euro und zwei neue Mitgliedsstaaten – Estland und Lettland – sind seit Beginn der Krise beigetreten. Die Ausweitung des

---

[99] Åslund, Anders und Dombrovskis, Valdis (2011). "How Latvia Came through the Financial Crisis", Washington DC: Institute of International Economics.

Euros trotz dieser schwierigen Bedingungen ist ein Beweis für die dem europäischen Projekt zugrunde liegende Stärke.

Irland

Irlands Fortschritt in Bezug auf sein Anpassungsprogramm wird in **Kapitel 1** eingehend behandelt, aber eine kurze Zusammenfassung sei hier erlaubt. Im Jahr 2008 – in der Anfangsphase der Krise – hatte Irland bereits Initiativen für den Beginn der finanzpolitischen Konsolidierung eingeleitet. Im Jahr 2009 wurde in Irland bereits daran gearbeitet, die Finanzregulierung einer Überholung zu unterziehen sowie Strukturreformen und Herausforderungen bei den öffentlichen Ausgaben anzugehen. Bis 2010 hatte Irland hier bereits große Fortschritte erzielt, trotz der in dem Jahr entstehenden Notwendigkeit, Unterstützung in Form eines Bailouts in Anspruch nehmen zu müssen. Viel früher als andere Länder, verbesserte Irland auch seine Leistungsbilanzergebnisse deutlich und frühzeitig, was eine maßgebliche Verbesserung der Wettbewerbsfähigkeit widerspiegelt. Das irische Anpassungsprogramm war erfolgreich, wenn auch nicht so abrupt und überfallartig wie das lettische. Bemerkenswert ist, dass die Bevölkerung trotz der Anpassungen in Irland aufgrund einer hohen Geburtenrate weiter wächst, und dass, obwohl die Auswanderungsquote unter jungen Menschen hoch ist, diese durch eine kontinuierliche und beträchtliche Einwanderung ausgeglichen wird.

Wie in **Kapitel 2** erwähnt, kombiniert das irische Geschäftsmodell ein ausgezeichnetes Umfeld für internationale Geschäfte mit einem wettbewerbsfähigen Steuersystem und Clustern aus der Hochtechnologie-Industrie. Irland profitiert auch von einer schnell anpassbaren Politik, die ständig bestrebt ist, die irische Wirtschaft zu erneuern und an neue Trends und Chancen der Weltwirtschaft auszurichten. Es hat den Rettungsschirm nun erfolgreich und ohne Rückgriff auf irgendwelche Notkreditfazilitäten verlassen. Irland ist auch in Bezug auf die Schaffung von Arbeitsplätzen vorangekommen und weist eine bemerkenswerte und ansehnliche Verringerung der Arbeitslosigkeit während der frühen Phasen der Erholung auf.

Irland hat sich dank seiner bereits vor der Krise stark liberalen und offenen Wirtschaft sehr schnell aus der Krise befreit. Die Last der Bankenrettung liegt aber weiterhin über der Wirtschaft. Als Exportnation Deutschland merken auch wir, dass es in einem schwierigen Umfeld auf dem „Heimatmarkt Europa" nicht einfach ist, die Exporte zu steigern. Dennoch, die Wirtschaft wächst, die Industrieproduktion ist stabil, und auch die Arbeitslosigkeit sinkt wieder langsam. Das Ende der Staatsschuldenkrise und der Unsicherheiten auf den Finanzmärkten ist damit aber noch nicht erreicht. Es bleibt noch viel zu tun. Auch müssen wir so manches Risiko im Auge behalten, das im Sinne der Krisenbewältigung von den Eurostaaten und der EZB eingegangen worden ist.

Schluss

Auf der halben Strecke stehenbleiben, führt nicht zum Ziel. Die vielen Reformen wären nur die Hälfte wert, wenn sie gebremst oder zurückgedreht würden. Die ersten Erfolge machen Mut. Sie sollten Anlass dazu geben, den Weg voranzuschreiten, jetzt sogar mit langsam zunehmendem Rückenwind.

Schluss

Die in diesem Buch versammelten Beiträge vertiefen unser Verständnis dessen, womit Irland und Deutschland in dieser Krise konfrontiert waren. Für jeden Autor galt als Ausgangspunkt: Wir müssen aus unseren Erfahrungen lernen, und zwar schnell, um eine Wiederholung der Krise zu vermeiden.

Die Krise war für uns nicht nur „eine Herausforderung". Sie war ein harter Schlag für viele Familien in Irland und in ganz Europa. Sie war außerdem eine ernste Bedrohung für das europäische Projekt an sich. Irland, Deutschland und ganz Europa schlug tiefe internationale Skepsis entgegen. Wir müssen anerkennen, dass sie mitunter berechtigt war.

Irlands wirtschaftliche Erholung und unser Ausstieg aus dem EU/IWF-Programm – planmäßig und ohne weitere Verpflichtungen – sind reale und beachtliche Zeichen des Fortschritts. Das mussten auch Europas Kritiker anerkennen. Diese Leistung war nur möglich, weil sich unser Volk entschlossen zeigte und wir die Unterstützung Deutschlands und unserer anderen Partner in Europa genossen.

Irlands Rückkehr auf einen nachhaltigen wirtschaftlichen Weg ist nicht die Art von Fortschritt, der mit zweifelhaften Versprechungen und Tricksereien erreicht werden kann. Dieser Prozess erforderte gewissenhafte Planung, gute Zusammenarbeit und zielstrebige Durchsetzung. Wir mussten eine Reihe sehr schwieriger Reformen umsetzen. Das hatte für viele Familien spürbare Auswirkungen auf ihr Haushaltsbudget. Wir mussten eine Anpassung der Besteuerung und der Ausgaben durchführen, die sich bis zum nächsten Jahr auf 20 Prozent unseres BIP summieren wird, und gleichzeitig versuchen, das Wirtschaftswachstum zu stützen und die Arbeitslosigkeit zu verringern.

Zum Glück wurde diese schwierige Realität von unseren Partnern in Europa anerkannt. Immer wieder erlebten wir Flexibilität, als es um die Neuverhandlung wichtiger Bedingungen des Programms und eine Verringerung des Zinssatzes ging. Wir konnten eine Lösung für das Problem der Schuldverschreibungen der Anglo Irish Bank finden. Dies waren wichtige Faktoren für Irlands erfolgreichen Ausstieg aus dem Hilfsprogramm.

Dieses Buch tut nicht so als sei Irlands Ausstieg aus dem EU/IWF-Programm das Ende dieser Geschichte. Auch liefert es keine Anweisung, wie unsere gemeinsamen Anstrengungen bewertet werden sollten. Stattdessen sollten wir uns daran messen lassen, ob uns eine wirtschaftliche Erholung gelingt, die in den Haushaltsbudgets der Familien in ganz Europa zu spüren ist - Arbeit, Wachstum und Vertrauen in die Zukunft.

Das Buch behandelt viele der Probleme, die einen Wiederaufschwung in Irland und Europa noch behindern. Als Entscheidungsträger Europas haben wir versprochen, den Teufelskreis aus Banken- und Staatsschulden zu durchbrechen. Wie wir das schaffen können, bleibt eine wichtige Frage. Irland bekam die Folgen dieser zerstörerischen Dynamik früher als die meisten anderen zu spüren, und zwar zu einem Zeitpunkt, als es noch keine Strukturen zum Schutz der europäischen Finanzstabilität gab. Die Iren leben mit der schweren Hinterlassenschaft dieser Zeit.

Ich möchte der Deutsch-Irischen Handelskammer unter Leitung von Ralf Lissek danken: Zum einen dafür, dass sie die Autoren dieses Buches zusammengeführt hat; aber auch für ihre fortdauernde Arbeit zur weiteren Stärkung der Beziehungen zwischen unseren Ländern.

Die Artikel dieses Buches verdeutlichen gemeinsam mit großer Klarheit eines der prägenden Merkmale des europäischen Projekts – nämlich, dass es eine dynamische Union kleiner wie auch großer Staaten ist. Was uns als Mitgliedsstaaten vor allem vereint, ist nicht eine vergleichbare Größe oder ähnliche Wirtschaftssysteme oder identische Interessen. Es ist eine tiefere Beziehung zwischen den Völkern und ein Bekenntnis zu einem besseren, sicheren, stabilen und gleichzeitig lebendigen Europa.

Irland wird auch weiterhin seinen Teil zu diesem Projekt beitragen und zu der unmittelbaren Aufgabe, Europas wirtschaftlichen Wiederaufschwung und seinen tieferen Zusammenhalt voranzubringen. In dieser Zusammenarbeit fühlen wir uns im Geiste wahrer Freundschaft und gegenseitiger Unterstützung mit Deutschland und unseren Partnern in ganz Europa verbunden.

Eamon Gilmore
Tánaiste (Vizeministerpräsident) und Außen- und Handelsminister

ANHANG I
Chronologie der Krise und Erholung

2008

14./15. März   Bear Stearns geht in Konkurs. George Bush spricht auf der Wirtschaftskonferenz in New York über die Weltwirtschaft.

15. September   Lehman Brothers geht in Konkurs. Eine weltweite Liquiditätskrise ist die Folge, die Kreditvergabe auf dem Interbankenmarkt friert ein.

18. September   Die irische Aufsichtsbehörde für Finanzdienstleistungen (Irish Financial Services Regulatory Authority – IFSRA) erlässt ein Verbot für Leerverkäufe von Finanzaktien.

30. September   Das irische Unterhaus garantiert für sechs inländische Finanzinstitute die Einlagen, Kredite und Anleihen im Wert von 440 Mrd. Euro: Allied Irish Banks, Anglo Irish Bank, Bank of Ireland, Irish Life and Permanent, EBS und Irish Nationwide.

14. Oktober   Die irische Regierung zieht den für Dezember vorgesehenen Haushalt um zwei Monate vor und setzt Steuererhöhungen und Ausgabenkürzungen durch. Dagegen gibt es einige friedliche Demonstrationen, die wirkungslos bleiben.

21. Dezember   Die Regierung gibt die Absicht bekannt, drei wichtige Kreditgeber mit einer Finanzspritze in Höhe von 5,5 Mrd. Euro zu versorgen: Bank of Ireland, Allied Irish Banks und Anglo Irish Bank.

2009

15. Januar   Die irische Regierung verstaatlicht die Anglo Irish Bank, um deren Zusammenbruch abzuwenden.

Januar   Im Rahmen eines Notstandsgesetzes führt die Regierung eine Abgabe für Beschäftigte im öffentlichen Dienst ein, um deren Pensionsansprüche finanzieren zu können.

11. Februar   Die irische Regierung gewährt der Bank of Ireland sowie der Allied Irish Banks eine Finanzspritze in Höhe von 7 Mrd. Euro und erhält Anteile in Höhe von je 25 Prozent an beiden Banken.

März	Um eine Kreditvergabe an Anglo Irish Bank – deren Sicherheiten nicht der Norm für geldpolitische Maßnahmen des Eurosystems entsprachen – zu ermöglichen, willigt die irische Zentralbank (Central Bank of Ireland) ein, eine „Sonderliquiditätshilfe" (siehe **Anhang II: Glossar**) zur Verfügung zu stellen. Diese Darlehen werden durch die irische Regierung gemäß dem „Credit Institutions Financial Stability Act, 2009" garantiert und führen dazu, dass der Staat Verpflichtungen übernimmt.
7. April	Im Rahmen des zweiten Notstandshaushaltes innerhalb von nur sechs Monaten führt die Regierung weitere erhebliche Steuererhöhungen ein.
April	Die Regierung gibt ihre Absicht bekannt, die staatliche Agentur zur Vermögensverwaltung (National Asset Management Agency, NAMA) zu gründen. NAMA übernimmt die Verwaltung von Immobiliendarlehen von fünf der im September 2008 geretteten Finanzinstitute (siehe **Anhang II: Glossar**).
29. Mai	Nach steigenden Verlusten des Kreditinstituts steckt die irische Regierung weitere 4 Mrd. Euro in die Anglo Irish Bank.
September	Die NAMA wird gegründet.
9. Dezember	Im Rahmen ihres dritten Haushaltes innerhalb von nur 14 Monaten setzt die irische Regierung Kürzungen der Gehälter im öffentlichen Dienst sowie der ausgezahlten Sozialleistungen durch. Im Folgejahr zeigt die Binnenwirtschaft einen moderaten Aufschwung in Bezug auf das Bruttonationaleinkommen (siehe **Kapitel 4**) von 0,5 Prozent gegenüber dem Vorjahr.

2010

19. Februar	Die Regierung erwirbt ihren ersten direkten Anteil an der Bank of Ireland.
März	Die Regierung schließt das sogenannte „Croke Park Agreement" (siehe **Anhang II: Glossar**) mit den Gewerkschaften des Öffentlichen Dienstes. Die Vereinbarung verpflichtet die Gewerkschaften zu Reformen und einer Nullrunde. Im Gegenzug verspricht die Regierung, Gehälter und Pensionen nicht weiter zu kürzen.

30. März	NAMA kauft das erste Bündel Immobilienkredite von irischen Banken mit einem Rabatt von 47 Prozent. Dieser höhere Nachlass erfordert von den betroffenen Banken eine höhere Kapitalbeschaffung als ursprünglich als notwendig erachtet. Die Zentralbank verlangt von Kreditgebern, bis Ende des Jahres mindestens 8 Prozent Kernkapital (Tier 1-Kapital) vorzuhalten. Die Regierung schießt weitere 8,3 Mrd. Euro in die Anglo Irish Bank und übernimmt die Kontrolle der Irish Nationwide.
31. März	Die Anglo Irish Bank meldet den höchsten Unternehmensverlust in der irischen Geschichte (12,7 Mrd. Euro).
13. Mai	Die Regierung übernimmt Anteile in Höhe von 18 Prozent an Allied Irish Banks.
9. Juni	Der Staat schießt weitere 3 Mrd. Euro in die Bank of Ireland.
25. August	Standard and Poor's reduziert Irlands langfristige Anleihenbewertung auf AA. Dies folgt einer Abstufung durch Moody's im Juli. Die Ratingsagenturen stellen weitere Abstufungen in Aussicht.
30. September	Die irische Zentralbank veröffentlicht eine Schätzung, wonach die Staatshilfe für das Bankensystem bis zu 34,3 Mrd. Euro betragen könnte - weitaus mehr als bis dahin erwartet.
Oktober	Mit dem Gesetz zur Zentralbankreform („Central Bank Reform Act, 2010") wird die Kontrolle der irischen Zentralbank über das irische Finanz- und Bankensystem ausgeweitet. Das Gesetz stellt auch Finanzdienstleister in die Verpflichtung der kontrollierten Kreditvergabe und Compliance.
November	Die Regierung vereinbart ein Rettungspaket mit der EU und dem IWF in Höhe von 85 Mrd. Euro und verpflichtet sich im Gegenzug zu einem Vierjahresprogramm von Steuererhöhungen und Ausgabenkürzungen.
7. Dezember	In Umkehrung der Vorjahrespolitik stellt die irische Regierung einen Haushalt vor, der Steuererhöhungen zum Schwerpunkt hat. Die Binnenwirtschaft, nach BNE gemessen, weist nach einem Jahr des moderaten Aufschwungs 2011 erneut ein Negativwachstum auf.

2011

Februar	Nachdem das irische Unterhaus die Haushaltsvorlage bewilligt hat, zerbricht die Regierung. Bei den Neuwahlen bleibt die wichtigste Oppositionspartei, Fine Gael, knapp unterhalb einer eigenen Mehrheit. Es kommt zur Koalition von Fine Gael und Labour unter Premierminister Enda Kenny.

1. Juli	Infolge einer gerichtlichen Anordnung wird die Irish Bank Resolution Corporation gegründet. Damit wird die staatliche Übernahme der Anglo Irish Bank und der Irish Nationwide Building Society formalisiert.
Juli	Moody's stuft Irlands Kreditwürdigkeit herab. Als Teil einer umfangreichen Reform richtet die Regierung den irischen unabhängigen Finanzbeirat (Irish Fiscal Advisory Council, IFAC) zur Überwachung der Finanzpolitik der Regierung ein.
Dezember	Die irische Regierung stellt einen Haushalt mit ausbalancierten Steuererhöhungen und Ausgabenkürzungen vor.

2012

Juni	Die irischen Wähler stimmen mit deutlicher Mehrheit dafür, den Vertrag über Stabilität, Koordinierung und Steuerung in der Wirtschafts- und Währungsunion (Fiskalvertrag) in die irische Verfassung aufzunehmen.
Dezember	Der Haushalt der irischen Regierung verfolgt einen Mix von Steuererhöhungen und Ausgabenkürzungen. Die Regierung installiert das Gesetz zur finanzpolitischen Verantwortung („Fiscal Responsibility Act, 2012") um der Billigung des *Fiskalvertrags* gesetzliche Wirksamkeit zu verleihen.

2013

Februar	Mit Billigung der EZB wird die Irish Bank Resolution Corporation (s. o.) abgewickelt. Ihre Schulden werden vom irischen Finanzministerium übernommen, allerdings zu günstigeren Bedingungen: Der Zinssatz für Schulden wird gesenkt und die Rückzahlung von 2023 auf 2053 aufgeschoben. Dadurch ergeben sich deutliche Einsparungen für die irische Staatskasse.
Juli	IFAC (s. o.) wird auf eine finanziell unabhängige Basis gestellt, um seinen Freiraum und seine Unabhängigkeit bei der Kommentierung der Haushaltspolitik zu verbessern.
19. September	Offizielle Wirtschaftsstatistiken bestätigen die Rückkehr des BIP zum Wachstum im zweiten Quartal 2012.
15. Oktober	Der IFAC bestätigt die Finanzprognosen der irischen Regierung für den kommenden Haushalt. Bei diesem Haushalt stehen Ausgabenkürzungen im Vordergrund.
26. November	Die offiziellen Beschäftigungszahlen bestätigen einen Anstieg von 3,8 Prozent bei den Vollzeitbeschäftigten. Der Statistik zufolge steigt auch die Rate des Beschäftigungswachstums.

18. Dezember   Die irische Regierung veröffentlicht „Eine Wachstumsstrategie" („A Strategy for Growth"). Sie formuliert als Ziel, zwischen 2014 und 2020 Vollbeschäftigung zu erreichen und die Staatsverschuldung um ein Viertel zu senken.

Glossar

Croke Park Agreement: Vertragliche Vereinbarung vom März 2010 zwischen der irischen Regierung und den irischen Gewerkschaften im öffentlichen Dienst. Das Abkommen betrifft den Bereich des öffentlichen Dienstes und der staatlichen Agenturen zwischen 2010 und 2014 und erhielt seinen Namen vom Verhandlungsort, einem Konferenzzentrum im Stadion Croke Park. Nachdem 2009 Gehälter und Pensionen im öffentlichen Dienst gekürzt worden waren, legte die Vereinbarung weitere Reformen im öffentlichen Dienst fest, darunter eine Verringerung der Zahl der Beschäftigten; im Gegenzug verzichtete die Regierung auf weitere Kürzungen der Gehälter oder Pensionen. Die Vereinbarung wurde weithin kritisiert, weil sie öffentliche Gehälter beibehielt, die vielerorts als zu hoch angesehen wurden. 2014 wurde das „Croke Park Agreement" durch das sogenannte „Haddington Road Agreement" abgelöst (siehe unten).

Eligible Liabilities Guarantee: Das „Credit Institutions (Eligible Liabilities Guarantee) Scheme" trat im Dezember 2009 in Kraft und sieht eine bedingungslose und unwiderrufliche staatliche Garantie für bestimmte Bankverbindlichkeiten (einschließlich Einlagen) mit einer Laufzeit von bis zu fünf Jahren für Kreditinstitute vor, die dem Programm beitreten. Das Programm steht unter der Leitung der National Treasury Management Agency (NTMA) (siehe unten). Die Aufnahme ungesicherter vorrangiger Anleihen und Schuldverschreibungen in das Programm war Gegenstand öffentlicher Kontroversen und führte zu Verpflichtungen in Höhe von gut 35 Mrd. Euro gegenüber Anleihe-Inhabern der Anglo Irish Bank und anderer Institute. Diese Verpflichtungen wurden in der irischen Bankenabwicklungsgesellschaft (Irish Bank Resolution Corporation) zusammengefasst und wurden 2013 nach einem Abkommen zur Umstrukturierung von Irlands bankenbedingter Verschuldung durch sogenannte Schuldverschreibungen („Promissory Notes") zu einem Teil der irischen Staatsverschuldung.

Europäische Finanzstabilisierungsfazilität (EFSF): Die EFSF wurde am 9. Mai 2010 von den Mitgliedsstaaten der Eurozone ins Leben gerufen. Sie soll die Finanzstabilität in Europa gewährleisten, indem sie Mitgliedsstaaten des Euroraums im Rahmen makroökonomischer Anpassungsprogramme Finanzhilfen gewährt. Dazu kann sie Kredite in Höhe von bis zu 440 Mrd. Euro aufnehmen und mit Unterstützung der Deutschen Finanzagentur Darlehen beschaffen. Ihre ersten Anleihen wurden im Januar 2011 ausgegeben. In den Jahren 2011 und 2012 stellte die EFSF Irland knapp 18 Mrd. Euro an Darlehen zur Verfügung. Seit September 2012 ist die EFSF auf die Abwicklung von

Geldtransfers und die Überwachung der Hilfsprogramme für Irland, Portugal und Griechenland beschränkt, ihre weiteren Funktionen sind im Europäischen Stabilitätsmechanismus (ESM) (siehe unten) aufgegangen.

Europäischer Finanzstabilisierungsmechanismus (EFSM): Seit Mai 2010 im Einsatz, wurde dieser Fonds als Reaktion auf die Eurokrise geschaffen. Er wird von den EU-Mitgliedsstaaten unterstützt und kann bis zu 60 Mrd. Euro beschaffen. Im Rahmen des „Troika-Programms" stellte der EFSM zwischen 2010 und 2013 Kredite für Irland in Höhe von 22,4 Mrd. Euro bereit. Seit September 2012 ist der EFSM auf die Abwicklung von Geldtransfers und die Überwachung der Hilfsprogramme für Irland, Portugal und Griechenland beschränkt, seine weiteren Funktionen sind im Europäischen Stabilitätsmechanismus (ESM) (siehe unten) aufgegangen.

Europäischer Stabilitätsmechanismus (ESM): Eingerichtet im September 2012, dient er zur Absicherung von in Not geratenen Mitgliedsstaaten der Eurozone, indem er für sofortigen Zugang zu Finanzhilfen sorgt. Hervorgegangen aus dem Europäischen Fiskalpakt (siehe unten), übernahm der ESM die meisten Funktionen des Europäischen Finanzstabilisierungsmechanismus (EFSM) und der Europäischen Finanzstabilisierungsfazilität (EFSF) (siehe oben). Er erhält gezeichnetes Kapital von Ländern der Eurozone in Höhe von bis zu 700 Mrd. Euro und kann Rettungspakete bis zu 500 Mrd. Euro genehmigen (wobei der Rest als Kapitalrücklage zurückbehalten wird). Das Rettungsprogramm für Irland nahm davon 67,5 Mrd. Euro in Anspruch.

Europäisches System der Zentralbanken (ESZB): Das ESZB ist die Gruppe aller Zentralbanken und schließt die EZB sowie die Zentralbanken aller EU-Mitgliedsstaaten ein (einschließlich derer, die nicht zur Eurozone gehören).

European Systemic Risk Board (Europäischer Ausschuss für Systemrisiken, ESRB): Eingerichtet im Dezember 2010, ist dieser Ausschuss mit der Makroaufsicht über das EU-Finanzsystem beauftragt. Der ESRB ist bei der Europäischen Zentralbank (EZB) angesiedelt und wird von dieser unterstützt.

Eurosystem: Das Eurosystem ist die Währungsbehörde der Eurozone und umfasst die Europäische Zentralbank (EZB) sowie die Zentralbanken der einzelnen Mitgliedsstaaten der Eurozone.

Exceptional Liquidity Assistance (Liquiditätsunterstützung in Sonderfällen, ELA): Dies war eine Kreditfazilität der irischen Zentralbank für die Anglo Irish Bank im Jahr 2009. Ende 2008 hatten die Finanzmärkte ihre Kreditvergaben an dieses Institut eingestellt. Als der Wert seiner Vermögenswerte drastisch fiel, war es nicht in der Lage, Sicherheiten für die vom Europäischen System der Zentralbanken (ESZB) (siehe oben) durchgeführten standardmäßigen Refinanzierungsmaßnahmen des Eurosystems zu stellen. Stattdessen erhielt die Anglo Irish Bank von der Zentralbank im Rahmen eines Rahmenvertrag über Kreditrückkauf („Master Loan Repurchase Agreement") eine Serie von Krediten. Der Gesamtwert dieser Kredite erreichte bis Mitte 2011 38,4 Mrd. Euro. Da eine Direktfinanzierung von Banken durch das Europäische System der

Zentralbanken (ESZB) gemäß den für das System geltenden Gesetzen verboten ist,[100] war es erforderlich, dass die irische Regierung die letztendliche Verantwortung für diese Kredite übernahm. Somit wurden sie zu einer Verpflichtung für den irischen Steuerzahler in Form einer Schuldverschreibung („Promissory Note") (siehe unten), die von der Regierung als eine Form der Sicherheit für Banken ausgegeben wurde, die von ELA-Krediten der irischen Zentralbank Gebrauch machten.

Europäischer Fiskalpakt: Siehe „Vertrag über Stabilität, Koordinierung und Steuerung in der Wirtschafts- und Währungsunion".

Haddington Road Agreement: Die Vereinbarung zwischen der irischen Regierung und den irischen Gewerkschaften im öffentlichen Dienst wurde im Mai 2013 abgeschlossen und trat am 1. Juli 2013 in Kraft. Gehälter von über 65.000 Euro pro Jahr sollen verringert werden, die Gewerkschaften verpflichteten sich zu grösserer Flexibilität in den Arbeitsabläufen. Die Umstrukturierung soll bis 2015 eine Verringerung der Kosten für Löhne und Gehälter im öffentlichen Dienst um 1 Mrd. Euro erreichen.

Irish Bank Resolution Corporation (Irische Bankenabwicklungsgesellschaft, IBRC): Die IBRC entstand im Jahr 2011 aus der Fusion der beiden am stärksten in Not geratenen irischen Banken, der Anglo Irish Bank und der Irish Nationwide Building Society. Gemäß dem Gesetz über die Stabilisierung der Kreditinstitute („Credit Institutions Stabilisation Act, 2010") wurden Vermögen und Schulden der letzteren auf die Anglo Irish Bank übertragen. Ergebnis war ein neues, fusioniertes Rechtsgebilde.

Irish Fiscal Advisory Council (Irischer Finanzbeirat, IFAC): Im Jahr 2011 eingerichtet, ist der IFAC ein unabhängiges Gremium, das Irlands Einhaltung der EU-Haushalts- und Finanzvorgaben überwacht. Nach der Ratifizierung des Europäischen Fiskalpaktes (siehe oben) wurde der IFAC 2013 auf eine gesetzliche Basis gestellt und genehmigte im Oktober 2013 erstmals den irischen Haushalt.

Irish Strategic Investment Fund (Irischer Strategischer Investmentfonds, ISIF): Der ISIF wird voraussichtlich 2014 eingerichtet. Er dient als Anlagevehikel, um Vermögenswerte des National Pension Reserve Fund (NPRF) (siehe unten) im Wert von 6,4 Mrd. Euro in Bereiche von strategischer Bedeutung für Irland zu leiten. Dadurch sollen das Wachstum unterstützt und neue Arbeitsplätze

---

[100] Artikel 32.4 der für das Eurosystem geltenden Satzung sieht jedoch vor, dass „der EZB-Rat beschließen [kann], dass die staatlichen Zentralbanken für Kosten in Verbindung mit der Ausgabe von Banknoten oder unter außergewöhnlichen Umständen für spezifische Verluste aus für das ESZB unternommenen währungspolitischen Operationen entschädigt werden". Dies wurde von einigen als vage Rechtfertigung für die Beteiligung des ESZB an Irlands Verlusten aus den ELA-Krediten interpretiert (Whelan, Karl (2012). „ELA, Promissory Notes and All That: The Fiscal Costs of Anglo Irish Bank", UCD Working Paper Series WP12/06, Februar).

geschaffen werden. Zu den Bereichen von Bedeutung gehören u. a.
Investitionen in Infrastruktur und die Kreditvergabe an kleine und
mittelständische Unternehmen.

**National Asset Management Agency (Staatliche Agentur zur
Vermögensverwaltung, NAMA):** Die NAMA wurde im Dezember 2009
gegründet. Sie sollte Immobilienkredite und die zugrundeliegenden
Vermögenswerte von irischen Banken in ihr Eigentum zu übernehmen und
somit bei der Sanierung von deren Bilanzen helfen. Von fünf in Not geratenen
Finanzinstituten wurden Kredite mit einem Buchwert von 77 Mrd. Euro – doch
einem geschätzten Marktwert im Jahr 2009 von 47 Mrd. Euro – für 54 Mrd.
Euro gekauft, im Austausch für Anleihen, die dann als Sicherheiten genutzt
wurden. Der für die Kredite gezahlte Zuschlag, der über den Marktwert von
2009 hinausging, war seinerzeit Ausdruck des Vertrauens darauf, dass Irlands
Wiederaufschwung eine Rendite auf diese Investition gewährleisten würde.

National Pension Reserve Fund (Staatlicher Pensionsrücklagenfonds, NPRF): Der
NPRF wurde 2001 eingerichtet, um soweit wie möglich die Kosten des irischen
Sozialsystems und der Pensionen im öffentlichen Dienst ab 2025 zu decken. Der
NPRF wird von der NTMA gesteuert und verwaltet. 2009 wurden Mittel des
NPRF für die Bankenrekapitalisierung verwendet und 2010 wurden die
regelmäßigen Einzahlungen in den Fonds ausgesetzt. Im September 2011 gab
die Regierung ihre Absicht bekannt, den Irish Strategic Investment Fund (ISIF)
(siehe oben) einzurichten, der Mittel aus dem NPRF in produktive Investitionen
in die irische Wirtschaft leiten soll.

**National Treasury Management Agency (Staatliche Finanzverwaltungsagentur,
NTMA):** Diese staatliche Stelle hat den kaufmännischen Auftrag, für die
Regierung Leistungen im Bereich der Vermögensverwaltung zu erbringen. Sie
hat sich von einer Agentur mit einer einzigen Funktion – der ausschließlichen
Verwaltung der irischen Staatsschulden – zur Verwalterin einer komplexen
Mischung aus Vermögen und Schulden der öffentlichen Hand, einschließlich
des National Pension Reserve Fund (NPRF) (siehe oben), der National Asset
Management Agency (NAMA) und anderer entwickelt.

Primary Budget Balance (Primärhaushaltssaldo): ein Messwert für den
Haushaltssaldo der Regierung, der die jährlichen Zahlungen für Zinsschulden
nicht berücksichtigt. Er hilft dabei, ein klareres Bild von der Fähigkeit des
Staates zu erhalten, die täglichen Ausgabenverpflichtungen der öffentlichen
Hand aus Steuern zu bestreiten.

Promissory Note (Schuldverschreibung): eine Rechtsurkunde, mit der ein
Schuldner schriftlich zusichert, einem Zahlungsempfänger eine Geldsumme zu
zahlen. Um irischen Banken den Zugang zu Finanzierungen über ELA zu
ermöglichen, gab die irische Regierung Schuldverschreibungen an sie aus, die
als Sicherheit bei der irischen Zentralbank genutzt werden konnten (siehe
„Exceptional Liquidity Assistance" oben). Diese Schuldverschreibungen wurden
auf die Irish Bank Resolution Corporation (IBRC) (siehe oben) übertragen; am

6. Februar 2013 wurde diese Bank abgewickelt und die Schulden aus diesen Schuldverschreibungen wurden in Anleihen der irischen Regierung umgewandelt.

Single Resolution Mechanism (Einheitlicher Mechanismus zur Bankenabwicklung, SRM): Vereinbart im Dezember 2013 (doch zum gegenwärtigen Zeitpunkt noch nicht zum Abschluss gebracht), wird die vorgeschlagene „Richtlinie über die Sanierung und Abwicklung von Kreditinstituten" („Banking Recovery and Resolution Directive") Verluste für Inhaber vorrangiger Anleihen und Großsparer zu einem dauerhaften Teil der EU-Reaktion auf Bankenkrisen machen. Ziel ist es, vom Steuerzahler finanzierte Rettungen europäischer Banken zu beenden. Eine der wichtigsten, noch zu klärenden Fragen ist, ob die irische Bankenrettung, die zu erheblichen Kosten für den Steuerzahler zur Rettung von Anleihe-Inhabern führte (siehe ELA oben), noch nachträglich den Bestimmungen des SRM unterworfen wird, wie es die Bestimmungen einer Vereinbarung auf dem EU-Gipfel im Juni 2012 vorsehen.

Single Supervisory Mechanism (Einheitlicher Bankenaufsichtsmechanismus, SSM): Dies ist ein Mechanismus zur Überwachung der Banken in der EU, der gemäß dem SRM (siehe oben) eingerichtet wurde. Der SSM wird bei der Europäischen Zentralbank angesiedelt sein und Ende 2014 die ersten Aufsichtsberichte vorlegen.

Structurally Adjusted Budget Balance (Strukturbereinigter Haushaltssaldo): Dies ist ein Messwert für den Haushaltssaldo einer Regierung, der Korrekturen für die Auswirkungen des Wirtschaftszyklus berücksichtigt, um ein klareres Maß der grundlegenden Finanzdisziplin der Regierung zu erhalten.

***Treaty on Stability, Co-ordination and Governance in the Economic and Monetary Union (*„Vertrag über Stabilität, Koordinierung und Steuerung in der Wirtschafts- und Währungsunion"):** Auch als Europäischer Fiskalpakt bezeichnet, ist dies ein zwischenstaatlicher Vertrag, der im März 2012 von allen EU-Mitgliedsstaaten mit Ausnahme der Tschechischen Republik und Großbritanniens unterzeichnet wurde und am 1. Januar 2013 in Kraft trat. Er verpflichtet die Unterzeichnerstaaten zur Einführung von „Ausführungsgesetzen", die Zielvorgaben, Richtlinien, Überwachungsverfahren und Sanktionen gemäß den im Pakt festgelegten Finanzzielen vorgeben. Irland hat als einziges Land den Pakt im Juni 2012 dem Volk zur Abstimmung vorgelegt.